# IBPS Bank PO QA Guide

# IBPS Bank PO QA Guide

dueNorth Academics
(AN IIM ALUMNI BODY)

BLOOMSBURY
NEW DELHI • LONDON • OXFORD • NEW YORK • SYDNEY

First published in India 2016



ISBN 978 93 85936 99 9
2 4 6 8 10 9 7 5 3 1

Bloomsbury Publishing India Pvt. Ltd
Second Floor, LSC Building No.4
DDA Complex, Pocket C – 6 & 7, Vasant Kunj
New Delhi 110070
www.bloomsbury.com

Typeset by Manipal Digital Systems
Printed and bound in India by Sanat Printers

# Contents


1. Intro to Numbers 01
2. LCM and HCF 17
3. Percentage 26
4. Profit and Loss 43
5. Simple Interest and Compound Interest 58
6. Ratio Proportion and Variation 71
7. Average 87
8. Time and Work 101
9. Pipes and Cisterns 120
10. Boats and Streams 127
11. Trains 138
12. Time Speed and Distance 151
13. Equation 164
14. Permutations and Combinations 175
15. Probability 193
16. Geometry 206
17. Mensuration 224
18. Set Theory 240
19. Quantitative Aptitude - Year 2014 257

    Quantitative Aptitude - Year 2013 269
20. MOCK QA Test 1 277

    MOCK QA Test 2 288

    MOCK QA Test 3 300

# 1 Intro to Numbers

Number is "a numeral or group of numerals". For Bank PO exams, we will confine ourselves with Real Numbers only.

## Real Number Tree:

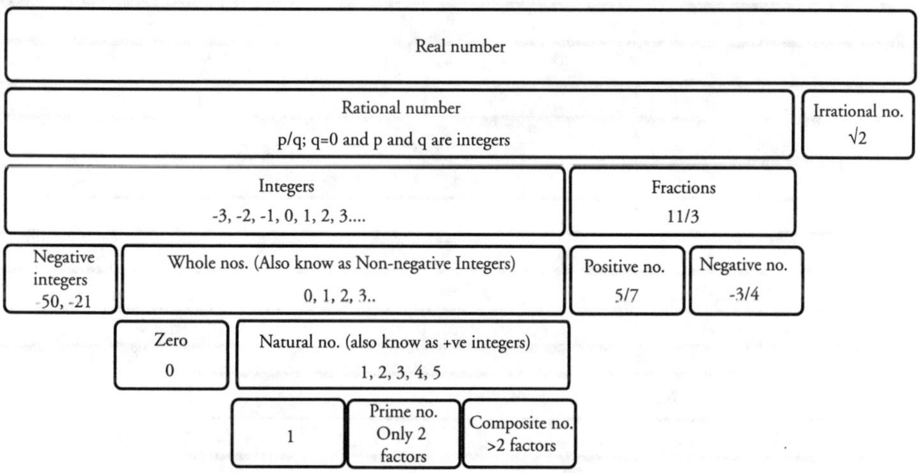


**Notes** - All the real numbers are either a rational number or an irrational number. No real number can be both a rational number and an irrational number.

Types of Rational numbers - (i) All the integers, (b) Terminating Decimals, (c) Recurring numbers.

All the real numbers other than Rational numbers are Irrational numbers.

> Note - $\pi$ is an Irrational Number, though $\frac{22}{7}$ is a rational number. It is all because the fact that is approximately equal to $\frac{22}{7}$.

**Some important properties related to numbers:**

1. Odd ± Odd = Even  Even ± Even = Even
   Odd ± Even = Odd  Even ± Odd = Odd
   $(\text{Odd})^{\text{Even}}$ = Odd  $(\text{Even})^{\text{Odd}}$ = Even
   Odd × Even = Even  Odd × Odd = Odd
   Even × Even = Even
2. All the prime numbers greater than 3 are of the format 6N ± 1. It means that all the prime numbers will give either a remainder of +1 or -1 when divided by 6.
3. (xy – yx) = 9 × (x-y) [where xy is a two digit number and yx is obtained by reversing it]
   For example, 51 – 15 = 9 × (5-1) = 36
4. Counting of Numbers in any Range:
   If N is a natural number, number of natural numbers in the range:

| Both the ends included | |
|---|---|
| $A \le N \le B$ | (B - A) + 1 |

| Only one end included | |
|---|---|
| $A \le N < B$ | B - A |

| Only one of the ends included | |
|---|---|
| $A < N \le B$ | B - A |

| None of the ends included | |
|---|---|
| $A < N < B$ | (B - A) - 1 |

| Both the ends included | |
|---|---|
| $10 \le N \le 20$ | (20 - 10) + 1 = 11 |

| Only one end included | |
|---|---|
| $10 \le N < 20$ | 20 - 10 = 10 |

| Only one of the ends included | |
|---|---|
| $10 < N \le 20$ | 20 - 10 = 10 |

| None of the ends included | |
|---|---|
| $10 < N < 20$ | (20 - 10) - 1 = 9 |

## Divisibility Rules

Divisibility Rules:

**Divisible by 2** – If unit digit of the number is 0, 2, 4, 6 or 8.

**Divisible by 3** - If sum of digits of the number is divisible by 3.

**Divisible by 4** - If last two digits of the number is divisible by 4.

**Divisible by 5** - If last digit of the number is either 5 or 0.

**Divisible by 6** - If last digit of the number is divisible by two and sum of all the digits of no. is divisible by 3.

**Divisible by 8** - If last 3 digits of the number is divisible by 8.

**Divisible by 9** - If sum of digits of the number is divisible by 9.

**Divisible by 10** – If the unit digit of the number is 0.

**Divisible by 11** - If the difference between the sum of the digits at the even places and the sum of the digits at the odd places is divisible by 11(zero is divisible by 11).

For example - 4553109 is divisible by 11 as the difference of $4 + 5 + 1 + 9 = 19$ and $5 + 3 + 0 = 8$ is 11.

**Divisible by 12** – If the number is divisible by 3 and 4, then the number will be divisible by 12.

**Divisible by 16** - if the number formed by the last 4 digits of the given number is divisible by 16.

## Unit Digit

Following results are true for unit digit:

(i) $(\text{Any digit})^{4n+1}$ = Same digit will be obtained

Example – Unit digit of $8^{53} = 8$, or, Unit digit of $7^{53} = 7$, or, Unit digit of $4^9 = 4$.

(ii) $(\text{Any odd digit})^{4n}$ – Unit digit obtained = 1, where n is any natural number.

Exception – If the odd digit = 5, then the unit digit obtained for $5^{\text{any natural number}} = 5$.

(iii) $(\text{Any even digit})^{4n}$ – Unit digit obtained = 6, where n is any natural number.

Exception – If the unit digit = 0, then the unit digit obtained for $0^{\text{any natural number}} = 0$.

## Rules of Powers

Rules of exponents:

1. $a^m \times a^n = a^{m+n}$
2. $a^m / a^n = a^{m-n}$

3. $(a^m)^n = a^{mn}$
4. $a^m \cdot b^m = (ab)^m$
5. $\frac{a^m}{b^m} = (\frac{a}{b})^m$
6. $a^0 = 1$
7. $a^{-b} = \frac{1}{a^b}$
8. $a^{\frac{m}{n}} = \sqrt[n]{a^m}$
9. $a^{b^c} = a^{[b^c]}$

For example, $2^{3^4} = 2^{81}$ (and not $2^{12}$).

## Rules of Factors

1. If a natural number N can be factorised like $N = a^p \times b^q \times c^r \times$......, where a, b and c are prime nos.then
   (a) Total number of factors = (p+1) (q+1) (r+1).....
   (b) Sum of factors = $\frac{(a^{p+1}-1)(b^{q+1}-1)\,(c^{r+1}-1)}{(a-1)(b-1)\,(c-1)}$
2. If an even natural number N can be factorised like $N = 2^p \times b^q \times c^r \times$......, where a, b and c are prime nos.then
   (a) Total number of even factors = (p) (q+1) (r+1).....
   (b) Total number of odd factors = (q+1) (r+1).....
3. Total number of factors for any perfect square will be odd. For example, total number of factors for 36 will be 9 (namely 1, 2, 3, 4, 6, 9, 12, 18, 36). Converse of this is also true.

## Worked Out examples:

Q1. Which is the lowest natural number divisible by 5 and 11 both?

**Solution** – Lowest natural number divisible by 5 and 11 both = LCM (5,11) = 55

Q2. Which is the lowest two digit natural number that gives a remainder 3 when divided by either 5 or 11?

**Solution** – We need to get 3 remainder after dividing i.e. number should be 3 greater than the number divisible by 5 and 11 both.

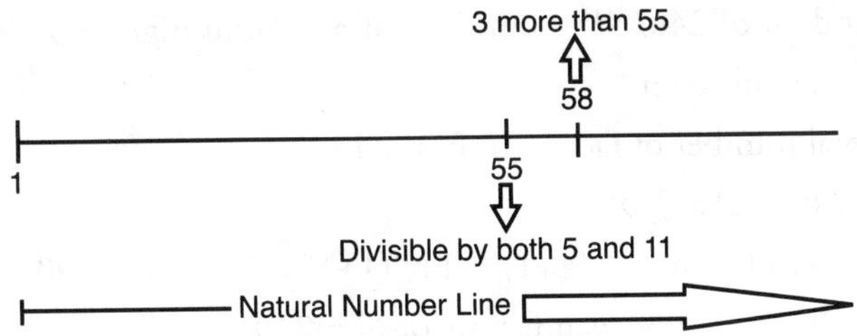


Hence required number = LCM (5,11) + 3 = 55 + 3 = 58.

Q3. If a and b are integers and $a^2 + b^2$ is even, which of the following is NOT possible?

(a) Both a and b are even (b) Both a and b are odd

(c)(a + b) is even (d) (a + b) is odd

**Solution** - If $a^2 + b^2$ is even, then either both $a^2$ and $b^2$ are even or both $a^2$ and $b^2$ are odd. Hence either both a and b are even or both a and b are odd. Clearly, options (a), (b) and (c) are possible. In any case, (a + b) cannot be odd. Hence option (d) is impossible and answer.

Q4. AB + CD = AAA, where AB and CD are two-digit numbers and AAA is a three digit number. A, B, C, and D are distinct natural numbers. What is the value of C?

**Solution** - Given that AB + CD = AAA. Maximum sum of two 2-digit numbers can be 198 (if both are same and equal to 99). Since AB and CD are two digit numbers, then AAA must be 111.

Therefore 1B + CD = 111

B can assume any value between 3 and 9

If B = 3, then CD = 111-13 = 98 and C = 9

If B = 9, then CD = 111-19 = 92 and C = 9

So for all B between 3 & 9, C = 9

Q5. If P represents the product of the first 15 positive integers, then P is not a multiple of:

(a) 99 (b) 84 (c) 72 (d) 57

**Solution** - If P represents the product of the first 15 integers, P would consist of the prime numbers that are below 15 namely 2, 3, 5, 7, 11, 13. Any value that has a prime higher than 13 would not be a value of P. In other words, P will not be divisible by that number. We can see that $57 = 3 \times 19$.

Since 19 is a prime greater than 13, hence option (d) is the answer.

Q6. What is the unit digit of $2463^{342}$?

**Solution** - To find out unit digit, we should be concerned only with the unit digit of the base and last two digits of the power.

Hence unit digit of $2463^{342}$ = unit digit of $3^{42}$ = unit digit of $3^{40} \times 3^2 = (....1) \times 9 = 9$.

Hence 9 is the unit digit.

Q7. Find the total number of factors of N = 240.

**Solution** - $240 = 2^4 \times 3^1 \times 5^1$

Hence number of factors = (4+1) (1+1) (1+1) = $5 \times 2 \times 2 = 20$.

Q8. Find the total number of even factors of N = 240.

**Solution** - $240 = 2^4 \times 3^1 \times 5^1$

Hence number of even factors = (4) (1+1) (1+1) = $4 \times 2 \times 2 = 16$

Q9. Find the total number of odd factors of N = 240.

**Solution** - $240 = 2^4 \times 3^1 \times 5^1$

**Method 1** : **Total number of odd factors = Total number of factors – total number of even factors = 20 – 16 = 4**

**Method 2** : Total number of odd factors = (1 + 1) (1 + 1) = 4 [we will consider only the powers of 3 and 5)

Q10. How many times would we write digit 4 when we write from 10 to 200?

**Solution** - For every 100 numbers, each of the digits form 1 to 9 occurs 10 times at the units place and 10 times at the tens place.

Hence 4 will occur 20 times at units place and 20 times at the tens place if we write from 1 to 200 i.e. total 40 times. But we are counting from 10, and hence remove '4' once.

Hence total number of times 4 will be written when we write from 10 to 200 = 40 – 1 = 39.

## Practice Exercise

Q1. How many numbers are there between 1000 and 2000 which are divisible by both 7 and 8 but not by 3?

(a) 11 (b) 12 (c) 13 (d) 14

Q2. The sum of four consecutive two-digit odd numbers, when divided by 10, becomes a perfect square. Which of the following can possibly be one of these four numbers?

(a) 21 (b) 25 (c) 41 (d) 67

Q3. The number of employees in an organization is a prime number and is less than 300. The ratio of the number of employees who are graduates and above, to that of employees who are not, can possibly be:

(a) 101 : 88 (b) 87 : 100 (c) 110 : 111 (d) 97 : 84

Q4. When you reverse the digits of the number 13, the number increases by 18. How many other two-digit numbers increase by 18 when their digits are reversed?

(a) 5 (b) 6 (c) 7 (d) 8

Q5. Suppose n is an integer such that the sum of digits on n is 2, and $10^{10} < n < 10^{11}$. The number of different values of n is

(a) 11 (b) 10 (c) 9 (d) 8

Q6. If a, a + 2 and a + 4 are prime numbers, then the number of possible solutions for a is

(a) one (b) two (c) third (d) more than three

Q7. Let x and y be positive integers such that x is prime and y is composite. Then,

(a) y - x cannot be an even integer (b) xy cannot be an even integer

(c) $\frac{(x+y)}{x}$ cannot be an even integer (d) None of these

Q8. The owner of a local jewellery store hired three watchmen to guard his diamonds, but a thief still got in and stole some diamonds. On the way out, the thief met each watchman, one at a time. To each he gave $\frac{1}{2}$ of the diamonds he had then, and 2 more besides. He escaped with one diamond. How many did he steal originally?

(a) 40 (b) 36 (c) 25 (d) None of these

Q9. A rich merchant had collected many gold coins. He did not want anybody to know about him. One day, his wife asked, ' How many gold coins do we have?" After a brief pause, he replied, "Well! if I divide the coins into two unequal numbers, then 48 times the difference between the two numbers equals the difference between the squares of the two numbers." The wife looked puzzled. Can you help the merchant's wife by finding out how many gold coins the merchant has?

(a) 96 (b) 53 (c) 43 (d) None of these

Q10. A child was asked to add first few natural numbers (i.e. 1 + 2 + 3 + ...) so long his patience permitted. As he stopped, he gave the sum as 575. When the teacher declared the result wrong, the child discovered he had missed one number in the sequence during addition. The number he missed was

(a) less than 10 (b) 10 (c) 15 (d) more than 15

Q11. Let x, y and z be distinct integers x and y are odd and positive, and z is even and positive. Which one of the following statements cannot be true?

(a) $y(x-z)^2$ is even (b) $y^2(x-z)$ is odd

(c) $y(x-z)$ is odd (d) $z(x-y)^2$ is even

Q12. Anil had to do a multiplication. Instead of taking 35 as one of the multipliers, he took 53. As a result, the product went up by 540. What is the new product?

(a) 1050 (b) 540 (c) 1440 (d) 1590

Q13. All the page numbers from book are added, beginning at page 1. However, one page number was added twice by mistake. The sum obtained was 1000. Which page number was added twice?

(a) 44 (b) 45 (c) 10 (d) 12

Q14. Let D be a recurring decimal of the form $D = 0.\ a_1a_2\ a_1a_2\ a_1a_2...$ where digits $a_1$ and $a_2$ lie between 0 and 9. Further, at most one of them is zero. Which of the following numbers necessarily produces an integer, when multiplied by D?

(a) 18 (b) 108 (c) 198 (d) 288

Q15. Let x, y and z be distinct integers, that are odd and positive. Which one of the following statements cannot be true?

(a) $xyz^2$ is odd (b) $(x-y)^2\ z$ is even

(c) $(x+y-z)\ (x+y)$ is even (d) $(x-y)(y+z)(x+y-z)$ is odd

Q16. If $n^2 = 123456787654321$, what is n?

(a) 12344321 (b) 1235789 (c)11111111 (d) 1111111

Q17. Let a, b, c be distinct digits. Consider a two digit number 'ab' and a three digit number 'ccb', both defined under the usual decimal number system. If $(ab)^2 = ccb$ and $ccb > 300$ then the value of b is

(a) 1 (b) 0 (c) 5 (d) 6

Q18. How many numbers are there between 500 and 600 in which 9 occurs only once?

(a) 19 (b) 18 (c) 20 (d) 21

Q19. The fuel indicator in a car shows one-fifth of the fuel tank as full. When 22 more litres of fuel are poured into the tank, the indicator rests at the three-fourth of the full mark. Find the capacity of the fuel tank.

(a) 25L (b) 35L (c) 30L (d) 40L

Q20. The highest score in an inning was $\frac{2}{9}$ of the total score and the next highest was of the remainder. These scores differ by 8 runs. What was the total score in the innings?

(a) 152 (b) 162 (c) 142 (d) 132

Q21. An army commander wishing to draw up his 5180 men in the form of a solid square found that he had 4 men less. If he could get four more men and form the solid square, the number of men in the front row is -

(a) 72 (b) 68 (c) 78 (d) 82

Q22. A tin of oil was $\frac{4}{5}$ full. When six bottles of oil were taken out and four bottles of oil were poured into it, it was $\frac{3}{5}$ full. How many bottles of oil can it contain?

(a) 20 (b) 10 (c) 30 (d) 40

Q23. To win an election, a candidate needs $\frac{3}{4}$ of the votes. If after $\frac{2}{3}$ of the votes have been counted, a candidates has $\frac{5}{6}$ of what he needs, then what part of the remaining votes does he still need?

(a) $\frac{1}{8}$ (b) $\frac{7}{12}$ (c) $\frac{1}{4}$ (d) $\frac{3}{8}$

Q24. Pintu dealt some cards to Mintu and himself from a full pack of playing cards and laid the rest aside. Pintu then said to Mintu, "If you gave me certain number of your cards, I will have 4 times as many cards as you have. If I give you the same number of cards, I will have thrice as many cards as you have." How many cards did Pintuhave.

(a) 31 (b) 32 (c) 29 (d) 30

Q25. There are four prime numbers written in ascending order. The product of the first three is 385 and that of the last three is 1001. The first number is

(a) 5 (b) 7 (c) 11 (d) 17

Q26. The remainder when $7^{84}$ is divided by 342 is

(a) 0 (b) 1 (c) 49 (d) 341

Q27. How many odd numbered pages are there in a book of 1089 pages.

(a) 545 (b) 544 (c) 546 (d) 542

Q28. Students of a class are preparing for a drill and are made to stand in a row. If 4 students are extra in a row, then there would be 2 rows less. But there would be 4 more rows if 4 students are less in a row. The number of students in the class.

(a) 96 (b) 56 (c) 69 (d) 65

Q29. A certain type of wooden board is sold only in lengths of multiples of 25 cm from 2 to 10 m. A carpenter needs a large quantity of this type of board in 1.65 m lengths. For the minimum waste, the lengths to be purchased should be

(a) 3.30 m (b) 6.60 m (c) 8.25 m (d) 9.95 m

Q30. A boy was asked to write $2^5 \times 9^2$ but he wrote 2592. The numerical difference between the two is

(a) 0 (b) 1 (c) 2 (d) 3

Q31. In a group of buffaloes and ducks, the number of legs are 24 more than twice the number of heads. What is the number of buffaloes in the group?

(a) 6 (b) 12 (c) 8 (d) None of these

Q32. If one-third of a number is 3 more than one-fourth of the number, then what is the number?

(a) 18 (b) 24 (c) 30 (d) 36

Q33. If one-eighth of a pencil is black, half of the remaining is yellow and the remaining $3\frac{1}{4}$ cm is blue, then what is the total length of the pencil?

(a) 6 cm (b) 7 cm (c) 8 cm (d) 11 cm

Q34. What is the unit digit of $7^{85}$?

(a) 7 (b) 3 (c) 9 (d) 1

Q35. What is the unit digit of $8^{47}$?

(a) 8 (b) 4 (c) 2 (d) 6

Q36. Find the total number of factors of N = 360.

(a) 24 (b) 12 (c) 36 (d) 48

## Answer Grid:

| Q. No. | 1 | 2 | 3 | 4 | 5 | 6 | 7 | 8 | 9 | 10 | 11 | 12 | 13 | 14 | 15 | 16 | 17 | 18 |
|---|---|---|---|---|---|---|---|---|---|---|---|---|---|---|---|---|---|---|
| Answer | b | c | d | b | a | a | d | b | d | d | a | d | c | c | d | c | a | b |
| Q. No. | 19 | 20 | 21 | 22 | 23 | 24 | 25 | 26 | 27 | 28 | 29 | 30 | 31 | 32 | 33 | 34 | 35 | 36 |
| Answer | d | b | a | d | b | a | a | b | a | a | c | a | b | d | c | a | c | a |

## Solutions and Explanations

Q1. LCM (7, 8) = 56 $1000 = 56 \times 17 + 48$ $2000 = 56 \times 35 + 40$

LCM (7, 8, 3) = 168 $1000 = 168 \times 5 + 160$ $2000 = 168 \times 11 + 152$

The numbers divided by 56 are (35 – 17) = 18 and the numbers divisible by 168 are (11 – 5) = 6

Hence, the numbers which are divisible by 56 but not by 168 are (18 – 6) = 12 in number

Hence option (b) is the answer.

Q2. Odd digits are 1, 3, 5, 7 and 9. If sum of four consecutive odd numbers is divisible by 10, then the digits should be 7, 9, 1 and 3.

Now using the option (c) – the numbers are 37, 39, 41 and 43.
Hence option (c) is the answer.

Q3. The sum of the numerator and denominator of the ratio should be a prime number.
Note that the number of employees is less than 300.
Consider options.
(1) 101 : 88
$101 + 88 = 189$
$189 \times 2 > 300 \Rightarrow$ Number of employees who are graduates and above = 101
and the others are 88 in number
189 is not a prime number. Option [1] is eliminated.
(2) 87 : 100
$87 + 100 = 187$, $187 \times 2 > 300$
187 is not a prime number.
(3) 110 : 111
$110 + 111 = 221$, $221 \times 2 > 300$
221 is not a prime number.
(4) 85 : 98
$85 + 98 = 183$, $183 \times 2 > 300$
183 is not a prime number.
Hence option (d) is the answer.

Q4. We know that xy – yx = 9 (x- y), where xy is a two digit number and xy ≥ yx.
So, x- y = 2
The possible pairs of (x, y) is (3, 1) (4, 2) (5, 3) (6, 4), (7, 5) (8, 6) (9, 7)
But we want the number other than 13 so, there are 6 possible numbers are there i.e. 24, 35, 46, 57, 68, 79.
So total possible numbers are 6.
Hence option (b) is the answer.

Q5. (1) $10^{10} < n < 10^{11}$

(2) Sum of the digits for 'n = 2 clearly

(n)min = 10000000001 (1 followed by 9 zeros and finally 1)

Obviously, we can form 10 such numbers by shifting '1' by one place from right to left again and again. Again, there is another possibility for n

n = 20000000000

So finally: No. of different values for n = 10 + 1 = 11

Hence option (a) is the answer.

Q6. As any prime number greater than 3 can be expressed in the form $6n \pm 1$ minimum difference between three consecutive prime numbers will be 2 and 4. The values that satisfy the given conditions are only 3, 5 and 7 i.e. only one set is possible.
Hence option (a) is the answer.

Q7. Let us solve this question through elimination

$9 - 7 = 2$ is even, therefore option (a) not possible.

$2 \times 9 = 18$ is even, therefore option (c) is not possible.

$\frac{3+9}{3} = \frac{12}{3} = 4$ is even, therefore option (c) is not possible.

The correct option is (d).

Q8. Since thief escaped with 1 diamond,

Before 3rd watchman he had $(1 + 2) \times 2 = 6$

Before 2nd watchman he had $(6 + 2) \times 2 = 16$

Before 1st watchman he had $(16 + 2) \times 2 = 36$

**Alternative method:**

Go through the options. Hence option (b) is the answer.

Q9. Let the number of gold coins $= x + y$

$48(x-y) = x^2 - y^2$

$48(x - y) = (x-y)(x+y) \Rightarrow x+y = 48$

Hence the correct choice would be none of these. Hence option (d) is the answer.

Q10. Following equation can be formed:

$1150 = n^2 + n - 2x$

$n(n+1) \geq 1150$. The smallest value for it is $n = 34$.

For $n = 34$, hence $40 = 2x \Rightarrow x = 20$. Hence option (d) is the answer.

Q11. Go through the options.

Odd × Odd = Odd

Odd × Even = Even

Even × Even = Even

Option (a) is the answer.

Q12. Let the number be x.

Increase in product $= 53x - 35x = 18x$, or $18x = 540$, so $x = 30$

Hence new product $= 53 \times 30 = 1590$. Hence option d is the answer.

Q13. Let the total number of pages in the book be n.

Let page number x be repeated. Then $\sum_{1=I}^{n} + x = 1000$

$$\frac{n(n+1)}{2} + x = 1000$$

Thus, $\frac{n(n+1)}{2} \leq 1000$ gives n = 44

Since $\frac{n(n+1)}{2} = 990$ (*For* n = 44)

Hence x = 10. Hence option (c) is the answer.

Q14. 99 × D = $a_1a_2$. Hence. So D must be multiplied by 198 as 198 is a multiple of 99. Hence c is the answer.

Q15. Take any three odd and positive numbers and check the options. Hence d is the answer.

Q16. $11^2 = 121$, $111^2 = 12321$, $1111^2 = 1234321$ and so on.

Hence $11111111^2 = 123456787654321$. Hence option (c) is the answer.

Q17. $(ab)^2 = ccb$, the greatest possible value of 'ab' to be 31, Since $31^2 = 961$ so 18 < ab < 31. So the possible value of ab which satisfies $(ab)^2 = ccb$ is 21. so $21^2 = 441$, a = 2, b = 1, c = 4. Hence option (a) is the answer.

Q18. Required numbers are 509, 519, 529, 539, .......... 1598

So there are 18 such numbers.

Hence option (b) is the answer

Q19. Let the capacity of the fuel tank be x L

Given, $\frac{x}{5} + 22 = x$ $\quad (\frac{5}{3} - \frac{1}{5})\,x = 22$

$\frac{11}{20}x = 22$ $\quad x = 40$ L

Hence option (D) is the answer

Q20. Let the total score in the innings be x. then Highest score = $\frac{2}{9}$ x

Next highest score = $\frac{2}{9}$ (x - $\frac{2}{9}$ x), or, $\frac{2}{9}$ x - $\frac{2}{9}$ (x - $\frac{2}{9}$ x) = 8.

Or, $x - x + \frac{2}{9} x = \frac{8\times9}{2}$ . Or, $x = \frac{8\times9\times9}{2\times2}$

Hence x = 162

Hence option (b) is the answer

Q21. Total number of men = 5180 + 4 = 5184

Number of men in first row = $\sqrt{5184}$ = 72

Hence option (a) is the answer

Q22. Let the tin oil contain x number of bottles.

$\frac{4}{5} x - 6 + 4 = \frac{3}{4} x$ $\frac{1}{20} x = 2$ x = 40 bottles

Hence option (d) is the answer

Q23. Let total number of votes cast be x. Total number of counted votes = $\frac{2}{3}$ x

Votes that candidate got = $\frac{5}{6} \times \frac{2}{3} x = \frac{5}{9} x$

Votes still need to win = $\frac{3}{4} x - \frac{5}{9} x = \frac{7}{36} x$

Remaining uncounted votes = $\frac{1}{3}$ x Remaining part = $\frac{7}{36} \times \frac{3}{1} = \frac{7}{12}$

Hence option (b) is the answer

Q24. Let P and M denote Pintu and Mintu respectively.

(P + n) = 4 (M – n) P – 4M = -5n ...........(i)

And (P – n) = 3 (M + n) P – 3M = 4n ........... (ii)

Solving eqs (i) and (ii), we get M = 9n and P = 31n

Put n = 1, we get P = 31

Hence option (a) is the answer

Q25. The four prime numbers are 5, 7, 11, 13

As $5 \times 7 \times 11 = 385$ and $7 \times 11 \times 13 = 1001$

So the first prime number is 5.

Hence option (a) is the answer

Q26. According to remainder theorem, 1 is the remainder

Hence option (b) is the answer

Q27. Number of odd numbered pages = $\frac{1089+1}{2} = 545$

Hence option (a) is the answer

Q28. Let the number of students in the class be x. let the number of rows in which they are made to stand is y. Number of students in each row will be $\frac{x}{y}$.

Given that $(\frac{x}{y} + 4)(y - 2) = (\frac{x}{y} - 4)(y + 4)$

$3x - 4y^2 - 4y = 0 \qquad x = \frac{4y2+4y}{3}$

The least value of y which satisfy the given condition is 8 ie: y = 8, x = 96

Hence option (a) is the answer

Q29. 1.65 m = 165 cm

Required length = LCM of 25 and 165 = 825 cm = 8.25 m

Hence option (c) is the answer

Q30. $2^5 \times 9^2 = 32 \times 81 = 2592$. Hence numerical difference is 0.

Hence option (a) is the answer

Q31. Let the number of buffaloes be x and number of ducks be y.

Then, Number of Legs = 4x + 2y, Number of Heads = x + y

Given, 4x + 2y = 2(x + y) + 24 2x = 24 x = 12

Hence option (b) is the answer

Q32. Let the number be x, Then $-\frac{x}{3} - \frac{x}{4} = 3$, or, $\frac{x}{12} = 3$

Hence x = 36. Hence option (d) is the answer

Q33. $\frac{1}{8}$ part of pencil is black. Half of remaining, ie: $\frac{1}{2} \times \frac{7}{8} = \frac{7}{16}$ is yellow. Now, the

part left = $\frac{7}{16}$ which is equal to $3\frac{1}{2} = 3.5$

Therefore, total length of pencil = $\frac{3.5}{\frac{7}{16}} = 8$ cm

Hence option (c) is the answer

Q34. We know that (any digit)$^{4n+1}$ = same digit will be obtained at the unit place.

In this question, 47 is a number of the format 4n + 1.

Hence unit digit of $7^{85}$ = Unit digit of $7^{4n+1}$ = 7. Hence option (a) is the answer.

Q35. We know that (any even digit)$^{4n}$ = 6 will be obtained at the unit place.

In this question, $8^{47} = 8^{44} \times 8^3$ = (....6) × (512) = 2. Hence option (c) is the answer.

Q36. $360 = 2^3 \times 3^2 \times 5^1$

Hence total number of factors = (3 + 1) (2 + 1) (1 +1) = 24. Hence option (a) is the answer.

# 2 LCM and HCF

## LCM (Least Common Multiple)

LCM is the lowest **positive** number divisible by all the numbers taken. In other words, it is the 1st number that occurs in the table of all the numbers taken.

LCM is defined only for positive numbers i.e. either positive integers or positive fractions. LCM for negative numbers is NOT possible.

## Factorization method to calculate LCM:

Step 1 –Do the prime factorization of the numbers.
Step 2 – Raise each prime factor to its maximum available power and multiply these.
For example, let us find out the LCM for 22 and 28.
Step 1 – $22 = 2^1 \times 11^1$ and $28 = 2^2 \times 7^1$
Step 2 – Prime Number present are 2, 11 and 7.
Maximum power of 2 occurs in $28 = 2^2$, maximum power of 11 occurs in $22 = 11^1$and maximum power of 7 occurs in $28 = 7^1$
LCM $= 2^2 \times 11^1 \times 7^1 = 308$

## HCF (Highest Common Factor)

HCF is the largest number that can divide the given set of numbers. In other words, HCF is the largest number that can be taken out common from the set of numbers.

For example – Consider the numbers 24, 30, 34. Largest number that can be taken out common from these three numbers is 2. Hence 2 is the HCF of these three numbers.

## Properties of HCF:

1. HCF (a, a) = a
2. HCF (a, b) = HCF (b, a)

3. If all the numbers are multiplies or divided by a non zero number n, then the HCF will also be multiplied / divided by n.
4. If HCF of (a, b) = N (where a and b are natural numbers and a > b), then HCF of [b, (a+b)] = [b, (a-b)] = N

For example, HCF of (403, 465) = 31

Hence HCF of [403, (465-403)] = HCF of [403, (62)] = 31

## Standard formula

1. LCM × HCF = Product of two nos.

   This formula can be applied only in case of two nos.
2. LCM of fractions = $\frac{LCM\ of\ numerators}{HCF\ of\ denominators}$
3. HCF of fractions = $\frac{HCF\ of\ numerators}{LCM\ of\ denominators}$
4. For the same set of number, LCM ≥ Each of the numbers ≥ HCF
5. LCM will be always divisible by HCF.
6. HCF of any two consecutive natural numbers = 1.
7. HCF of any two consecutive even natural numbers = 2
8. HCF of any two consecutive odd natural numbers = 1

## Application of LCM / HCF in Remainder based questions:

| Problem states that….. | Solution |
|---|---|
| 1. Find the Greatest Number that will exactly divide a, b and c | Required number = HCF of a, b and c (greatest divisor) |
| 2. Find the Greatest number that will divide x, y and z leaving remainders a, b and c respectively. | Required number (greatest divisor) = HCF of (x-a), (y-b) and (z-c) |
| 3. Find the least number which is exactly divisible by a, b and c | Required number = LCM of a, b and c |
| 4. Find the least number which when divided by x, y and z leaves the remainders a, b and c respectively, and (x-a) = (y-b) = (z-c) = N | Required number = LCM of (x, y and z) – N |
| 5. Find the least number which when divided by x, y and z leaves the same remainder 'r' each case. | Required number = (LCM of x, y and z) + r |

## Worked Out examples:

Q1. LCM of two natural numbers is 100 and its HCF is 30. How many sets of numbers are possible?

**Solution** - LCM has to be divisible by HCF. Since 100 is not divisible by 30, hence LCM = 100 and HCF = 30 are not possible.

Q2. HCF of two natural numbers A and B = 20 and product of A and B = 1200. How many sets of A and B are possible?

**Solution** - Since 20 is the HCF of the numbers, both A and B are divisible by 20.

Assume A = 20p and B = 20q

According to the question, $20p \times 20q = 1200$, or, $400pq = 1200$, or, $pq = \frac{1200}{400} = 3$

Since pq = 3, possible set of values of p and q = (3, 1) and (1, 3)

Hence there are two sets of A and B possible.

Q3 Three containers contain different quantities of rice, whose measurement are 403 kg, 434 kg and 465 kg. What biggest measure can be there to measure all the different quantities exactly?

**Solution** - Required measure = HCF of 403, 434 and 465 = 31 kg.

Q4. The LCM of two numbers is 4800 and their HCF is 160. If one of the numbers is 480, then the other number is?

**Solution** - LCM × HCF = Product of two numbers

Other number $= \frac{4800 \times 160}{480} = 1600$

Q5. Sum of two numbers is 200 and their HCF is 20. How many sets of two values are possible?

**Solution** - Since HCF is 20, assume the numbers are 20x and 20y.

According to the question, $20x + 20y = 200$, or, $(x+y) = 10$

For (x+y) = 10, following sets can be formed :- (1, 9), (2, 8), (3, 7), (4, 6) and (5, 5).

Out of these sets, for (2, 8), (4, 6) and (5, 5); HCF would not be equal to 20.

Only for (1, 9) and (3, 7), HCF will be 20. Hence two sets are possible.

Q6. LCM of two natural numbers is 230 and their HCF is 23. How many sets of values are possible?

**Solution** - Since HCF is 23, assume that the numbers are 23x and 23y.

LCM × HCF = Product of the numbers

Or, $230 \times 23 = 23x \times 23y$, or, $xy = 10$

It gives us the following set of values of x and y : (10, 1) and (5, 2).

Hence numbers are (230, 23) and (115, 46). Hence there are two sets possible.

Q7. There are three bells in a temple. 1st bell tolls after every 4 seconds, 2nd bell toll after every 6 seconds and 3rd bell tolls after every 9 seconds. After how much time all three bells will toll together?

**Solution** - Answer would be LCM of (4, 6, 9) = 36 seconds.

Q8. In the above question, how many times all three bells will toll together in 6 minutes?

**Solution** - 6 minutes = 360 seconds

Since all three bells toll together in 36 seconds, hence number of times they will toll together $= \frac{360}{36} = 10$ times. But we'll have to count T = 0 sec situation too when all three of them have toll together.

Hence answer = 1 + 10 = 11 times

Q9. A number when divided by 7 and 9 gives remainder 2 and 2 respectively. Which is the lowest such two digit natural number?

**Solution** - Using point (5) of **Application of LCM / HCF in Remainder based questions:**

Answer to this question will be = LCM (7, 9) + 2 = 65.

Q10. A natural number divided by 7 gives remainder 3, when divided by 13 gives remainder 9. Which is the lowest such natural number?

**Solution** - It can be seen that (7 – 3) = (13 – 9) = 4

Using point (4) of **Application of LCM / HCF in Remainder based questions:**

Answer = LCM (7, 13) – 4 = 87.

## Practice Exercise 1

Q1. The HCF and LCM of two numbers are 21 and 4641 respectively. If one of the number lies between 200 and 300, then the two numbers are

(a) 273, 357 (b) 273, 361

(c) 273, 359 (d) 273, 363

Q2. HCF of 3240, 3600 and a third number is 36 and their LCM is $2^4 \times 3^5 \times 5^2 \times 7^2$. The third number is

(a) $2^2 \times 3^5 \times 7^2$ (b) $2^2 \times 5^3 \times 7^2$

(c) $2^3 \times 3^5 \times 7^2$ (d) $2^5 \times 5^2 \times 7^2$

Q3. The sum of two numbers is 462 and their highest common factor is 22. What is the number of set of values satisfying the condition?

(a) 1 (b) 3 (c) 2 (d) 6

Q4. The LCM of two numbers is 280 and their ratio is 7:8. The two numbers are

(a) 70, 80 (b) 42, 48 (c) 35, 40 (d) 28, 32

Q5. Among how many students may 429 bats and 715 balls be equally divided?

(a) 143 (b) 153 (c) 183 (d) 13

Q6. What is the total of two natural numbers with LCM 36 and HCF 6, if the numbers are in the ratio 2 : 3 ?

(a) 30 (b) 10

(c) 35 (d) cannot be determined

Q7. Find the number of pairs of distinct natural numbers with LCM as 56.

(a) 3 (b) 4 (c) 10 (d) None of these

Q8. H and L are two natural numbers such that their HCF is same as their LCM then which of the following is necessarily true?

(a) H = L = 1 (b) H = L

(c) H divides L but H ≠ L (d) None of these

Q9. A commander can draw up his soldiers in the columns of 10, 15 and 18 soldiers and he can also draw them up in the form of a solid square. Find the least number of soldiers with the commander?

(a) 100 (b) 3600 (c) 900 (d) 90

Q10. The LCM and HCF of a pair of a numbers are 926 and 12 respectively. How many such distinct pairs are possible?

(a) 3 (b) 2 (c) 1 (d) 0

Q11. Seven drums beat at intervals of 2, 3, 4, 6, 8, 9 and 12 minutes respectively. They started ringing simultaneously at 6 in the evening. How many more times would all seven drum beats simultaneously till 5 in the morning of the same day?

(a) 8 (b) 9 (c) 12 (d) 18

Q12. An optical fibre wire is sold only in multiples of 1 metre and a person required several lengths of wire, each 85 cm long. To avoid any wastage and to minimize labour, he should purchase minimum length of

(a) 8.5 m (b) 17 m (c) 85 m (d) 1 m

Q13. There are 408 men and 312 women in a factory which are to be divided into equal sections of either men or women alone. Find the total number of sections thus formed

(a) 31 (b) 32 (c) 35 (d) 30

Q14. If P, Q and R are three numbers, such that, the LCM of P and Q is Q and the LCM of Q and R is R, then the LCM of P, Q and R is

(a) P (b) Q (c) R (d) $\frac{P+Q+R}{3}$

Q15. If two numbers are in the ratio of 2 : 3 and the product of their HCF and LCM is 33750, then the sum of the numbers is -

(a) 250 (b)425 (c) 325 (d) 375

Q16. The LCM and HCF of two numbers are 84 and 21 respectively. If the ratio of the two numbers is 1:4, then the larger of the two numbers is -

(a) 12 (b) 48 (c) 84 (d) 108

Q17. A number when divided by 7 and 5 gives remainder 3 and 3 respectively. Which is the lowest such two digit natural number?

(a) 23 (b) 38 (c) 73 (d) None of these

Q18. A number when divided by 11 and 7 gives remainder 7 and 3 respectively. Which is the lowest such natural number?

(a) 51 (b) 73 (c) 24 (d) None of these

Q19. At a bookstore, 'MODERN BOOK STORE' is a flashed using neon lights. The words as individually flashed at the intervals of $2\frac{1}{2}$ sec, $4\frac{1}{5}$ sec, and $5\frac{1}{8}$ sec respectively, and each word is put off after a second. The least time after which the full name of the bookstore can be read again is

(a) 49.5 sec (b) 73.5 sec (c) 1744.5 sec (d) 855 sec

Q20. Three pieces of cakes of weight $4\frac{1}{2}$ pound, $6\frac{3}{4}$ pound, and $7\frac{1}{5}$ pound respectively are to be divided into parts of equal weight. Each part must be as heavy as possible. If one such part is served to each guest, then what is the maximum number of guests that could be served?

(a) 54 (b) 72 (c) 20 (d) None of these

## Answer Grid:

| Q. No. | 1 | 2 | 3 | 4 | 5 | 6 | 7 | 8 | 9 | 10 |
|---|---|---|---|---|---|---|---|---|---|---|
| Answer | a | a | d | c | a | a | c | b | c | d |
| Q. No. | 11 | 12 | 13 | 14 | 15 | 16 | 17 | 18 | 19 | 20 |
| Answer | b | b | d | c | d | c | b | b | b | d |

## Solutions and Explanations:

Q1. Product of the numbers = HCF × LCM = $21 \times 4641 = 21 \times 3 \times 7 \times 13 \times 17 = 3 \times 7 \times 3 \times 7 \times 13 \times 17$

The numbers can be $3 \times 7 \times 13$ and $3 \times 7 \times 17$, i.e. 273 and 357

Hence option (a) is the answer

Q2. $3600 = 4 \times 9 \times 100 = 2^2 \times 3^2 \times 5^2 \times 2^2 = 2^4 \times 3^2 \times 5^2$

$3240 = 810 \times 4 = 3^2 \times 3^2 \times 2 \times 5 \times 2^2 = 3^4 \times 2^3 \times 5$

Third number = $2^2 \times 3^5 \times 7^2$

Hence option (a) is the answer

Q3. There are 6 such pairs (22, 440), (44, 418), (88, 374), (110, 352), (176, 286), (220, 242)

Hence option (d) is the answer

Q4. Let the number be 7x and 8x. HCF = x

LCM × HCF = Product of numbers

$280 \times x = 56\, x^2$, or, x = 5. Hence numbers are 35 and 40

Hence option (c) is the answer.

Q5. HCF (429, 715) = 143

Hence the number of children must be 143

Hence option (a) is the answer.

Q6. Let the number be 2x and 3x, then HCF (2x, 3x) = x = 6

The two numbers are $2 \times 6$ and $3 \times 6$ i.e. 12 and 18. Thus total of numbers are $(12 + 18) = 30$

Hence option (a) is the answer.

Q7. Let a, b be the two numbers with LCM 56. Since 56 is the LCM, a and b will be the divisors of 56. Following are the divisors of 56 = 1, 2, 4, 7, 8, 14, 28 and 56. Combining two of these at a time, the possible pairs with LCM as 56 are (1, 56), (2, 56), (4, 56), (7, 56), (8, 56), (14, 56), (28, 56), (8, 28), (8, 14) and (7, 8). Thus there are 10 pairs.

Hence option (c) is the answer.

Q8. For any two numbers, if their HCF is equal to LCM, then numbers have to be equal. Converse of this is also true i.e. if two numbers are equal, then its LCM is equal to HCF. Hence option (b) is the answer.

Q9. LCM (10, 15, 18) = 90. The least number of soldiers can be of the form 90k.

Since 90K should be a perfect square, hence minimum value of k = 10.

Hence option (c) is the answer.

Q10. HCF = 12 and LCM = 926. If the numbers be of the form 12a and 12b then LCM = 12ab.

LCM is always divisible by HCF. So in this question 926 is not divisible by 12, so no such pair exist.

Hence option (d) is the answer.

Q11. LCM (2, 3, 4, 6, 8, 9, 12) = 72 minutes. From 6 PM to 5 AM (11 hours), Number of times they will beat together = $\frac{11 \times 60}{72} = 9$

Since question is asking for "more number of times", we'll not count T = 0 situation.

Hence option (b) is the answer.

Q12. LCM (1000 cm, 85 cm) = 17000 cm = 17 m

Hence option (b) is the answer.

Q13. HCF (408, 312) = 24

Hence the number of men or women that can be placed in a section = 24

Thus the total number of sections are given by $\frac{408}{24} + \frac{312}{24} = 17 + 13 = 30$

Hence option (d) is the answer.

Q14. Option (c) is the answer.

Q15. The ratio of the two numbers is 2 : 3. So, the numbers are 2x and 3x.

$2x \times 3x = 33750$ (product of HCF and LCM), or, $x^2 = \frac{33750}{6} = 5625$

Hence x = 75

Thus, the sum of the numbers = $2 \times 75 + \times 3 \times 75 = 375$

Hence option (d) is the answer.

Q16. Let the number be x and 4x. Then, $84 \times 21 = x \times 4x$

Or, $4x^2 = 1764$, or, $x^2 = 441$. Hence $x = 21$

So the largest number is 4x i.e. $4 \times 21 = 84$

Hence option (c) is the answer

Q17. Lowest natural number = LCM (5, 7) + 3 = 38. Hence option (b) is the answer.

Q18. Lowest natural number = LCM (11, 7) – 4 = 73. Hence option (b) is the answer.

Q19. Because each word is lit for a second,

$$\text{LCM}\left(\frac{5}{2}+1, \frac{17}{4}+1, \frac{41}{8}+1\right) = \text{LCM}\left(\frac{7}{2}, \frac{21}{4}, \frac{49}{8}\right)$$

$$\frac{LCM(7,21,49}{HCM(2,4,8)} = 49\frac{49\times 3}{2} = 73.5S$$

Hence option (b) is the answer.

Q20. $\text{HCF}\left(\frac{9}{2}, \frac{27}{4}, \frac{36}{5}\right) = \frac{HCF(9,27,36)}{LCM(2,4,5)} = \frac{9}{20}$ Pound weight of each piece

Total weight = 18.45 pound

Maximum number of guests = $\frac{18.45\times 20}{9} = 41$

Hence option (d) is the answer.

# 3 Percentage

**Percentage expresses a quantity out of 100. It is represented by the symbol '%'.**

For example, 6% can be expressed like as shown in the diagram:

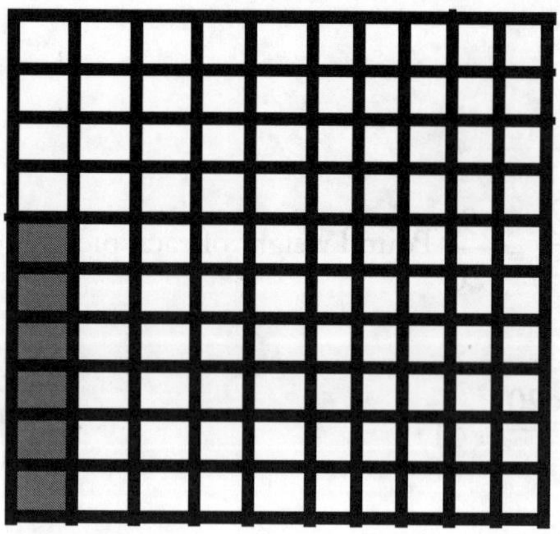

Out of 100 boxes, six of those are shaded which is equivalent to 6%.

(b) Percentage is also used to express a quantity out of 100.'

For example - if a student has scored 450 out of 600 total marks, then his percentage marks $= \frac{450}{600} \times 100 = 75\%$. It means that – had the full marks been 100, this student would have achieved 75 marks.

(c) Percentage is also a method to write down the ratios. For example, $15\% = \frac{15}{100}$

## Important Formula:

(a) Multiplications in percentage

$$x\% \text{ of } y = \frac{x}{100} \times y$$

x% of y% of z $\frac{x}{100} \times \frac{y}{100} \times z$

It should be noted that (a) x% of y = y% of x; (b) x% of y% of z = x% of z% of y = y% of z% of x

(b) Comparing one quantity as a percentage of other quantity

What percentage of salary of Ram is the salary of Shyam?

It can be seen that we are required to express salary of Shyam as a percentage of Salary of Ram. So salary of Ram will be the base or denominator.

$$\frac{Salary\ of Shyam}{SalaryofRam} \times 100$$

(c) Percentage change $\frac{Change}{InitialValue} \times 100$

(d) Successive percentage change

If there are two successive percentage increase of a% and b%, then net percentage change = $(a + b + \frac{ab}{100})\%$

Instead of increase, if there is percentage decrease, then minus sign will be used.

For example, if there are two successive percentage changes of a% increase and b% decrease, then net percentage change $(a - b + \frac{a(-b)}{100})\% = (a - b - \frac{ab}{100})\%$

Similarly, if there are two successive percentage changes of a% decrease and b% decrease, then net percentage change $(-a - b + \frac{(-a)(-b)}{100})\% = (-a - b + \frac{ab}{100})\%$

(e) Inter-conversion among percentage, ratio and decimal

$23\% = \frac{23}{100} = 0.23$

It is advisable to know the percentage equivalent of the reciprocals from 1 to 15:

$\frac{1}{1} = 100\%$ $\frac{1}{2} = 50\%$ $\frac{1}{3} = 33.33\%$ $\frac{1}{4} = 25\%$ $\frac{1}{5} = 20\%$

$\frac{1}{6} = 16.66\%$ $\frac{1}{7} = 14.28\%$ $\frac{1}{8} = 12.5\%$ $\frac{1}{9} = 11.11\%$ $\frac{1}{10} = 10\%$

$\frac{1}{11} = 9.09\%$ $\frac{1}{12} = 8.33\%$ $\frac{1}{13} = 7.69\%$ $\frac{1}{14} = 7.14\%$ $\frac{1}{15} = 6.66\%$

## Product Stability Relation:

In case of any relation where product of two quantities is a constant, product stability relation is useful.

For example, Speed × Time = Distance. Now if distance is constant, then we can use this relation to get the answer.

General Expression for Product Stability Relation:

If one quantity increases by ratio $\frac{a}{b}$, then other quantity will decrease by $\frac{a}{a+b}$.

Similarly, if one quantity decreases by ratio, then other quantity will increase by $\frac{a}{b-a}$.

For example, (a) if speed is increased by 30% = $\frac{3}{10}$, then time will decrease by $= \frac{3}{10+3} = \frac{3}{13}$

(b) if speed is decreased by 30% = $\frac{3}{10}$, then time will increase by $\frac{3}{10-3} = \frac{3}{7}$

## Worked out Examples:

Q1. Population of a town is 18 lacs. Out of this, 3% people are affected by viral fever. How many people are affected by viral fever?

**Solution** – Total number of people affected = 3% of 18 lacs = $\frac{3}{100} \times 18$ = 0.54 lacs = 54,000 persons

Q2. Salary of Bill is Rs. 12,000 per month and salary of Alex is Rs. 15,000 per month. What percentage of Bill's salary is Alex's salary?

**Solution** – Question is asking us to compare Alex's salary as a percentage of Bill's salary. Hence salary of Bill will the base or denominator.

Required percentage = $\frac{Bill'ssalary}{Alex'ssalary} \times 100 = \frac{15000}{12000} 100 = 125\%$

Q3. Salary of Bill is Rs. 12,000 per month and salary of Alex is Rs. 15,000 per month. What percentage of Alex's salary is Bill's salary?

**Solution** – Question is asking us to compare Bill's salary as a percentage of Alex's salary. Hence salary of Alex will the base or denominator.

Required percentage $\frac{Bill'ssalary}{Alex'ssalary} \times 100 = \frac{12000}{15000} \times 100 = 80\%$

Q4. In 2013, population of a town increased by 20% over the population in 2012. In 2014, population of this town increased by 10% over the population in 2013. What is the net percentage growth in the population from 2012 to 2014?

**Solution** – Using the formula for successive percentage increase:

Netpercentageincreaseforthegivenperiod= $(a + b + \frac{ab}{100})\% = (20 + 10 + \frac{20\times10}{100})\%$

$= 32\%$

Q5. Salary of A is 20% more than the salary of B and 10% less than the salary of C. If salary of B is Rs. 12,000, what is the salary of C?

**Solution** – Salary of A = Salary of B + 20% of salary of B = Rs. 12,000 + 20% of Rs. 12000

Or, Salary of A = Rs. 12,000 + $\frac{20}{100} \times$ 12,000 = Rs. 12,000 + Rs. 2400 = Rs. 14,400.

Now, salary of A = 10% less than the salary of C = Salary of C – 10% of salary of C = Rs. 14,400

Or, Salary of C – 10% of salary of C = Rs. 14,400

Or, 90% of the salary of C = Rs. 14400. Hence salary of C = Rs. 14400 $\times \frac{100}{90}$ = Rs. 16,000

Q6. Price of an article increases by 200% over the price last year. If its price was Rs. 80 now, what will be its price two years later?

**Solution** – Price of article after one year = Rs. 80 + 200% of Rs. 80 = Rs. 80 + $\frac{200}{100} \times$ Rs. 80 = Rs. 240

Price of the article after two years = Rs. 240 + $\frac{200}{100}$ × Rs. 240 = Rs. 720.

Q7. Aman got 273 marks in his graduation exam and got 5% more than the pass percentage. If Binod got 312 marks, then by what percentage above the pass marks, did he pass the exam?

**Solution** - Let us assume that pass marks = N marks. Since Aman got 5% more than the pass percentage, we can say the multiplier here is 1.05. So, 1.05 × N = 273 ⇒ N = 260. Binod got 312 marks ⇒ 52 marks more than the pass marks. So he obtained $\frac{52}{260} \times 100$ = 20% more marks than the pass marks.

Q8. Express 5:2 as percentage.

**Solution:** 5:2 = $\frac{5}{2}$. To covert this in percentage, we need to multiple the ratio by 100 = $\frac{5}{2}$ × 100 % = 250%.

Q9. A's income is 60% of B's income, and A's expenditure is 70% of B's expenditure. If A's income is 75% of B's expenditure, find the ratio of A's saving to B's saving.

**Solution** – Let us assume that Income of B = Rs. 100, then income of A = Rs. 60. Now using "A's income is 75% of B's expenditure", B's expenditure = 60/0.75 = Rs. 80. So, B's savings = Rs. 20

Expenditure of B = Rs. 80 ⇒ Expenditure of A = 70% of 80 = Rs. 56.

So savings of A = Income of A – Expenditure of A = Rs. 60 – Rs. 56 = Rs. 4

So Savings of A : savings of B = Rs 4 : Rs 20 = 1 : 5. Hence option (B) is the answer.

Q10. Savings of Samar and Aarna is 20% and 30% respectively less than Savings of Aadya. By what percentage is the Savings of Samar more than Savings of Aarna?

1. 33.33% 2. 50% 3. 10% 4. 14.28%

**Solution:** Assume that the Savings of Aadya = Rs. 100 ⇒ Savings of Samar = Rs. 80 and Savings of Aarna = Rs. 70

To calculate "By what percentage is the Savings of Samar more than Savings of Aarna", we would 1st calculate Savings of Samar is how much more than the Savings of Aarna = Rs. 10. Since "than the Savings of Aarna" is to be calculated, Savings of Aarna will be the base (denominator). Percentage increase $\frac{10}{70} \times 100 = 14.28\%$.

Q11. If 140 is 20% of a number, then 120% of that number will be:

**Solution – Method 1:** Let the number be x.

Then, 20% of x = 140, or, (20/100 × x) = 140, or, x = (140 × 100/20) = 700.

Hence 120% of x = (120/100 × 700) = 840.

**Method 2:** If 20% = 140, so 120 % will be six times of 140 = 840

Q12. Length of a rectangle is increased by 25%. By what percentage shall the breadth be decreased so that area remains constant?

**Solution** – Using Product Stability Relation:

$25\% = \frac{1}{4} \uparrow$ will result in other quantity getting decreased by $\frac{1}{1+4} = \frac{1}{5}$ = 20%. Hence breadth should be decreased by 20%.

## Percentage

Q1. In an examination, 40% marks are required to pass the exam. X obtains 10% less than the number of marks required to pass. Y obtains $11\frac{1}{9}\%$ less than X and Z obtained $41\frac{3}{17}\%$ less than the number of marks obtained by X and Y together. What marks did Z get?

a) 50 b) 40 c) 35 d) 45

Q2. Bittu spends 40% of his salary on food items, 50% of remaining on transport, 30% of remaining after spending on food and transport; he spends on clothes and saves the balance. If he saves Rs. 630 every month, what is his monthly salary?

a) 1500 b) 3000 c) 5000 d) 6500

Q3. The Rice sold by grocer contained 10% low quality rice. What quantity of good quality rice should be added to 150 kg of rice sold by grocer so that the percentage of low quality rice becomes 5%?

a) 50 b) 85 c) 135 d) 150

Q4. The present population of a town is 5500. If the number of males increased by 11% and the number of females increased by 20%, then the population will becomes 6330. What is the present population of females in the town?

a) 2000 b) 2500 c)3000 d) 3500

Q5. A Plant was planted 3 years ago. The rate of its growth is 30% per annum. If at present, the height of the plant is 670 cm, what was it when the plant was planted?

a) 305 cm b) 405 cm c) 500 cm d) 625 cm

Q6. When the price of salt was increased by 32%, a family reduced its consumption in such a way that the expenditure on salt was only 10% more than before. If 30 kg per month were consumed before, find the new monthly consumption?

a) 42 b) 35 c) 25 d) 16

Q7. A man income is increased by Rs. 1200 and at same time the rate of tax to be paid is reduced from 12% to 10%. He now pays the same amount of tax as before. What is his increased income, if 20% of his income is exempted from tax in both cases?

a) 6300 b) 7200 c) 4500 d) 6500

Q8. If J% of K is 100 and K% of L is 200, then find the relation between J and L.

a) L = J b) 2L = J c) L = 2J d) None of above

Q9. A factory kept increasing its output by the same percentage every year. Find the percentage increase per year if it is known that output is doubled after two years?

a) $100\sqrt{2}\%$ b) $100(\sqrt{2}+1)\%$ c) $100(\sqrt{2}-1)\%$ d) $50(\sqrt{3}-1)\%$

Q10. The tax on a commodity is diminished by 10% and its consumption increased by 10%. The effect on the revenue derived from it is P% change. Find the value of P?

a) 1 b) 2 c) -1 d) -2

Q11. A solution of Honey syrup has 15% honey. Another solution has 5% honey. How many liters of the second solution must be added to 20 L of first solution to make a solution of 10% honey ?

a) 10 L b) 5 L c) 15 L d) 20 L

Q12. Two gallons of a mixture of milk and water contain 12% of water. They are added to 3 gallons of another mixture, containing 7% of water and half a gallon of water is then added to the whole. Find the percentage of water in the resultant mixture?

a) $17\frac{3}{11}\%$ b) $16\frac{12}{11}\%$ c) $14\frac{1}{11}$ 1% d) None of these

Q13. The difference between 38% of a number and 24% of the same number is 135.10. What is 40% of that number?

a) 394 b) 370 c) 378 d) 386

Q14. In an examination Sohit obtained 20% more than Rohit but 10% less than Rajesh. If the marks obtained by Rohit are 1080, find the percentage marks obtained by Rajesh if the full marks are 2000?

a) 72% b) 78.33% c) 86.66% d) None of these

Q15. Out of the total production of copper from ore, 20% of the ore gets wasted. Out of remaining copper only 25% is pure copper. If the pure copper obtained in a year was 80000 kg, then the quantity of ore in year is

a) 400000 kg b) 500000 kg c) 450000 kg d) 600000 kg

Q16. The population of a City is 10000. If the population increased by 10% in first year, 20% in second year and decreases by 5% in third year, what will be its population after 3 year ?

a) 13860 b) 11540 c) 12860 d) 12540

Q17. A vessel full of spirit contains 40% water. A part of this spirit is replaced by containing 19% water now the percentage of water is found to be 26%. The quantity of spirit replaced is

a) $\frac{2}{3}$ b) $\frac{1}{3}$ c) $\frac{3}{7}$ d) $\frac{4}{7}$

Q18. One liter of water is evaporated from 6 L of solution containing 5% sugar. Find the percentage of sugar in the remaining solution?

a) 8% b) 10% c) 6% d) 4%

Q19. There are two candidates Anu and Manu for an election. Anu gets 65% of total valid votes. If total votes were 6000, what is the number of valid votes that the other candidate Manu gets if 25% of total votes were declared invalid?

a) 1575 b) 1625 c) 1675 d) 1525

Q20. In a medical certificate by mistake a person gave his height as 25% more than actual. In the interview, he clarified that his height was 5 ft 5 inches. Find the percentage correction made by candidate from his stated height to his actual height?

a) 28.56 b) 20 c) 25 d) None of these

Q21. In a Hindi exam, a student scored 30% in first paper out of total of 180. How much should he score in the second paper (out of 150) if he is to get at least 50% marks overall?

a) 75% b) 80% c) 74% d) 84%

Q22. The present worth of bill due 7 months hence is Rs. 1200. If the bill were due at the end of $2\frac{1}{2}$ year, its present worth would be Rs. 1016. The rate percent of the bill is

a) 16% b) 8% c) 10% d) 18%

Q23. Is A is 150% of B, then B is what percent of A + B?

a) $33\frac{1}{3}\%$ b) 40% c) 75% d) 80%

Q24. The price of diesel is increased by 25%. How much percent must a truck owner reduce the consumption of diesel so that expenditure on diesel remains the same?

a) 25% b) 50% c) 30% d) 20%

Q25. 50 g of an alloy of copper and lead contains 80% copper (by wt). The quantity of copper that is to be mixed up with this alloy, so that it may contain 95% copper is

a) 200 g b) 50 g c) 150 g d) 10 g

Q26. From the income of an employee, 10% is deducted as house rent, 15% of rest spend on chocolate and 10% of balance on toys. After this expenditure he is left with Rs. 1377. His income is

a) 2000 b) 2040 c) 2100 d) 2200

Q27. In a test, there were 2000 candidates, out of which 900 candidates were Men and the rest were Women. If 32% of men and 38% women passed, then the total percentage of failed candidates is

a) 68.5% b) 64.7% c) 35.3% d) 70%

Q28. If the price of milk increases by 30%, find how much the quantity of milk must be reduced so that expenditure remains the same as before?

a) 30% b) $23\frac{1}{3}\%$ c) $27\frac{2}{13}\%$ d) 19%

Q29. In a factory, there are 75% skilled workers and remaining unskilled. 80% of skilled and 20% of unskilled workers are permanent. If number of temporary workers is 126, then what is the number of total workers?

a) 480 b) 510 c) 360 d) 377

Q30. There were two parties in an election. 10% of voters did not vote. 60 votes were declared invalid. The elected party got 308 votes more than its opponent. If elected party got 47% of total votes, how many votes did each party get?

a) 2316 & 2012 b) 2629 & 2324 c) 2871 & 2575 d) 2914 & 2606

Q31. If the height of a triangle is decreased by 40% and base increased by 40%, what is the effect on its area?

a) No Change b) 8% decrease c) 16% decrease d) 16% increase

Q32. Population of a Colony is 296000 out of which 166000 are Boys. 50% of population is literate. If 70% boys are literate, then the number of Girls, who are literate, is

a) 32200 b) 31800 c) 66400 d) 48000

Q33. The population of a Country is increases at a rate of 4% per annum. There is an additional annual increase of 1% in the population due to new born babies. The percentage increase in the population after 2 year is

a) 10% b) 10.25% c) 10.50% d) 10.75%

Q34. The population of Virus culture doubles every 2 min. approximately, how many minutes will it take for the population to grow from 1000 to 500000 bacteria?

a) 10 min b) 12 min c) 14 min d) 18 min

Q35. If p% of S is equal to q% of T, then r% of T is what percent of S?

a) r% b) $\frac{pr}{100}$% c) $\frac{qr}{p}$% d) $\frac{rp}{q}$%

Q36. G% of H is H% of

a) G b) $\frac{H}{100}$ c) $\frac{G}{100}$ d) 100G

Q37. A person receives a 5% raise. A year later, the person receives a 2.5% cut in pay and now the amount is Rs. 22702.68. What was his amount to begin with?

a) 22000 b) 22176 c) 25000 d) 22193

Q38. A reduction of 20% in the price of Flour enables a purchaser to obtain 2kg more for Rs. 160. Find the original price per kg of Flour.

a) 12 b) 15 c) 16 d) 18

Q39. Which of the following multipliers will cause a number to be increased by 25.3%?

a) 12.53 b) 125.3 c) 1.253 d) 1253

Q40. When the price of a TV was reduced by 20%, its sale increased by 80%. What was the net effect on the sale?

a) 44% increase b) 44% decrease c) 66% increase d) 75% increase

**Answer Grid:**

| Q. No. | 1 | 2 | 3 | 4 | 5 | 6 | 7 | 8 | 9 | 10 | 11 | 12 | 13 | 14 | 15 | 16 | 17 | 18 | 19 | 20 |
|---|---|---|---|---|---|---|---|---|---|---|---|---|---|---|---|---|---|---|---|---|
| Answer | b | b | d | c | a | c | b | c | c | c | d | a | d | a | a | d | a | c | b | b |
| Q. No. | 21 | 22 | 23 | 24 | 25 | 26 | 27 | 28 | 29 | 30 | 31 | 32 | 33 | 34 | 35 | 36 | 37 | 38 | 39 | 40 |
| Answer | c | c | a | d | c | a | b | b | c | d | c | b | a | d | d | a | b | b | c | a |

## Solutions and Explanations:

Q1. Let the total marks be 100

then, minimum marks to be passed is 40

A obtained marks = $40 - 40 \times \frac{10}{100}$ = 36 marks

B obtained marks = $36 - \frac{10}{100} \times \frac{36}{100}$ = 32 marks

C obtained marks = $(36 + 32) - (36 + 32) \times \frac{700}{17 \times 100}$ = 40 marks

Hence (B) is the answer

Q2. Let monthly salary be Rs. X

According to the given condition, $\frac{4x}{10} + \frac{6x}{10} \times \frac{50}{100} + \frac{3x}{10} \times \frac{30}{100}$ saving money = $x$

$\frac{4x}{10} + \frac{3x}{10} + \frac{9x}{100}$ 630 = x

By solving this we get x = 3000

Hence (B) is the answer

Q3. Here, 10% of 150 kg = 15kg

Good quality of rice is 135

To become the 5% law quality of rice, we add 150 kg more rice

Hence (D) is the answer

Q4. Let the population of male and female be x and y respectively.

X + Y = 5500 .... (i)

And $\frac{111x}{100} + \frac{120y}{100}$ + = 633000 .... (ii)

Solving Equations (i) and (ii), we get Y = 2500

Hence (C) is the answer

Q5. Let the height of tree when it was planted be x cm

$X \times (\frac{1+30}{100})^3 = 670$

$X = 670 \times \frac{10 \times 10 \times 10}{13 \times 13 \times 13}$ = 305cm

Hence (A) is the answer

Q6. Let the price of salt be x per kg

Initial expenditure = Rs. 30x

New expenditure = Rs. 33x

New monthly consumption = $\frac{33x}{1.32x}$ = 25kg

Hence (C) is the answer

Q7. Let his increased income be x

$$(x-1200) \times \frac{80}{100} \times \frac{12}{100} = x \times \frac{80}{100} \times \frac{10}{100}$$

$\Rightarrow$ 12x – 14400 = 10x   X = 7200

Hence (B) is the answer

Q8. K% of L = 2(J% of K)= $\frac{KL}{100} = \frac{2JK}{100} \Rightarrow$ L = 2J

Hence option (C) is the answer

Q9. Let the output be x and percentage be a

Then, $X(1 + \frac{a}{100})^2 = 2x$

$$\Rightarrow 1+ \frac{a}{100} = \sqrt{2}$$

$$\Rightarrow \frac{a}{100} = \sqrt{2}-1 \quad a=(\sqrt{2}-1) \times 100\%$$

Hence (C) is the answer

Q10. Using formula K% = $-\frac{x+y-xy}{100}$

$$= -10 + 10 - 10 \times = \frac{10}{100} -1\%$$

Hence (C) is the answer

Q11. Let x L of second solution must be added

Then, $15 \times 20 + 5 \times \frac{x}{20} + x = 10$

$\Rightarrow$ 300 + 5x = 200 + 10x   X = $\frac{100}{5}$ = 20L

Hence (d) is the answer

Q12. Total quantity of mixture = 2 + 3 + 0.5 = 5.5 gallon

Total quantity of water

$$= 2 \times \frac{12}{100} + 3 \times \frac{7}{100} + 3 \times +0.5 = 0.95 \text{ gallon}$$

$$\text{Required percentage} = \frac{0.75}{5.5} \times 100 = \frac{232}{13} = 17\frac{11}{13}\%$$

Hence (A) is the answer

Q13. Let that number be x

Then, 0.38x – 0.24x = 135.10

$$X = \frac{135.10}{0.14} = 965 \; 0.4x = 0.4 \times 965 = 386$$

Hence (D) is the answer

Q14. Option (A) 72% is the answer.

Q15. Let the quantity of ore mined be x kg

$$\text{Then, } x \times \frac{80}{100} \times \frac{25}{100} = 80000$$

$$\Rightarrow X = 80000 \times \frac{100}{80} \times \frac{100}{25} = 400000\text{kg}$$

Hence (A) is the answer

Q16. Population after 3 yr

$$= 10000 \times \frac{110}{100} \times \frac{120}{100} \times \frac{95}{100} = 12540$$

Hence (D) is the answer

Q17. Let the quantity of milk replaced be x. Then, × (1-x) + = × 1

$$\Rightarrow 40 - 40x + 19x = 26 \; 21x = 14 \qquad X = \frac{2}{3}$$

Hence (A) is the answer

Q18. Quantity of salt in 6L of solution = $\frac{5}{100} \times 6 = 0.3$

Percentage of salt in 5L of solution = $\frac{0.3}{5} \times 100 = 6\%$

Hence (C) is the answer

Q19. Total number of votes = 6000

Total number of valid votes = 6000 × 0.75 = 4500

Total votes that Bhiku gets = 4500 × 0.65 = 2925

Total votes that Mhatre gets = 4500 – 2925 = 1575

Hence (B) is the answer

Q20. Required percentage correction = $\frac{1.25-1}{1.25} \times 100 = 20\%$

Hence (B) is the answer

Q21. Required marks ie 50% of (180 + 150) = 165

Marks scored in first paper = 54

Marks required to be scored in second paper = 111

Required % = $\frac{11}{150} \times 100 = 74\%$

Hence (C) is the answer

Q22. Let the rate of interest be r%

Then, A = $1200 + 1200 \times r \times \frac{7}{12} \times 100$ A = 1200 + 7r

Again, $1200 + 7r = 1016 + 1016 \times r \times \frac{25}{100}$

$\Rightarrow 1200 + 7r = 1016 + 25.4r$ 18.4r = 184

$\Rightarrow R = \frac{184}{18.4} = 10\%$

Hence (C) is the answer

Q23. Given S = 1.5T

Required percent = × 100 = $\frac{T}{1.5T+T} \times 100 = 40\ \%$

Hence (A) is the answer

Q26. Let his salary be Rs. X.

Then $x \times \frac{90}{100} \times \frac{85}{100} \times \frac{90}{100} = 1377$

$$x = 1377 \times \frac{100}{90} \times \frac{100}{85} \times \frac{100}{90} = \text{Rs } 2000$$

Hence (A) is the answer

Q27. Total candidates = 200

No. of men = 900 292-148

No. of women = 1100

No. of candidates who passed = $\frac{32 \times 900}{100} + \frac{38 \times 1100}{100}$ = 288 + 418 = 706

No. of candidates who failed = 2000 – 706 = 1294

Required percentage = $\frac{1294}{2000} \times 100 = 64.7\%$

Hence (B) is the answer

Q28. Required per cent decrease = $\frac{30}{130} \times 100 \ \frac{300}{13} = 23\frac{1}{3}\%$

Hence (B) is the answer

Q29. Let the total number of workers be 100

Number of skilled workers =75 of 100 =75

Number of unskilled workers = 100 – 75 = 25

Number of permanent workers = 80 % of 75 + 20% of 25

$$= \frac{80}{100} \times 75 + \frac{20}{100} \times 25 = 60 + 5 = 65$$

Number of temporary workers = 100 – 65 = 35

The number of temporary workers are, then total workers = 100

⇒ Number of total workers when number of temporary workers is 126

$$= \frac{100}{35} \times 126 = 360$$

Hence (C) is the answer

Q30. Only the option (d) gives the difference of votes between two candidates as 308.

Hence (D) is the answer

Q31. Let the height of the triangle be h and the base be b.

Area = $\frac{1}{2}$ bh

Decreased height = $\frac{6}{10}$ h

Increased base = $\frac{14}{10}$ b

New area = $\frac{1}{2}\times\frac{1}{6}h\frac{14}{10}b \quad = \frac{1}{2}\times\frac{84}{100}\times bh$

Decreased in area = $\frac{1}{2}bh\,(1 - \frac{84}{100}) = \frac{1}{2}bh \times \frac{16}{100}$

Percentage decrease = $\frac{1}{2}\times\frac{84}{100}\times\frac{2}{bh}\times 100 = 16\%$

Hence (C) is the answer

Q32. Number of literate girls = $29600\times\frac{50}{100} - 166000\times\frac{70}{100}$

$= 14800 - 116200 = 31800$

Hence (B) is the answer

Q33. Required % = $5 + 5 + \frac{5\times5}{100} = 10.25\%$

Hence (A) is the answer

Q34. In 2 min it becomes 2000.

In 4 min it becomes 4000.

In 6 min it becomes 8000.

Likewise in 18 min, it will become 512000.

Hence (D) is the answer

Q36. $\frac{G}{100}\times H = \times\frac{G}{100}$

Hence G% of H is H% of G.

Hence (A) is the answer

Q37. Let the original salary of the person be Rs. x.

Then, x × 1.05 x 0.975 = 22702.68

$\Rightarrow$ x × 1.02375 = 22702.68

$$\Rightarrow x = \frac{22702.68}{1.02373} = \text{Rs } 22176$$

Hence (B) is the answer

Q38. A reduction of 20 % means, now a person gets for Rs. 32 and this is the present price of that commodity.

$$\text{So, present price per kg} = \frac{32}{5} \times = \text{Rs } 12.8$$

Let the original price be ·· x, then price is arrived after reduction 20% of it.

x × 0.8 = 12.8 $\Rightarrow$ x = Rs 16

Hence (B) is the answer

Q39. Assume initial value = 1000. Since number is to be increased by 25.3%, final value = 1253

Hence multiplier = 1253/1000 = 1.253

Hence (C) is the answer

Q40. Let original price be x and sale be y.

Then, total revenue collected = x + y

New price = 0.8x, new sale = 1.8 y

New revenue collected = 1.44 xy

$$\text{Percentage increase in revenue} = \frac{0.44xy}{xy} \times 100\ 44\% \text{ increase}$$

Hence (A) is the answer

# 4 Profit and Loss

## Definition of the terms:

CP = Cost price = Price at which something is purchased or manufactured

## Types of Cost:-

1. Fixed cost – As obvious from the name, it is that kind of cost which is fixed in all the cases.
2. Variable cost – Variable costs are those costs which vary according to the no. of units produced.
3. Semi-variable cost – Semi variable costs are those costs which are fixed in one particular strata, but the costs varies among the different layers.

   One good example of Fixed Cost, Variable Cost and Semi-variable cost is the bill we receive for the telephone connections at our home. A part of that bill, rental, is fixed cost; and the rest part of the bill is calculated on the basis of the no. of calls made.

   SP = Selling Price = Price at which something is sold

   MP = Mark up price = Price which the shopkeeper fixes in the anticipation of some discount being asked by the customer. Mark up price is also known as Tag Price (price which is marked on tag) or List price.

## Important Formula:

(a) Profit = SP – CP

Loss = CP – SP

(b) $$\text{Profit percentage} = \frac{\text{Profit}}{\text{Cost Price}} \times 100$$

$$\text{Loss percentage} = \frac{\text{Loss}}{\text{Cost Price}} \times 100$$

(c) $CP = \frac{SP}{1 \pm \frac{R}{100}}$ [If there is a profit of R%, then +R will be used; there is a loss of R%, then -R will be used]

(d) If Selling prices of two articles are same, and one is sold at x% profit and other one is sold at x% loss, then in the whole transaction, there is a net loss = $\frac{x^2}{100}$ % of *sum of Cost prices of both the articles*

(e) If SP of x articles = CP of y articles

Then Net Profit percentage / Loss percentage = $\frac{\text{Absolute value (x - y)}}{\text{Number of Goods Sold (x)}} \times 100$

(f) Case of Faulty balance:

A shopkeeper professes to sell his goods at the cost price itself, but he sells only x grams at the place of 1000 grams.

Net profit percentage = $[\frac{1000-x}{x} \times 100]$ %

## Some important results:

## When SPs of two articles are same:

i. First article is sold at a profit of x% and second article is sold at a loss of x%. In this case, there will be always a loss.

Net Loss = $\frac{x^2}{100}$ % of CP

ii. First article is sold at a profit of x% and second article is sold at a profit of y%.
Ratio of $CP_1 : CP_2 = (100 + y) : (100 + x)$

iii. First article is sold at a profit of x% and second article is sold at a loss of y%.
Ratio of $CP_1 : CP_2 = (100 - y) : (100 + x)$
In this case, we cannot find if there will be net profit or loss.

iv. First article is sold at a loss of x% and second article is sold at a loss of y%.
Ratio of $CP_1 : CP_2 = (100 - y) : (100 - x)$

v. First article is sold at a loss of x% and second article is sold at a profit of y%.
Ratio of $CP_1 : CP_2 = (100 + y) : (100 - x)$
In this case, we cannot find if there will be net profit or loss.

## Worked Out Examples:

Q1. Cost price of an article is Rs. 120 and its selling price is Rs. 150. What is the profit percentage?

**Solution** – Profit = SP – CP = Rs. 150 – Rs. 120 = Rs. 30

$$\text{Profit percentage} = \frac{\textbf{Profit}}{\textbf{CP}} \times 100 = \frac{\textbf{Rs.30}}{\textbf{Rs.120}} \times 100 = 25\%$$

Q2. An article is sold for Rs. 180 after a loss of 20%. What is its cost price?

**Solution** – Using the formula, $CP = \dfrac{SP}{1 \pm \dfrac{R}{100}} = \dfrac{Rs.180}{1 - \dfrac{20}{100}} = \dfrac{Rs.180}{1 + \dfrac{1}{5}} = \dfrac{Rs.180}{\dfrac{4}{5}}$

$$= Rs.\ 180 \times = \frac{5}{4}\ Rs.\ 225$$

Q3. An article is sold for Rs. 400 after a profit of 25%. At what price shall it be sold so that there is a profit percentage of 40%?

**Solution** – Using the formula, $CP = \dfrac{SP}{1 \pm \dfrac{R}{100}} = \dfrac{Rs.\ 400}{1 + \dfrac{25}{100}} = \dfrac{Rs.\ 400}{1 + \dfrac{1}{4}} = \dfrac{Rs.\ 400}{\dfrac{5}{4}}$

$$= Rs.\ 400 \times = \frac{5}{4}\ Rs.\ 320$$

To earn a profit of 40%, new SP = CP + 40% of CP = Rs. 320 + 40% of Rs. 320 =

$Rs.\ 320 + \dfrac{40}{100} \times 320 = Rs.\ 448.$

Q4. A shopkeeper sells a mobile and a laptop at the same price. He earns a profit of 20% on the mobile and a loss of 20% on the laptop. What is his overall profit percentage or loss percentage?

**Solution** – If Selling prices of two articles are same, and one is sold at x% profit and other one is sold at x% loss, then in the whole transaction, there is a net loss = % of (Sum of Cost prices of both the articles)

$$\text{Net loss percentage} = \frac{20^2}{100}\% = 4\%$$

Q5. Selling price of 10 pens is same as cost price of 12 pens. What is the percentage profit?

**Solution** – Percentage Profit = $\frac{\text{Absolute value of (x - y)}}{\text{Number of Goods Sold (x)}} \times 100 = \frac{2}{10} \times 100 = 20\%$

Q6. A dishonest shopkeeper claims that he sells his goods at his cost price only. But he sells only 800 grams at the place of 1000 grams. What is his profit percentage?

**Solution** – If he sells x grams at the place of 1000 grams, net profit percentage =

$$[\frac{1000\text{-}x}{x} \times 100]\ \% = [\frac{1000\text{-}800}{800} \times 100]\ \% = 25\%$$

Q7. A dishonest shopkeeper claims that he sells his goods at his cost price only. But he sells only x grams at the place of 1000 grams and gains a profit of 40%. What is the value of x?

**Solution** – Method 1

$$[\frac{1000\text{-}x}{x}\ 100]\ \% = 40\%,\ \text{or},\ x = \frac{10000}{14} = 728\ \text{grams}$$

Method 2:

Answer is going to be simply: $\frac{1000}{1.4} = x$, hence x = 728 grams

[If profit percentage would have been 30%, answer would be $\frac{1000}{1.3} = x$, or, x = 769 grams)

## Practice Exercise

1. A shopkeeper bought a certain number of DVD writer for Rs. 1800. Keeping one to himself, he sold the remaining at a profit of Rs. 6 each. In total, she earned a profit of Rs. 114. The number of DVD writer she bought is

   a) 20 b) 28 c) 30 d) 32

2. A transistor is listed at Rs. 65. A customer bought this transistor for Rs. 56.16 with two successive discounts. One of them is 10%. The other discount of this discount scheme that was allowed by the shopkeeper is

   a) 6% b) 4% c) 3% d) 2.5%

3. A person bought two mobiles for Rs. 2200. He sells one at 5% loss and the other at 6% profit and in this transaction he neither gains nor loses. Find the cost price of each mobile.

   a) 500, 700 b) 2000, 200 c) 1200, 1000 d) 1100, 1100

4. A retailer sold a pen at a profit of 17.5%. If he had bought it at 8% less and sold it at 30% profit, he would have earned Rs. 11.55 more as profit. Cost price of the pen is

   a) 550 b) 675 c) 750 d) 1475

5. By selling a mobile at 80% of its marked price, a shopkeeper makes a loss of 12%. What will be the profit or loss percentage made by the shopkeeper if he sells the mobile at 95% of its marked price?

   a) 5.5% profit b) 1% loss c) 5% profit d) 4.5% profit

6. If the cost price of 12 chairs is equal to the selling price of 16 chairs, then the loss percent is

   (a) 20% (b) 25% (c) 30% (d) 35%

7. A seller gives 4% discount on the marked price and 1 book free with every 15 books bought and still gains 35%. The marked price is more than the cost price by

   a) 40% b) 39% c) 20% d) 50%

8. Ahmad got 30% concession on the labeled price of an article and sold it at Rs. 8750 with 25% profit on the price he bought. What was the labeled price?

   a)16000 b) 12000 c) 10000 d) 14000

9. The wholesale price of a microwave is Rs. 1265. if the manufacturer gain 10%, the manufacturer dealer gains 15% and the wholesaler gains 25%, then the cost of the product is

   a) 800 b) 900 c) 700 d) 600

10. What percent profit would be obtained if 34% of cost price of an item is 26% of selling price of the same item?

    a) 30.77% b) 74% c) 25.16% d) 88.40%

11. In a certain shop, the gain is 320% of the cost. If the cost price increased by 25% but the selling price remains same, what is the gain percentage of the selling price?

    a) 70% b) 80% c) 90% d) None of above

12. Anita bought a cooker with 24% discount on the selling price. If the cooker costs her Rs. 779, what is the marked price of the cooker?

    a) 1000 b) 950

    c) 1025 d) cannot be determined

13. A woman sells a chocolate at a profit of 20%. If she had bought it at 20% less and sold it for Rs.18 less, she would have gained 25%. The cost price of the chocolate is

a) 80 b) 70 c) 60 d) 90

14. Two-third of a plot was sold at a profit of 5% and the remainder at a loss of 2%. If the total profit was Rs. 400, the value of the plot was

a) 15000 b) 12000 c) 10000 d) 20000

15. By selling 12 Apple, the seller earns a profit equal to the selling price of 2 apple. What is his percentage profit?

a) 25% b) 20%

c) 16.67% d) Data inadequate

16. A retailer marks the price of his goods at 25% higher than the original price. She also allows a discount of 12%. What profit or loss did she get?

a) 15% profit b) 10% profit c) 10% Loss d) 15% Loss

17. Ramu purchased a bicycle for Rs. 5200 and expenditure of Rs. 800 on the repair of bicycle. He had to sell it for Rs. 5500. Find his profit or loss percent?

a) $7\frac{1}{2}$% gain b) $8\frac{1}{3}$ % loss c) 9% loss d) None of these

18. An old man buys apples at a certain price per dozen and sells them at 100 apples for Rs. 800. What is his profit or loss percentage?

a) 4% loss b) $8\frac{1}{4}$ % loss c) 4% gain d) $6\frac{1}{4}$ % gain

19. The cost price of 20 apples is the same as the selling price of x apple. If the profit is 25% then determine the value of x.

(a) 4 (b) 15 (c) 16 (d) 17

20. If the SP of a book is increased by Rs. 162, then seller would make a profit of 17% instead of a loss of 19%. What is the CP of the book?

(a) Rs. 540 (b) Rs. 450 (c)Rs. 360 (d) Rs. 600

21. The cost price of 20 articles is equal to the selling price of x articles. Find the value of x If the profit is 25%.

(a) 25 (b) 18 (c) 16 (d) 15

22. A man sells a flat at 5% profit. If he buys it at 5% less and sell it for Rs. 1 less, he would have gained by 10%. What is the cost price of the flat?

(a) Rs. 200 (b) Rs. 150 (c) Rs. 250 (d) Rs. 240

23. A company has 6435 bars of soap. If the company has sold 20% of its stock, then how many bars of soap did it sell?

(a) 1237 (b) 1257 (c) 1287 (d) 1300

24. A cycle originally costs Rs 100 and was discounted 10%. After three months, it was sold after being discounted 15%. What is the selling price of cycle?

(a) Rs. 55.5 (b) Rs. 95.25 (c) Rs. 76.5 (d) none of these

25. A shopkeeper sold a bag of rice for Rs. 17940, by giving a discount of 8% and gained 19.6%. If there is no discount allowed, then what is the profit per cent?

(a) 25% (b) 26.4% (c) 24.8% (d) 30%

26. By selling 33m of woolen cloth, a shopkeeper gains the price of 11m of woolen cloth. His gain% is

(a) 7% (b) 50% (c) 20% (d) 22%

27. If the cost of 12 pen is equal to the selling price of 10 pen, what is the profit per cent in the transaction.

(a) $16\frac{2}{3}\%$ (b) 18% (c) 20% d) 25%

28. Ravish sells a TV at a gain of $12\frac{1}{2}\%$. If he had sold it at Rs. 22.50 more, he would have gained 25%. The cost price of the TV is

(a) Rs. 162 (b) Rs. 140 (c) Rs. 196 (d) Rs. 180

29. The selling price of an apple including the sales tax is Rs. 616. The sales tax rate is 10%. If the shopkeeper has made a profit of 12%, then the cost price of the apple is

(a) Rs. 500 (b) Rs. 515 (c) Rs. 550 (d) Rs. 600

30. If selling price is doubled, the profit triples. Find the profit per cent.

(a) $66\frac{2}{3}\%$ (b) 100% (c) $105\frac{1}{3}\%$ (d) 120%

31. A house costs C rupees. Later it was sold for a profit of 25%. If the capital gains tax is 50% of the profit. Find the value?

(a) $\frac{C}{24}$ (b) $\frac{C}{8}$ (c) $\frac{C}{4}$ (d) $\frac{C}{2}$

32. What price should a shopkeeper mark up on an article which cost him Rs. 153 to gain a profit of 20% after giving a discount of 15%?

(a) Rs. 162 (b) Rs. 184 (c) Rs. 216 (d) Rs. 224

33. A pair of shoes was bought for Rs. 37.40 at a discount of 15%. What must be the marked price of each of the shoes?
(a) Rs. 15 (b) Rs. 20 (c) Rs. 22 (d) RS. 25

34. A shopkeeper markup his price of an item 35% above its cost price. What percentage of discount shall he allow so that profit percentage is 8%?
(a) 18% (b) 20% (c) 22% (d) 24%

35. A producer of wheat sells his two varieties of wheat, one costing Rs 18 per kg and another Rs. 20 per kg in the ratio 5: 3. If he sells the mixture of these two verities at Rs 21 per kg, then his gain percent is
(a) 12% (b) 13% (c) 14% (d) 15%

36. A shopkeeper sold a table for Rs. 2564.36. Approximately what was his profit percent if the cost price of the article was Rs. 2400?
(a) 4% (b) 5% (c) 6% (d) 7%

37. The cash difference between the selling prices of a car at a profit of 4% and 6% is Rs. 3. What is the ratio of selling price of both the car?
(a) 51:52 (b) 52:53 (c) 53:54 (d) 54:55

38. A shopkeeper sells a TV at Rs. 840 at a gain of 20% and another for Rs. 960 at the loss of 4%. Find his total gain percent.
(a) 5% (b) 4.2% (c) 5.88% (d) 4%

39. A woman gains 20% by selling a saree for a certain price. What is the percentage profit is she sells it at double price?
(a) 130% (b) 140% (c) 150% (d) 160%

40. If the cost price of 20 books is equal to the selling price of 10 books, then what is the profit percentage?
(a) 12% (b) 30% (c) 50% (d) 100%

## Answer Grid:

| Q. No. | 1 | 2 | 3 | 4 | 5 | 6 | 7 | 8 | 9 | 10 | 11 | 12 | 13 | 14 | 15 | 16 | 17 | 18 | 19 | 20 |
|---|---|---|---|---|---|---|---|---|---|---|---|---|---|---|---|---|---|---|---|---|
| Answer | a | a | c | a | d | b | d | c | a | a | a | c | d | a | b | b | b | a | c | b |
| Q. No. | 21 | 22 | 23 | 24 | 25 | 26 | 27 | 28 | 29 | 30 | 31 | 32 | 33 | 34 | 35 | 36 | 37 | 38 | 39 | 40 |
| Answer | c | a | c | c | d | d | c | d | a | b | b | c | c | b | a | d | b | d | b | d |

## Solutions and Explanations:

Q1. Let she bought x CDs

$(x - 1) \times 6 = 114$, or, $x - 1 = 19$. Hence $x = 20$

Hence option (A) is the answer.

Q2. Let the discount be x%

$$65 \times \frac{90}{100} \times \frac{100-x}{100} = 56.16 \qquad 100-x = \frac{56.16 \times 100 \times 100}{65 \times 90}$$

$\Rightarrow 100 - x = 96$ $\qquad X = 4\%$

Hence option (A) is the answer.

Q3. Let the cost price on one table be x

Then, cost price of other table will be (2200 - x)

$$X \times \frac{95}{100} + (2200-x) \times \frac{106}{100} = 2200$$

$\Rightarrow 95x + 233200 - 106x = 220000$ $\qquad 11x = 13200$

$X = 1200$ and $2200 - x = 1000$

Hence option (C) is the answer.

Q4. Let the cost of article be x

Then, $X \times \frac{117.5}{100} + 11.55 = x \times \frac{92}{100} \times \frac{130}{100}$

$$X = \frac{11.55}{(0.92 \times 130 - 117.5)} \times 100 = 550$$

Hence option (A) is the answer.

Q5. let the cost of article be x. Then, selling price of article = 0.88x

Marked price of $= \frac{0.88}{80} \times 100 \times x = 1.1x$

New selling price = 1.045x

Profit percent $= \frac{1.045x - x}{x} \times 100 = 4.5\%$

Hence option (D) is the answer.

Q6. Loss percentage = $\frac{\text{Absoulte value of (x-y)}}{\text{Number of Goods Sold (x)}} \times 100 = \frac{4}{16} \times 100 = 25\%$. Hence option (b) is the answer.

Q7. Discount on articles = $\frac{1}{16} \times 100 = 6.25\%$

Overall discount = $-4 - 6.25 + 4 \times \frac{6.25}{100} = -10\%$

Let the cost price = 100 then, Selling price = $135 \times \frac{100}{90} = 150$

So, 90% of marked price = 135 Marked price = $135 \times \frac{100}{90} = 150$

Marked price is increased by $\frac{150-100}{100} \times 100 = 50\%$

Hence option (D) is the answer.

Q8. SP of Ahmad = 8750

Labeled price = $\frac{125}{100} \times \frac{70}{100}$ MP = 8750 MP = 10000

Hence option (C) is the answer.

Q9. Let the cost of product be x

Then, $x \times \frac{110}{100} \times \frac{115}{100} \times \frac{125}{100} = 1265$

$\Rightarrow$ $X = 1265 \times \frac{100}{110} \times \frac{110}{115} \times \frac{125}{100} = 800$

$\Rightarrow$ Hence option (A) is the answer.

Q10. let the cost price and selling price be x and y respectively

$\frac{34x}{100} = \frac{26y}{100}$ $Y = \frac{17x}{13}$

Profit percent $= \frac{y-x}{x} \times 100 = 30.77\%$

Hence option (A) is the answer

Q11. Let C.P. = Rs. 100. Then, Profit = Rs. 320, S.P. = Rs. 420.

New C.P. = 125% of Rs. 100 = Rs. 125 New S.P. = Rs. 420.

Profit = Rs. (420 - 125) = Rs. 295

Required percentage = $\frac{295}{420} \times 100 = 70\%$(approx)

Hence option (A) is the answer

Q12. Let the marked price be x.

Then, $x \times \frac{76}{100} = 779$, or, $x = \frac{77900}{76} = 1025$

Hence option (C) is the answer.

Q13. Let the cost price be x

Then, (1.2x - 18) - 0.8x = 0.25x*0.8x

$0.4x - 18 = 0.20x$ => $x = \frac{18}{0.20} = 90$

Hence option (D) is the answer.

Q15. Let the selling price of a notebook be x

Then, cost price of 12 notebooks = 12x - 2x = 10x

Profit percent = $\frac{2x}{10x} \times 100 = 20\%$

Hence option (B) is the answer

Q16. Profit % or loss % = $+25 - 12 - \frac{25 \times 12}{100} = +10\%$

Hence option (B) is the answer

Q17. total cost price = 5200 + 800 = 6000 Selling price = 5500

Loss percent = $6000 - \frac{5500}{6000} \times 100 = \% \frac{25}{3}\%$

Hence option (B) is the answer

Q18. Let the cost price of 12 apples be 100. Then, selling price of 100 apples will be Rs. 800

CP of 1 apple = $\frac{100}{12} = \frac{25}{3}$ And SP of 1 apple = $\frac{800}{100}$ = Rs. 8

Loss= $(\frac{25}{3} - 8) = \frac{1}{3}$

Loss percent = $\frac{\text{Loss}}{\text{CP}} \times 100 = \frac{1}{3} \times \frac{3}{25} \times 100 = 4\%$

Hence option (A) is the answer

Q19. Let the cost price 1 article = Re 1

Cost price of x articles = x S.P of x articles = 20

Gain = 20 –x => $25 = (\frac{(20-x)}{x} \times 100)$ => 2000 – 100x = 25x => x = 16

Hence option (C) is the answer

Q20. (17 + 19 ) = 36 % of the cost price = 162

100% of the cost price = $\frac{162}{36}$

Hence option (B) is the answer

Q21. CP of 20 articles = SP of articles = 1(say)

CP of 1 article = $\frac{1}{20}$, SP of 1 articles = $\frac{1}{x}$

Profit per cent = $\frac{\frac{1}{x} - \frac{1}{20}}{\frac{1}{20}} = \frac{25}{100}$ $\frac{20-x}{x} = \frac{1}{4}$ $\Rightarrow$ 80-4x=x

$\Rightarrow$ 5x =80 $\Rightarrow$ x = 16

Hence option (C) is the answer

Q22. Let the CP of the article be Rs. 100. Then, SP = 105

New, CP = 95 New, SP = 104.5

If sells it for 0.5 less than CP = 100

If he sells it for 1 less than CP = $\frac{100}{0.5} \times 1$ = Rs 200

Hence option (A) is the answer

Q23. Required number = $6435 \times 20\% = 1287$

Hence option (C) is the answer

Q24. SP of bicycle = 100 x 0.9 x 0.85 = 76.50

Hence option (C) is the answer

Q25. SP = 17940, Discount = 8% $\therefore$ MP = $\frac{1790}{0.92}$ = Rs 1950

Gain = 19.6% (given) $\therefore$ CP = $\frac{17940}{1.196}$ = Rs 15000

New SP without discount = Rs. 19500 Gain = (19500 – 15000) = Rs. 4500

Gain per cent = $\frac{4500}{1500} \times 100 = 30\%$

Hence option (D) is the answer

Q26. SP of 33 m of cloth = CP of 33m + gain

SP of 33m = CP of 33m + SP of 11 m

$\Rightarrow$ SP of 22m = CP of 33m = 1 (say)

$\Rightarrow$ SP of 1 m = $\frac{1}{22}$ CP of 1 m = $\frac{1}{33}$

Gain = $\frac{1}{22} - \frac{1}{33} = \frac{11}{22\times33}$

Gain per cent = $\frac{\frac{11}{22\times33}}{\frac{1}{33}} \times 100 = \frac{11}{22\times33} \times 33 \times 100 = 50\%$

Hence option (D) is the answer

Q27. Let CP of 12 pencils = SP of 10 pencils = Rs. 1

Then, CP of 1 pencils = $\frac{1}{2}$ And SP of 1 pencil = $\frac{1}{10}$

Profit per cent = $\frac{\frac{60}{1}}{12} \times 100 = \frac{1}{60} \times 12 \times 100 = 20\%$

Hence option (C) is the answer

Q28. Let the CP of the article be Rs. x

According to the question, 125% of x – 112.5% of x = Rs. 22.5

Hence $x = \frac{100}{12.5} \times 22.5$ = Rs. 180

Hence option (D) is the answer

Q29. Let the CP of the article be x. Then, SP = x × 1.12 ×1.1

Given,

Hence option (A) is the answer

Q30. Let CP be x and SP be y. Then, profit = (y - x)

If SP = 2y, then profit = 3 (y - x)

Given, 2y – x = 3 (y - x)

Profit is 100%

Hence option (B) is the answer

Q31. Cost Price of house = C Profit = 25% of C = $\frac{C}{4}$

Capital gain tax = 50 % of $\frac{C}{4}$ = Rs $\frac{C}{8}$

Hence option (B) is the answer

Q32. CP = 153, gain 20% SP = 153 × 1.2 = 183.60

Let the marked price be x Then, x × 0.85 = 183.60

$\Rightarrow x = \frac{183.60}{0.85}$ = Rs 216

Hence option (C) is the answer

Q33. As question states that rate was of pair of sho*es, so rate of* shoes = $\frac{37.40}{2}$ = Rs. 18.70

Let Marked price = Rs X then 85% of X = 18.70

$\Rightarrow X = \frac{1870}{85}$ x = 22

Hence option (C) is the answer

Q34. Let the cost price = Rs 100. Then, marked price = Rs 135

Required gain = 8%, So Selling price = Rs 108

Discount = 135 - 108 = 27 Discount% = (27/135)′100 = 20%

Hence option (B) is the answer

Q35. Suppose he bought 5 kg and 3 kg of wheat.

Cost Price = Rs. (5 x 18 + 3 x 20) = Rs. 150. Selling price = Rs. (8 x 21) = Rs. 168.

Profit = 168 - 150 = 18 So, Profit % = $\frac{18}{150} \times 100 = 12\%$

Hence option (A) is the answer

**Q36.** Gain % = ( $164.36 \times \frac{100}{2400}$) = 6.84 % = 7% approx.

Hence option (D) is the answer

**Q37.** Let the Cost price of article is Rs. x

Required ratio = 104% of x106% of x = 104 : 106 = 52:53

Hence option (B) is the answer

Q38. C.P. of 1st *TV* = (100120 × 840) = 700

C.P. of 2nd *TV* = (10096 × 960) = 1000

Total C.P. = 1700 Total S.P. = 1800 Gain = 1800 – 1700 = 100

Gain% = ( $\frac{100}{1700} \times 100$) = *5.88%*

Hence option (D) is the answer

Q39. Let the C.P. = Rs. 100, then SP = Rs. 120. New SP = Rs. 240

New Profit% = ($\frac{\text{Profit}}{\text{CP}}$) × 100 = ( $\frac{140}{100} \times 100$) = 140 %

Hence option (B) is the answer

Q40. Percentage Profit = $\frac{\text{Absolute value of (x-y)}}{\text{Number of Goods Sold (x)}} \times 100 = \frac{10}{10} \times 100 = 100\%$

Hence option (d) is the answer.

# 5 Simple Interest and Compound Interest

Interest is defined as "Time Value of Money". It works under the basic principle that value of money is not fixed, and it will keep changing over the period of time. In this chapter, we are going to study two types of interest : (a) Simple Interest, (b) Compound Interest

## There are two types of Interest:

(1) Simple Interest – In case of Simple Interest, Interest as well as Principal remains fixed for every compounding period.

(2) Compound Interest – In case of Compound Interest, interest will be added to the initial principal after every compounding period. Hence compound interest keeps of increasing after every compounding period.

Differences between Simple Interest and Compound Interest:

| | *Simple Interest* | *Compound Interest* |
|---|---|---|
| (1) | Principal remains fixed for the whole period. | Principal keeps on increasing. |
| (2) | Interest is not added to the principal. | Interest is added to the principal after every compounding period. |
| (3) | Interest remains fixed. | Interest keeps on increasing. |
| (4) | Amount follows Arithmetic Progression. | Amount follows Geometric Progression. |
| (5) | Interest for next year is calculated over the original principal. | Interest for next year is calculated over the last year's amount. |

## For example:

(a) In case of S.I.:

Example - If the rate of interest = 10%, and the principal = Rs. 1000, Then:

Interest for 1$^{st}$ year = 10% of Rs 1000 = Rs. 100

Interest for $2^{nd}$ year = 10% of Rs 1000 = Rs. 100

Interest for $3^{rd}$ year = 10% of Rs 1000 = Rs. 100

It can be seen that Interest generated every year = Rs. 100

| Principal | Rate | Interest | |
|---|---|---|---|
| 1st Year | 1000 | 10% | 100 |
| 2nd Year | 1000 | 10% | 100 |
| 3rd Year | 1000 | 10% | 100 |

(b) In case of C.I.:

Principal of $1^{st}$ year (Initially) = P

Principal of $2^{nd}$ year = P + Interest of $1^{st}$ year

Principal of $3^{rd}$ year = P + Interest of $1^{st}$ year + Interest of $2^{nd}$ year

Example - If the rate of interest = 10%, and the principal = Rs. 1000, Then:

Interest for $1^{st}$ year = 10% of Rs 1000 = Rs. 100

| | *Principal* | *Rate* | *Interest* |
|---|---|---|---|
| 1st Year | 1000 | 10% | 100 |
| 2nd Year | 1000 + 100 = 1100 | 10% | 110 |
| 3rd Year | 1000 + 100 + 110 = 1210 | 10% | 121 |

## Expression for Simple Interest (SI) / Compound Interest (CI):

$$SI = \frac{\text{Principal} \times \text{RateofInterest} \times \text{Time}}{100}$$

$$CI = \text{Principal} \times \left[1 + \frac{R}{100}\right]^{N} - \text{Principal}$$

Principal = Sum invested or lent

R = Rate of Interest per annum

N = Number of years

It should be noted that the unit of Rate of interest and Time should be same. So, if rate of interest is "per year", then time should also be in "Year".

In case of Compound Interest, if the compounding is not done annually, then formula changes like the following:

(a) Half Yearly compounding – It means interest is given after every six months. In this case, after every six months, interest will be added to the principal.

| Rate of Interest | Compounding Period | Interest in 6 months (half Year) | Number of compounding period in a year |
|---|---|---|---|
| R% per year | Half Yearly | R%/2 | 2 (12 months / 6 months) |

$$CI = \text{Principal} \times \left[1 + \frac{R/2}{100}\right]^{2N} - \text{Principal}$$

(b) Quarterly compounding– It means interest is given after every three months. In this case, after every three months, interest will be added to the principal.

| Rate of Interest | Compounding Period | Interest in 3 months (quarter Year) | Number of compounding period in a year |
|---|---|---|---|
| R% per year | Quarterly | R%/4 | 4 (12 months / 3 months) |

$$CI = \text{Principal} \times \left[1 + \frac{R/2}{100}\right]^{4N} - \text{Principal}$$

## Important Points:

1. If the rate of Interest = R% per annum for both CI and SI, then the difference between CI and SI for 2 years will be equal to (R% of R)% of Principal = $\frac{R^2}{100}$% of Principal

   In the above case, R = 10%, so the difference between CI and SI for 2 years = 1%

2. If a sum doubles itself in n years at Simple Interest, then rate of interest = $\frac{100}{n}$

3. At S.I., if a sum of money amount to n times in t years, then rate of interest = $\frac{(n-1)}{r} \times$ 100%

## Comparison between CI and SI

Assume two different sums are getting double at their respective rates of S.I. and CI in 5 years. Following table gives us the mechanism of getting money *n* times in above situation:

| | After 5 years | After 10 years | After 15 years | After 20 years |
|---|---|---|---|---|
| At S.I. | 2 times | 3 times | 4 times | 5 times |
| At C.I. | 2 times | 4 times | 8 times | 16 times |

It happens because in case of S.I., amount follows Arithmetic Progression and in case of C.I., amount follows Geometric Progression.

## Worked Out examples:

Q1. At S.I., a sum of money amounts to twice its original value in 8 years. What is the rate of interest?

**Solution** – Rate of interest in this case = $\frac{100}{8} = 12.5\%$

Q2. At S.I., a sum of money amounts to three times its original value in 5 years. What is the rate of interest?

**Solution** – Method 1 – Equation method

Assume principal = Rs. 100.

According to the question, amount = three times the original value = Rs. 300. Hence interest = Rs. 300 – Rs. 100 = R. 200

Since interest remains same in case of S.I., interest obtained / year = $\frac{200}{5} = 40\%$

**Method 2** – Formula method

Rate of interest = $\frac{(n-1) \times 100}{T}\% = \frac{(3-1)}{5} \times 1000 = 40\ \%$

Q3. At C.I. , amount at the end of 1st year = Rs. 2400 and amount at the end of 2nd year = Rs. 2880.

What is (a) the rate of interest? (b) Principal? (c) Interest obtained in the 3rd year, (d) Amount at the end of 3rd year?

**Solution** - In case of C.I., Interest for next year is calculated over the last year's amount.

In this case, interest obtained in 2nd year = Rs. 2880 – Rs. 2400 = Rs. 480

(a) Hence rate of interest = $\frac{480}{2400} \times 100 = 20\%$

(b) To calculate Principal, we'll simply use the C.I. formula.

Amount = Principal × $\left[1+\frac{R}{100}\right]^{N}$ ,or, $2400 = P\ (1+\frac{20}{100})^{1}$. Solving it we get, P = Rs. 2000.

Hence principal = Rs. 2000

NOTE – A common mistake that students do in this question is to subtract 20% of 2400 from 2400 to get principal and form the following equation: 2400 – 20% of 2400 = P. This is wrong.

(c) Interest obtained in 3rd year = 20% of Rs. 2880 = Rs. 576

(d) Amount at the end of 3rd year = Rs. 2880 + Rs. 576 = Rs. 3456

Q4. The difference between SI and CI on a sum of money at the rate of 5% per annum for two years is Rs. 25. What is the principal?

**Solution** - Difference between CI and SI for two years = $\frac{R^2}{100}$ % of Principal = $\frac{5^2}{100}$ % of Principal

$\Rightarrow \frac{1}{4}$ % of Principal = Rs. 25 $\Rightarrow$ 1% of Principal = Rs. 100 $\Rightarrow$ Principal = Rs. 10,000

Q5. The rate of inflation is 1000%. What will be the cost of an article, which costs Rs 6 today, two years from now?

**Solution** - 1000% inflation means an increase of 10 times.

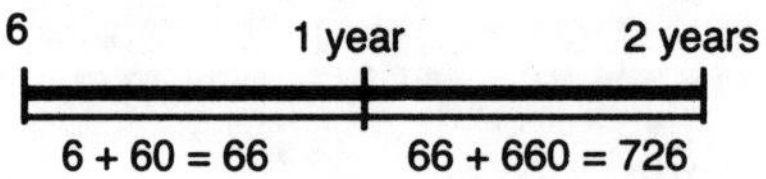


Hence price after two years = Rs. 726.

Q6. Simple interest on a certain sum at 5% per annum for 2 years is Rs. 60. What is the compound interest on the same sum for the same period of time?

**Solution –Method 1:**

$$\text{Principal} = 100 \times \frac{SI}{RT} = 100 \times \frac{60}{5 \times 2} = \text{Rs. } 600$$

$$\text{Compound Interest} = P(1 + \frac{R}{100})^{T} - P$$

$$600\,(1 + \frac{5}{100})^2 - 600 = 600(\frac{21}{20})^2 - 600 = 661.5 - 600 = \text{Rs. } 61.5$$

**Method 2**

**The difference between compound interest and simple interest on Rs. P for 2 years at R% per annum $= R \times \frac{SI}{2 \times 100}$**

**Difference between compound interest and simple interest $= R \times \frac{SI}{2 \times 100} = 5 \times \frac{60}{2 \times 100}$**

**= 1.5**

**Hence, compound interest = Simple Interest + 1.5 = 60 + 1.5 = Rs. 61.5**

**Hence option (B) is the answer**

## Practice Exercise

1. A scheme invests Rs.1000 at simple interest rate of 5% on the condition that interest will be added to the principal after 10 years. In how many years will it to amount to Rs. 2000?

   a) $16\frac{2}{3}$ yr  b) $16\frac{1}{4}$ yr  c) 16 yr  d) 11 yr

2. A woman borrows Rs.4000 from a bank at 7.50% compound interest. At the end of every year, she pays Rs.1500 as part repayment of loan and interest. How much does she still owe to the bank after three such installments?

   a) Rs. 123.25  b) Rs. 125  c) Rs. 400  d) Rs. 469.18

3. Anand borrowed a certain sum of money for 2 yr at 8% per annum on simple interest and immediately lent it to Ravish but at compound interest and gained Rs. 16. What amount did Anand borrow?

   a) Rs. 1600  b) Rs. 2500  c) Rs. 2400  d) Rs. 1800

4. The effective annual rate of interest corresponding to a compound interest rate of 8% per annum payable half yearly is

   a) 8%  b) 8.01%  c) 8.13%  d) 8.16%

5. A money lender lent out Rs. 25000 in two parts, one at 8% simple interest and the other at 8.5% simple interest. If the total annual income on the amount is Rs. 2031.25, the money lent at 8% is

   a) Rs. 12500  b) Rs. 6250  c) Rs. 10000  d) Rs. 18750

6. Asmita invests an amount of Rs. 9535 at the rate of simple interest 4% per annum, for how many years did she invest the amount to obtain the double her sum?

   a) 10 yr  b) 25 yr  c) 5 yr  d) 4 yr

7. The difference between the CI and SI on a certain sum of money for 2yr at 15% per annum is Rs. 45. Find the sum.
   (a) Rs. 7000 (b) Rs. 2750
   (c) Rs. 2000 (d) Rs. 2250
8. A man takes a loan of Rs10000 and pays back Rs. 13310 after 3yr. What is the rate of compound interest?
   (a) 8% (b) 9% (c) 10% (d) 11%
9. The ratio of the amount for two years under Compound Interest annually and for one year under Simple Interest is 6 : 5. When will be the ratio of interest is same, then find the value of the rate of interest.
   (a) 12.5% (b) 18% (c) 20% (d) 16.66%
10. At the rate of 12% the difference between the simple interest and the compound interest compounded annually on Rs. 5000 for two years will be -
    (a) Rs. 17.50 (b) Rs. 36 (c) Rs. 45 (d) Rs. 72
11. In 3 years the difference between the simple and the compound interest on same principal amount at the rate 20% is Rs. 48. What is the principal?
    (a) Rs. 650 (b) Rs. 300 (c) Rs. 375 (d) Rs. 400
12. I get an annual income of Rs. 688.25 from Rs. 10000 invested partly at the rate 8% per annum and partly by 5% per annum at the simple interest. How much of my money is invested by 5%?
    (a) Rs. 3725 (b) Rs. 4225 (c) Rs. 4800 (d) Rs. 5000
13. A sum of money becomes eight times in 3 yr, if the rate is compounded annually. In how much time the same amount at the same compound interest rate will become sixteen times?
    (a) 6 yr (b) 4 yr (c) 8 yr (d) 5 yr
14. The interest in the first two successive years was Rs. 400 and Rs. 420 when sum is invested at compound interest. Find the sum.
    (a) 8000 (b) 7500 (c) 8500 (d) 8200
15. Anand takes a certain sum from Manisha at a certain rate of simple interest for 2 years. He lent this sum to Sunita at the same rate of interest but compounded annually for the same period ie: two year. At the end of two years, he received Rs. 2400 as compound interest but paid Rs. 2000 as simple interest. What is the rate of interest.
    (a) 40% (b) 30% (c) 20% (d) 10%

16. If a sum on compound interest becomes three times in 4 years, then with the same interest rate, the sum will become 81 times in:

    (a) 12 yr (b) 18 yr (c) 16 yr (d) 14 yr

17. A sum is invested for 3 years compounded at 5%, 10% and 20 % per annum respectively. In three years, if the sum amounts to Rs. 1386, then find the sum.

    (a) 1500 (b) 1400 (c) 1200 (d) 1100

18. A sum of Rs. 6600 was taken as a loan. This is to be repaid in two annual installments. The rate of interest is 20% which compounded annually, then the value of each installment is

    (a) 4320 (b) 2220 (c) 4400 (d) 4420

19. If in a certain time period Rs. 10000 amount to Rs. 160000 at compound interest. What is the amount in half that time if principal is Rs. 10000?

    (a) 50000 (b) 40000 (c) 80000 (d) 60000

20. What will be the amount if a sum of Rs. 10000 is placed at compound interest for 3 years while rate of interest for the first, second and third years is 10%, 5% and 2% respectively?

    (a) 11781 (b) 11244 (c) 11231 (d) 11658

## Answer Grid:

| Q. No. | 1 | 2 | 3 | 4 | 5 | 6 | 7 | 8 | 9 | 10 |
|---|---|---|---|---|---|---|---|---|---|---|
| Answer | a | a | b | d | d | b | c | c | c | d |
| Q. No. | 11 | 12 | 13 | 14 | 15 | 16 | 17 | 18 | 19 | 20 |
| Answer | c | a | b | a | a | c | d | a | b | a |

## Solutions and Explanations:

Q1. SI for 10 yr $= 1000 \times 5 \times \frac{10}{100} = 500$

Now, Principal after 10 years = 1500 and final amount = 2000. So, SI = 500

$500 = 1500 \times 5 \times \frac{T}{100}$ $\quad T = \frac{500\times100}{1500\times5} = 6\frac{2}{3}$ yr

Hence option (A) is the answer

Q2. Amount remaining after:

$1\text{yr} = 4000\,(1 + \frac{7.5}{100}) - 1500 = 2800$

$2yr = 2800\ (1 + \frac{7.5}{100}) - 1500 = 1510$

$3yr = 1510\ (1 + \frac{7.5}{100}) - 1500 = 123.25$

Hence option (A) is the answer

Q3. Assume that Anand Borrows Rs. x

$X\,[\,(1 + \frac{8}{100})^2 - 1\,] - \frac{x \times 8 \times 2}{100} = 16$

Or, 0.1664x – 0.16x = 16. Hence $x = \frac{16}{0.0064} = 2500$

Hence option (B) is the answer

Q4. Rate of 8% per annum payable half yearly. So, effective rate = 4%

Effective annual rate= $4 + 4 + \frac{4 \times 4}{100} = 8.16\%$

Hence option (D) is the answer

Q5. Let the amount lend at 8% be x. Then, amount lend at 8.5% be (25000 - x)

$X \times 8 \times \frac{1}{100} + (250000 - x) \times 8.5 \times \frac{1}{100} = 2031.25$

Or, 8x + 212500 - 8.5x = 203125, or, -0.5x = -9375. Hence X = 18750

Hence option (D) is the answer

Q6. Let she invests for x yr. A sum will be double when interest is equal to principal.

$9535 = 9535 \times 4 \times \frac{x}{100}$ 4x = 100 X = 25yr

Hence option (B) is the answer

Q7. Difference between CI and SI for two years = $\frac{R^2}{100}$ % of Principal $\frac{15^2}{100}$ % of Prinicipal

Or, 2.25% of Principal = Rs. 45, hence Principal = Rs. 2000. Hence option (C) is the answer.

Q8. Let the rate of compound interest be r.

Then, $10000 \times \left(1 + \frac{r}{100}\right)^3 = 13310$

$\Rightarrow \left(1 + \frac{r}{100}\right) = \frac{1331}{1000}$ $\Rightarrow 1 + \frac{r}{100} = \frac{11}{10}$

$\Rightarrow \frac{r}{100} = \frac{1}{10}$ $\Rightarrow r = 10\%$

Hence option (C) is the answer

Q9. $\frac{P(1 + \frac{r}{100})^2}{(1+\frac{pr}{100})} = \frac{6}{5}$ $\Rightarrow \left(1 + \frac{r}{100}\right) = \frac{6}{5} \Rightarrow r = 20\%$

Hence option (C) is the answer

Q10. $\left[5000(1+\frac{12^2}{100}) - 500\right] - \frac{5000 \times 12 \times 2}{100}$

$= 5000\left(\frac{28}{25} \times \frac{28}{25} - 1\right) - 1200$ $= 5000\left(\frac{784 - 625}{625}\right) - 1200 = \text{Rs } 72$

Hence option (D) is the answer

Q11. Let principal amount be 100. Then,

$SI = \frac{100 \times 20 \times 3}{100} = \text{Rs}$ And $CI = 100\left(1 + \frac{20}{100}\right)3 - 100$

$= 100 \times \left(\frac{6}{3}\right)^3 - 100 = \frac{364}{5}$ $CI - SI = \frac{364}{5} - 60 = \frac{64}{5}$

If difference is $\frac{64}{5}$, principal = 100

If difference is 48, Principal $= \frac{100 \times 5}{64} \times 48 =$ Rs 375

Hence option (C) is the answer

Q12. Let money invested at 5% be Rs. x

$$\frac{x+1\times5}{100} + \frac{(100-x)\times1\times8}{100} = 688325$$

$\Rightarrow 5x - 8x + 8000 = 68825$ $\Rightarrow 3x = 11175$ x = Rs 3725

Hence option (A) is the answer

Q13. Let the sum of money be Rs. x. Then, $8x = x\left(1+\frac{r}{100}\right)^3$

$\Rightarrow \left(1+\frac{r}{100}\right)^3 = (2)^3$ $\Rightarrow 1 + \frac{r}{100} = 2$ ....................(i)

Again, let the sum will become 16 times in n yr.

Then, $16x = x\left(1 + \frac{r}{100}\right)n$ $16 = 2^n \Rightarrow 2^4 = 2^n$ [From Eq. (i)]

$\Rightarrow n = 4$yr

Hence option (B) is the answer

Q14. Difference in Interest between two years = Rs. 420 – Rs. 400 = Rs. 20

So, Rate % $= \frac{20}{100} \times 100 = 5\%$

Given that Rs. 400 is the interest on the sum for 1st year, Hence, sum $= 100 \times \frac{400}{5} \times 1 =$ Rs. 8000

Hence option (A) is the answer

Q15. Let the sum be x.

Simple interest on x for 2 years = Rs. 2000

Simple interest $= \frac{PRT}{100}$ $2000 = \frac{x \times R \times 2}{100}$ $\Rightarrow xR = 100000$ ....—(1)

Compound Interest on x for 2 years = 2400

$P(1 + \frac{R}{100})T - P = 2400$ $x(1 + \frac{R}{100})2 - x = 2400$

$x(1 + \frac{2R}{100} + \frac{2R}{10000}) - x = 2400$ $x(\frac{2R}{100} + \frac{2R}{10000}) = 2400$

$\frac{2xR}{100} + \frac{2xR}{10000} = 2400$ ......(2)

Substituting the value of xR from (1) in (2), we get

2000 + 10R = 2400 10R = 400 R = 40%

Hence option (A) is the answer

Q16. Let the sum be P. The sum P becomes 3P in 4 years on compound interest.

Method 1 –

$3P = P\left(1+\frac{R}{10}\right)^4$ $\Rightarrow 3 = \left(1+\frac{R}{10}\right)^4$

Let the sum P becomes 81P in n years, or, $81P = P(1 + \frac{R}{100})^n$

$\Rightarrow 81 = (1 + \frac{R}{100})^n$ $\Rightarrow (3)^4 = (1 + \frac{R}{100})^n$

$\Rightarrow ((1 + \frac{R}{100})^4)^4 = (1 + \frac{R}{100})^n$ $\Rightarrow (1 + \frac{R}{100})^{16} = (1 + \frac{R}{100})^n$ n=16

i.e, the sum will become 81 times in 16 years

Method 2 -

We know that amount follows Geometric Progression in case of Compound Interest.

Hence $P \xrightarrow{4\,years} 3P \xrightarrow{4\,years} 9P \xrightarrow{4\,years} 27P \xrightarrow{4\,years} 81P$

Hence option (C) is the answer

Q17. Amount = $1386 = (1+\frac{5}{100})(1 + \frac{10}{100})(1+\frac{20}{100})$, or, $1386 = P(\frac{21}{20})(\frac{11}{10})(\frac{6}{5})$

Solving it, we get P = Rs.1000

Hence option (D) is the answer

Q18. Present worth of Rs. x due T years = $x/(1 + \frac{R}{100})^T$

Let x be the annual payment. Then, present worth of x due 1 year hence + present worth of x due 2 year hence = 6600

$$\left(\frac{x}{1+20100}\right) + \left(\frac{x}{1+20100}\right)^2 = 6600, \text{ or, } \frac{x}{6/5} + \left(\frac{x}{6/5}\right)^2 = 6600$$

$$\frac{5x}{6} + \frac{25x}{36} = 6600, \text{ or, } \frac{55x}{36} = 6600. \text{ Hence } x = 6600 \times \frac{36}{55} = 4320$$

Hence option (A) is the answer

Q19. Let the rate of interest be R% per annum.

Assume that Rs. 10000 amount to Rs. 160000 in T years $10000(1 + \;)^T = 160000$

$$\Rightarrow (1 + \frac{R}{100})^T = \frac{16000}{10000} = 16 \Rightarrow (1 + \frac{R}{100})^{T/2} = \sqrt{16} = 4 \quad \text{—(1)}$$

In T/2 years, Rs.10000 amounts to $10000(1+\frac{R}{100})^{T/2} = 10000 \times 4$

Hence option (B) is the answer

Q20. When rates are different for different years $A = P(1 + \frac{R1}{100})(1 + \frac{R2}{100})(1 + \frac{R3}{100})$

Amount after 3 years = $10000(1+\frac{2}{100})(1+\frac{5}{100})(1+\frac{10}{100}) = 10000\,(\frac{102}{100})(\frac{105}{100})$

$(\frac{110}{100}) = 102 \times 105 \times \frac{11}{10} = \text{Rs. } 11781$

Hence option (A) is the answer.

# 6 Ratio Proportion and Variation

**Ratio is the comparison between two quantities or among several quantities. In other words, ratio tells that one quantity is how much bigger or smaller than the other quantity, without actually revealing the exact value of the quantities.**

## Important Formula:

(a) If A : B = x : y and B : C = p : q
Then A : B : C = xp : yp : yq
This can be seen below through the following diagram:

A : B = x : y

B : C = p : q

**A : B : C = xp : yp : yq**

**Note from Authors** – In the above ratios, B is known as 'middle term'. Ratio among different quantities can be established only if there is a middle term present.

(b) Continued proportion

a, b and c are said to be in continued proportion if $\frac{a}{b}=\frac{b}{c}$

So, $b^2$ = ac. Here b is known as the mean proportion.

Similarly if a, b, c and d are in continued proportion, then we get $\frac{a}{b}=\frac{b}{c}=\frac{c}{d}$

(c) Componendo:

If $\frac{a}{b}=\frac{c}{d}$, then $\frac{a+b}{b}=\frac{c+d}{d}$

(d) Dividendo:

If $\frac{a}{b} = \frac{c}{d}$, then $\frac{a-b}{b} = \frac{c-d}{d}$

(e) Componendo and Dividendo:

If $\frac{a}{b} = \frac{c}{d}$, then $\frac{a+b}{a-b} = \frac{c+d}{c-d}$

(f) $\frac{a}{b} = \frac{c}{d} = \frac{a+c}{b+d}$

(g) Partnership:

Consider the case where A, B and C have invested $M_1$, $M_2$ and $M_3$ sum for the time period $T_1$, $T_2$ and $T_3$. Then out of total profit, their shares are in the ratio:

Profit of A : profit of B : Profit of C = $M_1T_1 : M_2T_2 : M_3T_3$

In case time period is same, then the ratio of profit will be in the same ratio as that the ratio of sum invested.

For example, if A, B and C invest $M_1$, $M_2$ and $M_3$ sum for the same time period (say one year), then

Profit of A : profit of B : Profit of C = $M_1 : M_2 : M_3$

(h) If we multiply or divide each term of a ratio by the same non- zero number, it would not affect the ratio.

## Worked Out examples:

Q1. Ratio of salary of A and salary of B = 2:3 and ratio of salary of B and salary of C = 4:5. What is the ratio of salary of A, B and C?

**Solution –**

A : B = 2 : 3

B : C = 4 : 5

A : B : C = 2×4 : 3×4 : 3×5

So, A : B : C = 8 : 12 : 15

Q2. Ratio of salary of A and salary of B = 2:5 and ratio of salary of C and salary of D = 1:3. What is the ratio of salary of A, B, C and D?

**Solution** – There is no middle term here. Hence ratio among A, B, C and D cannot be established.

Q3. Three friends Aman, Parth and Manoj purchased a music system for Rs. 6000 by pooling in money. Aman contributed half of what Parth and Manoj contributed combined. How much did Aman contribute?

**Solution** – Since Aman contributed half of what Parth and Manoj contributed combined, hence Aman contributed $1/3^{rd}$ of total.

[An easier way of understanding this goes as follows:

Assume the sum contributed by Parth and Manoj combined = Rs. 2x

Since Aman contributed half of the sum contributed by Parth and Manoj combined, hence he contributed ½ × 2x = Rs. x. So, total sum = Rs. 2x + Rs. x = Rs. 3x ⇒ Out of this Aman contributed Rs. x, hence he contributed $1/3^{rd}$ of the total.]

According to the question, Rs. 3x = Rs. 6000. Hence x = Rs. 2000.

Q4. A man distributed his wealth among his three children in the ratio of their ages. Ages of the children are 9 years, 12 years and 18 years. What proportion of the whole wealth did the eldest son get?

**Solution** – Age of eldest son = 18 years.

Ratio of ages of sons = 9 : 12 : 18 = 3 : 4 : 6

According to the question, wealth distributed is in the ratio of their ages ⇒ 3x : 4x : 6x

Hence total wealth distributed = 3x + 4x + 6x = 13x

Hence proportion of the whole wealth did the eldest son get = $\frac{6x}{13x} = \frac{6}{13}$

Q5. Given that $\frac{x}{y}$ = 3: 2. What is the value of (2x – y): (3x + 2y)?

**Solution** – Best way to solve such questions is "through assuming the values".

Given that $\frac{x}{y}$ = 3: 2, so assume x = 3 and y = 2.

Hence (2x – y): (3x + 2y) = (2 × 3 – 2): (3 × 3 + 2 × 2) = 4:13

Q6. Zimmer and Christopher enter into a partnership to produce a movie. Zimmer invests Rs. 2 million and Christopher invests Rs. 10 million. It takes 2 years to produce the movie. Movie earns a total profit of Rs. 36 million. What will be the share of Zimmer out of the whole profit?

**Solution** – Ratio of profit between them = $M_1T_1 : M_2T_2$

Ratio of profit between Zimmer and Christopher = 2 × 24 : 10 × 24 = 1 : 5

Assume their profit are x and 5x.

According to the question, x + 5x = Rs. 36 million ⇒ 6x = Rs. 36 million

Hence x = 6 million = Zimmer's profit

Q7. What is the mean proportion of the numbers 3 and 27?

**Solution** – Let a = 3 and b = 27.

Using the formula for mean proportion, we get mean proportion = $(3 \times 27)^{½} = 9$

Q8. Given that 3x = 4y = 5z. What is the value of x : y : z?

**Solution** – Easier way of solving such questions is to assume 3x = 4y = 5z = LCM (3, 4, 5) = 60

Now, 3x = 60 ⇒ x = 20; 4y = 60 ⇒ y = 15; 5z = 60 ⇒ y = 12

Hence x : y : z = 20 : 15 : 12.

Q9. Given that 2x = 3y = 4z. What is the ratio of x : y : z?

**Solution** – Assume that 2x = 3y = 4z = LCM (2, 3, 4) = 12

Now 2x = 12, so, x = 6; 3y = 12, so, y = 4; 4z = 12, so, z = 3.

Hence x : y : z = 6 : 4 : 3.

Q10. Given that $x : y : z = \frac{1}{2} : \frac{1}{3} : \frac{1}{4}$. What is the ratio of x : y : z?

**Solution** – Given that $x : y : z = \frac{1}{2} : \frac{1}{3} : \frac{1}{4}$: = k, or, x : y : z = 2k : 3k : 4k = 2 : 3: 4

Q11. $\frac{x}{2} = \frac{y}{3} = \frac{z}{4}$. What is the ratio of x : y : z?

**Solution** – $\frac{x}{2} = \frac{y}{3} = \frac{z}{4}$ = K. Hence x = 2k, y = 3k, z = 4k. Hence x : y : z = 2 : 3 : 4.

NOTE – Mathematically, Q10 and Q11 are same.

Q12. Given that $\frac{x}{y} = \frac{2}{3}$ = , what is the value of $(2x^2 - 3y^2)/(2x^2 + y^2)$?

**Solution** – Best way to solve such questions is to put x = 2 and y = 3 in the expression given in the question.

$(2x^2 - 3y^2)/(2x^2 + y^2) = (2 \times 2^2 - 3 \times 3^2)/(2 \times 2^2 + 3^2) = (8 - 27) / (8 + 9) = -19/17$.

Q13. Ratio of daily pocketmoney of two friends Anu and Anam is 3: 4. Both the friends spend Rs. 12 each on eating noodles. After spending money on noodles, the remaining sum with them is in the ratio 9: 14. How much daily pocketmoney does Anu get?

**Solution** – Assume the pocket money obtained by Anu and Anam is 3x and 4x respectively. After spending Rs. 12 each on noodles, they are left with Rs. (3x – 12) and Rs. (4x – 12) respectively.

According to the question, $\frac{3x-12}{4x-12}=\frac{9}{14}$

Or, 14 ( 3x – 12) = 9 (4x – 12), or, 42x – 168 = 36x – 108

Or, 6x = 60. Hence x = Rs. 10. So, pocket money obtained by Anu = 3x = 3 × Rs. 10 = Rs. 30

## Practice Exercise

Q1. In a mixture of 60 L, the ratio of milk and water is 2:1. If this ratio is to be 1:2, then the quantity of water to be further added is

a) 30 L b) 20 L c) 40 L d) 60 L

Q2. The ratio between the number of passengers travelling by I and II classes between the two bus stations is 1:50, whereas the ratio of I and II classes fares between the same stations is 3:1. If on a particular day, Rs. 1325 were collected from the passengers, then what was the amount collected from the II class passengers?

a) Rs. 750 b) Rs. 1000 c) Rs. 850 d) Rs. 1250

Q3. A man's saving and expenditure is in the ratio 2:3. His income increases by 10%. His expenditure also increases by 12%. By how much percent do his savings increase?

a) 7% b) 9% c) 10% d) 13%

Q4. A bottle contains $\frac{3}{4}$ of soda and the rest water. What amount of the mixture must be taken away and replaced by an equal quantity of water so that the mixture has half soda and half water?

a) 25% b) 33% c) 45% d) 50%

Q5. A mixture of 45 L of spirit and water contains 20% of water in it. How much water must be added to it make the water 25% in the new mixture?

a) 5 L b) 3 L c) 4 L d) 6 L

Q6. Divide Rs. 671 among Anil, Binit and Chinu such that if their shares be decreased by Rs. 3, Rs. 7 and Rs. 9 respectively, then the remainder shall be in the ratio 1 : 2 : 3.

a) Rs. 110, Rs. 220, Rs. 336 b) Rs. 112, Rs. 223, Rs. 336
c) Rs. 105, Rs. 223, Rs. 330 d) None of the above

Q7. Three partners invested capital in the ratio 2:7:9. The time period for which each of them invested was in the ratio of the reciprocals of the amount invested. Find the share of the partner who brought in the maximum capital, if gain is Rs. 1080.

a) Rs. 120 b) Rs. 360 c) Rs. 540 d) Rs. 420

Q8. The ratio of the ages of the father and the son at present is 7:1. After 4 yr, the ratio will become 4:1. What is the sum of the present ages of the father and the son?

a) 20 yr b) 35 yr c) 32 yr d) None of these

Q9. M and N enter into a partnership with Rs. 50000 and Rs. 60000 respectively. O joins them after x months contributing Rs. 70000 and N leaves x months before the year's end. The ratio of their profit is 20: 18: 21, and then the value of x is

a) 3 b) 9 c) 6 d) 8

Q10. A person has a chemical of Rs. 25 per liter. In what ratio should water mixed in that chemical, so that after selling the mixture at Rs. 20 per liter he may get a profit of 25%?

a) 13:16 b) 12:15 c) 16:9 d) 19:22

Q11. Ritu, Reshu, Rohin and Neha rented a house and agreed to share the rent as follows

Ritu: Reshu = 8:15

Reshu: Rohin = 5:8 and Rohin: Neha = 4:5. The part of rent paid by Rohin will be

a) 24/77 b) 13/66 c) 12/55 d) 13/77

Q12. In a proportion the multiplication of first and last terms is 40 and that of second and third terms is 2.5x, then the value of x is

a) 16 b) 36 c) 75 d) 90

Q13. Plane fares of 3rd, 2nd and 1st classes between two cities were in the ratio of 3:6:8. The fares of 2nd and 1st class were subsequently reduced by 1/12 and 1/6, respectively. If during a year, the ratio between the passengers of 3rd, 2nd and 1st classes was 26:12:9 and total amount collected by the sale of tickets was Rs. 1088, then find the collection from the passengers of 1st class.

a) Rs. 260 b) Rs. 280 c) Rs. 300 d) Rs. 320

Q14. Three tubs G, H and I have mixtures of juice and water in the ratio 1:5, 3:5 and 5:7 respectively. If the capacities of the tub are in the ratio 5:4:5 then find the ratio of the juice to the water if the mixtures of the entire three tubs are mixed together.

a) 51:115 b) 52:115 c) 53:115 d) 54:115

Q15. Salaries of Anu, Banu and Chamu were in the ratio 3:5:7 respectively. If their salary were increased by 50%, 60% and 50% respectively, what will be the new ratio of their respective salaries?

a) 4:5:7 b) 3:6:7 c) 4:15:18 d) 9:16:21

Q16. The ratio of the rate of flow of water in tunnels varies inversely as the square of the radius of the tunnels. What is the ratio of the rates of flow in 2 tunnels of diameter 2 cm and 4 cm?

a) 1:2 b) 2:1 c) 1:8 d) 4:1

Q17. If y/(x-z) = (y+x)/z = x/y, then find x: y: z.

a) 1:2:3 b) 3:2:1 c) 4:2:3 d) 2:4:7

Q18. Half the women and one-third of the men of a college reside in the Paying Guest. What fractional part of the student body are PG dwellers if the total number of women in the college is 100 and is 1/4 of the total strength?

a) 2/5 b) 5/12 c) 1/5 d) None of these

Q19. Given that 24 carat gold is pure gold, 18 carat gold is 3/4 gold and 20 carat gold is 5/6 gold, tha ratio of pure gold in 18 carat gold to the pure gold in 20 carat gold is

a) 5:8 b) 9:10 c) 15:24 d) 8:5

Q20. The ratio of coins in a bag contains Rs. 216 in the form of one rupee, 50 paisa and 25 paisa coins are 2:3:4. The number of 50 paisa coins is

a) 96 b) 144 c) 114 d) 141

Q21. The ratio of monthly income of two workers are is 4:5 and their monthly expenditures are 7:9. If each saves Rs. 50 a month, then what is their monthly income?

a) Rs. 100, Rs. 125 b) Rs. 200, Rs. 250

c) Rs. 300, Rs. 375 d) Rs. 400, Rs. 500

Q22. In a mixture of 60 l, the ratio of Juice and soda is 2:1 . If the ratio of the juice and soda is to be 1 : 2, then the amount of soda to be further added must be

a) 40 L b) 30 L c) 20 L d) 60 L

Q23. A woman left one half of the property for his husband. One third to his son and the remainder to his daughter. Share of daughter was worth Rs. 45,000. How much money did the woman leave?

a) Rs. 2,45,000 b) Rs. 2,60,000 c) Rs. 2,70,000 d) Rs. 2,75,000

Q24. A flower bouquet contains pink roses, red roses, pink carnations, and red carnations. One third of the pink flowers are roses, three fourths of the red flowers are carnations, and six tenths of the flowers are pink. What percentage of the flowers are carnations?

(a) 15 (b) 30 (c) 40 (d) 70

Q25. A fruit salad consists of blueberries, raspberries, grapes, and cherries. The fruit salad has a total of 280 pieces of fruit. There are twice as many raspberries as blueberries, three times as many grapes as cherries, and four times as many cherries as raspberries. How many cherries are there in the fruit salad?

(a) 8 (b) 16 (c) 25 (d) 64

Q26. 60 kg of an alloy A is mixed with 100 kg of alloy B. If alloy A has lead and iron in the ratio 3: 2 and alloy B has iron and copper in the ratio 1: 4, then the amount of iron in the new alloy is:

a) 36 kg b) 44 kg c) 53 kg d) 80 kg

Q27. Number of students for Mathematics, Physics and Biology in a school are in the ratio 5: 7: 8. If number of these seats is increased by 40%, 50% and 75% respectively, what will be the ratio of students after the increase?

a) 2: 3: 4 b) 6: 7: 8 c) 6: 8: 9 d) None of these

Q28. Rs. 366 are divided amongst A, B and C so that A may get 1/2 as much as B and C together, B any get 2/3 as much as A and C together, then the share of A is:

a) Rs. 122 b) Rs. 129.60 c) Rs. 146.60 d) Rs. 183

Q29. Three jars have their volumes in the ratio 3: 4: 5. They are full of mixtures of milk and water. The mixtures contain milk and water in the ratio of (4: 1), (3: 1) and (5: 2) respectively. The contents of all these three jars are poured into a fourth jar. The ratio of milk and water in the fourth jar is:

a) 4: 1 b) 151: 48 c) 157: 53 d) 5: 2

Q30. Ratio of income of A and B is 5: 4 and the ratio of their expenditures is 3: 2. At the end of the year, each saves Rs. 1600. What is the income of A?

a) Rs. 3400 b) Rs. 3600 c) Rs. 4000 d) 4400

Q31. The incomes of Chandni and Kiran are in the ratio 9:4 and their expenditure is in the ratio 7:3. If each saves Rs. 2, 000, then Chandni expenditure is

a) Rs. 60, 000 b) Rs. 80,000 c) Rs. 70,000 d) None of these

Q32. N and M entered into partnership with Rs. 600 and Rs. 700 respectively. After 6 months, M withdraws 28.56% of his stock but after 3 months, he puts back 60% of what he had withdrawn. The gain at the end of the year is Rs. 726. How much of this should M receive?

a)Rs. 336 b)Rs. 366 c)Rs. 633 d)Rs. 663

Q33. At the start of a Project the ratio of the number of boys to the number of girls was 3:1. During the tea break, 16 boys left and 6 more girls registered. The ratio of the boys to the girls became 2:1. The total number of boys and girls at the start of the seminar was

a) 112 b) 48 c) 54 d) 72

Q34. The number that must be added to each of the numbers 8, 21, 13 and 31 to make the ratio of last two numbers equal to the ratio of first two numbers is

a) 7 b) 5 c) 9 d) None of these

Q35. The least number which when subtracted from the ratio 6 : 7 to give a ratio less than 16 : 21, is

a) 3 b) 4 c) 5 d) 6

## Answer Grid:

| Q. No. | 1 | 2 | 3 | 4 | 5 | 6 | 7 | 8 | 9 | 10 | 11 | 12 | 13 | 14 | 15 | 16 | 17 | 18 |
|---|---|---|---|---|---|---|---|---|---|---|---|---|---|---|---|---|---|---|
| Answer | d | d | a | b | b | b | b | c | a | c | a | a | d | c | d | d | c | d |
| Q. No. | 19 | 20 | 21 | 22 | 23 | 24 | 25 | 26 | 27 | 28 | 29 | 30 | 31 | 32 | 33 | 34 | 35 | |
| Answer | b | b | d | d | c | d | d | b | a | a | c | a | c | b | a | b | a | |

## Solution and Explanation

Q1. Quantity of milk in mixture = $\frac{2}{3} \times 60 = 40$ L

Quantity of water in mixture = $\frac{1}{3} \times 60 = 20$ L

Let the Quantity of water to be further added be x

Then, = $\frac{40}{20+x} = \frac{1}{2}$ 20 + x = 80 X = 60 L

Hence option (D) is the answer

Q2. Let the number of passengers travelling by class I and class II be x and 50x respectively

Then, amount collected from class I and class II will be Rs. 3x and Rs. 50x respectively

Given, 3x + 50x = 1325 53x = 1325 X = 25

Amount collected from class II = 50 × 25 = Rs. 1250

Hence option (D) is the answer

Q3. Let expenditure be Rs. 60 and savings be Rs. 40

Total Income = Rs. 100, New Income = Rs. 110

New expenditure = Rs. 67.2, New Savings = 100 – 67.2 = Rs. 42.8

Percentage increase in savings = $\frac{28}{40} \times 100 = 7\%$

Hence option (A) is the answer

Q4. Soda = $\frac{3}{4}\times 100 = 75$

Ratio of soda and water = 3 : 1

Water = $\frac{1}{4}\times 100 = 25$

Let x Ltr of mixture is taken away, then quantity of soda left = $\left(3-\frac{3x}{4}\right)$

and water left = $\left(1-\frac{x}{4}\right)+x$

Given, $3-\frac{3x}{4}=1-\frac{x}{4}+x$ $\quad 3-1=\frac{3x}{4}-\frac{x}{4}+x$

$2=\frac{6x}{4}x$ $\quad =\frac{4}{3}$

required percentage = $\frac{\frac{4}{3}}{4}\times 100 = 33\frac{1}{3}\%$

Hence option (B) is the answer

Q5. Quantity of water in the mixture = $\frac{20}{100}\times 45 = 9$ ltr

Let x ltr of water must be added to make the water 25% in the solution

$\frac{9+x}{45+x}\times 100 = 25$ $\quad 36 + 4x = 45 + x$

$3x = 9$ $\quad x = 3$ ltr

Hence option (B) is the answer

Q6. Let the share of Anil, Binit and Chinu be (x - 3), (2x - 7) and (3x - 9) respectively

Then, (x - 3) + (2x - 7) + (3x - 9) = 671, or, 6x = 690, or, x = 115

Anil = Rs. 112 Binit = Rs. 223 Chinu = Rs. 336

Hence option (B) is the answer

Q7. Ratio of Capital = 2:7:9 $\quad$ Ratio of Time $=\frac{1}{2}:\frac{1}{7}:\frac{1}{9}$

Ratio of Investment $= 2\times\frac{1}{2}:7\times\frac{1}{7}:9\times\frac{1}{9}$

Share of each partner = $\frac{1}{3} \times 1080$ = Rs. 360

Hence option (B) is the answer

Q8. Let the present age of father and son be 7x yr and x yr respectively.

After 4 year, Age of father = (7x + 4) yr And Age of Son = (x + 4) yr

Given, $\frac{7x+4}{x+4} = \frac{4}{1}$ = 7x + 4 = 4x + 16

3x = 12 x = 4

7x + x = 28 + 4 = 32 yr

Hence option (C) is the answer

Q9. Investment of M = 50,000 × 12 = Rs. 6,00,000

Investment of N = 60,000 × (12 – x)

Investment of O = 70,000 × (12 – x)

$$\frac{60,000}{60,000 \times (12-x)} = \frac{20}{18} \qquad 180 = 240 - 20x \qquad x = 3$$

Hence option (A) is the answer

Q10. Selling price of Mixture = Rs. 20 Cost price of Mixture = $\frac{100}{125} \times 20$ = Rs. 16

By the rule of allegation, required ratio = 16 :9

Hence option (C) is the answer

Q11. Ritu : Reshu = 8 : 15

Reshu : Rohin = 5 : 8

Rohin : Neha = 4 : 5

Ritu: Reshu : Rohin : Neha = 8 : 15 : 24 : 30

Part of rent paid by Rohin = $\frac{24}{8+15+24+30} = \frac{24}{77}$

Hence option (A) is the answer

Q12. In a proportion, Multiplication of 1st and 4th terms = Multiplication of 2nd and 3rd terms

40 = 2.5x x = 16

Hence option (A) is the answer

Q13. New ratio of fares (1st, 2nd and 3rd) = $8\times\frac{5}{6}:6\times\frac{11}{12}:3\times1$ = 80 : 66 : 36 = 40 : 33 : 18

Ratio of passengers = 9 : 12 : 26

Ratio of Amount collected = 40 × 9 : 33 × 12 : 18 × 26 = 90 : 99 : 117

Amount collected from 1st class fares = $\frac{90}{306}$ × 1088 = Rs. 320

Hence option (D) is the answer

Q14. Ratio of juice and water

$$\left(\frac{1}{6}\times5+\frac{3}{8}\times4+\frac{5}{12}\times5\right):\left(\frac{5}{6}\times5+\frac{5}{8}\times4+\frac{7}{12}\times5\right)$$

106 : 230 = 53 : 115

Hence option (C) is the answer

Q15. New ratio = $3\times\frac{150}{100}:5\times\frac{160}{100}:7\times\frac{150}{100}=\frac{9}{2}:8:\frac{21}{2}=9:16:21$

Hence option (D) is the answer

Q16. Radius of tunnels is 1cm and 2cm. Hence required ratio = $\left(\frac{1}{(1)}\right)^2:\left(\frac{1}{(2)}\right)^2$ = 4 : 1

Hence option (D) is the answer

Q17. Use options to solve this question. Only option (c) satisfy the equations.

Hence option (C) is the answer

Q18. Total student = 400

No. of Women = 100 No. of men = 300

No. of PG dwellers = $\frac{1}{2}$ × 100 + $\frac{1}{3}$ × 300 = 150

Required fraction = $\frac{150}{400}=\frac{15}{40}$

Hence option (D) is the answer

Q19. 18 carat Gold = $\frac{3}{4}$ Pure Gold = $\frac{3}{4} \times 24 = 18$

20 carat gold = $\frac{5}{6}$ pure gold = $\frac{5}{6} \times 24 = 20$

Required ratio = 18 : 20 = 9 : 10

Hence option (B) is the answer

Q20. Amount of 50 paisa coins = $\frac{3}{9} \times 216$ = Rs. 72

No. of 50 paisa coins = 72 × 2 = 144 (as Rs. 1 has 2 fifty paisa coins)

Hence option (B) is the answer

Q21. Let the income of two workers be 4x and 5x and their expenses be 7y and 9y.

Then, $4x - 7y = 50$ ..... (i) and $5x - 9y = 50$ ..... (ii)

Solving eqs (i) and (ii), we get $x = 100$ and $y = 50$

Hence option (D) is the answer

Q22. Quantity of juice = $\frac{2}{3} \times 60 = 40$ L

Quantity of soda = $\frac{1}{3} \times 60 = 20$ L

Quantity of soda added = x L (suppose)

Now, $\frac{40}{20+x} = \frac{1}{2}$ Hence, x = 60 L

Hence option (D) is the answer

Q23. Let that woman left Rs. x

Share of Daughter = $x - \frac{x}{2} - \frac{x}{3} = 45000 = \frac{x}{6} =$ $x$ = Rs 270000

Hence option (C) is the answer

Q24. We are given that $\frac{6}{10} = \frac{3}{5}$ = of the flowers are pink, so we know $\frac{2}{5}$ of the flowers are red.

Since $\frac{1}{3}$ of the pink flowers are roses, $\frac{2}{3}$ of the pink flowers are carnations.

We are given that $\frac{3}{4}$ of the red flowers are carnations.

The number of carnations are $\frac{3}{5}\times\frac{2}{3}+\frac{2}{5}\times\frac{3}{4}=\frac{2}{5}+\frac{3}{10}=\frac{7}{10}$ =70%. Hence option (d) is the answer.

Q25. Let the number of blueberries be b the number of raspberries be r the number of grapes be g and finally the number of cherries be c

Observe that since there are 280 pieces of fruit, so, b + r + g + c = 280

Since there are twice as many raspberries as blueberries, 2b = r.

Given that that there are three times as many grapes as cherries ⇒ 3c = g.

Because there are four times as many cherries as raspberries ⇒ 4r = c.

Note that we are looking for c. So, we try to rewrite all of the other variables in terms of c. The third equation gives us the value of g in terms of c already. We divide the fourth equation by 4 to get that r = $\frac{c}{4}$. Finally, substituting this value of r into the first equation provides us with the equation b = $\frac{c}{8}$ and substituting yields: $\frac{c}{4}+\frac{c}{8}$ + 3c + c = 280.

Multiply this equation by 8 to get:

2c + c + 24c + 8c = 8 × 280,

35c = 8 × 280, ⇒ c = 64. Hence option (d) is the answer.

Q26. Quantity of iron in 60 kg of A = (60 × 2/5) kg = 24 kg.

Quantity of iron in 100 kg of B = (100 × 1/5) kg = 20 kg.

Quantity of iron in the new alloy = (24 + 20) kg = 44 kg.

Q27. Originally, let the number of students for Mathematics, Physics and Biology be 50, 70 and 80 respectively.

New number of students = (140% of 50), (150% of 70) and (175% of 80)

Hence Required ratio = 70: 105: 140 = 2: 3: 4. Hence option (A) is the answer.

Q28. A: (B + C) = 1: 2, or, A's share = Rs. (366 × 1/3) = Rs. 122.

Hence option (a) is the answer.

Q29. Let the three jars contain 30, 40 and 50 litres of mixtures respectively.

Milk in 1st mixture= (30 × 4/5) litres = 120/5 litres.

Water in 1st mixture= (30 – 12x/5) litres = 30/5 litres.

Milk in 2nd mixture= (40 × 3/4) litres = 30 litres.

Water in 2nd mixture= (40 – 30) litres = 10 litres.

Milk in 3rd mixture = (50 × 5/7) litres = 250/7 litres.

Water in 3rd mixture = (50 – 25x/7) litres = 100/7 litres.

Total milk in final mixture = (120 /5 + 30 + 250/7) litres = 3140/35 litres.

Total water in final mixture = (30/5 + 10 + 100/7) litres = 1060/35 litres.

Ratio of milk and water in 4th jar = 3140/35: 1060/35 = 157: 53.

Q30. Let the incomes of A and B be Rs. 5x and Rs. 4x respectively and let their expenditures be Rs. 3y and Rs. 2y respectively.

Then, 5x – 3y = 1600 .... (i) and 4x – 2y = 1600 ..... (ii)

Solving (i) and (ii), we get: 2x = 1600 ⇒ x = 800.

Hence A's income = Rs. 5x = Rs. (5 × 800) = Rs. 4000.

Q31. Let incomes of Chandni and Kiran are 9x and 4x respectively

And their expenditure are 7y and 3y respectively,

9x – 7y = 2000 .....(i) and 4x – 3y = 2000 .....(ii)

on solving (i) and (ii), we get y = 10000

Chandni expenditure = 7 × 10000 = Rs 70000

Hence option (C) is the answer

Q32. M's investment = $(700 \times 3) + (700 \times \frac{5}{7} \times 3) + (500 + 200 \times \frac{3}{5}) \times 6$ = Rs 7320

N's investment = 600 × 12 = Rs. 7200

M's share from profit = $\frac{7320}{7320+7200} \times 726$ = Rs. 366

Hence option (B) is the answer

Q33. Let number of boys and girls at the start of seminar be 3x and x respectively

Then, $\frac{3x-16}{x+6} = \frac{2}{1}$ = 3x – 16 = 2x + 12 x = 28

Total number of Boys and Girls at the start of seminar = 3x + x = 4 × 28 = 112

Hence option (A) is the answer

Q34. Let that number be x.

Then, $\frac{13+x}{31+x} = \frac{8+x}{21+x}$ = Or, $248 + 31x + 8x + x^2 = 273 + 21x + 13x + x^2$

Or, $5x = 25$. Hence $x = 5$

Hence option (B) is the answer

Q35. Let x is subtracted from each one of the numbers.

According to the question, $(6-x) : (7-x) < 16 : 21$

Or, $21(6-x) < 16(7-x)$, or, $5x > 14$, or, $x > 2.8$

Least such number is 3.

Hence option (A) is the answer

# 7 Average

Average is calculated by dividing the sum of all the numbers by the number of numbers.

$$\text{Average} = \frac{\text{Sum of numbers}}{\text{Number of numbers}}$$

**e.g.1:** A student obtained 76, 65, 82, 67 and 85 marks (out of 100) in English, Maths, Physics, Civics and Biology. What are his average marks in all the mentioned subjects?

**Solution** - $\text{Average} = \frac{76+65+82+67+85}{5} = \frac{375}{5} = 75$

**e.g.2:** Average of ten two digits numbers is S. However when we reverse one of the numbers AB as BA from the given 10 numbers, then the average becomes (S + 1.8). What is the value of B - A?

**Solution** - Average of 10 numbers is increasing by 1.8, so it can be assumed that 1.8 has been added up to all the numbers.

So, BA is 1.8 × 10 = 18 more than AB.

There are so many two-digit numbers which satisfy above condition. Using hit and trial, number can be 13, 24, 35, 46, 57, 68, 79. In every case, difference between the digits = 2

Otherwise, we can use the formula

(BA – AB) = 9 × (B-A)

Where BA and AB are two-digit nos.

## Properties of average:

1. Average always lies in between maximum and minimum value. It can be equal to the maximum or minimum value only in case of all the numbers being equal.
2. When weights of different quantities are same, then we use simple method to find the average however when we take different weights of different quantities, then it is known as weighted average and we use the method of weighted average to find the average.

3. If the value of the each quantity is increased or decreased by the same value S, then the average will also increase or decrease respectively by S.
4. If the value of each quantity is multiplied by the same value S. Then the average will also be multiplied by S.
5. If the value of each quantity is divided by the same value S(S ≠ 0) then the average will also be divided by S.

## Some Special Cases:

### 1. If the series is in Arithmetic Progression:

$$\text{Average} = \frac{\text{1st Number + Last Number}}{2}$$

[Arithmetic Progression is a series in which difference between any two consecutive terms is same. To know more, go through the chapter – Sequence and Series in this book]

**e.g.3.** Average of first seven multiples of 5 is:

**Solution –**

**Method 1** – Using general definition of Average = 5 (1 + 2 + 3 + 4 + 5 + 6 + 7) / 7 = 140/7 = 20

**Method 2** – Since consecutive multiples will be in Arithmetic Progression,

$$\text{Average} = \frac{\text{1st Number + Last Number}}{2}$$

1st Number = 1st multiple of 5 = 5, and last number = 7th multiple of 5 = 35

$$\text{Hence Average} = \frac{5+35}{2} = 20$$

**e.g.4.** Average of 5 observations p, p + 2, p + 4, p + 6 and p + 8 is 11. What is the average of last three observations?

**Solution –**

**Method 1** – It can be seen that numbers are in AP. Hence average = Middle Number

Hence middle number = Average = p + 4 = 11 þ p = 7

Average of last three observations = Middle Number = p + 6 = 7 + 6 = 13

**Method 2** – Going through general approach:

[p + (p + 2) + (p + 4) + (p + 6) + (p + 8)] /5 = 11 or 5p + 20 = 55 or p = 7.

So, the numbers are 7, 9, 11, 13, 15.

Hence Required mean = (11 + 13 + 15) /3 = 39/3 = 13.

## 2. Average involving Time Speed and Distance:

General formula for Average speed = $\frac{\text{Total.distance}}{\text{Total.time}}$

### Particular Cases:

(a) If a person covers the same distance with different speeds A and B,

Average speed for the whole journey = $\frac{2AB}{A+B}$ Harmonic Mean of A and B.

(b) If a person covers some distance with different speeds A and B for equal time,

Average speed for the whole journey = $\frac{A+B}{2}$ Arithmetic Mean of A and B.

**e.g.5.** Kitti goes to Patna from New Delhi at a speed of 40 kmph and returns with a speed of 60 kmph. His average speed during the whole journey is -

Since the distance covered is same, Average speed = $\frac{2AB}{A+B} = \frac{2 \times 40 \times 60}{40 + 60}$ = 48 kmph

**e.g.6.** Kitti is going form Patna to New Delhi. For half the time, his speed was 40 kmph and for other half of the time, his speed was 60 kmph. His average speed during the whole journey is -

Since time taken is same, Average speed = $\frac{AB}{2} = \frac{40+60}{2}$ = 50 kmph.

**e.g.7.** Sudhir goes from A to B at an speed of 60 kmph and comes back with a speed of x kmph. During his whole journey, his average speed = 120 kpmh. What is the value of N?

**e.g. 7.** This is not possible. Average speed has to be less than twice the lower speed. In this case, lower speed = 60 kmph, hence average speed will be less than 120 kmph. Hence option (D) is the answer.

## 3. Average involving Age:

If Average of a group of n persons is given at any point of time and we are required to find out the average of same group consisting same n persons, then it is done in the following way:

| 5 years back | 10 years back | Now | 10 yrs. later | 5 years later |
|---|---|---|---|---|
| N – 5 | N –10 | N | N + 10 | N + 5 |

## 4. Average involving No. system:

(a) Average of 1st n consecutive natural nos. = $\frac{n+1}{2}$

e.g. – Average of 1st five natural nos. = 3

(b) Average of 1st n consecutive even natural nos. = n +1

Sum of 1st n consecutive even natural nos. = n(n +1)

e.g. – Average of 1st five even natural nos. = 6

(c) Average of 1st n consecutive odd natural nos. = n

Sum of 1st n consecutive odd natural nos. = $n^2$

e.g. – Average of 1st five odd natural nos. = 5

## Weighted Average

Let us see a general scenario for two groups:

| *Group No.* | *No. of members* | *Average age of group* |
|---|---|---|
| $G_1$ | $N_1$ | $A_1$ |
| $G_2$ | $N_2$ | $A_2$ |

If we combine both the groups, then average age of all the members = $(N_1 \times A_1 + N_2 \times A_2)/ (N_1 + N_2) = A_w$

We write this in the Conventional "Criss-Cross" method as given below:

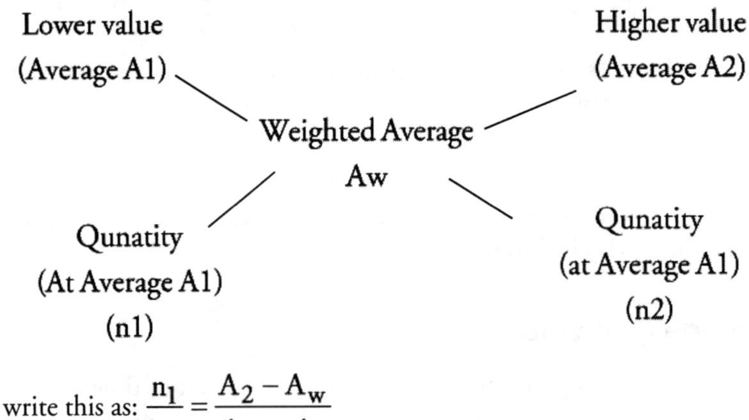


And we write this as: $\frac{n_1}{n_2} = \frac{A_2 - A_w}{A_w - A_1}$

i.e. $\frac{\text{Quantity (Lower.Priced)}}{\text{Quantity (Higher.Priced)}} = \frac{\text{Higher.Price-Averge.Price}}{\text{Average.Price-Lower Price}}$

**e.g.8.** Two mixtures of 70% milk solution and 30% milk solution are mixed to from 45% milk solution. In what ratio they have been mixed?

**Solution –**

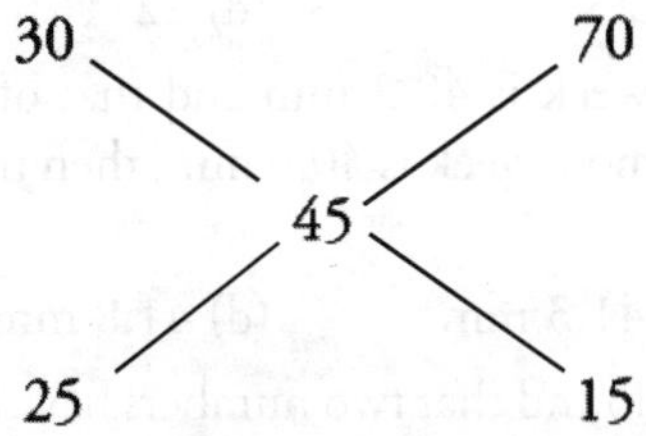


Hence quantity of 30% milk solution : 70% milk solution = 25 : 15 = 5 : 3.

**e.g.9.** In a class of 60 students, the average height of 30 students is x cms and that of the remaining students is y cms. Find the average height of the whole class.

**Solution** - Since the number of students is same, hence the average age = (x + y) / 2 years.

## Practice Exercise

Q1. Some students planned for a party. The budget for food was Rs. 5000. But 5 of them failed to go and thus the cost of food for each member increased by Rs. 50. How many students attended the party?

(a) 15 (b) 25 (c) 20 (d) 30

Q2. The average marks of boys in in a school is 71 and that of the girls is 73. The average marks of all the students of the school are 71.8. The ratio of the number of boys to that of the girls in the school?

(a) 1:2 (b) 3:2 (c) 2:3 (d) 4:2

Q3. The mean monthly salary paid to 75 workers in a factory is Rs. 5680. The mean salary of 25 of them is Rs. 5400 and that of 30 others is Rs. 5700. The mean salary of the remaining workers is

(a) Rs. 5000 (b) Rs. 7000 (c) Rs. 6000 (d) Rs. 8000

Q4. The average monthly expenditure of a family was Rs. 2200 during the first 3 months; Rs. 2250 during the next 4 months and Rs. 3120 during the last 5 months of a year. If the total savings during the year was Rs. 1260, then the average monthly income was

(a) Rs. 2605 (b) Rs. 2805 (c) Rs. 2705 (d) Rs. 2905

Q5. A number of friends decided to go on a picnic and planned to spend Rs. 96 on eatables. Four of them, did not turn up. As a consequence, the remaining ones had to contribute Rs. 4 each extra. The number of those who attended the picnic was

(a) 8 (b) 16 (c) 12 (d) 24

Q6. The average salary of all the workers in a company is Rs. 8000. The average salary of 7 Workers is Rs. 12000 and the average salary of the rest of the worker is Rs. 6000. The total number of workers in the company is

(a) 21 (b) 20 (c) 23 (d) 22

Q7. The average rain of the first four days of a week is 40.2 mm and that of the last four days is 41.3 mm. If the average rain for the whole week is 40.6 mm, then the rain on the fourth day is

(a) 40.8 mm (b) 38.5 mm (c) 41.3 mm (d) 41.8 mm

Q8. The average of 10 numbers is 40.2. Later it is found that two numbers have been wrongly added. The first is 18 greater than the actual number and second number added is 13 instead of 31. Find the correct average.

(a) 40.2 (b) 40.4 (c) 40.6 (d) 40.8

Q9. The average of 11 numbers is 10.9. If the average of the first six numbers is 10.5 and that of last six numbers is 11.4, then find the middle number?

(a) 11.5 (b) 11.4 (c) 11.3 (d) 11.0

Q10. The mean of 1, 7, 5, 3, 4 and 10 is m. The mean of 10, 12, 3, 5, 1, 7 and p is m+1 and their median is q. Then, q is equal to (median is defined as the middle number when all the numbers are arranged in either ascending order or descending order):

(a) 4 (b) 5 (c) 10 (d) 12

Q11. In a class, the average score of girls in an examination is 73 and that of boys is 71. The average score for the whole class is 71.8. The percentage of the girls in the class is

(a) 60% (b) 40% (c) 1.8% (d) 18%

Q12. In the first 10 over of a IPL cricket match, the run rate was only 3.2. What should be the run rate in the remaining 40 over's to reach the target of 282 runs?

(a) 6.25 (b) 6.50 (c) 6.75 (d) 7

Q13. The average (arithmetic mean) of x and y is 40. If z = 10, then what is the average of x, y and z?

(a) $16\frac{2}{3}$ (b) 30 (c) 25 (d) $17\frac{17}{2}$

Q14. There are 30 students in a class. The average age of the first 10 students is 12.5 yr. The average age of the next 20 students is 13.1 yr. The average age of the whole class is

(a) 12.5 yr (b) 12.7 yr (c) 12.8 yr (d) 12.9 yr

Q15. The weight in kilograms of 10 students are 52, 45, 31, 35, 40, 55, 60, 38, 44, 36. If 44 is replaced by 46 and 40 is replaced by 35, then the new median will be

(a) 42 (b) 40.5 (c) 40 (d) 41.5

Q16. The average of three numbers is 135. The largest number is 180 and the difference between the others is 25. The smallest number is

(a) 130 (b) 125 (c) 120 (d) 100

Q17. Of the three numbers, the first is twice the second and the second is twice the third. The average of these numbers is 21. Find the largest number out of these.

(a) 36 (b) 38 (c) 47 (d) 48

Q18. During a census, it is found that the average age A of the oldest child is 20 years less than ½ the sum of the ages of the two parents. If F represents the age of father and M is the age of mother, then which of the following is equivalent to A?

(a) $\frac{F+M-20}{2}$ (b) $\frac{F+M}{2}+20$ (c) $\frac{F+M}{2}-20$ (d) F + M – 10

Q19. In three numbers, the first is twice the second and thrice the third. If the average of these three numbers is 44, then the first number is

(a) 72 (b) 24 (c) 36 (d) 44

Q20. The batting average of 40 innings of a cricket player is 50 runs. His highest score exceeds his lowest score by 172 runs. If these two innings are excluded the average of the remaining 38 innings is 48. His highest score was

(a) 172 (b) 173 (c) 174 (d) 176

Q21. Nine persons went to a hostel for taking their meals. Eight of them spent Rs. 12 each over their meals and ninth spent Rs. 8 more than the average expending of all the nine. Total money spent by them was

(a) Rs. 104 (b) Rs. 105 (c) Rs. 116 (d) Rs. 117

Q22. A batsman makes scores of 98 runs in the $19^{th}$ innings and thus increases his average by 4. What is his average after $19^{th}$ innings?

(a) 22 (b) 24 (c) 28 (d) 26

Q23. The average weight of 45 students in a class is 52kg. 5 of them whose average weight is 48kg leave the class and other 5 students whose average weight is 54kg join the class. What is the new average weight (in kg) of the class?

(a) 52.6 (b) $52\frac{2}{3}$ (c) $52\frac{1}{3}$ (d) none of these

Q24. The average weight of 29 students in a class is 48 kg. If the weight of the teacher is included, the average weight rises by 500g. Find the weight of the teacher ?

(a) 57kg (b) 60 kg (c) 65kg (d) 63 kg

Q25. The average of marks obtained by 120 candidates was 35. If the average of the all the candidates who passed the exam was 15, then the number of candidates who passed the examination was

(a) 100 (b) 110 (c) 120 (d) 150

Q26. The number of observation in group is 40. If the average of the first 10 is 4.5 and that of the remaining 30 is 3.5, then the average of the whole group is

(a) $\frac{15}{4}$ (b) $\frac{1}{5}$ (c) 8 (d) 4

Q27. An investor earns 3% return on 1/4th of his capital, 5% on 2/3rd and 11% on the remainder. What is the average rate of return he earns on his total capital?

(a) 10% (b) 5% (c) 5.5% (d) 10.5%

Q28. The average of 11 results in 50. If the average of first six result is 49 and that of last six 52, the sixth result is

(a) 60 (b) 56 (c) 64 (d) 70

Q29. The average age of a husband, his wife and son 3 yr ago was 27 yr and that of his wife and son 5 yr ago was 20 years. What is the husband's present age?

(a) 35 yr (b) 32 yr (c) 37 yr (d) 40 yr

Q30. The average temperature from Monday to Thursday is 48° and from Tuesday to Friday is 52°. If the temperature on Monday is 42°, what was the temperature on Friday (in °C)

(a) 55 (b) 52 (c) 58 (d) 51

Q31. If a, b, c, d, e are five consecutive odd numbers, their average is:

(a) 3(a + 4) (b) abcde/5

(c) 5(a + b + c + d + e) (d) none of these

Q32. The average of 7 consecutive numbers is 20. The largest of these numbers is:

(a) 20 (b) 22 (c) 23 (d) 24

Q33. The sum of three consecutive odd numbers is 38 more than the average of these numbers. What is the first of these numbers?

(a) 13 (b) 17 (c) 19 (d) 21

Q34. A library has an average of 510 visitors on Sundays and 240 on other days. The average number of visitors per day in a month of 30 days beginning with a Sunday is:

(a) 31 (b) 32

(c) 31.7 (d) cannot be determined

Q35. The average weight of 16 boys in a class is 50.25 kgs and that of the remaining 8 boys is 45.15 kgs. Find the average weight of all the boys in the class.

a) 47.55 kgs b) 48 kgs c) 48.55 kgs d) 49.25 kgs

## Answer Grid:

| Q. No. | 1 | 2 | 3 | 4 | 5 | 6 | 7 | 8 | 9 | 10 | 11 | 12 | 13 | 14 | 15 | 16 | 17 | 18 |
|---|---|---|---|---|---|---|---|---|---|---|---|---|---|---|---|---|---|---|
| Answer | c | b | c | c | a | a | d | a | a | b | b | a | b | d | d | d | a | c |
| Q. No. | 19 | 20 | 21 | 22 | 23 | 24 | 25 | 26 | 27 | 28 | 29 | 30 | 31 | 32 | 33 | 34 | 35 | |
| Answer | a | c | d | d | b | d | a | c | b | b | d | c | d | a | b | c | | |

## Solutions and Explanations:

Q1. Let there were x students, then contribution of one student = $\frac{5000}{x}$

Contribution of each student when 5 of them have failed to go = $\frac{5000}{x-5}$

Given, = $\frac{5000}{x} - \frac{5000}{x-5} = 5$

Using options, we find x = 25 satisfies the equation. Therefore, number of students who attended the picnic = (25 - 5)= 20

Hence option (C) is the answer.

Q2. Let the total number of boys and girls be B and G respectively,

Total score of boys = 71B and Total score of girls = 73G

Total score of the class = 71.8 (B + G)

So, 71B + 73G = 71.8(B + G) or 0.8G = 1.2B or $\frac{B}{G} = \frac{1.2}{0.8} = \frac{3}{2}$

Hence option (B) is the answer.

Q3. Total salary of 75 workers = 426000, Total salary of 25 workers = 135000

Total salary of 30 workers = 171000

So, Total salary of remaining 20 workers = 426000 – (135000 + 171000) = 120000

Hence, mean salary of 20 workers = $\frac{120000}{20} = 6000$

Hence option (C) is the answer.

Q4. Total expenditure for the year = {2200 3 + 2250 × 4 + 3120 × 5}= 6600 + 9000 + 15600 = 31200

Total saving = 1260

Total income = expenses + savings, Therefore 31200 + 1260 = 32460

Average income = $\frac{32460}{12}$ = 2705

Hence option (C) is the answer.

Q5. Let there were x friends, then contribution of one friend = $\frac{96}{x}$

If four friends have left, then contribution of each friend = $\frac{96}{x-4}$

So, $\frac{96}{x-4} - \frac{96}{x} = 4$ Hence, x = 12

Number of friends who attended the picnic = 12 – 4 = 8

Hence option (A) is the answer.

Q6. Let total no. of workers be x. Then, 8000x = 7 × 12000+ (x-7) × 6000

or x = $\frac{42000}{2000}$ = 21

Hence option (A) is the answer.

Q7. Temperature on the fourth day = (40.2 × 4) + (41.3 × 4) – (40.6 × 7), or, 41.8°C

Hence option (D) is the answer.

Q8. Sum of 10 numbers = 402

Correct sum of 10 numbers = 402 – 13 + 31 – 18 = 402

Hence, new average = $\frac{402}{10}$ = 40.2

Hence option (A) is the answer.

Q9. Sum of 11 numbers = 11 × 10.9

Sum of first six numbers = 6 × 10.5 Sum of last six numbers = 6 × 11.4

Then the middle number = 6× 10.5 + 6 × 11.4 –11 × 10.9 = 11.5

Hence option (A) is the answer.

Q10. Given, $m = \frac{1+7+5+3+4+10}{6} = 5$ and $(m+1) = \frac{10+12+3+5+1+7+p}{7}$

or $\frac{38+p}{7} = m+1$

So, 38 + p = 7m + 7. Hence, p = 42 – 38 = 4

Hence the numbers are as follows:- 1, 3, 4, 5, 7, 10, 12 and Median m is 5.

Hence option (B) is the answer.

Q11. Let the number of boys be x and thus of girls be y

Then, Total score of boys = 71x and Total score of girls = 73y

Therefore $\therefore \frac{71x+73y}{(x+y)} = 71.8$ or 71x + 73y = 71.8x + 71.8y or 0.8x = 1.2y

and $\frac{x}{y} = \frac{1.2}{0.8} = \frac{3}{2}$

Percentage of girls in the class = $\frac{2}{5} \times 100 = 40\%$

Hence option (B) is the answer.

Q12. Total runs in the first 10 over's = 10 × 3.2 = 32

$\therefore$ Run rate in the remaining 40 over's = $\frac{282-32}{40} = \frac{250}{40} = 6.25$

Hence option (A) is the answer.

Q13. Total of x and y = 40 × 2 = 80 and Average of x, y and z = $\frac{80+10}{3} = \frac{90}{3} = 30$

Hence option (B) is the answer.

Q14. Total age of 10 students = 125 yr and Total age of 20 students = 262 yr

So, $\therefore$ average age of 30 students = $\frac{125+262}{30} = 12.9$ yr

Hence option (D) is the answer.

Q15. Replacing the two number and arranging them in ascending order, we get 31, 35, 35, 36, 38, 45, 46, 52, 55, 60. Hence the $\therefore$ Median = $\frac{38+45}{2} = 41.5$

Hence option (D) is the answer.

Q16. Given, $\frac{(x-25)+(x)+180}{3} = 135$ or 2x + 155 = 405 or $x = \frac{250}{2} = 125$

Hence, the smallest number = 125 – 25 = 100

Hence option (D) is the answer.

Q17. Let the numbers be a, b and c. Then, a = 2b and b = 2c or c = $\frac{b}{2}$

Then, = 21$\frac{2b+b+\frac{b}{2}}{3}$ = 21 or $\frac{7b}{6}$ = 21 or b = 18

Hence the Numbers are 36, 18 and 9. The largest number is 36.
Hence option (A) is the answer.

Q18. It is given in the question that, A = $\frac{F+M}{2}$ – 20

Hence option (C) is the answer.

Q19. Let the three numbers be a, b and c. a = 2b = 3c ∴ b = $\frac{a}{2}$ and c = $\frac{a}{3}$

Given, $\frac{a+\frac{a}{2}+\frac{a}{3}}{3} = 44$ or $\frac{11a}{18} = 44$ or a = 72

Hence option (A) is the answer.

Q20. Total of 40 innings = 40 × 50 = 2000, Total of 38 innings = 38 × 48 = 1824
∴ Sum of highest and lowest score is x + y = 2000 – 1824 = 176
or x + y = 176 ...(i) x – y = 172 ...(ii)
Solving equations we get, x= 174
Hence option (C) is the answer.

Q21. Let the ninth person spent x. Then, average of all the nine = =

Given, x = $\frac{96+x}{9}$ + 8 or 9x = 96 – x + 72 or 8x = 168 or x = 21

Hence, Total money spent = 96 + 21 = 117
Hence option (D) is the answer.

Q22. Let the average of 18 innings be x. Then, $\frac{18x+98}{19}$ = x + 4

Thus, average after 19$^{th}$ innings = x + 4 = 22 + 4 = 26
Hence option (D) is the answer.

Q23. Total weight of 45 students = 45 × 52 = 2340
Total weight of 5 students who leave = 5 × 45 = 240
Total weight of 5 students who join = 5 × 54 = 270
New total weight of 45 students = 2340 – 240 + 270 = 2370.

Therefore Average = $\frac{2370}{45} = 52\frac{2}{3}$ kg

Hence option (B) is the answer.

Q24. Total weight of 29 students =29 x 48=1392 kg. If teacher weight is included, then Total weight = 30 x 48.5 = 1455 kg. so the Weight of teacher =1455 – 1392 = 63 kg
Hence option (D) is the answer.

Q25. Total marks obtained by the candidates = 120 × 35 = 4200. Let passed students be x, Then 4200 = x × 39 + (120 – x) 15 or 4200 = 24x + 1800 or 2400 = 24x or x = 100
Hence option (A) is the answer.

Q26. Required average = $\frac{10\times4.5-30\times3.5}{40} = \frac{45+105}{40} = \frac{150}{40} = \frac{15}{4}$

Hence option (A) is the answer.

Hence, $(x_2 - 4)(x_2 - 7) = 0$ or $x_2 = 4, 7$ and $x_1 = 7, 4$

So the observations are as follows 4, 7.
Hence option (C) is the answer.

Q28. Total of eleven results = 11 × 50 = 550
Total of first six results = 49 = 294, Total of last six results = 52 × 6 = 312
Required sixth result = 294 + 312 – 550 = 56
Hence option (B) is the answer.

Q29. Let present age of husband, his wife and son be x, y and z respectively

According to the given condition, $\frac{(x-3)+(y-3)+(z-3)}{3} = 27$

or x + y + z = 90 ………(i)

And, $\frac{(y-5)+(z-5)}{2} = 20$ or y + z =50 ……….(ii)

From equation (i) and (ii) we get, x = 90 – 50 = 40 yr
Hence option (D) is the answer.

Q30. Given, $\frac{Mon + Tues + Wed + Thu}{4} = 48°$ or $42° + Tues + Wed + Thu = 192°$ and Tues+ Wed + Thu = 150°

Also given, $\frac{Tues + Wed + Thu + Fri}{4} = 52°$ or 150° + Fri = 208°. Hence, Temp. on Fri = 58

Hence option (C) is the answer.

Q31. Assume numbers to be 1, 3, 5, 7, 9. Obviously Average = Middle Number = 5 (Since the series is in AP). We will check which option = 5 for a = 1, b = 3, c = 5, d = 7 and e = 9.

None of these options given 5. Hence (d) None of these is the answer.

Q32. We have taken the consecutive numbers, hence the series is in AP ⇒ Average = Middle number of the Series = 4$^{th}$ Number = 17.

Since 4$^{th}$ Number = 17, 5$^{th}$ Number = 18, 6$^{th}$ number = 19 and 7$^{th}$ Number = 20. Hence option (a) is the answer.

Q33. Let the numbers be x, x + 2 and x + 4.

Then, (x + x + 2 + x + 4) – (x + x + 2 + x + 4/3) = 38

Or (3x + 6) – (3x + 6/3) = 38 or 2 (3x + 6) = 114 or 6x = 102 or x = 17.

So, first number = x = 17.

Q34. Since the month begins with a Sunday, so there will be five Sunday in the month.

Hence, required average = (510 × 5 + 240 × 25 / 30) = $31^{5}/_{7}$ years. Hence option (c) is the answer.

Q35. Required average = (50.25 × 16 + 45.15 × 8 / 16 + 8) = (804 + 361.20 / 24) = 1165.20 / 24 = 48.55.

# 8 Time and Work

In this chapter we are going to learn the relationship among Time, Work and number of persons doing the job.

## 1. Concept of Man-hour or man-days

(a) If number of hours of work done per day is same but work done are different:

$$\frac{M_1D_1}{W_1}=\frac{M_2D_2}{W_2}$$

Where $M_1$ and $M_2$ are the number of persons involved in doing two works $W_1$ and $W_2$ in $D_1$ and $D_2$ days respectively.

(b) If number of hours of work done per day are different but work done are different:

$$\frac{M_1D_1T_1}{W_1}=\frac{M_2D_2T_2}{W_2}$$

Where $M_1$ and $M_2$ are the number of persons involved in doing two works $W_1$ and $W_2$ in $D_1$ and $D_2$ days working $T_1$ hours per day in 1st case and $T_2$ hours per day in 2nd case.

(c) If work done in two cases are same: $M_1D_1 = M_2D_2$
Where $M_1$ and $M_2$ are the number of persons involved in doing the same work in $D_1$ and $D_2$ days.

## 2. Concept of Individual Work and efficiency

(a) If A can do a job in 10 days, work done by A in one day = $\frac{1}{10}$ of the total work

In general, if A can finish a work in 'x' days, then work done by him in one day = 1/x.

Similarly, work done by him in 'y' days = $\frac{y}{x}$ part of the whole job.

(b) If ratio of efficiency of two persons is x : y, then the ratio of time taken by them in doing the same work $\frac{1}{x}:\frac{1}{y}=y:x$

Vice versa of this is also true i.e. if ratio of days taken by A and B in doing the same work is a : b, then ratio of efficiency of A and B $=\frac{1}{b}:\frac{1}{b}=b:a$

(c) Payment of wages is always done in ratio of efficiency.

(d) If A can do a work in (z + x) days alone, B can do the same work in (z + y) days alone, and A and B together take z days, then $z = \sqrt{xy}$

(e) If A is x% more efficient than B, then

Number of days taken by A alone = $\dfrac{\textit{Number of days taken byB alone}}{\dfrac{100+x}{100}}$

For example, if A is 25% more efficient than B, and B takes **x** days in finishing a work alone, then number of days taken by A alone = $\frac{x}{1.25}$

## Worked Out examples:

Q1. 20 men can cut 15 trees in 12 days. In how many days can 8 men cut 24 trees?

**Solution** – We are going to use following formula in this question: $\frac{M_1D_1}{W_1}=\frac{M_2D_2}{W_2}$

In this question, $M_1$ = 20 men, $D_1$ = 12 days, $W_1$ = 15 trees ; $M_2$ = 8 men, $W_2$ = 24 trees and $D_2$ is to be calculated.

$\frac{M_1D_1}{W_1}=\frac{M_2D_2}{W_2}$, or, $\frac{20\times12}{15}=\frac{8\times D_2}{24}$, $D_2$ = 48 days

Q2. 40 men can plough 12 fields in 18 days. How many men are required to plough 24 fields in 10 days working same number of hours per day?

**Solution** – Let us identify the terms involved here:

$M_1$ = 40 men, $W_1$ = 12 fields and $D_1$ = 18 days. Similarly, $M_2$ = N men (assume), $W_2$ = 24 fields and $D_2$ = 10 days

Using the formula:

$$\frac{M_1D_1}{W_1}=\frac{M_2D_2}{W_2}$$

$$\Rightarrow \frac{40\times18}{12}=\frac{N\times10}{24}$$

Solving it, we get N = 144 men.

Q3. A contractor estimated that a project will be finished by 60 workers in 50 days. He employs 60 men. However, after 40 days, he realizes that work in only 3/5 complete. How many extra men should he employ now so that project is finished on time?

**Solution** – Let us identify the terms involved here:

$M_1$ = 60 men, $W_1$ = 3/5 and $D_1$ = 40 days. Similarly, $M_2$ = N men (assume), $W_2$ = Remaining work = 1 - 3/5 = 2/5 and $D_2$ = Remaining days = 10 days (50 days – 40 days)

Using the formula:

$\frac{M_1D_1}{W_1}=\frac{M_2D_2}{W_2}$ Or $\frac{60\times40}{3/5}=\frac{N\times10}{2/5}$. Hence N = 160 men.

Hence number of extra men to be employed = 160 – 60 = 100 men.

Q4. Sudhir can do a work in 20 days working alone and Samar can do the same work in 40 days working alone. In how many days both of them will finish the work together?

**Solution** – Method 1: Reciprocal calculation method

Sudhir can do a work in 20 days working alone ⇒ Work done by Sudhir in one day = $\frac{1}{20}$ part of total work

Similarly, Samar can do the same work in 40 days working alone ⇒ Work done by Samar in one day = $\frac{1}{40}$ part of total work

Hence work done by Sudhir and Samar together in one day = $\frac{1}{20}+\frac{1}{40}=\frac{3}{40}$ part of total work

Hence days taken by both of them in finishing the work together = $\frac{40}{3}$ days = $13\frac{1}{3}$ days.

**Method 2 – LCM method**

Assume total units of work = LCM (20, 40) = 40 units

Sudhir can do a work in 20 days working alone ⇒ Work done by Sudhir in one day = $\frac{40}{20}$ = 2 units

Similarly, Samar can do the same work in 40 days working alone ⇒ Work done by Samar in one day = $\frac{40}{40}$ = 1 unit

Hence work done by Sudhir and Samar together in one day = 2 units + 1 unit = 3 units

Hence days taken by both of them in finishing the work together = $\frac{40}{3}$ days = $13\frac{1}{3}$ days.

Q5. A can do a job in 18 days and B can do the same job in 24 days, working individually. They started working together, and worked for 2 days. After this, A quit the job, and B finished the remaining work on his own. In how many days will the whole work be finished?

**Solution – Method 1: Reciprocal calculation method**

Work done by A in one day = $\frac{1}{18}$ of the total work; work done by B in one day = $\frac{1}{24}$ of the total work.

Work done by both of them in one day = $\frac{1}{18}+\frac{1}{24}=\frac{7}{72}$ of the whole work

Since they worked together for 2 days, total work done by them = $2\times\frac{7}{22}$ of the whole work = $\frac{7}{36}$ of the whole work.

Remaining work = 1 - $\frac{7}{36}$ of the whole work = $\frac{29}{36}$ of the whole work.

Days taken by B in finishing the remaining work = $\frac{\frac{29}{36}}{\frac{1}{24}}=\frac{58}{3}$ days

Hence days taken in finishing the whole job = 2 days + $\frac{58}{3}$ days = $\frac{64}{3}$ days

**Method 2 – LCM method**

Assume total units of work = LCM (18, 24) = 72 units

A can do a work in 18 days working alone $\Rightarrow$ Work done by A in one day = $\frac{72}{18}$ = 4 units

Similarly, B can do the same work in 24 days working alone $\Rightarrow$ Work done by B in one day = $\frac{72}{24}$ = 3 units

Following timeline can be made:

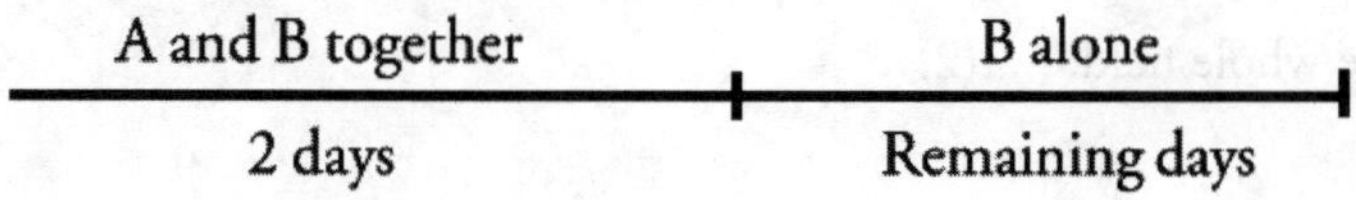


Work done (in units) by A and B together in one day = 4 units + 3 units = 7 units

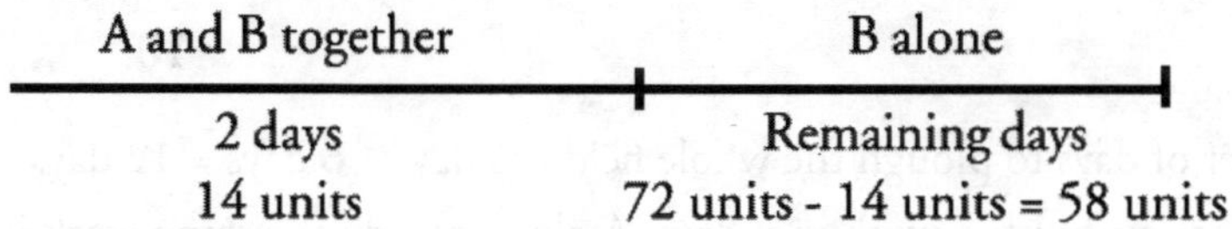


Days taken by B in finishing 58 units on his own = $\frac{58}{3}$ days

Hence days taken in finishing the whole job = 2 days + $\frac{58}{3}$ days = $\frac{64}{3}$ days

Q6. Mohan can plough a field in 15 days. Ram can plough the same field in 30 days. Mohan and Ram start working together. They worked for initial few days together, but Ram quit the job 6 days before the whole field was ploughed. In how many days the whole field is ploughed?

**Solution** – Part of the field ploughed by Mohan in one day = $\frac{1}{15}$ of the whole field and part of the field ploughed by Ram in one day = $\frac{1}{30}$ of the whole field.

Part of the field ploughed by Ram and Mohan together in one day = $\frac{1}{15}+\frac{1}{30}=\frac{2+1}{30}$ $=\frac{1}{10}$ of the whole field .......(1)

According to the question:

| Ram and Mohan together | Mohan alone |
|---|---|
| Initial few days | Last six days |

Given that Ram quit the job 6 days before the whole field was ploughed. Hence only Mohan has worked in the last six days.

Part of the field ploughed by Mohan in last six days = $6 \times \frac{1}{15} = \frac{6}{15}$ of the whole field

Remaining part of the field was ploughed by Ram and Mohan both in initial few days =

$1 - \frac{6}{15} = \frac{9}{15}$ of the whole field. .....(2)

Using (1) and (2), number of days Ram and Mohan worked together = $\frac{\frac{9}{15}}{\frac{1}{10}}$ days = 6 days

So, total number of days to plough the whole field = 6 days + 6 days = 12 days

Q7. A and B together can finish a work in x days. A alone can do the same work in x + 4 days and B alone can do the same work in x + 9 days. What is the value of x?

**Solution** – Using:

If A can do a work in (z + x) days alone, B can do the same work in (z + y) days alone, and A and B together take z days, then $z = \sqrt{xy}$

A takes x + 4 days and B takes x+9 days, whereas A + B together take x days in finishing the work.

Hence $x = \sqrt{4 \times 9} = 6$ days.

Q8. A is thrice as efficient as B and hence takes 20 days less than B in doing the same work. In how many days both of them will finish the work together?

**Solution** – Assume that A alone takes x days, then B alone takes 3x days.

According to the question, 3x – x = 20 days, or, 2x = 20 days. Hence x = 10 days.

So A takes 10 days and B takes 30 days in finishing the work alone.

Assume total work = LCM (10, 30) = 30 units

So, work done by A alone in one day = $\frac{30}{10}$ = 3 units and work done by B alone in one day

= $\frac{30}{30}$ = 1 unit.

Hence time taken by both of them in finishing the work together = $\frac{30}{4}$ = 7.5 days

Q9. A is 20% more efficient than B. If B takes 60 days in doing the work alone, in how many days will A finish the work alone?

**Solution** – Number of days taken by A alone in finishing the work = $\frac{60}{1.2}$ = 50 days

Q10. An skilled labour is twice as efficient as a mason. 24 skilled labours take 15 days in building a wall of height 10 meter. How many masons should be added to the group of 10 skilled labours so that they can build a wall of height 18 meters in 6 days (assume width and length of the wall remains same)?

**Solution** – Assume number of masons to be added = 2x

Since an skilled labour is twice as efficient as a mason, hence 2x masons = x skilled labours

$$= \frac{24 \times 15}{10} = \frac{(10+x) \times 6}{18}$$

Solving it we get, x = 98. Hence number masons required = 98 × 2 = 196 masons

## Practice Exercise

Q1. M and N weave a mat in 10 days and 15 days respectively. They begin to work together but N leaves after 2 days. In how much time will M complete the remaining work?

(a) $6\frac{1}{3}$ days (b) $6\frac{2}{3}$ days (c) 7 days (d) 8 days

Q2. P can do a work in 18 days, Q in 9 days and R in 6 days. P and Q start work together and after 2 days R joins them. What is the total number of days taken to finish the work?

(a) 4.33 (b) 4.0 (c) 4.66 (d) 5.33

Q3. The work done by a woman in 8 hr is equal to the work done by a man in 6 hr and by a boy in 12 hr. If working 6hr per day 9 men can complete a work in 6 days, then in how many days can 12 men, 12 women and 12 boys together finish the same working 8 hr per day?

(a) $2\frac{1}{2}$ days (b) $1\frac{1}{2}$ days

(c) $3\frac{1}{2}$ days (d) none of the above

Q4. A sum of Rs.1500 was paid for a work which J can do in 32 days, K in 20 days, K and L in 12 days and M in 24 days. How much (in Rs.) did L receive if all four worked together?

(a) 50 (b) $\frac{104}{3}$ (c) 640 (d) 320

Q5. A job can be done by 3 skilled women in 20 days or by 5 boys in 30 days. How many days will they take if they work together?

(a) 11 days (b) 10 days (c) 8 days (d) 12 days

Q6. A, B and C working together completed a job in 10 days. The ratio of their efficiency is 2:3:6. How many days would be required by the fastest worker to complete the entire work?

(a) 15 days (b) 20 days (c) 30 days (d) 40 days

Q7. 8 women and 12 men complete a certain piece of work in 9 days. If each women takes twice the time taken by a man to finish the work, 12 men will finish the same work in -

(a) 12 days (b) 15 days (c) 14 days (d) 8 days

Q8. If 15 men or 24 women or 36 boys can do piece of work in 12 days, working 8 hr a day, how many men must be associated with 12 women and 6 boys to do a piece of work $2\frac{1}{4}$ times as in 30 days working 6 hr a day?

(a) 4 (b) 8 (c) 6 (d) 10

Q9. Group of 4 boys and 10 girls are put on a work. They completed 1/3 of the work in 4 days. After this, 2 boys and 2 girls were added to the existing group. They completed 2/9 more of the work in 2 days. If the remaining work is to be completed in 3 days, then how many more girls must be increased?

(a) 32 (b) 8 (c) 50 (d) 55

Q10. R is twice as efficient as P. Q takes thrice as many days as R. P takes 12 days to finish the work done alone. If they work in pairs (i.e, PQ, QR, RA) starting with PQ on the first day, QR on the second day and PR on the third day and so on, then how many days are required to finish the work?

(a) $6\frac{1}{5}$ days (b) $4\frac{1}{2}$ days (c) $5\frac{1}{9}$ days (d) 8 days

Q11. A can build up a wall in 8 days while B can break it in 3 days. A has worked for 4 days and then B joined to work with A for another 2 days only. In how many days will A alone build up the remaining part of wall?

(a) $13\frac{1}{3}$ days (b) $6\frac{1}{3}$ days (c) $7\frac{1}{3}$ days (d) 7 days

Q12. Ajju can do a piece of work in 10 days, while Bijju alone can do it in 15 days. They work together for 5 days and the rest of the work is done by Chajju in 2 days. If they get Rs. 450 for the whole work, what should be their respective shares?

(a) Rs. 225, Rs 150, Rs 75 (b) Rs. 250, Rs 100, Rs 100
(c) Rs. 200, Rs 150, Rs 100 (d) Rs. 175, Rs 175, Rs 100

Q13. Annu and Bannu can finish a job in 10 days while Bannu and Channu can do it in 18 days. Annu started the job worked for 5 days, then Bannu worked for 10 days and the remaining job was finished by Channu in 15 days. In how many days could Channu alone have finished the whole job?

(a) 30 days (b) 15 days (c) 45 days (d) 24 days

Q14. In climbing a 21m long round pole, a gorilla climbs 6 m in the first minute and slips 3 m in the next minute. What time (in minute) the gorilla would take to reach the top of the pole?

(a) 11 (b) 14 (c) $14\frac{2}{3}$ (d) 9

Q15. Running at the same constant rate, 6 identical Machines can produce a total of 270 Toys per min. At this rate, how many Toys could 10 such Machine produce in 4 min?

(a) 648 (b) 1800 (c) 2700 (d) 10800

Q16. A worker makes a basket in *2/3* of an hour. If he works for 80 hours, then how many baskets will he make?

(a) 60 (b) 120 (c) $12\frac{1}{2}$ (d) None of these

Q17. If 5 men take an hour to dig a ditch, the how long should 12 men take to dig a ditch of the same dimension?

(a) 25 min (b) 30 min (c) 28 min (d) 20 min

Q18. Two women and 7 children complete a certain piece of work in 4 days while 4 women and 4 children complete the same work in only 3 days. The number of days required by 1 woman to complete the work is

(a) 60 days (b) 15 days (c) 6 days (d) 51 days

Q19. Machine A produces bolts at a uniform rate of 120 every 40 seconds and machine B produces bolts at a uniform rate of 100 every 20s. If the two machines run simultaneously, then how many seconds will it take them to produce a total of 200 bolts?

(a) 28 (b) 25 (c) 22 (d) 32

Q20. In a footwear factory, a team of employees was to finish 360 pairs of shoes in a certain number of days. Making four more pairs per day that was planned, they could complete the job a day ahead of the schedule. How many days did they take to complete the job?

(a) 8 days (b) 10 days (c) 9 days (d) 12 days

Q21. A certain job was assigned to a group of women to do it in 20 days. But 12 women did not turn up for the job and the remaining women did the job in 32 days. The original number of women in the group was -

(a) 32 (b) 34 (c) 36 (d) 40

Q22. A father and a son working together can complete a work in 4 days. But if the father works alone he can complete the work in 6 days. Both of them worked for one day and then the father had to leave. How long will the son take to complete the remaining work?

(a) 7 days (b) 8 days (c) 9 days (d) 10 days

Q23. Ram is twice as good a workman as Suresh and finished a piece of work in 3 h less than Suresh. In how many hours they together could finish that piece of work?

(a) $2\frac{1}{3}$ (b) 2 (c) $1\frac{2}{3}$ (d) None of these

Q24. Machine P can print one lakh books in 8 hours. Machine Q can print the same number of books in 10 hours while machine R can print the same in 12 hours. All the machines started printing at 9 A.M. Machine P is stopped at 11 A.M. and the remaining two machines complete work. Approximately at what time will the printing of one lakh books be completed?

(a) 3pm (b) 2 pm (c) 1:00 pm (d) 11 am

Q25. P can finish a work in 18 days. Q can finish the same work in 15 days. Q worked for 10 days and left the job. How many days does P alone need to finish the remaining work?

(a) 8 (b) 5 (c) 4 (d) 6

Q26. 3 men and 7 women can complete a work in 10 days. But 4 men and 6 women need 8 days to complete the same work. In how many days will 10 women complete the same work?

(a) 50 (b) 40 (d) 30 (d) 20

Q27. A can complete a work in 12 days with a working of 8 hours per day. B can complete the same work in 8 days when working 10 hours a day. If A and B work together, working 8 hours a day, the work can be completed in — days.

(a) $5\frac{5}{11}$ (b) $4\frac{5}{11}$ (c) $6\frac{4}{11}$ (d) $6\frac{5}{11}$

Q28. P is 20% more efficient than Q. P can complete a work in 25 days. If P and Q work together, then on which day the work will be finished?

(a) $9^{th}$ day b) $11^{th}$ day (c) $13^{th}$ day (d) $14^{th}$ day

Q29. In Nuts And Bolts factory, one machine produces only nuts at the rate of 100 nuts per minute and needs to be cleaned for 5 minutes after production of every 1000 nuts. Another machine produces only bolts at the rate of 75 bolts per minute and needs to cleaned for 10 minutes after production of every 1500 bolts. If both the machines start production at the same time, what is the minimum duration required for producing 9000 pairs of nuts and bolts?

(a) 130 minutes (b) 135 minutes (c) 170 minutes (d) 180 minutes

Q30. A chemical plant has four tanks (A, B, C and D), each containing 1000 litres of a chemical. The chemical is being pumped from one tank to anther as follows.

From A to B @ 20 litres/minute

From C to A @ 90 litres/minute

From A to D @ 10 litres/minute

From C to D @ 50 litres/minute

From B to C @ 100 litres/minute

From D to B @ 110 litres/minute

Which tank gets emptied first, and how long does it take (in minutes) to get empty after pumping starts?

(a) A, 16.66 (b) C, 20 (c) D, 20 (d) D, 25

**Answer Grid:**

| Q. No. | 1 | 2 | 3 | 4 | 5 | 6 | 7 | 8 | 9 | 10 | 11 | 12 | 13 | 14 | 15 | 16 | 17 | 18 |
|---|---|---|---|---|---|---|---|---|---|---|---|---|---|---|---|---|---|---|
| Answer | b | b | b | d | d | b | a | b | b | c | c | a | c | a | b | b | a | b |
| Q. No. | 19 | 20 | 21 | 22 | 23 | 24 | 25 | 26 | 27 | 28 | 29 | 30 | | | | | | |
| Answer | b | b | a | c | b | c | d | b | a | d | c | c | | | | | | |

## Solutions and Explanations:

Q1. (A + B)'s one day's work = $\frac{1}{10}+\frac{1}{15}=\frac{1}{6}$

(A + B)'s two day's work = $\frac{2}{6}=\frac{1}{3}$

Hence, remaining 2/3 of the work is done by A alone in $10 \times \frac{2}{3}=\frac{20}{3}$ = days

Hence option (B) is the answer.

Q2. (A + B)'s 2 days work = $2\left(\frac{1}{18}+\frac{1}{9}\right)=\frac{1}{3}$

So, remaining work $=1-\frac{1}{3}=\frac{2}{3}$

(A + B + C)'s one day's work = $\left(\frac{1}{18}+\frac{1}{9}+\frac{1}{6}\right)=\frac{1}{3}$

$\frac{1}{3}$ *rd* work is completed working all of them together in 1 day, so, total number of days taken to finish the work in 4 days.

Hence option (B) is the answer.

Q3. Given that work done by 8 women = 6 men = 12 boys

12 women = $\frac{6}{8} \times 12 = 9$ men

12 boys = $\frac{6}{12} \times 12 = 6$ men

Using $M_1D_1T_1=M_2D_2T_2$

Or, 9 × 6 × 6 = (12 + 9 + 6) × D2 × 8. Hence $D_2 = 9 \times 6 \times \frac{6}{27} \times 8 = 1\frac{1}{2}$ Days

Hence option (B) is the Answer

Q4. L's 1 day's work = $\frac{1}{12}-\frac{1}{12}=\frac{1}{30}$

Ratio of their efficiencies = $\frac{1}{32}:\frac{1}{20}:\frac{1}{30}:\frac{1}{24}$ 15:24:16:20

L's share = $\frac{16}{15+24+16+20} \times 1500$ = Rs. 320

Hence option (D) is the Answer

Q5. Required time $=20 \times \dfrac{30}{20+30} = 12$ days

Hence option (D) is the Answer

Q6. Ratio of efficiency = 2 : 3 : 6

Ratio of time required = $\dfrac{1}{2}:\dfrac{1}{3}:\dfrac{1}{6}=3:2:1$

Let, A, B and C can complete the work in 3x, 2x and x days respectively.

Then, $\dfrac{3x\times 2x\times x}{3x\times 2x\times 3x\times x\times 2x\times x} = 10$, or, $\dfrac{6x\times x}{11x\times x} = 10$. Hence x = 20 days

Hence option (B) is the answer.

Q7. Given that each women takes twice the time taken by a man, hence efficiency of 2 women = Efficiency of 1 man

According to the question, (4 + 12) men can complete the work in 9 days.

Hence 12 men can complete the work in $\dfrac{9\times 16}{12} = 12$ days

Hence option (A) is the Answer

Q9. Let one boy takes X days to complete the work and one girl takes Y days to complete the work independently.

Then, $\dfrac{4\times 4}{X}+\dfrac{10\times 4}{Y}=\dfrac{1}{3}$ and $\dfrac{6\times 2}{X}+\dfrac{12\times 2}{Y}=\dfrac{2}{9}$

Solving above equations, we get X = 108 and Y = 216

Let Z girl be added to complete the work in 3 days.

Then, $\dfrac{6\times 3}{108}+\dfrac{3(12+z)}{216}=1-\left(\dfrac{1}{3}+\dfrac{2}{9}\right)=\dfrac{4}{9}$

$36 + 36 + 3Z = \dfrac{216\times 4}{9} = 96$, or, $3Z = 96 - 72 = 24$. Hence Z = 8

Hence option (B) is the answer.

Q10. Given that ratio of efficiency of P, Q and R is 3 : 2 : 6. So ratio of number of days = 2 : 3 : 1 respectively.

Number of days taken by P = 12, number of days taken by Q = 18 and number of days taken by R = 6.

1 day's work of (P + Q) = $\frac{5}{36}$

1 day's work of (Q + R) = $\frac{8}{36}$ and 1 day's work of (R + P) = $\frac{9}{36}$

In 5 days total work = $\frac{35}{36}$

Now, the rest of the work (i.e.) is done by PR, so, number of days taken by PR for the remaining work = $\frac{1}{36}/\frac{9}{36}=\frac{1}{9}$

Therefore, total time taken to complete the work $=5+\frac{1}{9}=5\frac{1}{9}$ days

Hence option (C) is the answer.

Q11. Work done by A in 4 days $=\frac{4}{8}=\frac{1}{2}$

Net work done by (A + B) in 1 day $\frac{1}{8}-\frac{1}{3}=\frac{5}{24}$

Work done by (A + B) in 2 days $=\frac{5}{24}\times 2=-\frac{5}{12}$

Work done by (A + B) in 6 days $=\frac{1}{2}-\frac{5}{12}=\frac{1}{12}$

Remaining of the wall is built by A in $\frac{8\times 11}{12}=\frac{88}{12}=\frac{22}{3}$ days

Hence option (C) is the answer.

Q12. Work done by Ajju and Bijju in 5 days = $\left(\frac{1}{10}+\frac{1}{15}\right)\times 5=\frac{5}{6}$

Remaining work = $1\frac{5}{6}=\frac{1}{6}$

Chajju alone can do the work in 6 × 2 = 12 days

Ratio of their work = $\frac{5}{10}:\frac{5}{15}:\frac{2}{12} = 3 : 2 : 1$

Share of money = 225, 150, 75

Hence option (A) is the answer.

Q13. Let C complete the work in X days.

Work done by (A + B) in day = $\frac{1}{10}$ work

Work done by (B + C) in day = $\frac{1}{18}$ work

A's 5 day's work + B's 10 day's work + C's 15 days work =1

OR, (A + B)'s 5 day's work + (B + C)'s 5 day's work + C's 10 days work =1

Or, $\frac{5}{10}+\frac{5}{18}+\frac{10}{x} = 1$. Hence X = 45 days

Hence option (C) is the answer.

Q14. Net distance travelled by gorilla in 2 min = 3m

In 10 min, distance travelled (climbed) = 15m

It is given in the question that in first min it climbs 6 m and in other min it slips down 3 m.

Hence, gorilla will travel remaining 6m in next min.

Total time taken = (10 + 1) = 11 min

Hence option (A) is the answer.

Q15. $M_1 \times T_1 \times W_2 = M_2 \times T_2 \times W_1$

6 × 1 × X = 10 × 4 × 270

Or, x = $\frac{10 \times 4 \times 270}{6}$ = Hence x = 1800

Hence option (B) is the answer.

Q16. In $\frac{2}{3}$ hr he makes 1 basket.

In 80 hours he will make $\frac{1}{2} \times 3 \times 80$ baskets = baskets.

Hence option (B) is the answer.

Q17. Using $M_1 \times D_1 = M_2 \times D_2$, or, $5 \times 60 = 12 \times D_2$

So, $D_2 = 25$ minutes. Hence option (A) is the answer.

Q18. (2M + 7C)'s 1 day work = $\frac{1}{4}$

It means that 1 work will be finished by (8M + 28C) in one day.

Again, (4M + 4C)'s 1 day's work = $\frac{1}{3}$, so, 1 work will be completed by 12M +12C in one day.

Hence 8M + 28C = 12M + 12C, or, 4M = 16C, so, M = 4C

Since, 5 men complete a work in 3 days, 1 man will complete it in 15 days.

Hence option (B) is the answer.

Q19. Option (B) is the answer.

Q20. Let they makes x pairs per day.

Then, $\frac{360}{x} - \frac{360}{x+4} = 1$, or, $360\left(\frac{4}{x(x+4)}\right) = 1$

Or, x(x + 4) = 1440 = 36 × 40. Hence x = 36

Required number of days = $\frac{360}{36}$ = 10 days

Hence option (B) is the Answer.

Q21. Let originally there were x women in the group. Given that (x–12) men did the job in 32 days

So, 20x = 32(x–12). Hence x = 32

Hence option (A) is the answer.

Q22. (Man + Son)'s one day work = $\frac{1}{4}$. So, remaining work = $\frac{3}{4}$

Man's one day work = $\frac{1}{6}$. So, Son's one day work = $\frac{1}{4}-\frac{1}{6}=\frac{1}{12}$

$\frac{1}{12}$ th of the work is done by the son in 1 day. Hence $\frac{3}{4}$ th of the work will be done by the son in 9 days. Hence option (C) is the answer.

Q23. Let Suresh finishes the job in x hr. So, Ram will finish the job in $\frac{x}{2}$ hr.

Given that x – $\frac{x}{2}$ = 3. Hence x = 6

Time taken by Suresh to finish the work alone = 6 hours and time taken by Ram to finish the work alone = 3 hours

Work done by both of them in an hour $=\frac{1}{6}+\frac{1}{3}=\frac{1}{2}$ hr

They together could finish the work in 2 hours.
Hence option (B) is the answer.

Q24. Work done by P in 1 hour = $\frac{1}{8}$, Work done by Q in 1 hour = $\frac{1}{10}$

Work done by R in 1 hour = $\frac{1}{12}$

Work done by P, Q and R in 1 hour = $\frac{1}{8}+\frac{1}{10}+\frac{1}{12}=\frac{37}{120}$

Work done by Q and R in 1 hour = 1/10 + 1/12 = 22/120 = 11/60
From 9 am to 11 am, all the machines were operating.
Ie, they all operated for 2 hours and work completed = 2 × (37/120) = 37/60
Pending work = 1– 37/60 = 23/60
Hours taken by Q an R to complete the pending work = (23/60) / (11/60) = 23/11 which is approximately equal to 2

Hence the work will be completed approximately 2 hours after 11 am which is around 1 pm

Hence option (C) is the answer

Q25. Work done by P in 1 day = 1/18, work done by Q in 1 day = 1/15 and work done by Q in 10 days = 10/15 = 2/3.

Remaining work = 1 – 2/3 = 1/3

Number of days in which P can finish the remaining work = (1/3) / (1/18) = 6

Hence option (D) is the answer

Q26. Work done by 4 men and 6 women in 1 day = 1/8

Work done by 3 men and 7 women in 1 day = 1/10

Let one man does m work in one day and one woman does w work in one day. The above equations can be written as:

$4m + 6w = 1/8$ —(1) $3m + 7w = 1/10$ —(2)

Solving equation (1) and (2) , we get m=11/400 and w=1/400

Amount of work 10 women can do in a day = 10 × (1/400) = 1/40

It means that 10 women can complete the work in 40 days. Hence option (B) is the answer

Q27. A can complete the work in 12 days working 8 hours a day

⇒ Number of hours A can complete the work = 12×8 = 96 hours

⇒ Work done by A in 1 hour = 1/96

B can complete the work in 8 days working 10 hours a day

⇒ Number of hours B can complete the work = 8×10 = 80 hours

⇒ Work done by B in 1 hour = 1/80

Work done by A and B in 1 hour = 1/96 + 1/80 = 11/480, so, A and B can complete the work in 480/11 hours.

A and B work 8 hours a day, hence total days to complete the work with A and B working together = (480/11)/ (8) = 60/11 days = $5\,^{5}D_{11}$ days

Hence option (A) is the answer

Q28. Time taken by Q to complete the work alone = 25 × 1.2 = 30 days

Hence work done by P and Q in one day = 1/25 + 1/30 = 11/150

Hence time taken by P and Q in finishing the work together = 150/11 @ 14th day

Hence option (d) is the answer.

Q29. Machine I:

Number of nuts produced in one minute = 100

To produce 1000 nuts time required = 10 mm

Cleaning time for nuts = 5 mm

Over all time to produce 1000 nuts = 15 mm.

Over all time to produce 9000 = 138 mm - 5mm = 133mm ... (1)

**Machine II:**

To produce 75 bolts time required = 1 mm

To produce 1500 bolts time required = 20 mm

Cleaning time for bolts = 10 in.

Effective time to produce 1500 bolts = 30 mm

Effective time to produce 9000 bolts = 30 x 6 – 10 = 170mm ... (2)

From (1) and (2), Minimum time = 170 minutes. Hence option (c) is the answer.

Q30. Option (c) is the answer.

# 9 Pipes and Cisterns

Concept of Pipes and Cisterns is just an extension of concept of Individual work.

## Basic Statement :

If tap A can fill a tank in 20 hours, then part of tank filled by tap A in one hour = $\frac{1}{20}th$ of the total tank. Similarly, if leakage B can empty the whole tank in 25 hours, then part of tank vacated by leakage in one hour = $\frac{1}{25}th$ of the total tank. It should be noted that sign of the work done by leakage is 'negative'.

## Worked out examples:

Q1. Pipe A can fill a tank in 10 hours and pipe B can fill the same tank in 12 hours. In how much time both the pipes will fill the tank working together?

**Solution** – Work done by pipe A in 1 hour = 1/10 and Work done by pipe B in 1 hour = 1/12.

Hence work done by both the pipes together in one hour = 1/10 + 1/12 = 11/60

Hence total time taken in filling the tank = 60/11 hour = $5\frac{5}{11}$ hour

Q2. Pipe A can fill a tank in 10 hours and pipe B can fill the same tank in 12 hours. A leakage at the bottom of the tank takes 20 hours to empty the full tank. In how much time the tank will be filled if both the pipes and leakage are working together?

**Solution** – Work done by pipe A in 1 hour = 1/10 and Work done by pipe B in 1 hour = 1/12 and work done by leakage in 1 hour = 1/20

In this question, works done by pipes are positive and work done by leakage is negative.

Hence work done by both the pipes and leakage together in one hour = 1/10 + 1/12 – 1/20 = 8/60

Hence total time taken in filling the tank = 60/8 hour = $7\frac{1}{2}$ hour

Q3. Tap A can fill a tank in 5 hours. Due to a leakage at the bottom, tap A now takes 6 hours to fill the same tank. In how much time tank will be emptied by the leakage if tap A is closed and tank is full?

**Solution** – Work done by leakage in one hour = 1/5 – 1/6 = 1/30

Hence time taken by leakage to empty the full tank = 30 hours.

Q4. An inlet pipe A can fill a tank in x hours, and outlet pipe B can empty the full tank in y hours. What is the work done by inlet and outlet pipes in one hour ($x < y$)?

**Solution** – Work done by inlet pipe A in one hour = 1/x

Work done by outlet pipe B in one hour = 1/y

Hence work done by both the pipes in one hour = 1/x – 1/y = (y – x)/xy

Q5. In above question, if capacity of pipe is z litres, then in how much time the tank will be full?

**Solution** – Work done by both the pipes in one hour = z/x – z/y = z(y – x)/xy

Since capacity of tank = z litres, hence time taken = $\frac{z}{z(y-x)/xy} = \frac{xy}{(y-x)}$ hours

## Practice Exercise

Q1. Tap A can fill a tank in 25 hours. A drainage pipe B at the bottom of the tank can empty the full tank in 40 hours. Initially tank is empty. How many hours will it take for tap A to fill the whole tank if drainage pipe B is also working?

(a) 200 hours (b) 200/3 hours (c) 100 hours (d) 75 hours

Q2. Tap A can fill a tank in 20 hours. Because of a leakage, it now takes 25 hours to fill the same tank. How much time will the leakage take to empty the full tank?

(a) 200 hours (b) 200/3 hours (c) 100 hours (d) 75 hours

Q3. Two pipes A and B can separately fill a cistern in 40 minutes and 30 minutes respectively. There is a third pipe in the bottom of the cistern to empty it. If all the three pipes are simultaneously opened, then the cistern is full in 20 minutes, in how much time, the third pipe alone can empty the cistern?

(a) 120 min (b) 100 min (c) 140 min (d) 80 min

Q4. Two pipes A and B can fill a tank in 9 hours and 3 hours respectively. If they are opened on alternate hours and if pipe A is opened first, how many hours, the tank shall be full?

(a) 4 hr (b) 5 hr (c) 2 hr (d) 6 hr

Q5. 13 buckets of water fill a tank when the capacity of each bucket is 51 litres. How many buckets will be needed to fill the same tank, if the capacity of each bucket is 17 litres?

(a) 33 b) 29 (c) 39 (d) 42

Q6. Pipe A can fill a tank in 8 hours, pipe B in 4 hours and pipe C in 24 hours. If all the pipes are open, in how many hours will the tank be filled?

(a) 2.4 hr (b) 3 hr (c) 4 hr (d) 4.2 hr

Q7. First pipe can fill tank in 15 min and second in 10 min. Third pipe can empty the tank in 5 min. The first two pipes are kept open for 4 min in the starting and then the third pipe is also opened. In what time the tank will empty?

(a) 35 min (b) 15 min
(c) 20 min (d) cannot be determined

Q8. Pipes P and R can fill a tank in 5 and 6 h respectively. Pipe S can empty it in 12 h. The tank is half full. All the three pipes are in operation simultaneously. After how much time the tank will be full?

(a) $3\frac{9}{7}$ h (b) 11 h (c) $2\frac{8}{11}$ h (d) $1\frac{13}{17}$ h

Q9. A pipe can fill a tank in 16 min and another empty it in 8 min. If the tank is already ½ full and both the pipe are open together, will the tank be filled or emptied? How long will it take before the tank is either filled or emptied completely as the case may be?

(a) Emptied, 16 min (b) Filled, 8 min (c) Emptied, 8 min (d) Filled, 12 min

Q10. Pipe M is 3 times faster than second pipe N and takes 32 min less than the pipe N. When will the cistern be full if both pipes are opened together?

(a) 12min (b) 24min (c) 30min (d) Data inadequate

Q11. A cistern has a leak which would empty it in 8hr. A tap is turned on which admits 6L in a minute into the cistern and now empty in12 hr. The Holding capacity of cistern is

(a) 7860 L (b) 6840 L (c )8640 L (d) None of these

Q12. A tank is filled in 10 hours by three pipes M, N and O. Pipe O is twice as fast as N and N is twice as fast as M. How much time will pipe M alone take to fill the tank?

(a) 70 hrs (b) 30 hrs (c) 35 hrs (d) 50 hrs

Q13. One pipe can fill a tank 4 times as fast as another pipe. If together they fill the tank in 36 minutes, then the slower pipe alone will fill the tank in:

(a) 180 min (b) 144 min (c) 126 min (d) 144 min

Q14. A pipe can fill a tub in 4 hours. After half the tub is filled, three more similar pipes are opened. What is the total time taken to fill the tub completely?

(a) 3 hrs (b) 1hr 30 min (c) 2 hr 30 min (d) 2 hr

Q15. A pipe can fill a tank in 4 hours. After half the tub is filled, two more similar pipes are opened. What is the total time taken to fill the tub completely?

(a) 1 hr 20 min (b) 4 hr (c) hr (d) 2hr 40 min

Q16. Bucket P has thrice the capacity as bucket Q. It takes 80 turns for bucket P to fill an empty drum. How many turns it will take for both the buckets P and Q, having each turn together to fill the empty drum?

(a) 30 (b) 45 (c) 60 hr (d) 80 hr

## Answer Grid:

| Q. No. | 1 | 2 | 3 | 4 | 5 | 6 | 7 | 8 | 9 | 10 | 11 | 12 | 13 | 14 | 15 | 16 |
|---|---|---|---|---|---|---|---|---|---|---|---|---|---|---|---|---|
| Answer | b | c | a | b | c | a | c | d | c | a | c | a | a | c | d | c |

## Solutions and Explanations:

Q1. Work done by tap A in one hour = $\frac{1}{25}$ of whole tank

Work done by drainage pipe B in one hour = $\frac{1}{40}$ of whole tank

Net work done by pipe A and drainage pipe B in one hour = $\frac{1}{25} - \frac{1}{40} = \frac{8-5}{200} = \frac{3}{200}$ part of the whole tank

Hence time taken in filling the whole tank = hours. Hence option (b) is the answer.

Q2. Work done by tap A in one hour = $\frac{1}{20}$ of whole tank

Work done by tap A and leakage in one hour = $\frac{1}{25}$ of whole tank

Hence work done by leakage alone in one hour = $\frac{1}{20} - \frac{1}{25} = \frac{5-4}{100} = \frac{1}{100}$ of the whole tank

Hence time taken by leakage to empty the full tank = 100 hours. Hence option (c) is the answer.

Q3. Part filled by pipe A in 1 minute = 1/40

Part filled by pipe B in 1 minute = 1/30

Net part filled by pipe A, pipe B and the third pipe in 1 hour = 1/20

⇒ Part emptied by the third pipe in 1 hour = 1/40 + 1/30–1/20 = (3 + 4 – 6)/120 = 1/120 i.e., third pipe alone can empty the cistern in 120 minutes

Hence option (A) is the answer

Q4. Part filled by pipe A in 1 hour = 1/9

Part filled by pipe B in 1 hour = 1/3

Pipes A and B are opened alternatively.

Part filled in every 2 hour = 1/9 + 1/3 = (1 + 3)/9 = 4/9

Part filled in 4 hour = 2 × 4/9 = 8/9

Remaining part = 1 – 8/9 = 1/9

Now it is pipe A's turn.

Time taken by pipe A to fill the remaining 1/9 part = 1 hour

Total time taken = 4 hour + 1 hour = 5 hour

Hence option (B) is the answer

Q5. Capacity of the tank = (13 × 51) Litre

Number of buckets required of capacity of each bucket is 17 litre = (13 × 51)/17 = 13 × 3 = 39

Hence option (C) is the answer

Q6. Part filled by pipe A in 1 hour = 1/8

Part filled by pipe B in 1 hour = ¼

Part filled by pipe C in 1 hour = 1/24

Part filled by pipe A, pipe B and pipe C in 1 hour = 1/8 + 1/4 + 1/24 = 10/24 i.e, pipe A, pipe B and pipe C together can fill the tank in 24/10 hours = 2.4 hours

Hence option (A) is the answer

Q7. Work done by both the pipes in 4 min = $4\left(\frac{1}{15}+\frac{1}{10}\right)=\frac{2}{3}$ of tanks work done by all the pipes working together = $\frac{1}{15}+\frac{1}{10}-\frac{1}{5}=\frac{1}{30}$ tank. It means that $\frac{1}{30}$ tank is emptied in 1 min, or, $\frac{2}{3}$ of tank can be emptied in $30 \times \frac{2}{3}$ = 20 mins

Hence option (C) is the answer.

Q8. In one hr work done by all the pipes together = $\frac{1}{5}+\frac{1}{6}-\frac{1}{12}=\frac{17}{60}$ tank

In other word, tank is filled by all the pipes working together in $\frac{60}{17}\times\frac{1}{2}$ ie $\frac{30}{17}$ h

Hence option (D) is the answer.

Q9. If both the pumps are working together then the tank will be emptied because the working efficiency of pump emptied is more than that of pump filling it.

Hence , in 1 min net work done = $\frac{1}{8}-\frac{1}{16}=\frac{1}{16}$ tanks

so, 1 tank will be emptied in 16 min.

Hence, $\frac{1}{2}$ tank will be emptied in 8 min.

Q10. Let, pipe M takes x min to fill the cistern.

Then, pipe N takes 3x min to fill the cistern.

3x – x = 32, so, x = 16 min and 3x = 48 min

So, both the pipes can fill the cistern in $\left(\frac{48\times16}{48+16}\right)$ min = 12 min

Hence option (A) is the Answer

Q11. Let the tap can fill the cistern in x hr.

$\frac{x\times8}{x-8}$ = 12 8x = 12x – 96 X = 24 hr

Hence capacity of cistern = 24 × 60 × 6 = 8640 ltr

Hence option (C) is the Answer

Q12. Let the pipe A can fill the tank in x hours. Then pipe B can fill the tank in x/2 hours and pipe C can fill the tank in x/4 hours.

Part filled by pipe A in 1 hour = 1/x, Part filled by pipe B in 1 hour = 2/x, Part filled by pipe C in 1 hour = 4/x. Part filled by pipe A, pipe B and pipe C in 1 hour = 1/x + 2/x + 4/x = 7/x i.e., pipe A, pipe B and pipe C can fill the tank in x/7 hours.

Given that pipe A, pipe B and pipe C can fill the tank in 10 hours, x/7 = 10 ⇒ x = 10 × 7 = 70 hours

Hence option (A) is the answer

Q13. Let the slower pipe alone can fill the tank in x minutes. Then the faster pipe can fill the tank in x/4 minutes. Part filled by the slower pipe in 1 minute = 1/x, Part filled by the faster pipe in 1 minute = 4/x, Part filled by both the pipes in 1 minute = 1/x + 4/x

It is given that both the pipes together can fill the tank in 36 minutes ⇒ Part filled by both the pipes in 1 minute = 1/36.

Hence 1/x + 4/x = 1/36. Hence x = 5 × 36 = 180 i.e., the slower pipe alone fill the tank in 180 minutes

Hence option (A) is the answer

Q14. A tap can fill a tank in 4 hours, or, the tap can fill half the tank in 2 hours.

Remaining part = 1/2

After half the tank is filled, three more similar taps are opened. Hence, total number of taps becomes 4.

Part filled by one tap in 1 hour = ¼, Part filled by four taps in 1 hour = 4 × 1/4 = 1 i.e., 4 taps can fill remaining half in 30 minutes

Total time taken = 2 hour + 30 minute = 2 hour 30 minutes

Hence option (C) is the answer

Q15. A tap can fill a tank in 4 hours. Hence the tap can fill half the tank in 2 hours.

Remaining part = 1/2 After half the tank is filled, two more similar taps are opened. Hence, total number of pipes becomes 3.

Part filled by one tap in 1 hour = ¼, Part filled by three taps in 1 hour = 3 × 1/4 = 3/4

Time taken to fill ½ tank by 3 pipes = (1/2)/(3/4) = 4/6 = 2/3 hour = 40 minutes

Total time taken = 2 hour + 40 minute = 2 hour 40 minutes

Hence option (D) is the answer

Q16. Let capacity of bucket P = x, then capacity of bucket Q = x/3

Given that it takes 80 turns for bucket P to fill the empty drum, hence capacity of the drum = 80x

Number of turns required if both P and Q are used = 60

Hence option (C) is the answer

# 10 Boats and Streams

## What is Downstream Movement:

When the direction of the movement of river and boat is same.

**Downstream Movement**

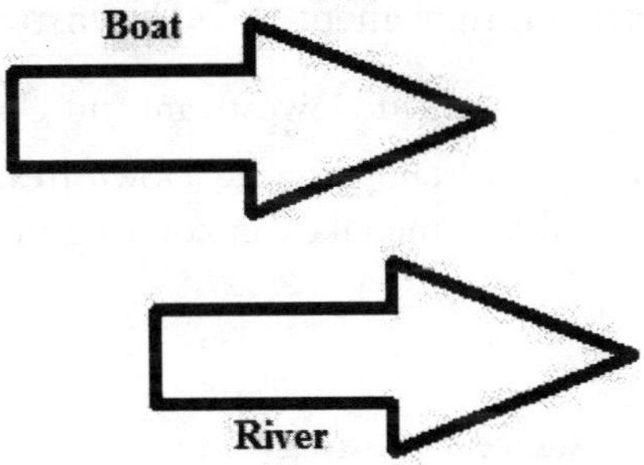


Distance covered in this case is known as Downstream Distance.
If speed of River = R and speed of boat = B, then Downstream Speed = B + R

## What is Upstream Movement:

**When direction of movement of river and boat is opposite.**

**Upstream Movement**

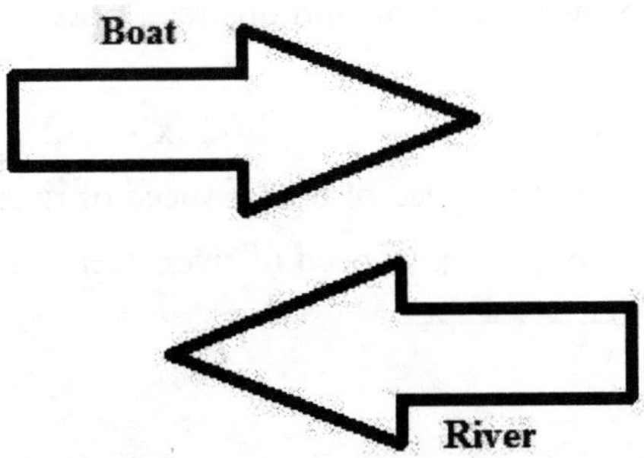

Distance covered in this case is known as Upstream Distance.
If speed of River = R and speed of boat = B, then Upstream Speed = B – R
[Conventionally we take speed of boat more than speed of river and if this would not have been the case, boat would not be able to go back.)

## Important Points:

(1) Speed of boat = ½ (Downstream Speed + Upstream Speed) = ½ (B + R + B – R) = B
And speed of river = ½ (Downstream Speed – Upstream speed) = ½ (B + R – B + R) = R
For example - if Downstream speed and upstream speed are given as 20 kmph and 10 kmph, then speed of boat = 15 km/h and speed of river = 5 km/h.

(2) If distances covered downstream and upstream are same, then ratio of time taken becomes inversely of the ratio of the speeds.

$$\frac{\text{Time taken in Downtream movement}}{\text{Time taken in Upstream movement}} = \frac{\text{Upstream Speed}}{\text{Downstream Speed}}$$

[Assuming same distance is travelled Downstream and Upstream]

(3) If time taken in covering a certain distance Downstream and Upstream = x hours and y hours respectively, then time taken in covering the same distance in still water

$= \frac{2xy}{x+y}$ hr.

(4) A man rows a certain distance downstream in $t_1$ hours and returns the same distance upstream in $t_2$ hours. If the speed of the stream is y km/hr, then the speed of the man in still water $= y\left(\frac{t2+t1}{t2-t1}\right)$ km/hr

(5) When distance is constant, average speed $= \frac{2 \times \text{Downstream speed} \times \text{Upstream Speed}}{\text{Downstream Speed} + \text{Upstream Speed}}$

## Worked Out Examples:

Q1. Speed of boat in still water is x kmph and upstream speed is y kmph. What is the speed of river (in kmph)?

(a) y – x (b) x – y (c) (x – y)/2 (d) (y – x)/2

**Solution** - Upstream speed = Speed of boat – speed of river

According to the question, y = x – speed of river. Hence speed of river = x – y. Hence option (b) is the answer.

Q2. Downstream speed is 4 kmph and upstream speed is 2 kmph. What is the ratio of speed of boat to the speed of river?

(a) 4 : 2 (b) 3 : 1

(c) 3 : 2 (d) 4 : 1

**Solution** - Downstream speed = B + R = 4 kmph, and upstream speed = B – R = 2 kmph

Hence speed of boat (B) = $\frac{4+2}{2}$ = 3 kmph and speed of river (R) = 1 kmph. Hence ratio = 3 : 1. Hence option (b) is the answer.

Q3. Sudhir takes 5 hours downstream to cover a certain distance. He can cover the same distance in 10 hours going upstream. What is the time taken by him to cover the same distance in still water?

**Solution** - Using point 3 as given above,

Time taken in still water = $\frac{2xy}{x+y}$ hr. = $\frac{2\times5\times10}{5\times10}$ hours = 6.66 hrs

Q4. Downstream speed is 20 km/hr and upstream speed is 10 kmph. Find his average speed for total journey.

**Solution** - When distance is constant, average speed =

$$\frac{2 \times \text{Downstream speed} \times \text{Upstream Speed}}{\text{Downstream Speed} + \text{Upstream Speed}} = \frac{2\times20\times10}{20+10} = 13.33 \text{ kmph}$$

Q5. A man can row 30 km upstream and 44 km downstream in 10 hr. Also, he can row 40 km upstream and 55km downstream in 13 hr. The rate of the current is

(a) 3 km/hr (b) 3.5 km/hr (c) 4 km/hr (d) 4.5 km/hr

**Solution** - Let the speed of the man and current be x km/h and y km/h respectively.

Then, $\frac{30}{x-y} + \frac{44}{x+y} = 10$ .....(i) And $\frac{40}{x-y} + \frac{55}{x=y} = 13$ + =13

....(ii)

Solving equation (i) and (ii),

→ x + y = 11 .....(iii) And x – y = 5 ......(iv)

Solving equations (iii) and (iv), Y = 3 km/h

Hence option (A) is the answer.

Q6. Speed of a boat in still water is 10 km/hr. If it can travel 78 km downstream and 42 km upstream in the same time, the speed of the stream is

**Solution** - Let the speed of the stream be x km/hr. Then

Speed upstream = (10 – x) km/hr    Speed downstream = (10 + x) km/hr

Time taken to travel 78 km downstream = Time taken to travel 42 km upstream

$$\Rightarrow \frac{78}{10+x} = \frac{42}{10-x} \quad \Rightarrow = \frac{14}{10-x}$$

Or, $\frac{13}{10+x} = \frac{7}{10-x}$, or, 130 – 13x = 70 + 7x. Hence 20x = 60, or, x = 3 km/hr.

Hence speed of stream = 3 kmph.

## Practice Exercise

Q1. Ratio of Downstream speed to the upstream speed = x : y. In covering the same distance, what will be the ratio of time taken?

(a) x : y (b) y : x (c) $x^2 : y^2$ (d) None of these

Q2. A man rows 8 km/hr in still water. If the river is running at 2 km/hr, he takes 32 min to row to a place and back. How far is the pace?

(a) 1.5 km (b) 2.5 km (c) 2 km (d) 3 km

Q3. A woman is swimming in a river which flows with the speed of $1\frac{1}{2}$ km/hr. It is given that she can swim twice as far with the river as she can against it in the same time. At what rate does she swim?

(a) $4\frac{1}{2}$ km/hr (b) $5\frac{1}{2}$ km/hr

(c) $7\frac{1}{2}$ km/hr (d) None of the these

Q4. A boat travels upstream from N to M and downstream from M to N in 3 hr. If the speed of the boat in water is 9 km/hr and the speed of the tide is 3 km/hr, the distance between M and N is

(a) 4 km (b) 8 km (c) 6 km (d) 12 km

Q5. A motor boat can travel at 10 km/hr in still water but it travelled 91 kilometer downstream in a river and then returned, taking altogether 20 hours. Find the rate of flow of the river.

(a) 6 km/hr (b) 5 km/hr (c)8 km/hr (d) 3 km/hr

Q6. A woman who can swim 48 m/min in still water, swims 200 m against the flow and 200 m with the flow. If the difference between these two times is 10 min, find the speed of the flow.

(a) 30 m/min (b) 29 m/min (c) 31 m/min (d) 32 m/min

Q7. Speed of a boat when moving in the direction perpendicular to the direction of the current is 16 km/h, speed of the flow is 3km/h. So, the speed of the boat against the current will be

(a) 22 km/h (b) 9.5 km/h (c) 10 km/h (d) none of these

Q8. A boat while going downstream in a river covered a distance of 50 miles at an average speed of 60 miles per hour. While returning because of the water force, it took 1 h 15 min to cover the same distance. What was the average speed during the whole journey?

(a) 40 miles/h (b) 48 miles/h (c) 50 miles/h (d) 55 miles/h

Q9. A ship goes 24 Km upstream and 28 Km downstream in 6 h. It goes 30 Km upper in opposite side and 21 Km down in same side in 6 h and 30 min. The speed of the ship in still water is

a) 10 Km/h b) 4 Km/h c) 14 Km/h d) 6 Km/h

Q10. A motor boat whose speed is 15 Km/h in still water goes 30 Km downstream and come back in four and a half hours. The speed of the stream is

a) 45 Km/h b) 6 Km/h c) 7 Km/h d) 5 Km/h

Q11. A boat takes 90 minutes less to travel 36 miles downstream than to travel the same distance upstream. If the speed of the boat in still water is 10 mph, the speed of the stream is:

a) 4 mph b) 2.5 mph c) 3 mph d) 2 mph

Q12. A boatman can row 3 km against the stream in 20 minutes and return in 18 minutes. Find the rate of current.

(a) $\frac{1}{2}$ km/hr (b) 1 km/hr (c) $\frac{1}{3}$ km/hr (d) $\frac{2}{3}$ km/hr

Q13. In a river flowing at 2 km/hr, a boat travels 32 km upstream and then returns downstream to the starting point. If its speed in still water be 6 km/hr, find the total journey time.

(a) 10 hr (b) 12 hr (c) 14 hr (d) 16 hr

Q14. A man can row at a speed of 12 km/hr in still water to a certain upstream point and back to the starting point in a river which flows at 3 km/hr. Find his average speed for total journey.

(a) 12.5 km/hr (b) 11.5 km/hr (c) 12.25 km/hr (d) 11.25 km/hr

Q15. A boat covers a certain distance downstream in 4 hours but takes 6 hours to return upstream to the starting point. If the speed of the stream be 3 km/hr, find the speed of the boat in still water

(a) 15 km/hr (b) 12 km/hr (c) 13 km/hr (d) 14 km/hr

Q16. If a man rows at the rate of 5 kmph in still water and his rate against the current is 3 kmph, then the man's rate along the current is:

(a) 5 kmph (b) 7 kmph (c) 12 kmph (d) 8 kmph

Q17. A man can row 8 km/hr in still water. If the river is running at 3 km/hr, it takes 3 hours more in upstream than to go downstream for the same distance. How far is the place?

(a) 32.5 km (b) 25 km (c) 27.5 km (d) 22.5 km

Q18. A man can row 4 kmph is still water. If the river is running at 2 kmph it takes 90 min to row to a place and back. How far is the place?

(a) 2 km (b) 4 km (c) 5 km (d) 2.25 km

Q19. At his usual rowing rate, Rahul can travel 12 miles downstream in a certain river in 6 hours less than it takes him to travel the same distance upstream. But if he could double his usual rowing rate for his 24-mile round trip, the downstream 12 miles would then take only one hour less than the upstream 12 miles. What is the speed of the current in miles per hour?

(a) 213 mph (b) 113 mph (c) 123 mph (d) 223 mph

Q20. A man can row 40 kmph in still water and the river is running at 10 kmph. If the man takes 1 hr to row to a place and back, how far is the place?

(a) 16.5 km (b) 12.15 km (c) 2.25 km (d) 18.75 km

Q21. A boatman can row 96 km downstream in 8 hr. If the speed of the current is 4 km/hr, then find in what time will be able to cover 8 km upstream?

(a) 6 hr (b) 2 hr (c) 4 hr (d) 1 hr

Q22. A man can walk up an upwards moving escalator in 90 seconds and walk down an upwards moving escalator in 30 seconds. In how much time will he be able to walk up the escalator if it is not moving (assume his speed is constant in all the cases)?

(a) 45 seconds (b) 60 seconds (c) 75 seconds (d) 30 seconds

## Answer Grid:

| Q. No. | 1 | 2 | 3 | 4 | 5 | 6 | 7 | 8 | 9 | 10 | 11 |
|---|---|---|---|---|---|---|---|---|---|---|---|
| Answer | b | c | a | d | d | d | c | b | a | d | d |
| Q. No. | 12 | 13 | 14 | 15 | 16 | 17 | 18 | 19 | 20 | 21 | 22 |
| Answer | a | b | d | a | b | c | d | d | d | b | a |

## Solutions and Explanations:

Q1. Since distance is constant, speed will be inversely proportional to the time. Hence ratio of time taken will be y : x. Hence option (b) is the answer.

Q2. Let the place be x km. Then, $\frac{x}{8} - 2 + \frac{x}{8} + 2 = \frac{32}{60}$

Or, $\frac{5x-3x}{30} = \frac{32}{8}$ → $x = \frac{32}{60} \times \frac{32}{8} = 2$ km

Hence option (C) is the answer

Q3. Let the woman was swimming at the rate of x km/h and she can swim D km upstream.

$\frac{D}{x-1\frac{1}{2}} = \frac{2D}{x+1\frac{1}{2}}$ → $x+\frac{3}{2} = 2x-3$ → $x = 4\frac{1}{2}$ km/h

Hence option (A) is the answer

Q4. Let the distance between M and N be x km. Given
Speed of Boat in still water = 9km/hr and Speed of current = 3km/hr
Upstream speed = (9 – 3) = 6 km/hr and Downstream speed = (9 + 3) = 12 km/hr

$\frac{x}{6} + \frac{x}{12} = 3$ $x = 12$ km

Hence option (D) is the answer

Q5. Let the rate of flow of river be x km/hr. Then
Downstream speed = (10 + x) km/hr and Upstream speed = (10 – x) km/hr

Given, $\frac{91}{(10+x)} + \frac{91}{(10+x)} = 20$ for x = 3 above expression holds true.

Hence option (D) is the answer

Q6. Let the speed of flow be x m/min. Then,
Speed with flow = (48 + x) m/min and Speed against flow = (48 – x) m/min

$= \frac{200}{(48-x)} + \frac{200}{(48-x)} = 10$ $40x = (48)^2 - x^2$

$x^2 + 40x - 2304 = 0$ $(x + 72)(x - 32) = 0$ $x = 32$ m/min

Hence option (D) is the answer

Q7. Speed of speed boat = 16 – 3 = 13 km/h

Speed of boat against the current = 13 – 3 = 10 km/h

Hence option (C) is the answer

Q8. Time taken by boat downstream = $\frac{50}{60} = \frac{5}{6}$ hr and time taken by boat in Upstream $= \frac{5}{4}$ hr

$$\text{Average speed} = \frac{2\times50}{\frac{5}{4}+\frac{5}{6}} = \frac{100\times24}{50} = \textbf{48 miles/h}$$

Hence option (B) is the answer

Q9. Lets the speed of the Ship in still water be x km/h and speed of the current be y km/h.

then, upward speed = (x – y) km/h and downward speed = (x + y)km/h

24 / (x – y) + 28 / (x + y) = 6 ...........(1) and 30 / (x – y) + 21 / (x + y) = 13 / 2 ...........(2)

Solving equations (1) and (2), we get x = 10 km/h and y = 4 km/h.

Hence option (A) is the answer

Q10. Let the speed of stream be x km/h

Then, upward speed = (15 – x)km/h and downward speed = (15 + x)km/h

Or, 30/(15 + x) + 30/(15 – x) = 4.5. Using options we find that x = 5 km/h

Hence option (D) is the answer

Q11. Speed of the boat in still water = 10 mph

Let speed of the stream be x mph. Then, speed downstream = (10 + x) mph

speed upstream = (10 – x) mph

Time taken to travel 36 miles upstream - Time taken to travel 36 miles downstream

= 9060 hrs ⇒ 3610 – x – 3610 + x = 32 ⇒ 1210 – x – 1210 + x = 12

⇒ 24(10 + x) – 24(10 – x) = (10 + x)(10 – x) ⇒ 240 + 24x – 240 + 24x = $(100 – x^2)$

⇒ 48x = $100 – x^2$ ⇒ $x^2 + 48x – 100 = 0$ ⇒ (x + 50)(x – 2) = 0 ⇒ x = –50 or 2

Hence option (D) is the answer.

Q12. Speed upstream = $3(\frac{60}{20})$ = 9 km/hr and Speed downstream = $3(\frac{60}{18})$ = 10 km/hr

Rate of current = $\frac{10-9}{2} = \frac{1}{2}$ **km/hr**

Hence option (A) is the answer

Q13. Speed of the boat = 6 km/hr

Speed downstream = (6 + 2) = 8 km/hr    Speed upstream = (6 – 2) = 4 km/hr

Distance travelled downstream = Distance travelled upstream = 32 km

Total time taken = Time taken downstream + Time taken upstream

$$= \frac{32}{8} + \frac{32}{4} = \frac{32+64}{8} = \frac{96}{8} = 12 \text{ hr}$$

Hence option (B) is the answer

Q14. Speed downstream = (12 + 3) = 15 km/hr

Speed upstream = (12 – 3) = 9 km/hr

When distance is constant, average speed = $\frac{2 \times \text{Downstreamspeed} \times \text{UpstreamSpeed}}{\text{Downstreamspeed} + \text{UpstreamSpeed}}$

Average Speed = $\frac{2 \times 15 \times 9}{15+9} = \frac{45}{4}$ = 11.25 km/hr

Hence option (D) is the answer

Q15. **Solution 1** :- Let the speed of the water in still water = x

Given that speed of the stream = 3 kmph

Speed downstream = (x + 3) kmph    Speed upstream = (x – 3) kmph

He travels a certain distance downstream in 4 hour and come back in 6 hour.

ie, distance travelled downstream in 4 hour = distance travelled upstream in 6 hour

since distance = speed × time, we have    $(x + 3)4 = (x - 3)6$

$\Rightarrow (x + 3)2 = (x - 3)3$    $\Rightarrow 2x + 6 = 3x - 9$    $\Rightarrow x = 6 + 9 = 15$ kmph

**Solution 2** :- A man rows a certain distance downstream in $t_1$ hours and returns the same distance upstream in $t_2$hours. If the speed of the stream is y km/hr, then the speed of the man in still water = $y\left(\frac{t2 + t1}{t2 - t1}\right)$ km/hr

$t_1$ = 4 hour,    $t_2$ = 6 hour,    y = 3 km/hr

By using the above formula, Speed of the boat in still water

$= y\left(\frac{t2 + t1}{t2 - t1}\right)$ $= 3\left(\frac{6+4}{6-4}\right)$ $= 15$ km/hr

Hence option (A) is the answer

Q16. Let the rate along with the current is x km/hr. $\frac{x+3}{2} = 5$ $\Rightarrow x + 3 = 10$

$\Rightarrow x = 7$ kmph

Hence option (B) is the answer

Q17. Let the speed downstream = x and speed upstream = y

Then, $\frac{x+y}{2} = 8$ $\Rightarrow x + y = 16$ —(Equation 1)

$\frac{x-y}{2} = 3$ $\Rightarrow x - y = 6$ —(Equation 2)

(Equation 1 + Equation 2) $\Rightarrow 2x = 22$ $\Rightarrow x = 11$ km/hr

(Equation 1 – Equation 2) $\Rightarrow 2y = 10$ $\Rightarrow y = 5$ km/hr

Time taken to travel upstream = Time taken to travel downstream + 3

Let distance be x km. Then, $\frac{x}{5} = \frac{x}{11} + 3$

$\Rightarrow 11x = 5x + 165$ $\Rightarrow 6x = 165$ $\Rightarrow 2x = 55$ $\Rightarrow x = 27.5$

Hence option (C) is the answer.

Q18. Speed in still water = 4 kmph Speed of the stream = 2 kmph

Speed upstream = (4 – 2) = 2 kmph Speed downstream = (4 + 2) = 6 kmph

Total time = 90 minutes = $\frac{90}{60}$ hour = $\frac{3}{2}$ hour

Let L be the distance. Then, $\frac{L}{6} + \frac{L}{2} = \frac{3}{2}$

$\Rightarrow L + 3L = 9$ $\Rightarrow 4L = 9$ $\Rightarrow L = 2.25$ km

Hence option (D) is the answer

Q19. Hence option (D) is the answer

Q20. **Method 1: Using equations**

Let the distance be x kms.

Speed upstream = (40 – 10) = 30 kmph and Speed downstream = (40 + 10) = 50 kmph

Total time taken = 1 hr

$\frac{x}{50} + \frac{x}{30} = 1 \quad \Rightarrow \frac{8x}{150} = 1 \quad \Rightarrow x = \frac{150}{8} = 18.75$ km

Hence option (D) is the answer

**Method 2 – Using average speed**

When distance is constant, average speed = $\frac{2 \times \text{Downstream Speed} \times \text{Upstream Speed}}{\text{Downstream Speed} + \text{Upstream Speed}}$

Average Speed for the whole journey = $\frac{2 \times 50 \times 30}{50 + 30} = 37.5$ km/hr

Hence total distance traveled (up and down) = Average speed for the whole journey × total time of the journey = 37.5 × 1 = 37.5 kms

Hence distance one way = 37.5/2 = 18.75 kms. Hence option (d) is the answer.

Q21. Speed downstream = $\frac{96}{8} = 12$ kmph Speed of current = 4 km/hr

Speed of the boatman in still water = 12 – 4 = 8 kmph

Speed upstream = 8 – 4 = 4 kmph Time taken to cover 8 km upstream = $\frac{8}{4} = 2$ hours

Hence option (B) is the answer

Q22. This question is just another way of putting up the question from boats and streams. When direction of movement of man and escalator is same, it is downstream movement and when direction of movement of man and escalator are different, it is upstream movement.

As given in the concepts (important points 3), If time taken in covering a certain distance Downstream and Upstream = x hours and y hours respectively, then time taken in covering the same distance in still water = $\frac{2xy}{x+y}$ hr = $\frac{2 \times 90 \times 30}{90 + 30}$ seconds

= 45 seconds.

Hence option (a) is the answer.

# 11 Trains

Let us 1st understand that why do we need to study concept of trains separately despite this concept is a part of Time Speed Distance.

## Consider the following case:

1a. A and B are two man running towards each other. Speed of A is 15 m/s and speed of B is 5 m/s. If the distance between them is 100 m, in how much time will they *meet* each other?

1b. A and B are two man running towards each other. Speed of A is 15 m/s and speed of B is 5 m/s. If the distance between them is 100 m, in how much time will they *cross* each other?

A ——————— 100 m ——————— B

⇨ 15 m/s ⇦ 5 m/s

It can be seen that answer to both 1a and 1b will be same i.e. meeting and crossing each other are same in this case. Time = $\frac{\text{Distance}}{\text{Relative Speed}} = \frac{100}{20} = 5$ secs

## Now consider the following case:

2a. A and B are two trains running towards each other. Speed of train A is 15 m/s and speed of train B is 5 m/s. Length of train A is 150 m and length of train B is 50 m. If the distance between them is 100 m, in how much time will they *meet* each other?

2b. A and B are two trains running towards each other. Speed of train A is 15 m/s and speed of train B is 5 m/s. Length of train A is 150 m and length of train B is 50 m. If the distance between them is 100 m, in how much time will they *cross* each other?

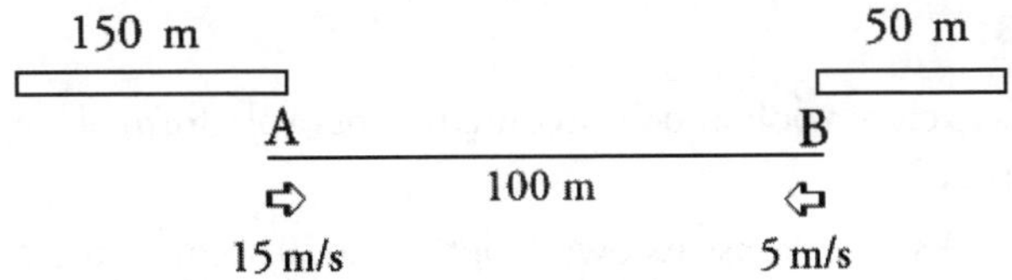


Will the answers to questions 2a and 2b same?

It will not be same because in case of (2a) total distance travelled by trains = 100 m,

$$\text{Time} = \frac{\text{Distance}}{\text{Relative Speed}} = \frac{100}{20} 5 \text{ secs}$$

In case of (2b) total distance travelled by trains = 150 m + 100 m + 50 m = 300 m

$$\text{Time} = \frac{\text{Distance}}{\text{Relative Speed}} = \frac{300}{20} \; 15 \text{ secs}$$

## Standard Cases:

(a) If a train of length 'L' is crossing a pole (or any stationery object of negligible width) at a speed of v m/s, then the train covers a distance equal to its length = L meters. Hence time taken by train in crossing a pole = $\frac{\text{Length of train}}{\text{Speed of train}} = \frac{L}{v}$

(b) If a train of length is crossing a platform at a speed of v m/s, then the train covers a distance equal to (its own length + length of platform). Hence time taken by train in crossing a platform = $\frac{\text{Length of train + length of platfrom}}{\text{Speed of train}}$

(c) If two train or two bodies of length $l_1$ and $l_2$ m are moving in *opposite* direction on parallel path with $v_1$ m/s and $v_2$ m/s, then time taken by the trains or bodies to cross each other = $\left(\frac{L1+L2}{v1+v2}\right)$ second

(d) If two trains of length $l_1$ and $l_2$ are moving in *same* direction at $v_1$ m/s and $v_2$ m/s then the time taken by the faster body to cross the slower body = $\left(\frac{L1+L2}{|v1-v2|}\right)$ second

**Note that – Distance will be always added up irrespective of the direction of the movement of the objects.**

## Worked Out Examples:

Q1. A train takes 10 seconds to cross a pole and 20 seconds to cross a platform of length 200 m. What is the length of train?

**Solution** – Train takes 10 secs to cross its own length and 20 seconds to cross its own length and length of platform.

So, it infers that train takes 10 seconds to cross platform and 10 secs to cross its own length.

Since time taken to cross platform = time taken to cross its own length. So, length of platform = length of train = 200 m

Q2. Speed of a train is 36 kmph. It takes 25 secs to cross a pole. What is the length of this train?

**Solution** – Speed of train = 10 m/s (36x 5/18). Distance covered = 10 × 25 = 250 m. So, length of train = 250 m

Q3. A man running with a speed of 18 kmph crosses a train of length 280 m running in the opposite direction in 20 secs. What is the speed of train?

**Solution** – Total distance covered = 280 m, and time taken = 20 secs

Hence relative speed = $\frac{280}{20}$ = 14 m/s

Speed of man = 18 kmph = 5 m/s

Hence speed of train = 9 m/s

Q4. Two trains of length 200 m and 220 m are running on parallel tracks in the same direction. Speed of 1st train is 72 kmph and speed of second train is 54 kmph. What is the time taken by both the trains to cross each other?

**Solution** – Relative Speed = 72 kmph – 54 kmph = 18 kmph = 5 m/s

Total distance to be covered = 200 + 220 = 420 m [Distance will be always added].

So time taken = $\frac{420}{5}$ = 84 secs

Q5. In the above question, what would have been the time taken had their direction of movement been the opposite direction?

**Solution** – Relative Speed = 72 kmph + 54 kmph = 126 kmph = 35 m/s

Total distance to be covered = 200 + 220 = 420 m [Distance will be always added].

So time taken = $\frac{420}{35}$ = 12 secs

Q6. How much time the train will take to cross a pole along the railway track if length of the train is 180 m and it is running at the speed of 54 km/h?

**Solution** – When a train crosses a pole, distance travelled by train = Length of train = 180 m

Speed of train = 54 km / h = $54 \times \frac{5}{18}$ = 15 m /s

Time = Distance / Speed = $\frac{180}{15}$ = 12 seconds

Q7. The lengths of a train and a platform are 120 m and 180 m respectively. Train takes 6 seconds to cross the platform. Find the speed of train.

**Solution** – When a train crosses a platform, distance covered by train = Length of train + length of platform = 120 m + 180 m = 300 m

Train takes 6 seconds to cross the platform, hence speed of train = $\frac{\text{Distance}}{\text{Time}} = \frac{300}{6}$ 50 m/s

Q8. Length of a goods train is 287 m and it passes a bridge in 38 sec running at the speed of 90 km/h. What is the length of the bridge?

**Solution** – Total distance covered = $90 \times \frac{5}{18} \times 38$ = 950 m

When a train crosses a bridge, distance covered = Length of bridge + length of train = 950 m

Hence length of bridge = 950 m – 287 m = 663 m.

Q9. A train 75 meters long overtook a person who was walking at the speed of 6 kmph in the opposite direction and passed him in $7\frac{1}{2}$ seconds. Subsequently, it overtook a second person, walking in the same direction as the first person and passed him in $6\frac{3}{4}$ seconds. At what rate was the second person travelling?

**Solution – Case I:**

Relative speed = $\frac{\text{length of train}}{\text{time taken}} = \frac{75}{15/2}$ = 10 m/s

10 m/s × $\frac{18}{5}$ = 36 km/hr

Speed of train = 36 – 6 = 30 km/hr

Now distance travelled by X in 1.5 hr is = $6 \times \frac{3}{2} = 9$ km

Thus at 6.30 pm X has travelled = (9 + 18) km = 27 km.

**Case II:**

With 2nd person

Relative speed = $\frac{75}{27/4} = \frac{300}{27}$ m/s

Or, $\frac{300}{27}\frac{m}{s} = \frac{300}{27} \times \frac{18}{5}$ km/h = 40 km/hr

Thus speed of 2nd person = 40 – 30 = 10 km/hr

Q10. A train, 225 m long, is running at 45 km/hr. In what time does it cross a man running at 18 km/hr in the same direction?

1. 20 secs 2. 30 secs 3. 25 secs 4. 15 secs

**Solution** – Speed of train = 45 km/h and speed of man = 18 km/h

Since they are in the same direction, relative speed = 45 – 18 = 27 km/h = $27 \times \frac{5}{18}$ m/sec

$= \frac{45}{2}$ m/sec

Hence time taken to cross the man = $\frac{\text{Length of train}}{\text{Relative speed}} = \frac{225}{45/2}$ sec $= \frac{225 \times 2}{45}$ sec = 30 sec.

## Practice Exercise

Q1. A man sitting in a train travelling at the rate of 50km/hr observes that it takes 9sec for a goods train travelling in the opposite direction to pass him. If the goods train is 187.5 m long, find its speed.

(a) 25 km/hr (b) 40 km/hr (c) 35km/hr (d) 36km/hr

Q2. A train started form Ajabgarh and proceded towards Bahadurgarh at a speed of 28 km/hr. 45 min later another train started from Bahadurgarh and proceeded towards Ajabgarh at 50 km/hr. If the distance between them is 232 km, at what distance from station will the trains meet?

(a) 108 km (b) 144 km (c) 132 km (d) None of these

Q3. A railway passenger counts the electric poles the rail road as he passes them. The electric poles are at a distance of 50m. What will be his count in 4 hr if speed of train is 45 km/hr?

(a) 2500 (b) 600 (c) 3600 (d) 5000

Q4. A train driver, driving in a fog, passes a child who was walking at the rate of 2 km/hr in the same direction. The child could see the train for 6 min and it was visible to him up to a distance of 0.6 km. What was the speed of the train?

(a )15 km/hr (b) 30 km/hr (c) 20 km/hr (d) 8 km/hr

Q5. A train crosses a platform in 36 sec and a man standing on the platform in 20 sec. If the speed of the train is 54 km/hr, find the length of the platform.

(a) 225 m (b) 235 m (c) 230 m (d) 240 m

Q6. Two Bullet trains, 130 m and 110 m long, are going in the same direction. The faster Bullet train takes one minute to pass the other bullet train completely. If they are moving in opposite directions, they pass each other in 3sec. Find the speed of the faster bullet train.

(a) 38 m/sec (b) 46 m/sec (c) 42 m/sec (d) 50 m/sec

Q7. Two stations Panipat and Sonipat are 110 km apart on a straight track. One train starts from Panipat at 7 a.m. and travels towards Sonipat at 20 kmph. Another train starts from Sonipat at 8 a.m. and travels towards Panipat at a speed of 25 kmph. At what time will they meet?

(a) 10:30 am (b) 10 am (c) 9:10 am (d) 11 am

Q8. A train overtakes Ajay and Vijay walking along a track. Ajay walks at 4.5 km/hr and Vijay walks at 5.4 km/hr. The train needs 8.4 and 8.5 seconds respectively to overtake them. What is the speed of the train if Ajay and Vijay are walking in the same direction as the train travelling?

(a) 81 km/hr (b) 88 km/hr (c) 62 km/hr (d) 46 km/hr

Q9. A Train of length 110 meter is running at a speed of 60 kmph. In what time, it will pass a man who is running at 6 kmph in the direction opposite to the train?

(a) 10 sec (b) 8 sec (c) 6 sec (d) 4 sec

Q10. A 300 m long train crosses a bridge in 39 seconds while it crosses a electric post in 18 seconds. What is the length of the bridge?

(a) 150 m (b) 350 m (c) 420 m (d) 600 m

Q11. A train crosses an electric post in 15 seconds and crosses a stationary train of 100 m long in 25 seconds. Its length is

(a) 150 m (b) 300 m (c) 400 m (d) 180 m

Q12. A train, 800 meter long travelling at a speed of 78 km/hr. It crosses a platform in 1 minute. What is the length of the platform (in meters)?

(a) 440 m (b) 500 m (c) 260 m (d) 430 m

Q13. Two train each of 500 m, running in opposite directions on parallel tracks. If their speeds are 45 km/hr and 30 km/hr respectively, then the time taken by slower train to pass the engine of the faster one is

(a) 50 sec (b) 58 sec (c) 24 sec (d) 22 sec

Q14. Two trains are running at 40 km/hr and 20 km/hr respectively in the same direction. If the express train completely passes a woman sitting in the local train in 5 seconds, the length of the express train is

(a) 19 m (b) 1329 m (c) 33 m (d) None of these

Q15. Two trains of length 120 meter each are running in opposite directions by the same speed. If they cross each other in 12 seconds, the speed of each train (in km/hr) is

(a) 42 (b) 36 (c) 28 (d) 20

Q16. A train has a length of 108m is moving at a speed of 50 km/hr. It crosses a train in 6 second coming from opposite direction of length 112 m. What is the speed of the $2^{nd}$ train?

(a) 82 km/hr (b) 76 km/hr (c) 44 km/hr (d) 58 km/hr

Q17. How many seconds will a 500 meter long train take to cross a man walking with a speed of 3 kmph in the direction of the train?

(a) 42 (b) 50 (c) 30 (d) 28

Q18. Two trains starting at the same time from two stations, 200 km apart going in opposite directions, cross each other at a distance 110 km from one of them. What is the ratio of their speed?

(a) 11 : 20 (b) 9 : 20 (c) 11 : 9 (d) 19 : 20

Q19. A certain distance is covered by a train with a certain speed. If half the distance is covered in double time, then the ratio of this speed to that of the original is

(a) 1 : 4 (b) 4 :1 (c) 1 : 2 (d) 2 : 1

Q20. A train running between two stations A and B arrives at its destination 10 min late when its speed is 50 km/h and 50 min late when its speed is 30 km/h. What is the distance between the stations A and B?

(a) 40 km (b) 50 km (c) 60 km (d) 70 km

Q21. Two trains are 2 km apart and their lengths are 200m and 300m. They are approaching towards each other with a speed of 23 m/s and 30 m/s respectively. After how much time will they cross each other?

(a) 50 s (b) 100 s (c) $\frac{25}{3}$ s (d) 150 s

Q22. A train with 90 km/h crosses a bridge in 36 s. Another train 100 m shorter crosses the same bridge at 45 km/h. What is the time taken by the second train to cross the bridge?

(a) 61 s (b) 63 s (c) 62 s (d) 64 s

Q23. A train travels 25 km /h faster than a bike for a journey of 500 km. If the bike takes 10 h more than the train, then the speeds of the bike and the train are

(a) 25 km/h and 40 km/h respectively (b) 25 km/h and 60 km/h respectively

(c) 25 km/h and 50 km/h respectively (d) None of these

Q24. A train 100 m long passes a bridge at the rate of 72 Km/h in 25 s. the length of the bridge is

(a) 150 m (b) 400 m (c) 300 m (d) 200 m

Q25. A train 110 m length travels at 60 Km/h. How much time does the train take in passing a man walking at 6 Km/h against the train?

(a) 6 s (b) 12 s (c) 10 s (d) 8 s

## Answer Grid:

| Q. No. | 1 | 2 | 3 | 4 | 5 | 6 | 7 | 8 | 9 | 10 | 11 | 12 | 13 | 14 | 15 | 16 | 17 | 18 | 19 | 20 |
|---|---|---|---|---|---|---|---|---|---|---|---|---|---|---|---|---|---|---|---|---|
| Answer | a | c | c | d | d | c | b | a | c | b | a | b | c | d | b | a | c | c | a | b |
| Q. No. | 21 | 22 | 23 | 24 | 25 | | | | | | | | | | | | | | | |
| Answer | d | d | c | b | a | | | | | | | | | | | | | | | |

## Solutions and Explanations:

Q1. Let the speed of goods train be x km/h. As the trains are running in opposite direction,

$$187.5 = (50 + x) \times \frac{5}{18} \times 19$$

Or, 50 + x = 75. Hence x = 25 km/h

Hence option (A) is the answer

Q2. Let the trains will meet x h after the train from station B started.

According to the question,

48 × (x + ) + 50 × x = 232, or, 48x + 36 + 50x = 232, or, x = 2 h

Distance travelled by the train starting from station A at the meeting point $= 48 \times \left(2 + \frac{45}{60}\right)$

= 132 km

Hence option (C) is the answer

Q3. Distance travelled by train in 4hr = 45 × 4 = 180 km

No. of electric poles = $\frac{180 \times 1000}{50}$ = 3600

Hence option (C) is the answer

Q4. Let the speed of the train be x km/hr. as the child is walking in the same direction

Or, (x – 2) = $\frac{0.6}{6}$ × 60, or, x = 6 + 2 = 8m/hr

Hence option (D) is the answer

Q5. Train with a speed of 54 km/hr passes the man in 20 sec.

Length of train = 54 × $\frac{5}{18}$ × 20 = 300 m

Let the length of platform be x m, then (300 + x) = 54 × $\frac{5}{18}$ × 36. Or, x = 540 – 300 = 240 m

Hence option (D) is the answer

Q6. Let the speed of the faster bullet train be x km/hr and that of slower bullet train be y km/hr.

Then, in first case, relative speed = (x – y) km/hr

(130 + 110) = (x – y) × $\frac{5}{18}$ × 60 (x – y) = 14.4 ..........(i)

In second case, relative speed = (x + y) km/hr

(130 + 110) = (x + y) × $\frac{5}{18}$ × 3 (x + y) = 288 .......... (ii)

Using equations (i) and (ii), 2x = 302.4. Hence x = $\frac{302.4}{2}$ = 151.20 km/hr and 42 m/sec

Hence option (c) is the answer

Q7. Assume both trains meet after x hours after 7 am.

Distance covered by train starting from P in x hours = 20x km

Distance covered by train starting from Q in (x – 1) hours = 25(x – 1)

Total distance = 110

$\Rightarrow$ 20x + 25(x – 1) = 110 $\Rightarrow$ 45x = 135 $\Rightarrow$ x = 3

Means, they meet after 3 hours after 7 am, ie, they meet at 10 am

Hence option (B) is the answer

Q8. Let x is the length of the train in meter and y is its speed in kmph.

$$\frac{x}{8.4} = (y-4.5)\frac{10}{36} \quad ......(1) \qquad \frac{x}{8.5} = (y-5.4)\frac{10}{36} \quad ......(2)$$

Dividing 1 by 2

$$\frac{8.5}{8.4} = \frac{5-4.5}{y-5.4} \qquad \Rightarrow 8.4y - 8.4 \times 4.5 = 8.5y - 8.5 \times 5.4$$

0.1y = 8.5 × 5.4 – 8.4 × 4.5 $\Rightarrow$ 0 .1y = 45.9 – 37.8 = 8.1 $\Rightarrow$ y = 81 km/hr

Hence option (A) is the answer

Q9. Distance = 110 m, Relative speed = 60 + 6 = 66 kmph (Since both the train and the man are in moving in opposite direction) = $66 \times \frac{10}{36}$ mps = $\frac{110}{6}$ mps

Time = distance/speed = 110 / (110/6) = 6 s

Hence option (C) is the answer

Q10. Length of the train = distance covered in crossing the post = speed × time = speed × 18

Speed of the train = $\frac{300}{18}$ m/s = $\frac{50}{3}$ m/s

Time taken to cross the platform = 39 s

(300 + x) / (50/3) = 39 s where x is the length of the platform

300 + x = (39 × 50) / 3 = 650 meter x = 650 – 300 = 350 meter

Hence option (B) is the answer

Q11. Assume x is the length of the train and v is the speed $\frac{x}{v} = 15$ $\Rightarrow v = \frac{x}{15}$

$\frac{x+100}{v} = 25$ $\Rightarrow v\ \frac{x+100}{25}$

Or, $\frac{x}{15} = \frac{x+100}{25}$ $\Rightarrow$ 5x = 3x + 300 $\Rightarrow x = \frac{300}{2} = 150$

Hence option (A) is the answer

Q12. Distance = 800 + x meter where x is the length of the tunnel.

Time = 1 minute = 60 seconds

Speed = 78 km/hr = $78 \times \frac{10}{36}$ m/s = $\frac{130}{6} = \frac{65}{3}$ m/s

Speed = $\frac{\text{Distance}}{\text{time}}$ $\frac{65}{3} = \frac{800+x}{60} \Rightarrow 800 + x = 20 \times 65 = 1300 \Rightarrow x = 1300 - 800 = 500$ m

Hence option (B) is the answer

Q13. Relative speed = 45 + 30 = 75 km/hr = $\frac{750}{36}$ m/s = $\frac{125}{6}$ m/s

We are calculating the time taken by the slower train to pass the driver of the faster one. Hence the distance = length of the slower train = 500 m

Time = $\frac{\text{Distance}}{\text{speed}}$ = 500 / (125/6) = 24 s

Hence option (C) is the answer

Q14. Relative speed = 40 – 20 = 20 km/hr = $\frac{200}{36}$ m/s = $\frac{100}{18}$ = m/s Time = 5 s

Distance = speed × time = $\frac{100}{18} \times 5 = \frac{250}{9}$ = m = length of the fast train

Hence option (d) is the answer

Q15. Distance covered = 120 + 120 = 240 m Time = 12 s

Let the speed of each train = v. Then, relative speed = v + v = 2v

2v = $\frac{\text{Distance}}{\text{Time}} = \frac{240}{12}$ = 20 m/s

Speed of each train = v = $\frac{20}{2}$ = 10 m/s = $10 \times \frac{36}{10}$ km/hr = 36 km/hr

Hence option (B) is the answer

Q16. Total distance = 108 + 112 = 220 m Time = 6s

Relative speed = $\frac{\text{Distance}}{\text{Time}} = \frac{220}{6}$ m/s = $\frac{110}{3}$ m/s $= \frac{110}{3} \times \frac{18}{5}$ km/hr = 132 km/hr

$\Rightarrow$ 50 + speed of second train = 132 km/hr

$\Rightarrow$ Speed of second train = 132 – 50 = 82 km/hr

Hence option (A) is the answer

Q17. Distance = 500m Speed = 63 – 3 km/hr = 60 km/hr = $\frac{600}{36}$ m/s = $\frac{50}{3}$ m/s

Time taken = $\frac{\text{Distance}}{\text{Speed}}$ = 500 / (50/3) = 30 s

Hence option (C) is the answer

Q18. Let the speed of trains be s1 and s2 km/h.

When they cross each other, time taken by both the trains will be equal

then, s1 / 110 = s2 / 90 , so, s1 : s2 = 11 : 9

Hence option (C) is the answer

Q19. Let distance x be covered in t time. Then, required ratio = { (x/2) / 2t } / (x / t) = 1 / 4

Hence option (A) is the answer

Q20. Let the distance between two station be X km. Then, $\frac{x}{50}-\frac{1}{6}=\frac{x}{30}-\frac{5}{6}$

Or, $\frac{x}{30}-\frac{x}{50}=\frac{2}{3}$. Hence x = 50 km

Hence option (B) is the answer

Q21. Let the length of first train be X m and that of bridge is Y m. Speed = 90km/h = $\frac{90\times5}{18}$

= 25m/s

We know that distance = Speed × Time, hence (x + y) = 25 × 36 = 900

Length of another train = (x – 100).

Speed = $\frac{45\times5}{18}$ m/s

D = S × T, or, (X – 100 + Y) = $\frac{45\times8}{18}$ × t. Hence (900 – 100) = $\frac{25}{2}$ × t, or, t = 64 sec.

Hence option (D) is the answer

Q23. Let the of the train be X km/h

Speed of the bike = (X + 25)km/h.

According to the question, $\frac{500}{x} = \frac{500}{x+25} + 10$, or, $X^2 + 25X - 1250 = 0$.

Solving, X = 25 km / h = Speed of the train. So, Speed of the bike = 50 km/h

Hence option (C) is the answer

Q24. Let the length be x m.

According to the question, (x + 100) = 72 × 25 × (5/18) = 500

Or, x = 500 – 100 = 400m

Hence option (B) is the answer

Q25. Relative speed = (60 + 6) kmph = 66 kmph = (66 × 5)/18 m/s

Distance = 110 m. Hence time = (110 × 18)/(66 × 5) = 6s

Hence option (A) is the answer

# 12 Time Speed and Distance

## Time Speed and Distance

Speed is defined as the distance travelled in unit time. Mathematically, Speed = $\frac{\text{Distance}}{\text{Time}}$

**Distance:** If a person is moving at a speed of v m/s for t seconds, the distance covered by him will be = Speed × Time

Or, Distance = Speed × Time

Most commonly used units of Speed are meter per second OR km per hour.

To convert Km/h unit into m/s we multiply it by a factor of $\frac{5}{18}$ and if we have to convert m/s to Km/h, it is multiplied by $\frac{18}{5}$.

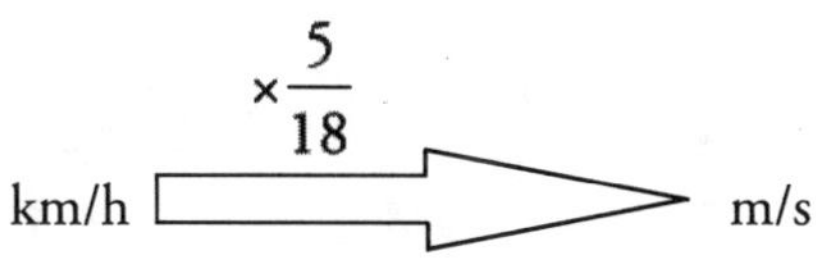


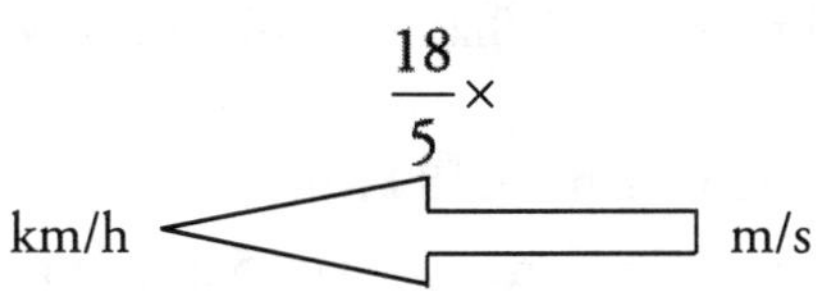


## 1. Motion in a straight line

### Important formula:

(1) If the ratio of the speeds of two moving objects is (x: y) then the ratio of the times taken by them to cover same distance is (y: x)

(2) Average Speed for the whole journey = $\dfrac{\text{Total distance}}{\text{Total Time taken}}$

Corollary to point (2):

(a) However, if a moving object covers a certain distance with a speed of 'a' kmph and an equal distance at 'b' kmph, then the average speed for the whole journey = $\left(\dfrac{2ab}{a+b}\right)$ kmph

(b) If a moving object travels for 't' hours with a speed of 'a' kmph, and another 't' hours with a speed of 'b' kmph, then the average speed for the whole journey = $\left(\dfrac{a+b}{2}\right)$ kmph

(3) When two objects are travelling in the same direction, Relative Speed = Difference of the speeds

(4) When two objects are travelling in the opposite direction, Relative Speed = Sum of the speeds

## Worked Out Examples:

Q1. A man covers 70 m in 35 second. What is the speed of this man?

**Solution** – Speed = $\dfrac{\text{Distance}}{\text{Time}}$

Distance = 70 m and time = 35 seconds

So speed = $\dfrac{70}{35}$ = 2 m/s

Q2. A car is moving with a speed of 90 kmph for 2 hours. What is the distance covered by car in that time?

**Solution** – Distance = Speed × Time = 90 kmph × 2 hrs = 180 Km

Q3. A man covers a distance of 245 meters while moving with a speed of 5 m/s. What is the time taken by the man?

**Solution** – Time = Distance/Speed = $\dfrac{145}{5}$ = 49 second

Q4. Samar travelled from point A to point B at the rate of 30 kmph and walked back to 'A' at the rate of 50 kmph. What was his average speed during the whole journey?

**Solution** – As distance covered is same in both the cases, Average speed $=\left(\dfrac{2ab}{a+b}\right)$

$=\left(\dfrac{2\times30\times50}{30+50}\right)= 37.5$ kmph

Q5. Tinki travels for 3 hours at the speed of 25 kmph and another 3 hours at the speed of 33 kmph. What is his average speed for the whole journey?

**Solution** – As time invested is same in both the cases, Average speed $=\dfrac{a+b}{2}=\dfrac{25+33}{2}$

= 29 kmph

Q6. A thief escaped from a jail at 11 AM. After realizing the escape at 1 PM same day, a cop starts chasing the thief in his direction. If speed of thief is 30 kmph and speed of cop is 50 kmph, at what time will the thief be caught?

**Solution** – Since the escape was unreported till 1 PM, the distance thief has covered from 11 AM (since his escape) till cop starts chasing (1 PM) = 30 kmph × 2 hrs = 60 kms

Since cop and thief are travelling the same direction, relative speed of cop over thief = 50 kmph – 30 kmph = 20 kmph

Time taken by cop to catch the thief $=\dfrac{\text{Distance}}{\text{Relative Speed}}=\dfrac{60 \text{ kms}}{20 \text{ kmph}}=3$ hours

Since cop starts chasing the thief at 1 PM, he would catch thief 3 hours later at 4 pm.

Q7. In previous question, how much distance cop has travelled before catching the thief?

**Solution** – Cop started chasing the thief at 1 PM and caught him at 4 PM. So time taken by cop in catching the thief = 3 hours

Distance = Speed × Time = 50 × 3 = 150 kms

## Practice Exercise

Q1. A Biker goes from Mumbai to Pune, a distance of 192 km at an average speed of 32 km/hr. A man starts from Mumbai by car to Pune, 2 hr after the first and reaches Pune half an hour earlier. What is the ratio of the speeds of the Biker and the car?

(a) 10:27 (b) 1:3 (C) 1:2 (d) 5:4

Q2. Two cyclists start on a circular track from a given point but in opposite directions with speeds of 7 cm/sec and 8 cm/sec respectively. If the circumference of the circle is 300 cm, after what time will they at the starting point?

(a) 20 sec (b) 100 sec (c) 300 sec (d) 200 sec

Q3. A car travels a distance of 45 km at the speed of 15 km/hr. It covers the next 50 km of its journey at the speed of 25 km/hr and the last 25 km of its journey at the speed of $8\frac{1}{3}$ km/hr. What is the average speed of the car?

(a) 40 km/hr (b) 24 km/hr (c) 15 km/hr (d) 18 km/hr

Q4. A car travels a distance of 170 km in 2 hr partly at a speed of 100 km /hr and partly at 50 km/hr. The distance travelled at a speed of 50 km/hr is

(a) 50 km (b) 40 km (c) 30 km (d) 60 km

Q5. A bike is scheduled to cover the distance between two points 46 km apart in one hour. If it travels 25 km with a speed of 40 km/hr, find the speed for the remaining journey.

(a) 66 km/hr (b) 56 km/hr (c) 46 km/hr (d) 36 km/hr

Q6. A cyclist moving on a circular track of radius 100m completes one revolution in 2 min. What is the approximate speed of the cyclist?

(a) 200 m/min (b) 314 m/min (c) 300 m/min (d) 900 m/min

Q7. The speeds of three cars are in the ratio 2:3:4. The ratio of the time taken by cars to cover the same distance is :

(a) 4:3:2 (b) 2:3:4 (c) 4:3:6 (d) 6:4:3

Q8. Alok walks to a viewpoint and returns by his car and thus takes a total time of 6 hours 45 min. He would have taken for him to walk both ways?

(a) 7 hr 45 min (b) 8 hr 45 min (c) 5 hr 30 min (d) None the these

Q9. Two round wheels of which one has 16 cogs and the other 27 cogs, work into each other. If the later turns 80 times in three quarters of a minute, how often does the other turn in 8sec?

(a) 18 (b) 30 (c) 24 (d) 36

Q10. A cart travels distances 2500m, 1200m and 500m at the rate of 500 m/hr, 400 m/hr and 250 m/hr respectively. The average speed is -

(a ) 420 km/hr (b) 405 km/hr (c) 410 km/hr (d) 575 km/hr

Q11. Anil and Binit run 5 km race on a round circle of 400 m. If ratio of their speeds be 5:4, how often does the winner pass the other?

(a ) $4\frac{1}{2}$ times (b) $2\frac{3}{4}$ times (c) $3\frac{1}{2}$ times (d) $2\frac{1}{2}$ times

Q12. A racer starts running with the initial speed of 40 km/min, with its speed increasing every min by 5 km/min. How many hours will it take to cover a distance of 385 km?

(a) 9 min (b) $9\frac{1}{2}$ min (c) $8\frac{1}{2}$min (d) 7 min

Q13. Points R and S are 70 Km apart on a highway. One man starts from R and the other one from S at the same time. If they travel in the same direction, they meet in 7 h. But if they travel towards each other, they meet in one hour. The speeds of the two men are

a) 45 and 25 Km/h b) 70 and 10 Km/h

c) 40 and 30 Km/h d) 60 and 40 Km/h

Q14. Dinesh travel 760 Km to his home by train and by bus. He takes 8 h if he travels 160 Km by the train and the rest by the bus. He takes 12 min more if he travels 240 Km by train and the rest by the bus. The speed of the train and the bus respectively are

a) 80 Km/h, 100 Km/h b) 100 Km/h, 80 Km/h

c) 120 Km/h, 100 Km/h d) 100 Km/h, 120 Km/h

Q15. A train starts from Delhi at 6:00 am and reaches Ambala at 10 am. Another train starts from Ambala at 8 am and reaches Delhi at 11:30 am. If the distance between Delhi and Ambala is 200 km, at what time did the two trains meet each other?

(a) 8:56 am (b) 8:46 am (c) 7:56 am (d) 8:30 am

Q16. Ramesh travels 760 km to his home, partly by bike and partly by car. He takes 8 h, if he travels 160 km by bike and the rest by car. He takes 12 min more, if he travels 240 km by bike and the rest by car. What are the speeds of the bike and the car?

(a) speed of car = 25 km/h, speed of bike = 40 km/h respectively

(b) speed of car = 100 km/h, speed of bike = 80 km/h respectively

(c) speed of car = 80 km/h, speed of bike = 90 km/h respectively

(d) speed of car = 100 km/h, speed of bike = 90 km/h respectively

Q17. A Bus covered a certain distance at a uniform speed. If the bus had been 6 km/h faster, it would have taken 4h less than the scheduled time and if the bus were 6 km/h slower, the bus would have taken 6 h more than the scheduled time. The length of the bus journey is -

(a) 700 km (b) 740 km (c) 720 km (d) 760 km

Q18. Wheels of diameter 7 cm and 14 cm start rolling simultaneously from X and Y, which are 1980 cm apart, towards each other in opposite directions. Both of them make same number of revolutions per second. If both of them meet after 10 s, the speed of the smaller wheel is

(a) 44 cm/s (b) 22 cm/s (c) 66 cm/s (d) 132 cm/s

Q19. In a flight, an airplane was slowed down by bad weather. Due to this, the average speed for the journey was reduced by 100 Km/h and the time increased by one hour. If the total distance travelled by airplane was 3000 km, find the original duration of journey.

a) 5 h b) 6 h c) 4 h d) None of these

Q20. The diameter of a cycle wheel is 70 cm. A cyclist takes 30 h to reach a destination at the speed of 22 Km/h. How many revolutions will the wheel make during this journey?

a) 3 lacs b) 3 lacs c) 4 lacs d) None of these

Q21. Two rockets approach each other, one at 41000 mile/h and the other at 18000 mile/h. They start 3256 miles apart. How far are they a part (in miles) 1 min before impact?

a) 1628 b) 1000 c) 826 d) 1200

Q22. Two cyclists start on a circular track from a given point but in opposite directions with speed of 7 m/s and 8 m/s respectively. If the circumference of the track is 300 m after what time will they meet at the starting point for the first time?

(a) 20 s (b) 100 s (c) 300 s (d) 200 s

Q23. A clock gains 15 min per day. It is set right at 12 night, what time will the clock show at 4:00 pm in the next day?

(a) 4 :10 pm (b) 4 :15 pm (c) 4 :30 pm (d) 5 :00 pm

Q24. During a trip of 80 km, a bus covers first 60 km with a speed of 40 km/h and completes the remaining distance with a speed of 20 km/h. What is the average speed of the bus during the whole tour?

(a) 30 km/h (b) 32 km/h (c) 36 km/h (d) 40 km/h

Q25. If a man travels at 30 km/h, he reaches his destination late by 10 min but if he travels at 42 km/h, then he reaches 10 min earlier. What is the distance travelled by him?

(a) 36 km (b) 35 km (c) 40 km (d) 45 km

Q26. A student rides on a motorcycle at 8 km/h and reaches his college 2.5 min late. The next day he increases his speed to 10 km/h and reaches the college 5 min early. How far is the college from his house?

(a) 1.25 km (b) 8 km (c) 5 km (d) 10 km

Q27. A jet plane can travel at 320 m/h. The wind is blowing at a constant speed of 40 m/h. The total time for a journey against the wind is 135 min. what will be the time in minutes for the return journey with the flow of wind?

(a) 94.5 (b) 105 (c) 108.125 (d) 120

Q28. The jogging track in the sport complex is 726 m in circumference. Mahesh and his father start from the same point and walk in opposite direction at 4.5 Km/h and 3.75 Km/h respectively. When would they meet for the first time?

a) 5.5 min b) 6.0 min c) 5.28 min d) 4.9 min

Q29. There are 20 poles with the constant distance between each pole. Starting from the 1st pole, a car takes 24 s to reach the 12th pole. How much more time will it take to reach the last pole?

a) 25.25 s b) 17.45 s c) 35.74 s d) 41.45 s

Q30. A bus driver travels from the plains to the hill station, which is 200 km apart at an average speed of 40 Km/h. In the return journey, he covers the same distance at an average speed of 20 Km/h. The average speed of the Bus over the entire distance of 400 Km is

a) 16.56 km/h b) 17.89 Km/h c) 26.67 Km/h d) 35 km/h

Q31. A man in a bus notices that he can count 21 electric posts in one minute. If two poles are known to be 50 m apart, then at what speed is the bus travelling?

a) 57 Km/h b) 60 Km/h c) 63 Km/h d) 55 Km/h

Q32. A round running path is 726 m in circumference. Two women start from the same point and walk in opposite direction at the rate of 3.75 Km/h and 4.5 Km/h respectively. When will they meet first time on the track?

a) 5.5 min b) 6.0 min c) 5.28 min c) 4.9 min

Q33. A gun is fired at a distance of 3.32 Km from a man, who hears it 10 s later. Find the speed of the sound.

a) 301 m/s b) 302 m/s c) 332 m/s d) 340 m/s

Q34. X and Y start from the same point and run around a circular stadium, whose circumference is 4200 m, at the rate of 500 m/min by X and 700 m/min by Y in the opposite direction. They will meet each other in

a) 3.5 min b) 6.0 min c) 8.4 min d) 21 min

Q35. It takes eight hours for a 600 Km journey, if 120 Km is done by train and the rest by car. It takes 20 min more, If 200 Km done by train and the rest by car. The ration of the speed of the train to that of the speed of the car is

a) 4 : 3 b) 3 : 4 c) 3 : 2 d) 2 : 3

## Answer Grid:

| Q. No. | 1 | 2 | 3 | 4 | 5 | 6 | 7 | 8 | 9 | 10 | 11 | 12 | 13 | 14 | 15 | 16 | 17 | 18 |
|---|---|---|---|---|---|---|---|---|---|---|---|---|---|---|---|---|---|---|
| Answer | c | c | c | c | b | b | d | b | c | a | d | d | c | a | a | b | c | c |
| Q. No. | 19 | 20 | 21 | 22 | 23 | 24 | 25 | 26 | 27 | 28 | 29 | 30 | 31 | 32 | 33 | 34 | 35 | |
| Answer | a | b | b | c | a | b | b | c | b | c | d | c | b | c | c | a | b | |

## Solutions and Explanations

Q1. Time taken by bike = $\frac{192}{32}$ = 6 hrs and time taken by car = 6 – (2.5 + 0.5) = 3hrs

Ratio of the speed of Bike : car = 3 : 6 = 1 : 2
Hence option (C) is the answer.

Q2. Time taken by 1st cyclist to complete one round = $\frac{300}{7}$ s

Time taken by 2nd cyclist to complete one round = $\frac{300}{8}$ S

Required time = LCM of $\frac{300}{7}$ and $\frac{300}{8}$ =300 s
Hence option (C) is the answer

Q3. Average speed of car = 45 + 50 + 25/ $\frac{45}{15}+\frac{50}{25}+25\times\frac{3}{25}=\frac{120}{3+2+3}$ =15 km/h

Hence option (C) is the answer

Q4. Let the distance travelled at the speed of 50 km/h be x km and (170 – x) km at the speed of 100km/h. Then, $\frac{x}{50}+\frac{170-x}{100}$ = 2x + 170 - x = 200, or x = 30km

Hence option (C) is the answer

Q5. Time taken to cover 25 km = $\frac{25}{40}\text{h}=\frac{5}{8}\text{h}$

Required speed = $\frac{\text{Remaining Distance}}{\text{Remaining Time}}=\frac{46-25}{1-\frac{5}{8}}=\frac{21}{\frac{3}{8}}$ = 56km/h

Hence option (B) is the answer

Q6. Distance travelled = 2 × $\frac{22}{7}$ × 100, Hence the Speed = $\frac{2\times\frac{22}{7}\times100}{2}$ = 314.28 m/min = 314 m/min

Hence option (B) is the answer

Q7. Ratio of speeds = 2:3:4. So, ratio of time taken by the cars respectively = $\frac{1}{2}:\frac{1}{3}:\frac{1}{4}$

= 6 : 4 : 3

Hence option (D) is the answer

Q8. Time taken by Alok for one way = $\frac{\text{6hr 45 min - 2hr}}{2}$ = 2hr 22.5min

Time taken in walking to go one way = 6hr 45min – 2hr 22.5min = 4hr 22.5min

Time taken in walking to go both ways = 2(4hr 22.5min) = 8hr 45min

Hence option (B) is the answer

Q9. When two wheels work together, then the number of rotation of smaller wheel will be more. It means if 27 cogged wheels make one rotation, then 16 cogged wheel will make $\frac{27}{16}$ rotation. Given, 27 cogged wheel make 80 turns in 45 sec.

16 cogged wheel make 80 × $\frac{27}{16}$ turns in 45 sec. In 8 sec, it will make $\frac{80\times27}{45\times16}\times8=24$ turns

Hence option (C) is the answer

Q10. Average speed = $\frac{\text{Total Distance}}{\text{Total Time}}$, Total time = $\frac{2500}{500}+\frac{1200}{400}+\frac{500}{250}$ = 5 + 3 + 2 = 10hr

Average speed = 2500 + 1200 + 500/10 = 420 km/hr

Hence option (A) is the answer

Q11. It is clear from the question that when Anil covers 500 m, Binit covers 400 m ie, Anil takes a lead of 100m in every 500 m of distance. Therefore, Anil lead of 400 m will be taken in travelling a distance of 2000 m or in other words Anil passes Binit every after 2000 m.

Hence total number of such pass = $\frac{5000}{2000}=\frac{5}{2}=2\frac{1}{2}$ times

Hence option (D) is the answer

Q12. We have $\frac{n}{2}$[2 × 40 + (n – 1)5] = 385 or $\frac{n}{2}$(80 + 5n – 5) = 385 or $5n^2$ + 75 – 770 = 0 or N = 7

Hence option (D) is the answer.

Q13. Let the speed of the men be x km/h and y km/h.

Relative speed in same direction = (x – y) km/h. Relative speed in opposite direction = (x + y) km/h.

Now, 70 / (x + y) = 1 x + y = 70 .............(1)

and 70 / (x - y) = 7 x - y = 10 .............(2)

Solving equations (1) and (2), we get x = 40 km/h and y = 30 km/h

Hence option (C) is the answer

Q14. Let the speed of the train be x km/h and of bus be y km/h

Then, 160/x + 600/y=8 ....................(I) 240/x + 520/y = 41/5 ......................(II)

Solving equations (I) and (II), we get x = 80 and y = 100

Hence option (A) is the answer

Q15. Average speed of the train leaving Delhi = $\frac{200}{4}$ = 50km/h

Average speed of the train leaving Ambala = $\frac{200 \times 2}{7} = \frac{400}{7}$ = km/h

By the time the other train starts from Ambala the first train had travelled 100 km

Hence, the trains meet after = $\frac{100}{50+\frac{400}{7}} = \frac{100 \times 7}{750} = \frac{2 \times 7}{15}\text{hr} = \frac{14}{15} \times 60$ = 56 min

Hence, they meet at 8:56 am. Option (A) is the answer

Q16. Let the speed of train be X km/h and the speed of car be Y km/h

Then $\frac{160}{x} + \frac{600}{y} = 8$, ...(1) And $\frac{240}{x} + \frac{520}{y} = \frac{41}{5}$ ...(2)

From equation (1) and (2), X = 80 and Y = 100

Therefore, speed of the train = 80 km/h and Speed of car = 100 km/h

Hence option (B) is the answer

Q17. Let the length of the journey be X km and speed of train be X km/h

Then, $\frac{x}{v+6} = t - 4$ ........(1) And $\frac{x}{v-6} = t + 6$ ....(2) $\frac{x}{v-6} - \frac{x}{v+6} = 10$ ...(3)

Solving equations, we get V = 30 and X = 720 km

Hence option (C) is the answer

Q18. Let no. of revolutions per second be x. Then, $\{2\times\frac{22}{7}\times\frac{7}{2}) + 2\times(\frac{22}{7}\times\frac{14}{2}\}\ 10\times X$

$= 1980\ (22 + 44)10X = 1980$, or, $X = \frac{1980}{66\times10} = 3$

Rate of smaller wheel = $3\times2\times\frac{22}{7}\times\frac{7}{2}\times = 66$ cm/s

Hence option (C) is the answer

Q19. Let the original time taken by the plane is x hours. Then, original speed = $\frac{3000}{x}$ km/h

So, 3000 kms = $\left[\frac{300}{x}-100\right](x+1)$. Solving it, we get, x = 5 hours

Hence option (A) is the answer

Q20. Circumference of the wheel $=2\times\pi\times r = 2\times\pi\times35 = 220$ cm.

Number of revolutions made by the wheel during the journey $= \frac{2200000}{220}\times30 = 3000000$

= 3 lacs. Hence option (B) is the answer

Q21. Relative speed of rocket = 42000 + 18000 = 60000, it means both of them together cover a distance of 60000 mile between then in 60 min or 1000 miles in 1 min.

Hence option (B) is the answer

Q22. Relative speed = (8 – 7) = 1 m/s and distance = 300 m. Hence, time taken to cover this distance = $\frac{300}{1}$ = 300 sec

Hence option (C) is the answer

Q23. The clock gains 15 m in 24hr. Then, in 16 hr it will gain 10 min. Hence, the time shown by this clock will be 4 : 10 am.

Hence option (A) is the answer

Q24. Average speed = Total distance / Total time = 80 / (60 / 40 ) + (20 / 20)
= 80 / 2.5= 32 km/h
Hence option (B) is the answer

Q25. Let the distance be x km. Then, correct time at a speed of 30 km/h = $\frac{x}{30}-\frac{10}{60}$

Correct time at a speed of 42 km/h

$=\frac{x}{42}+\frac{10}{60}$ or $\frac{x}{30}-\frac{10}{60}=\frac{x}{42}+\frac{10}{60}$ or $\frac{x}{30}-\frac{x}{42}=\frac{2}{6}$ or $x=35$ km

Hence option (B) is the answer

Q26. Let the distance be x km. Then, $\frac{x}{8}-\frac{2.5}{60}=\frac{x}{10}+\frac{5}{60}$ or $\frac{x}{8}-\frac{x}{10}=\frac{5}{60}+\frac{2.5}{60}$

Hence, $\frac{2x}{80}=\frac{7.5}{60}$ or $x=\frac{7.5\times 80}{2\times 60}$ = 5 km

Hence option (C) is the answer

Q27. Speed of Jetplane against the wind = (320 – 40) = 280 km/h. Let the distance be x km.

Then, $\frac{135}{60}=\frac{x}{280}$ = 630 km, speed of Jetplane with the wind = (320 + 40) = 360 km/h

Time taken by jetplane with the wind = $\frac{630}{360}$ x 60 min = 105 min

Hence option (B) is the answer

Q28. Let both of them meet after X min. 4500 m are covered by Mahesh in 60 mins. In X min, he will cover $(\frac{4500}{60})$X m. Similarly, In X min Mahesh father will cover $(\frac{3700}{60})$X m

Given, $(\frac{4500}{60})X+(\frac{3700}{60})X=726$ or X = 5.28 mins

Hence option (C) is the answer

Q29. Let the distance between each pole be X m. Then, distance up to 12th pole = 11X m

Speed = $\frac{11x}{22}$ sec, Time to cover total distance up to 20th pole = $\frac{19x \times 24}{11x}$ = 41.45 sec

Hence option (D) is the answer

Q30. Average speed = $\frac{2xy}{x+y}$ where X and Y are two different speeds covering same distance.

Average speed = $\frac{2 \times 40 \times 20}{40+20}$ = 26.67 km/h

Hence option (C) is the answer

Q31. Distance between 21 poles = (21 – 1) × 50 = 1000 m, Speed of Bus = 1km/h = 60 km/h

Hence option (B) is the answer

Q32. Relative speed = (4.5 + 3.75)km/h = 8.25 km/h, Distance = 726m = $\frac{726}{1000}$ = 0.726km

Therefore, Required time = $\frac{0.726}{8.29}$ × 60 = 5.28 mins

Hence option (C) is the answer

Q33. Distance = 3.32 × 1000 = 3320m, Time = 10 sec, speed = $\frac{3320}{10}$ = 332 m/s

Hence option (C) is the answer

Q34. Relative speed = (500 + 700) = 1200 m/min, time taken = $\frac{4200}{1200}$ = 3.5 mins.

Hence option (A) is the answer

Q35. Let the speed of the train be x km/h and car br y km/h.

Then, $\frac{120}{x}+\frac{480}{y}=8$ ...........(1) And $\frac{200}{x}+\frac{400}{y}=\frac{25}{3}$ ...........(2)

From eqns (1), 120 y + 480 x = 8 xy. Using equations (2), 200 y + 400 x = $\frac{25}{3}$ xy

Hence, $\frac{120y+480x}{8}=3\frac{200y+400x}{25}$ or 15y + 60x = 24y + 48x or 12x = 9y

or $\frac{x}{y}=\frac{3}{4}$

Hence option (B) is the answer

# 13 Equation

## Opening Puzzle:

A girl leaves home with x flowers to offer equal number of flowers in two different temples. Before offering the flowers to the deity at the first temple, she dips all the flowers to the nearby pond which doubles the number of flowers. She offers a part of these to the deity in the 1st temple and dips the remaining flower in the river making it double the existing number of flowers again. She offers the remaining flowers to the deity in the second temple. After offering the flowers, she does not have any flower left with her. If she leaves home with 12 flowers, how many flowers did she offer at each of the temples?

An equation equates two quantities. It is represented by the symbol '='. **Generally**, on the left hand side of the equation, there will be variable/s and on the right hand side will be numbers. Through an equation, we find the value of those variable/s.

## Equation in One variable:

If on the left hand side, there is only one variable, then it is known as equation in one variable.

For example, $2x + 3 = 5$ .....(1)

## Equation in Two variables:

If on the left hand side, there are two variables, then it is known as equation in two variables.

For example, $2x + 3y = 10$ .....(2)

To get the unique value of the variables involved in an equation, number of equations should be equal to the number of variables.

For example, we can get the unique value of x in equation (1), but in equation (2) we do not get the unique values of x and y because there is only one equation given.

[Note from authors: However it should be noted that two equations in case of two variables does not always guarantee the unique solution.

Consider the examples given below:

| | Case 1 | Case 2 | Case 3 |
|---|---|---|---|
| Equation 1 | $2x + 3y = 10$ | $2x + 3y = 10$ | $2x + 3y = 10$ |
| Equation 2 | $4x + 6y = 20$ | $4x + 6y = 15$ | $4x + 5y = 20$ |
| Remarks | Both the equations are same | Data Inconsistent | Different equations |
| Number of solutions | Infinite | Zero | Unique |
| Graphical Meaning | Same line | Parallel Lines | Intersecting Lines |

It can be seen that we'll get unique solution only if co-efficient of x and co-efficient of y are not in the same ratio, irrespective of the value of constant term.]

## Degree of an equation:

Highest power of the variable is known as degree of an equation.

For examples,

Degree of equation $5x^2 + 3 = 10$ is 2 because highest power of variable $x = 2$.

Degree of equation $3x^2 - 4x^3 + 2 = 10$ is 3 because highest power of variable $x = 3$.

[Degree of an equation = Number of values of variable that will satisfy the equation.]

## For example:

$2x + 3 = 5$ has degree of equation = 1, and hence there will be only one value of x that will satisfy this equation.

$x^2 + 9 = 13$ has degree of equation = 2, and hence there will be two values of x that will satisfy this equation.

$X^3 + 2x^2 + 1 = 15$ has degree of equation = 3, and hence there will be three values of x that will satisfy this equation.

Note from authors: When we say number of value/s of variable that will satisfy the equation, those values can be same or distinct. For example, look at the equation $x^2 - 4x + 4 = 0$. For this equation, there are two values of $x = 2, 2$ that will satisfy this equation. If question is asked that how many solutions of x is/are there, our answer will be two. However if it is asked that how many **distinct** solutions of x is/are there, our answer will be one.

## Format of Linear equation:

(1) $ax + bx + c = 0$, where a, b and c are real numbers and 'a' & 'b' are not both zero is called a linear equation in two variables 'x' & 'y'

(2) $y = mx + c$, where 'm' and 'c' are constants. These equations are called linear equation because the set of solutions of such an equation forms a straight line. In this equation constant 'm' denotes the slope of the line and the constant 'c' determines the point at which the line crosses the y-axis.

## Format of Quadratic Equation:

$ax^2 + bx + c = 0$ is the standard quadratic equation. There will be two roots / values of x that will satisfy this equation.

## Properties of Roots:

(a) Complex roots or irrational roots always occur in pair.
For example: If $3 + \sqrt{5}$ is one root of a quadratic equation, then $3 - \sqrt{5}$ will be the other root of that equation.

(b) Any equation whose sum of all of the coefficients = 0, will have 1 as its one of the roots.
For example, $x^2 - 3x + 2 = 0$ will have 1 as one of its roots.

## Nature of roots of a Quadratic Equation:

Assuming that $\alpha$ and $\beta$ are the roots of this equation.

Then $\alpha = \dfrac{-b + \sqrt{b^2 - 4ac}}{2a}$ and $\beta = \dfrac{-b - \sqrt{b^2 - 4ac}}{2a}$

Nature of roots depends upon the value of $b^2 - 4ac$ = **Discriminant(D)** of the quadratic equation $ax^2 + bx + c = 0$.

If D = 0

- Roots are real
- Roots are equal

If D > 0

- Roots are real
- Roots are un-equal

If D < 0

- Roots are not real

If D is a perfect square (including D = 0) and a, b and c are rational, then roots will be rational.

## Quadratic Equation

$f(x) = ax^2 + bx + c = 0$

Assume that the roots are $\alpha$ and $\beta$.

$$\alpha + \beta = -\frac{b}{a}$$

$$\alpha\beta = \frac{c}{a}$$

## Worked Out Examples:

Q1. Four times the salary of Ramesh is equal to Rs. 5000. How much is Ramesh's salary?

**Solution:** Assume that the salary of Ramesh by 'Rs. x'.

Now the situation can be represented by following linear equation:

$4x = 5000$

Or x=1250. Hence Ramesh's salary is Rs. 1250.

Q2. Sum of two numbers is 16 and their difference is 10. Find the numbers.

**Solution:** let the two numbers be x and y respectively,

Then according to situation: $x + y = 16$........ (1)

$x - y = 10$..........(2)

Adding equation (1) and equation (2), we get $2x = 26 \Rightarrow x = 13$.

Putting the value of x in equation (1), we get $y = 3$.

Hence the numbers are 13, 3.

Q3. Mahesh bought 2 mangoes and 3 oranges for Rs. 28. Pankaj bought 4 mangoes and 5 oranges for Rs. 50. What is the price of 1 mango and 1 orange?

**Solution:** Let price of one mango be Rs. x Rs and that of one orange be Rs. y.

According to the question, equation becomes:

$2x + 3y = 28$ ———(1)

$4x + 5y = 50$ ———(2)

Multiply equation (1) by 2 and subtract equation (2) from it:

Equation (1) $\times$ 2 will give $4x + 6y = 56$ ———(3)

Subtracting equation (2) from equation (3) gives us: y = Rs. 6 and x = Rs. 5.

Hence price of one mango = Rs. 5 and price of one orange = Rs. 6.

Q4. Haresh and Mahesh together have 25 toys. Both of them lost 7 toys each and the product of the number of toys they now have is 130. How many toys each of them had in the beginning?

**Solution:** Let the number of toys with Haresh = x, then the number of toys with Mahesh = (25 – x)

The number of toys left with Haresh after he lost 7 toys = (x – 7)

The number of toys left with Mahesh after he lost 7 toys = 25 – x – 7 = 18 – x

According to the question, $(x - 7)(18 - x) = 130$

Or, $-x^2 + 18x + 7x - 126 = 130$ ,or, $-x^2 + 25x - 126 = 130$

Finally, we obtain the equation $-x^2 + 25x - 256 = 0$, or, $x^2 - 25x + 256 = 0$

Factorizing it, we obtain, $(x - 12)(x - 13) = 0 \Rightarrow x = 12$ or 13.

So, if Haresh had 12 toys, then Mahesh had 13 toys and if Haresh had 13 toys, then Mahesh had 12 toys.

Q5. Find the roots of the equation $2x^2 - 5x + 3 = 0$

**Solution:** Middle term of the equation = – 5x which can be broken as –2x and –3x as $(-2x) \times (-3x) = 6x^2 = 2x^2 \times 3$.

Or, $2x^2 - 5x + 3 = 2x^2 - 2x - 3x + 3 = 2x(x - 1) - 3(x - 1) = (2x - 3)(x - 1)$

Now it can be rewritten as $(2x - 3)(x - 1) = 0$.

Hence values of x are: $x = \frac{3}{2}$ or $x = 1$.

Q6. What is the sum of the roots of the quadratic equation $2x^2 + 5x - 3 = 0$?

**Solution:** Sum of roots of the equation $ax^2 + bx + c = 0$ is $\frac{-b}{a}$.

Hence sum of roots of the equation $2x^2 + 5x - 3 = 0$ is $\frac{-5}{2}$.

Q7. What is the product of the roots of the quadratic equation $2x^2 + 5x - 3 = 0$?

**Solution:** Product of roots of the equation $ax^2 + bx + c = 0$ is $\frac{c}{a}$.

Hence product of roots of the equation $2x^2 + 5x - 3 = 0$ is $\frac{-3}{2}$.

Q8. For what minimum value of p, will the quadratic equation $x^2 - px + 9 = 0$ have real roots?

**Solution:** Discriminant = $b^2 - 4ac = p^2 - 4 \times 1 \times 9 = p^2 - 36$

For roots to be real, Discriminant $\geq 0$.

Or, $p^2 - 36 \geq 0$, or, $p^2 \geq 36$. Hence $p \geq 6$. Hence minimum value of p = 6.

Solution to the opening puzzle:

Assume number of flowers offered by her at each of the temples = x

After she has dipped the number of flowers to the deity at the 1st temple, remaining number of flowers with her = 12 – x. She dips these flowers in the pond making it double = 2(12-x).

Now, she offers x flowers to the deity in the second temple, and this leaves her with no flower.

Hence 2(12-x) – x = 0, or, 24 – 2x – x = 0, or, 24 – 3x = 0. Hence x = 8. So, she offered 8 flowers at each of the temples.

## Formation of quadratic equation from its Roots:

If roots of a quadratic equation are $\alpha$ and $\beta$, then there can be infinite such quadratic equations.

In general, we have the following equation $a(x - \alpha)(x - \beta) = 0$, where a is the co-efficient of $x^2$.

### Practice Exercise

Q1. Amit has Rs. 5 more than Vinit. Which of the following equations correctly depicts this statement?

(a) Sum with Amit = Rs. 5 + Sum with Vinit

(b) Sum with Amit + Rs. 5 = Sum with Vinit

(c) Sum with Amit = Rs. 5 × Sum with Vinit

(d) None of these

Q2. Three times of a number x is 6 less than twice a number y. Which of the following equations correctly depicts this statement?

(a) 3x - 6 = 2y (b) 3x + 6 = 2y (c) 3x = 2y + 6 (d) None of these

Q3. Anam earns Rs. n daily and spends Rs. m daily (where n > m). She wants to save Rs. y in some days. Which of the following options rightly depicts the number of days required by Anam to save Rs. y?

(a) $\frac{n-m}{y}$ (b) $\frac{y}{n-m}$ (c) $\frac{m-n}{y}$ (d) $\frac{y}{m-n}$

Q4. Price of 3 chairs and 5 tables is Rs. 2520 and price of 4 chairs and 3 tables is Rs. 2040. What is the price of one table?

(a) Rs. 240 (b) Rs. 300 (c) Rs. 360 (d) Rs. 380

Q5. Given that $x - y = 4$. Which of the following statements is definitely true?

(a) If x is a positive number, then y is also a positive number.

(b) If x is a negative number, then y is also a negative number.

(c ) If x is a negative number, then y is a positive number.

(d) If x is a positive number, then y is a negative number.

Q6. I have some Rupees with me. If I buy 14 candies with this money, shopkeeper will return me Rs. 2. However, if I had Rs. 5 more, I could have bought 15 candies. What is the price of one candy?

(a) Rs. 6 (b) Rs. 7

(c) Rs. 8 (d) cannot be determined

Q7. In previous question, how much money do I have?

(a) Rs. 90 (b) Rs. 100

(c) Rs. 105 (d) cannot be determined

Q8. I can buy 5 apples and 3 bananas and 6 oranges for Rs. 40. My friend Vijay can buy 2 apples and 4 bananas and 1 orange for Rs. 30. How much is required to be paid for 4 apples, 4 bananas and 4 oranges?

(a) Rs. 20 (b) Rs. 30

(c) Rs. 40 (d) cannot be determined

Q9. Samar, a baby boy, says that his father's age now is equal to the square of his age. Though, three years back, his father's age was 11 times of baby Samar's age. What is the present age of baby Samar?

(a) 5 years (b) 6 years

(c) either 5 years or 6 years (d) None of these

Q10. Which of the following quadratic equations will NOT have real roots?

(a) $x^2 + 5x + 8 = 0$ (b) $2x^2 - 5x + 3 = 0$

(c) $x^2 + 7x - 8 = 0$ (d) $3x^2 + 5x - 8 = 0$

Q11. What is the sum of roots of the quadratic equation $2x^2 + 14x - 8 = 0$?

(a) 5 (b) 7 (c) -5 (d) -7

Q12. What is the product of roots of the quadratic equation $3x^2 + 5x - 16 = 0$?

(a) $\frac{5}{3}$ (b) $\frac{16}{3}$ (c) $\frac{-5}{3}$ (d) $\frac{-16}{3}$

Q13. Roots of a quadratic equation $ax^2 + bx + c = 0$ are 2 and 5. What is the value of a + b + c?

(a) 5 (b) 4

(c) -5 (d) cannot be determined

Q14. One root of a quadratic equation is $2 + \sqrt{3}$. What is other root of this quadratic equation?

(a) $2 + \sqrt{3}$ (b) $2 - \sqrt{3}$ (c) 2 (d) None of these

Q15. A quadratic equation $2x^2 - 5x + p = 0$ has one of its roots as 1. What is the value of p?

(a) 3 (b) 2 (c) 5 (d) 1

Q16. Sum of three whole numbers taken in pairs are 12, 17, and 19. What is the middle number?

(a) 4 (b) 5 (c) 6 (d) 7

Q17. What is the remainder when $f(x) = 2x^3 + 3x^2 - 4x - 2$ is divided by $(x - 2)$?

(a) 22 (b) 20 (c) 16 (d)18

Q18. Five bananas, three apples and one mango cost Rs. 20 whereas two bananas, four apples and six mangoes cost Rs. 15. What is the price of two bananas, two apples and two mangoes?

(a) Rs. 10 (b) Rs.15

(c) Rs. 20 (d) cannot be determined

Q19. Tom, Dorothy, and Sammy went on a vacation and agreed to split the costs evenly. During their trip Tom paid Rs. 105, Dorothy paid Rs. 125, and Sammy paid Rs. 175. In order to share the costs equally, Tom gave Sammy Rs. t, and Dorothy gave Sammy Rs. d. What is the value of (t-d)?

(a) 15 (b) 20 (c) 25 (d) 30

Q20. Sum of the squares of marbles the three children have is 600 and the sum of products taken two at a time of marbles is 150. Then what is the sum of all the three numbers?

(a) 30 (b) 35 (c) 40 (d) 45

## Answer Grid:

| Q. No. | 1 | 2 | 3 | 4 | 5 | 6 | 7 | 8 | 9 | 10 |
|---|---|---|---|---|---|---|---|---|---|---|
| Answer | a | b | b | c | b | b | b | c | d | a |
| Q. No. | 11 | 12 | 13 | 14 | 15 | 16 | 17 | 18 | 19 | 20 |
| Answer | d | b | d | b | a | d | d | a | b | a |

## Solution and Explanation:

Q3. Anam's daily saving = Income – expenditure = Rs. n – Rs. m

To save Rs. y, she would take $\frac{y}{n-m}$ days. Hence option (b) is the answer.

Q4. Assume price of one chair = Rs. x and price of one table = Rs. y

According to the question,

$3x + 5y$ = Rs. 2520 ——————(1)

$4x + 3y$ = Rs. 2040 ——————(2)

To solve these equations, multiply equation (1) by 4 and equation (2) by 3:

$12x + 20y$ = Rs. 10080 ——————(3)

$12x + 9y$ = Rs. 6120 ——————(4)

Subtracting equation (4) from equation (3):

$11y$ = Rs. 3960. Hence y = Rs. 360. Hence option (c ) is the answer.

Q5. Except option (b), none of the options are definitely true. Options (a) and (d) are probably true. Option (c) is definitely false. Hence option (b) is the answer.

Q6. Assume that the price of one candy = Rs. x

So, $14x + 2 = 15x - 5$ Þ x = Rs. 7. Hence option (b) is the answer.

Q7. Price of one candy = Rs. 7. Hence sum of money with me = $14x + 2$ = Rs. 100. Hence option (b) is the answer.

Q8. According to the question,

5 apples + 3 bananas + 6 oranges = Rs. 40

2 apples + 4 bananas + 1 orange = Rs. 30

Adding both the equations, we get 7 apples + 7 bananas + 7 oranges = Rs. 70

Hence 1 apple + 1 banana + 1 orange = Rs. 10

So, price of 4 apples, 4 bananas and 4 oranges = Rs. $10 \times 4$ = Rs. 40. Hence option (c) is the answer.

Q9. Assume baby Samar's present age = x years. So his father's age = $x^2$

Three years back, baby Samar's age = $(x - 3)$ years and his father's age = $(x^2 - 3)$ years

According to the question, $(x^2 - 3) = 11 \times (x - 3)$

Or, $(x^2 - 3) = 11x - 33$, or, $x^2 - 11x + 30 = 0$, or, $x^2 - 6x - 5x - 30 = 0$

Hence $(x - 5)(x - 6) = 0$

Hence baby Samar's age now could be either 5 years or 6 years. Hence option (c) is the answer.

**Note from Authors :** In our opinion, best way to solve such questions is by going through the options.

Q10. Except option (a), all the other options have Discriminant > 0. Hence only option (a) will NOT have real roots. Hence option (a) is the answer.

Q11. Sum of roots of the equation $ax^2 + bx + c = 0$ is $\frac{-b}{a}$.

Hence sum of roots of the equation $2x^2 + 14x - 8 = 0$ is $\frac{-14}{2} = -7$. Hence option (d) is the answer.

Q12. Product of roots of the equation $ax^2 + bx + c = 0$ is $\frac{c}{a}$.

Hence product of roots of the equation $3x^2 + 5x - 16 = 0$ is $\frac{16}{3}$. Hence option (b) is the answer.

Q13. If roots of a quadratic equation are $\alpha$ and $\beta$, then there can be infinite such quadratic equations.

In general, we have the following equation $a(x - \alpha)(x - \beta) = 0$, where a is the co-efficient of $x^2$.

In this case, we do not have the value of a, hence option (d) cannot be determined is the answer.

Note from authors : $(x - 2)(x - 5) = 0 \Rightarrow x^2 - 7x + 10 = 0$ is only one such equation. There can be infinite such equations with the roots as 2 and 5. For example, $2x^2 - 14x + 20 = 0$ is another such equation. You may observe that value of (a + b + c) will be different in this case.

Q14. Irrational roots always occur in conjugate pairs. Since $2 + \sqrt{3}$ is one root, other root will be $2 - \sqrt{3}$ Hence option (b) is the answer.

Q15. For '1' to be root of any quadratic equation, sum of co-efficient should be equal to 0.

In this question, co-efficient of $x^2 = 2$, co-efficient of $x = -5$, and constant term = p

So, $2 - 5 + p = 0$. Hence $p = 3$. Hence option (a) is the answer.

Q16. Let the three numbers be equal to a, b, and c. We can now write three equations:

$a + b = 12$

$b + c = 17$

$a + c = 19$

Adding these equations together, we get that $2(a + b + c) = 48 \Rightarrow a + b + c = 24$

Substituting the original equations into this one, we find

$c + 12 = 24$

$a + 17 = 24$

$b + 19 = 24$

Hence, our numbers are 12, 7, and 5. The middle number is 7. Hence option (d) is the answer.

Q17. When f(x) is divided by g(x), remainder is obtained by putting the value of x obtained by g(x) = 0.

In this question, $f(x) = 2x^3 + 3x^2 - 4x - 2$ is divided by $(x - 2)$

Step 1 : we will put $x - 2 = 0$. So, $x = 2$

Step 2 : Now we'll put x = 2 in $f(x) = 2x^3 + 3x^2 - 4x - 2 = 2 \cdot 2^3 + 3 \times 2^2 - 4 \times 2 - 2 = 18$. Hence option (d) is the answer.

In normal cases, we know that if there are three variables, then we need three equations to find out the value of individual variables. In this question, you are not supposed to find out the value of individual variables.

Q18. Let us frame the equations:

(5 bananas + 3 apples + 1 mango) = Rs. 20 ——————(1)

(2 bananas + 4 apples + 6 mango) = Rs. 15 ——————(2)

Adding both the equations, we get :

(7 bananas + 7 apples + 7 mango) = Rs. 35

Hence (1 banana + 1 apple + 1 mango) = Rs. 5.

Hence price of (2 bananas + 2 apples + 2 mangoes) = Rs. 5 × 2 = Rs. 10. Hence option (a) is the answer.

Q19. Add up the amounts that Tom, Dorothy, and Sammy paid to get Rs. 405, and divide by 3 to get Rs. 135, the amount that each should have paid.

Tom, having paid Rs. 105, owes Sammy Rs. 30, and Dorothy, having paid Rs.125, owes Sammy Rs. 10. Thus, t-d = 30 – 10 = 20. Hence option (b) is the answer.

Q20. This question is the simple application of the following formula:

$(a + b + c)^2 = (a^2 + b^2 + c^2) + 2(ac + bc + ab)$

Assume that the number of marbles with the children are a, b and c.

Using the formula given above:

$(a + b + c)^2 = (600) + 2(150) = 900$

Hence $(a + b + c) = 30$. Hence option (a) is the answer.

# 14 Permutations and Combinations

## Meaning of Permutation and Combination

Dictionary meaning of the words Permutation and Combination are as follows:- Permutation is the number of ways in which a set or number of things can be ordered or arranged and Combination means the number of ways in which a group of things can be chosen from a larger group without giving regard to their arrangement.

For example, consider the following statements:

***My fruit salad is made up of "apples, oranges and bananas" We can observe that*** We don't care what order the fruits are in, they could also be "bananas, oranges and apples" or "oranges, apples and bananas", it is the same fruit salad. Here order of occurrence of elements does not matter.

**It is Combination.**

***My bank locker's password is 317"***. Now we **do** care about the order. "713" or "137" would not workIt has to be exactly **3-1-7. Here order or occurrence of elements is significant.**

**It is Permutation.**

Look at the following picture of a combination lock as an example of permutation:

Let us go through another example:

Suppose there are four different batsmen A, B, C and D. And we have to select a group of three batsmen out of these four batsmen. Now, we can select any combination of three batsmen so that no set of batsmen has all the three batsmen same. These set of batsmen will be – ABC, BCD, ABD, ACD. This is a case of combination as for every set of selection of three batsmen, order of selection does not play any role (i.e. we can select anybody first or second or third and it creates no difference in the final selection as well as the total no. of selection).

Now, if we try to define their batting order also, i.e. who bats first and 2[nd] and so on, then corresponding to every selection of a set of three batsmen, we will have six different arrangements of their batting. It can be seen below that corresponding to selection of ABC as a team, following is the list of different batting orders:

ABC, ACB, BAC, BCA, CAB, CBA.

**Now it is a case of permutation since order of occurrence has become important.**

Since there are four different ways of selecting a group of three batsmen and every selection can be arranged in 6 different ways, so total no. of ways of arranging 3 batsmen(or, distinct things) out of 4 batsmen(or, distinct things) = $4 \times 6 = 24$ ways.

Consider the examples of hand shake and Gifts exchange to understand Permutation and Combination better: Assume that there are 20 persons in a party and everybody shakes hand with each other and presents a gift also.

Now if we take a case of two persons A and B, then the event of shaking hand between them is a case of Combination because when A shakes hand with B or B shakes hand with A, the number of hand shake is just one. So, we can say that order of occurrence is not important and hence it is a case of Combination.

Similarly, event of presenting the gift is a case of Permutation because gift given to B by A and gift given to A by B are two different gifts. So, the order of case plays a role here and hence it is a case of Permutation.

## Standard Meanings and Definitions:

(a) n! =Product of all the natural numbers from n to 1 = $n(n-1)(n-2)(n-3)\ldots\times 3\times 2\times 1$.

(b) $0! = 1$

***Note*** – Factorials are defined only for whole numbers, and not for negative numbers or fractions.

## Fundamental principle of Counting: Two basic theorem

1. **Multiplication theorem** – If there are two jobs in such a way that one of them can be done in *m* ways and when it is completed in any of the ways out of *m* ways, second job can be completed in *n* ways, then the whole job can be done in $m \times n$.
2. **Addition theorem** – If there are two jobs in such a way that one of them can be done in *m* ways and second one can be done in *n* ways independently, then either of the jobs can be done in $(m + n)$ ways.

   Basically, there's one point where these two theorems differ. –in multiplication the job does not get completed while in addition it gets completed. In layman's language, we multiply the no. of ways when job has not been completed and we add the no. of ways when jobs have been completed.

## Permutations

As we have seen, each of the arrangements that can be made by taking some or all elements out of a number of things is called a Permutation. Permutation implies "arrangement" or that" order of the things" is important.

The permutations of three things a. b and c taken two at a time are ab, ba, ac, ca, cb and bc. Since the order in which the things are taken is important, ab and ba are counted as two different arrangements.

The number of permutations of n things taking r at a time is denoted by $^nP_r$.

## Combinations

As we have seen, each of the groups or selections which can be made by taking some or all out of a number of things is called a Combination. In combinations, the order in which the things are taken is not important.

The combination of three things a, b and c taken two at a time are ab, bc and ca. Here, ab and ba are same because the order in which a and b are taken is not important. What is required is only a combination including a and b. The words "combination" and "selection" can be used without any differentiation.

The number of combinations of n things taking r at a time is denoted by $^nC_r$.

## Meaning and derivation of $^nP_r$ and $^nC_r$

**Number of Permutations of n different things taken r at a time = $^nP_r$**

In this statement, we are doing following two assumptions:

- All the n things are distinct or distinct (or no two things are of the same type)
- each thing is used at most once(i.e.,no thing being repeated in any arrangement)

The number of arrangements of n distinct things taken r things at a time is ${}^nP_r = \frac{n!}{(n-r)!}$

If we take n things at a time, then we get ${}^nP_n$. From a discussion similar to that we had for filling the r boxes above. We can find that ${}^nP_n$ is equal to n! The first box can be filled in n ways, the second one in (n – 1) ways, the third one in (n – 2) ways and so on, then the n[th] box in 1 way; hence, all the n boxes can be filled in ${}^nP_n = n!$

But if we substitute r = n in the formula for ${}^nP_n$ then we get ${}^nP_n = \frac{n!}{0!}$; since we already found that ${}^nP_n = n!$

## We can conclude that 0! = 1

Number of combinations of n distinct things taken r at a time = ${}^nC_r$ and ${}^nC_r = \frac{n!}{(n-r)!} \times \frac{1}{r!}$

**It can also be deduced from here that the number of selections of n distinct things taken all at a time will be equal to 1(Since there is only one way in which all the articles can be selected)**

Alternatively ${}^nC_n = \frac{n!}{0! \times n!} = 1$

Out of n things kept in a bag, if we select r things and remove them from the bag, we are left with (n - 1) things inside the bag – that is, whenever r things are selected out of n things, we automatically have another selection of the (n - 1) things. Hence, the number of ways of making combinations taking r out of n things is the same as selecting (n - r) things out of n given things, i.e., ${}^nC_r = {}^nC_{n-r}$

**Before we move ahead, lets make it clear once again that whenever we are using ${}^nC_r$ and ${}^nP_r$, our assumption is that all the things are distinct i.e. no two of them are same.**

**e.g.1.** A team of 5 players is required to be chosen out of 10 players. In how many ways this can be done?

**Solution** - Number of ways 5 players can be chosen from 10 players = ${}^{10}C_5$.

**e.g.2.** A teacher has 6 students in his class. He takes 3 of them to the museum at a time as often as he can, but he does not take the same three children to the museum more than once. How many times the teacher will be required to go to museum?

1. 10 2. 20 3. 90 4. 40

**Solution** - Number of times (read ways) 3 children(read distinct things) can be selected from 5 children(read distinct things) = ${}^6C_3$. So, he will be required to go ${}^6C_3$ times = 20.

**e.g.3.** A team of total 5 players is required to be chosen out of 10 players including the captain who has to be chosen certainly. In how many ways remaining players can be chosen?

**Solution** – Since captain has to be chosen, we are required to select 4 players out of 9 players.

Number of ways 4 players can be chosen from 9 players = ${}^9C_{4.}$

**e.g.4.** A team of 5 players is required to be chosen out of 10 players. However, there are two players A and B who do not gel well, and do not agree to be in the same time at the same time. In how many ways this can be done?

**Solution** – Our solution in this question is = Total number of cases without any condition – Number of cases where both the players A and B have been chosen.

Total number of cases without any condition = ${}^{10}C_5$

Number of cases where both the players A and B have been chosen = ${}^8C_3$ [we are required to select only three players out of remaining 8 players because both the players A and B have already been chosen]

So, number of ways it can be done as per the condition in the question = ${}^{10}C_5 - {}^8C_3$

**e.g.5.** In a party, where everybody shakes hand with everybody else, total number of handshake = 66. How many people are there at the party?

**Solution** – Total number of handshake = $\dfrac{n(n-1)}{2}$ = 66, hence n = 12.

**e.g.6.** In a chess competition involving some boys and girls of a school, every student had to play exactly one game with every other student. It was found that in 45 games both the players were girls, and in 190 games both were boys. The number of games in which one player was a boy and the other was a girl is:

1. 200 2. 216 3. 235 4. 256

**Solution**–Lettherebemboysandngirls.$^{n}C_2 = 45 = \dfrac{n(n-1)}{2} \Rightarrow n(n-1) = 90 \Rightarrow n = 10$

$$^{m}C_2 = 190 \Rightarrow \frac{m(m-1)}{2} = 190 \Rightarrow m(m-1) = 380 \Rightarrow m = 20$$

Number of games between one boy and one girl = 10 × 20 = 200. Hence option (1) is the answer.

e.g.7. In how many ways can three persons be seated on five chairs?

**Solution** – This question is a very fundamental problem of arrangements without repetition. The first person can seat in 5 ways (into any of the five chairs), the second person can take place in 4 ways (into any of the remaining 4 chairs) and the third person can seat in 3 ways.

So, total number of ways in which these 3 persons can arrange themselves on 5 chairs is $5 \times 4 \times 3 = 60$.

## Circular Permutation

When n distinct things are to be arranged in a straight line, we can do this in n! ways. However, if these n things are arranged in a circular manner, then the number of arrangements will **NOT** be n!.

Let us understand this:

Number of ways A, B and C can be arranged in a straight line = 3! = 6

The possible arrangements are – ABC, ACB, BAC, BCA, CAB, CBA

Now arrange these three people A, B and C in a circle –

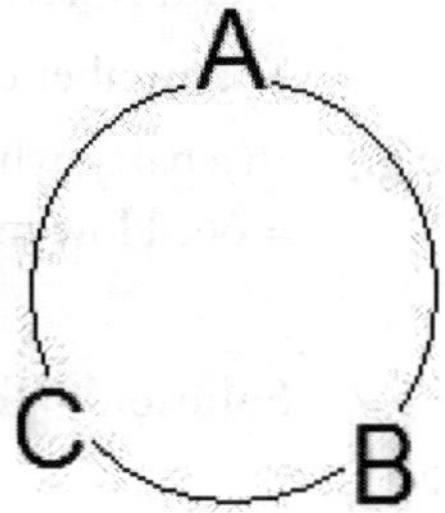


What we can observe here is that arrangements ABC, BCA and CAB are same. And similarly arrangements ACB, CBA and BAC are same. So, there are only two permutations in this case of circular permutation. To derive the formula for Circular Permutation, We first fix the position of one thing. Then the remaining (n - 1) things can be arranged in (n - 1)! ways.

**Hence, the number of ways in which n distinct things can be arranged in a circular arrangement is (n – 1)!**

1. **Fundamental Principle of counting:**
   (a) Multiplication rule: If a work is done only when all of a number of works are done, then number of ways of doing that work is equal to the product of number of ways of doing separate works.
   (b) Addition rule: If a work is done only when any one of a number of works is done, then number of ways of doing that work is equal to the sum of number of ways of doing separate works.
   Thus if a work is done when exactly one of a member of works is done, then number of ways of doing this work = sum of number of ways of doing all the works.
2. If ${}^nC_x = {}^nC_y$ then either x = y or x + y = n.

3. $\lfloor n = 1.2.3...n;\ \lfloor 0 = 1$

4. (a) Number of permutation of n different articles taken r at a time is denoted by

$$^{n}P_{r} \text{ and } ^{n}P_{r} = \frac{\lfloor n}{\lfloor n-r}$$

(b) Number of permutations of n different articles taking all at a time = $\lfloor n$.

(c) Number of permutations of N articles, out of which P are alike and are of one type, Q are alike and are of second type and rest are all different = $\frac{N!}{P!Q!}$.

5. Number of permutations (arrangements) of n different articles taking r at a time when articles can be repeated any number of times = n × n × … r times = $n^r$.

6. Circular permutations:
Number of circular permutations (arrangements) of n different articles = $\lfloor n-1$.

7. Number or combinations of n different articles taken r at a time is denoted by

$$^{n}C_{r} \text{ and } ^{n}C_{r} = \frac{\lfloor n}{\lfloor r \lfloor n-r}.$$

8. Number of selections of r articles (r ≤ n) out of n identical articles is 1.

9. Total number of selections of zero or more articles from n distinct articles = $^{n}C_{0} + ^{n}C_{1} + ^{n}C_{2} + ... ^{n}C_{n} = 2^{n}$.

10. Total number of selections of zero or more articles from n identical articles = 1 + 1 + 1 +… to (n + 1) terms = n + 1.

11. Number of ways of distributing n identical articles among r persons when each person may get any number of articles = $^{n+r-1}C_{r-1}$

12. Number of ways of dividing m + n different articles in two groups containing m and n articles respectively $(m \neq n) = ^{m+n}C_{n} \times ^{m}C_{m} = \frac{\lfloor m+n}{\lfloor m \lfloor n}$

13. Number of ways of dividing 2m different articles each containing m articles $= \frac{\lfloor 2m}{\lfloor m \lfloor m \lfloor 2}$

14. $^{n}C_{r-1} + ^{n}C_{r} = ^{n+1}C_{r}$

15. Number of diagonals in an n-sided regular polygon = $^{n}C_{2} - n = n(n-3)/2$

16. Maximum number of point of intersection among n lines = $^{n}C_{2}$

## Some Standard Formats of Questions:

**Word Formation –**

Order of occurrence of letters decide the formation of words. For example, word "WON" and word "NOW" are two different words. Hence Word Formation is one standard example of Permutation.

## Rules –

(a) Number of arrangements of n letters when all the n letters are distinct = n!

(b) Number of arrangements of n letters out of which m letters are alike and remaining all are distinct = $\frac{n!}{m!}$

Let us understand with the help of some examples:

**e.g.8.** How many words can be formed using the letters of the word 'DELHI'?

**Solution** – Total number of letters = 5, and each one is a distinct letter.

Hence total number of words that can be formed using the letters of the word 'DELHI' = 5! = 120

**e.g.9.** How many new words can be formed using the letters of the word 'DELHI'?

**Solution** – Total number of letters = 5, and each one is a distinct letter.

Hence total number of words that can be formed using the letters of the word 'DELHI' = 5! = 120

Since question is asking for new words, we'll subtract 'DELHI' from the list of words.

Hence total number of new words = 120 – 1 = 119.

**e.g.10.** How many words can be formed with the word 'LUCKNOW' which will have

(i) No restriction.

(ii) L is the $1^{st}$ letter of the word.

(iii) All the vowels are together

(iv) Vowels are at even places.

(v) L always occurs before U

**Solution –**

(i) Total number of distinct letters = 7 (L, U, C, K, N, O, W)

So, total number of words that can be formed = 7!

(ii) Now we can arrange only 6 letters(As place of L is restricted),

So, total number of words that can be formed = 6!

(iii) U and O should be together, so we will assume these two letters to be tied up with each other.

Now we have 6 distinct things to be arranged - (L, UO, C, K, N, W)

So, number of arrangements = 6!

But place of U and O can be interchanged between themselves.

So, total number of words that can be formed = 5! × 2!

(iv) Total number of even places can be seen below:

— — — — — — —
2nd 4th 6th

Out of these three places, we'll have to choose two places for vowels namely U and O, and then arrange the same.

This can be done in 3P2 ways. Remaining 5 places can be used by remaining 5 letters. Total arrangement of 5 letters at 5 places = 5!

Hence total number of ways = 3P2 × 5! = 360.

So, total number of words that can be formed = 7!/2

(v) There are six possible arrangements (3!) corresponding to L, U and W. However only one out of these six will be in the prescribed order: L always occurs before U and U always occurs before W.

So, corresponding to 7! arrangements, no. of ways in which the condition will be satisfied = 7!/3! ways.

**e.g.11.** How many total words can be formed with the word 'DEHRADUN'?

**Solution** - Total number of letters = 8, out of which D occurs twice.

So, total number of words that can be formed = 8!/2!

**e.g.12.** How many words can be formed with the word 'ALLAHABAD'?

**Solution** – Letters are – A – Four times

L –Twice

H, B and D are occurring once.

So, total number of words = $\frac{9!}{4!2!}$

## Number Formation –

Number Formation is another standard example of Permutation. Here we will introduce BOX Diagram method of solving the questions.

If a three digit number is to be constructed, then we will use

| Hundred's Place | Ten's place | Unit's place |
|---|---|---|

If a four digit number is to be constructed, then we will use

| Thousand's Place | Hundred's Place | Ten's place | Unit's place |
|---|---|---|---|

And so on.

While solving questions related to **Number Formation**, we should have two things very clearly in our mind:

(i) While using box diagram, we should start with the digit which is having any restriction, i.e. some condition is imposed on that digit.

(ii) When nothing about repetition of digits is mentioned in the question, we will have to assume that repetition is allowed.

**e.g.13.** How many different 3 digit numbers can be formed using the digits 1, 3, 5, 7 and 9?

(i) When repetition is not allowed,

(ii) When repetition is allowed

**Solution** – Below given Box represents the respective positioning of digits in a three digit number.

| Hundred's Place | Ten's place | Unit's place |
|---|---|---|

(i) Since repetition of the digits is not allowed, we can fill Unit's place in 5 ways, Ten's place in 4 ways and Hundred's place in 3 ways.

| 3 | 4 | 5 |
|---|---|---|

Using Multiplication Theorem, Total number of numbers which can be formed = $5 \times 4 \times 3 = 60$

Alternatively, 3 digits can be selected out of 5 digits in ${}^5P_3 = 60$

(ii) Since repetition of the digits is allowed here, we can fill each of the hundred's, ten's and Unit's place in 5 ways.

| 5 | 5 | 5 |
|---|---|---|

Using Multiplication Theorem, Total number of numbers which can be formed $= 5 \times 5 \times 5 = 125$

**e.g.14.** How many 4–digit numbers divisible by 4 can be formed from the digits 0, 1, 2, 3, 4, 5?

**Solution** – Any number divisible by 4 will have number formed by its last two digits divisible by 4.

In this case, last two digits of the number can be 00, 04, 12, 20, 24, 32, 40, 44, 52.

Corresponding to any one of 00, 04, 12, 20, 24, 32, 40, 44, 52, we can have the following digits at its Hundred's and Thousand's place:

| 5 | 6 | 1 | 1 |
|---|---|---|---|

Thousand's place cannot be filled by 0, so it can be filled in 5 ways.

Hundred's place can be filled by any of the 0, 1, 2, 3, 4, 5; hence 6 ways.

So, corresponding to any one of 00, 04, 12, 20, 24, 32, 40, 44, 52, total number of ways = $5 \times 6 = 30$

So, total number of numbers which can be formed = $30 \times 9 = 270$

**e.g.15.** How many odd integers from 1000 to 8000 have none of its digits repeated?

**Solution** – There are two restrictions operating in this questions:

(i) For a number to be odd, unit digit should be either 1 or 3 or 5 or 7 or 9.

(ii) Thousand's place cannot be filled with 8 or 9.

For unit's digit - When it is filled with 9, thousand's place can be filled in 7 ways namely any digit from 1 to 7, and remaining two places can be filled in $8 \times 7 = 56$ ways.

So, total number of numbers formed in this way = $56 \times 7 = 392$

Now, if unit's place is filled with any of the four digits 1, 3, 5 or 7, the thousand's place can be filled in 6 ways (0 will be excluded), and remaining two places can be filled in $8 \times 7 = 56$ ways.

So, total number of numbers formed in this way = $56 \times 6 \times 4 = 1344$

So, total number of numbers = $392 + 1344 = 1736$

## Practice Exercise

Q1. From a group of persons the number of ways of selecting 5 persons is equal to that of 8 persons. The number of persons in the group is

(a) 13 (b) 40 (c) 18 (d) 21

Q2. At a get-together, it was found that a total of 66 handshakes took place at the conclusion of the party. If each guest shook hand only once will with all the others, how many people were present.

(a) 33 (b) 22 (c) 12 (d) 13

Q3. Greatest possible number of points of intersection of 8 straight lines and 4 circles is

(a) 32 (b) 64 (c) 76 (d) 104

Q4. There are 20 questions in a question paper. If no two students solve the same combination of questions but solve equal number of questions then the maximum number of students who appeared in the examination is

(a) $20C_9$ (b) ${}^{20}C_{11}$ (c) ${}^{20}C_{10}$ (d) None of these

Q5. Two out of six papers set for an examination are of mathematics. What is the number of ways in which the papers can be set so that the two mathematics papers are not together?

(a) 480 (b) 520 (c) 492 (d) 512

Q6. The number of all three distinct digit numbers which are divisible by 4 that can be formed from the digits 1, 2, 3, 4 and 5 is

(a) 8 (b) 12 (c) 16 (d) None of these

Q7. The Governing Council of an institute has fifteen members and wants to hold its annual meeting. In how many ways can the council be seated around a round table if the Chairman and the Vice-Chairman of the council are always seated together?

1. 10 x 12 ! 2. 14 x 10 ! 3. 13! 4. None of these

Q8. Akshay is planning to give a birthday party at his place. In how many ways can he invite one or more of five friends and seat them at a circular table?

1. 84 2. 89 3. 78 4. 81

Q9. In the above question, in how many ways can he invite one or more of five friends and seat them at a circular table with him?

1. 325 2. 205 3. 265 4. 320

Q10. A cricket team of eleven is to be chosen from among 8 batsmen, 6 bowlers and 2 wicket-keepers. In how many ways can the team be chosen if there must be at least four batsmen, at least four bowlers and exactly one wicket-keeper?

1. 1681 2. 5304 3. 1652 4. None of these

Q11. How many words can be formed using the letters of the word "CORRESPONDENCE"?

1. $\frac{8!}{(2!)^4(3!)^1}$ 2. 14! 3. $\frac{14!}{(2!)^4(3!)^2}$ 4. $\frac{14!}{(2!)^5(3!)^1}$

Q12. How many words can be formed using the letters of the word "CORRESPONDENCE" if the consonants are always written together?

1. 182 2. 184 3. $216 \times 9!$ 4. None of these

Q13. If six persons are selected out of ten, in how many ways will a particular person be found among those six?

(a) 124 (b) 126 (c) 144 (d) 84

14. There are 8 different locks, with exactly one key for each lock. All the keys have been mixed up. What is the maximum number of trials required in order to determine which key belongs to which lock?

1. 44 2. 28 3. 24 4. 32

Q15. How many natural numbers less than a million can be formed using the digits 0, 7 and 8?

(a) 729 (b) 728 (c) 462 (d) 461

Q16. You are going to set up a stereo system by purchasing separate components. You find 3 different receivers, 6 different compact disc players, and 10 different speaker systems. If you want one of each of these components, how many different stereo systems are possible?

(a) 180 (b) 60 (c) 540 (d) None of these

Q17. There are five chairs kept in a row for five dignitaries. In how many ways can they sit on the chairs?

(a) 5! (b) $5^5$ (c) 5 (d) 1

Q18. There are five chairs kept in a row for five toys to be kept on them. It is known that one chair can hold one or more than one toys. In how many ways can toys be kept on chairs?

(a) 5! (b) $5^5$ (c) 5 (d) 1

**Directions for questions 19 and 20: Answer the questions on the basis of the information given below.**

A string of three English letters is formed as per the following rules:

I. The first letter is any vowel.

II. The second letter is m, n or p.

III. If the second letter is m, then the third letter is any vowel which is different from the first letter.

IV. If the second letter is n, then the third letter is e or u.

V. If the second letter is p, then the third letter is the same as the first letter.

Q19. How many strings of letters can possibly be formed using the above rules?

a. 40 b. 45 c. 30 d. 35

Q20. How many strings of letters can possibly be formed using the above rules such that the third letter of the string is e?

a. 8 b. 9 c. 10 d.11

## Answer Grid:

| Q. No. | 1 | 2 | 3 | 4 | 5 | 6 | 7 | 8 | 9 | 10 |
|---|---|---|---|---|---|---|---|---|---|---|
| Answer | a | c | d | c | a | b | d | b | a | d |
| Q. No. | 11 | 12 | 13 | 14 | 15 | 16 | 17 | 18 | 19 | 20 |
| Answer | c | d | b | b | b | a | a | b | d | c |

Q1. Assume the number of people = x. Hence $= {}^{x}C_{5} = {}^{x}C_{8}$

It is possible only if x = 5 + 8 = 13. Hence option (a) is the answer.

Q2. Number of handshake in a party among n persons where everybody shakes hand with every other person = ${}^{n}C_{2} = \frac{n(n-1)}{2}$

Given that = 66. Solving this, we get x = 12. Hence option (c) is the answer.

Q3. Number of maximum points of intersection among n straight lines = ${}^{n}c_{2}$

Number of maximum points of intersection among n circles = ${}^{n}P_{2}$

Number of maximum points of intersection between one straight line and one circle = 2 points

Answer to this question = ${}^{8}c_{2} + {}^{4}P_{2} + 2 \times 8 \times 4 = 104$. Hence option (d) is the answer.

Q4. This question is asking for maximum value of ${}^{n}c_{r}$ for n = 20. This is equal to = ${}^{20}C_{10}$. Hence option (c) is the answer.

Q5. To solve this question, we'll find out the total number of ways of setting the paper and then subtract the number of ways in which both the mathematics paper are together.

Total number of ways of setting the paper = n! = 6!

Total number of ways of setting the paper in which both the maths paper are together = 5! × 2!

Hence required value = 6! – 5! × 2! = 240. Hence option (a) is the answer.

Q6. Numbers which are divisible by 4 will have the following last two digit numbers:

12, 24, 32, 52.

When last two digits are 12, hundred's place can be fixed in 3 ways (by namely digits 3, 4 and 5).

So numbers formed will be 312, 412, 512 = 3 numbers.

Similarly,

Numbers formed with last two digits as 24 = 3 numbers

Numbers formed with last two digits as 32 = 3 numbers

Numbers formed with last two digits as 52 = 3 numbers

Hence total number of numbers = 12. Hence option (b) is the answer.

Q7. Total number of members to be arranged = 13 members + (one pair of Chairman + Vice Chairman) = 14

Number of ways circular arrangement can be done = (14 – 1) ! × 2! = 13! × 2!. Hence option (d) is the answer.

Q8. He can invite either one or two or three or four or all five friends. Question is asking "for the friends (seat them) arrangements:

(a) Number of ways One friend can be chosen = 5C1 = 5

Circular arrangements possible if there is only one friend = (1 – 1)! = 0! = 1

Hence total number of arrangements = 5 × 1 = 5 ......................(i)

(b) Number of ways two friends can be chosen = 5C2 = 10

Circular arrangements possible if there are two friends = (2 – 1)! = 1! = 1

Hence total number of arrangements = 10 × 1 = 10 ......................(ii)

(c) Number of ways three friends can be chosen = 5C3 = 10

Circular arrangements possible if there are three friends = (3 – 1)! = 2! = 2

Hence total number of arrangements = 10 × 2 = 20 ......................(iii)

(d) Number of ways four friends can be chosen = 5C4 = 5

Circular arrangements possible if there are four friends = (4 – 1)! = 3! = 6

Hence total number of arrangements = 5 × 6 = 30 ......................(iv)

(e) Number of ways five friends can be chosen = 5C5 = 1

Circular arrangements possible if there are five friends = (5 – 1)! = 4! = 24

Hence total number of arrangements = 1 × 24 = 24 ......................(v)

Total number of ways = Sum of all these five = 5 + 10 + 20 + 30 + 24 = 89. Hence option (2) is the answer.

Q9. He can invite either one or two or three or four or all five friends. In this question, Question is asking for arrangements alongwith him.

(a) Number of ways One friend can be chosen = 5C1 = 5

Circular arrangements possible if there is only one friend and Akshay = (2 – 1)! = 1! = 1

Hence total number of arrangements = 5 × 1 = 5 ......................(i)

(b) Number of ways two friends can be chosen = 5C2 = 10

Circular arrangements possible if there are two friends and Akshay = (3 – 1)! = 2! = 2

Hence total number of arrangements = 10 × 2 = 20 ......................(ii)

(c) Number of ways three friends can be chosen = 5C3 = 10

Circular arrangements possible if there are three friends and Akshay = (4 – 1)! = 3! = 6

Hence total number of arrangements = 10 × 6 = 60 ......................(iii)

(d) Number of ways four friends can be chosen = 5C4 = 5

Circular arrangements possible if there are four friends and Akshay = (5 – 1)! = 4! = 24

Hence total number of arrangements = 5 × 24 = 120 ......................(iv)

(e) Number of ways five friends can be chosen = 5C5 = 1

Circular arrangements possible if there are five friends and Akshay = (6 – 1)! = 5! = 120

Hence total number of arrangements = 1 × 120 = 120 ......................(v)

Total number of ways = Sum of all these five = 5 + 20 + 60 + 120 + 120 = 325. Hence option (1) is the answer.

Q10. Following cases are possible:

| | Batsman | Bowler | Wicketkeeper | Total |
|---|---|---|---|---|
| Case 1 | 6 | 4 | 1 | 11 |
| Case 2 | 5 | 5 | 1 | 11 |
| Case 3 | 4 | 6 | 1 | 11 |
| Case 4 | 6 | 4 | 1 | 11 |
| Case 5 | 5 | 5 | 1 | 11 |
| Case 6 | 4 | 6 | 1 | 11 |

Q11. In this word:

| Letter | Number of times occurs |
|---|---|
| R | 2 |
| O | 2 |
| E | 3 |
| C | 2 |
| S | 1 |
| P | 1 |
| N | 2 |
| D | 1 |

So total number of words formed = $\frac{14!}{(2!)^4(3!)^1}$

Hence option (3) is the answer.

Q12. Vowels are – O, E

Consonants are – R, C, S, P, N, D. Consonants will be in one group.

So, total entities to be arranged = O, E, (Group of consonants) = 3

Total ways of arrangements = $\frac{3!\times 9!\times 5!}{(2!)^4(3!)^1}$. This is option (4). Hence option (4) is the answer.

Q13. Since one particular player has already been selected, we are required to select only 5 persons out of 9 persons. This can be done in $^9C_5$ways = $\frac{9!}{4!5!}$ = 126. Hence option (b) is the answer.

Q14. Maximum total number of trials for the key to be identified of 1st lock = 7 (Once you have used all the seven keys and lock has not opened, it means 8th key is the right key). And so on.

Maximum total number of trials = 7 + 6 + 5 + 4 + 3 + 2 + 1 = 28. Hence option (2) is the answer.

Q15. Numbers formed would be of Single digit, Two digits, Three digits, Four digits, Five digits and six digits.

Single digit numbers = 7 and 8

For two digits numbers,

| 2 | 3 |
|---|---|

= 2 × 3 = 6 numbers

For three digits numbers,

| 2 | 3 | 3 |
|---|---|---|

= 2 × 3 × 3 = 18 numbers

For four digits numbers,

| 2 | 3 | 3 | 3 |
|---|---|---|---|

= 2 × 3 × 3 × 3 = 54 numbers

For five digits numbers,

| 2 | 3 | 3 | 3 | 3 |
|---|---|---|---|---|

= 2 × 3 × 3 × 3 × 3 = 162 numbers

For six digits numbers,

| 2 | 3 | 3 | 3 | 3 | 3 |
|---|---|---|---|---|---|

= 2 × 3 × 3 × 3 × 3 × 3 = 486 numbers

So, total number of numbers = 728

Q16. Answer = 3C1 × 6C1 × 10C1 = 1880. Hence option (a) is the answer.

Q17. 1st person can choose hit seat in 5 ways, then second person can choose his seat in 4 ways, then 3rd person can choose hit seat in 3 ways, then 4th person can choose his seat in 4 ways and 5th person will sit on the last remaining 5th seat.

Hence total number of ways they can choose the seats = $5 \times 4 \times 3 \times 2 \times 1 = 5!$. Hence option (a) is the answer.

Q18. 1st toy can be kept one any of the five chairs in 5 ways. Now, since a chair can hold more than one toy, 2nd toy can also be kept in 5 ways, and similarly, 3rd toy can also be kept in 5 ways, 4th toy can also be kept in 5 ways and 5th toy can also be kept in 5 ways.

Hence total number of ways toys can be kept on chairs = $5 \times 5 \times 5 \times 5 \times 5 = 5^5$. Hence option (b) is the answer.

## Solution to questions 19 – 20:

Q19. (d) Case I: ___m___

First place can be selected in five ways and hence the third in four ways

So, 5 x 4 = 20 ways.

Case II: ___n___

First place can be selected in 5 ways and third in 2 ways

So, 5 x 2 = 10 ways

Case III: ___p___

First place can be selected in 5 ways and last letter will same, i.e. one way

So, 5 x 1 = 5 way

Total ways = 20 + 10 + 5 = 35 ways

Q20. (c) As third letter is e that can be selected in one way only

Case I: 4 m e = 4 ways

Case II: 5 n e = 5 ways

Case III: e p e = 1 ways

Hence total number of ways = 10 ways

# 15 Probability

## Consider the following case:

During the recent cricket tournament held in my city, during the toss of coin, captain of team A chose "Heads" but lost the toss because it was "Tails." In next match, he again chose "Heads" but lost the toss again. So, next time, in the 3rd match, he chose "tails". Does he have more chances of winning the toss because in the last two tosses, coin has showed "tails"?

Answer is – NO. And the reason is simple – In a toss of a coin, occurrence of head or tail are equally likely, and it really does not matter that how many times the coin has already showed head or tail previously.

Probability of head in a toss of a coin = Probability of tail in a toss of a coin = $\frac{1}{2}$

In fact in our day to day life, we often use a lot of words that contain "unclear extent" of occurrence of something. For example, (a) it is **very likely** that Indian cricket team will win world cup cricket; (b) **most probably** I will go for a vacation next year, (c) It has **rarely** rained at Jodhpur. In these statements, words in **bold** show subjectivity or an "unclear extent" of occurrence of that particular event.

Now we'll define probability – Probability is "Possibility Quantified". In other words, we want to remove the subjectivity from the occurrence of an event through **a number** - either through percentage or a ratio.

This ratio used to express probability is calculated by dividing total number of desired outcomes by total number of possible outcomes.

$$\text{Probability of an event} = \frac{\textit{Number of desired outcomes}}{\textit{Total number of possible outcomes}}$$

Now consider the same statements given above:

(a) it is **60% likely** that Indian cricket team will win world cup cricket; (b) **90% sure,** I will go for a vacation next year, (c) **Only 1% of** the year, It has rained at Jodhpur. In these statements, words in **bold** present the exact extent of occurrence of that particular event.

Important notations and Formula:

(a) Probability of occurrence of an event is shown as P(E).

(b) Probability of non - occurrence of an event is shown as P'(E).

(c) P(E) + P'(E) = 1

(d) Certain event is an event which has probability = 1 or which are 100% certain. In other words, it is bound to happen. For example, if I throw a ball up in the air, probability that it will fall on the earth (unless it has been thrown with escape velocity) = 1.

(e) Impossible event is an event which has probability = 0 or which is 0% probable. In other words, it will never happen. For example, probability that there will be 55 Sundays in a year = 0.

(f) Playing cards:

There are 52 playing cards in a pack – 13 each from Heart, Club, Diamond and Spade. These 13 cards are Ace, no. 2, no. 3, no. 4, no.5, no. 6, no. 7, no. 8, no. 9, no. 10, Jack, Queen and King.

(g) **ODDS in FAVOUR and ODDS in AGAINST**

$$\text{Odds in Favour} = \frac{\text{Number of favourable cases}}{\text{Number of Unfavourable cases}}$$

$$\text{Odds in Against} = \frac{\text{Number of Unfavourable cases}}{\text{Number of favourable cases}}$$

(h) **Understanding AND/OR**

To understand the role played by And / Or in our questions, let us take an example of throwing an unbiased die. Let A and B be two events associated with it such that

Event A = getting an odd number, event B = getting a multiple of 3.

Then A = {1, 3, 5}, and B = {3, 6}.

We now define a new event "A or B" which occurs if event A or event B or both occur i.e. **at least one** of event A or event B occurs. Clearly the event "A or B" occurs if the outcome is any one of the outcomes {1, 3, 5, 6}. Thus, the event "A or B" is represented by the $A \cup B$.

Similarly, "A and B" means occurrence of both A and B which is possible if the outcome is {3}.

Hence it is represented by the subset $A \cap B$.

## Worked Out examples:

Q1. Using the data from the previous years, a school predicts that 6 out of total 300 students will get above 95% marks in $10^{th}$ board. This year school has 400 students. How many of them are expected to get above 95% marks in $10^{th}$ board?

**Solution** – Probability that a student will get above 95% marks = $\frac{6}{300} = \frac{1}{50}$

There are 400 students this year in school.

Hence expected number of students with above 95% marks = $\frac{1}{50} \times 400 = 8$ students

Q2. In a single throw of a die, what is the probability that the number shown is either an even number or a prime number?

**Solution** – Following numbers are even numbers = 2, 4, 6

Following numbers are prime numbers = 2, 3, 5

Hence numbers which are either an even number or a prime number = 2, 3, 4, 5, 6. So number of favorable outcomes = 5, and number of total outcomes = 6

Hence desired probability $= \frac{5}{6}$

Q3. In a single throw of a die, what is the probability that the number shown is an even number and a prime number both?

**Solution** – Following numbers are even numbers = 2, 4, 6

Following numbers are prime numbers = 2, 3, 5

Hence numbers which is/are an even number and a prime number both = 2. So number of favorable outcomes = 1, and number of total outcomes = 6

Hence desired probability $= \frac{1}{6}$

Q4. In a single throw of two die, what is the probability that the sum on the top face of both the die will be 8?

**Solution** – When two die are thrown, sum of the numbers appearing on the faces can be anything from 2 to 12. To find out the number of favourable cases we will be required to find out the cases in which sum = 8.

Following are the case – (6, 2), (2, 6), (5, 3), (3, 5), (4,4)

So, total number of favourable cases = 5

Total number of possible outcomes = $6 \times 6 = 36$

Hence probability = $\frac{5}{36}$

Q5. Three coins are tossed simultaneously. What is the probability that exactly one of them shows a head?

**Solution** – To get exactly one head, following ways are possible – (HTT), (THT), (TTH).

Hence total number of favourable cases = 3

Total number of possible outcomes = $2 \times 2 \times 2 = 8$

Hence probability = $\frac{3}{8}$

Q6. Three coins are tossed simultaneously. What is the probability that atleast one of them shows head?

**Solution** – At least one head = 1 – Probability that all three coins are showing tails = $1 - \frac{1}{8} = \frac{7}{8}$

Q7. In an examination, probability that A passes the exam = 1/3, probability that B passes the exam = ¼ and probability that C passes the exam = 2/5. What is the probability that

(a) None of them pass the exam?

(b) At least one of them passes the exam?

(c) Exactly one of them passes the exam?

(d) All of them pass the exam?

**Solution** – If three students are appearing at an examination, following EIGHT cases are possible:

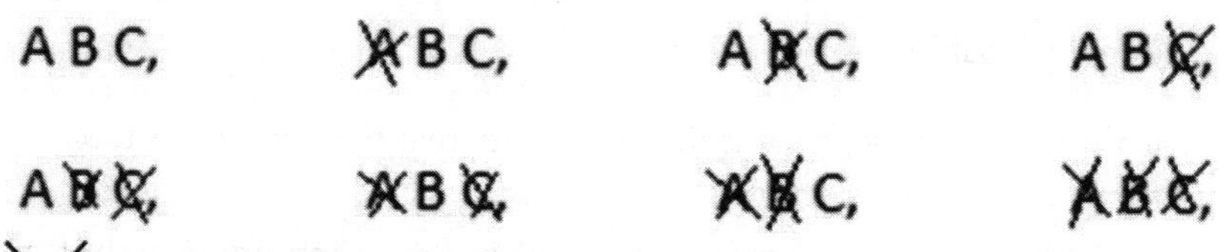

 **means student fails the exam.**

(a) Probability that A fails the exam = 1 – 1/3 = 2/3, probability that B fails the exam = 1 – ¼ = ¾ and probability that C fails the exam = 1 – 2/5 = 3/5

None of them pass the exam = 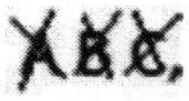

Hence probability that none of them pass the exam = 2/3 × ¾ × 3/5 = 18/60 = 3/10

(b) At least one of them passes the exam = 1 – None of them pass the exam = 1 – 3/10 = 7/10

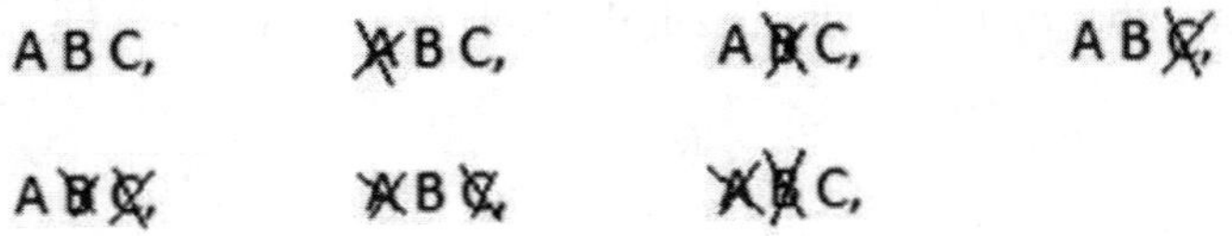

(c) Exactly one of them passes the exam = (1/3 × ¾ × 3/5) + (2/3 × ¼ × 3/5) + (2/3 × ¾ × 2/5) = 27/60

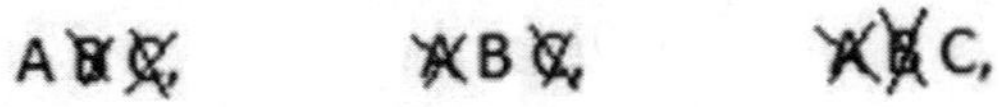

(d) All of them pass the exam = A B C = 1/3 × ¼ × 2/5 = 2/60 = 1/30

Q8. A box contains 9 red, 7 white and 4 pink balls. If 2 balls are drawn at random, find the probability that

(i) Both the balls are red

(ii) Exactly one ball is white

**Solution:**

There are 20 balls in the bag out of which 2 balls can be drawn in ${}^{20}C_2$ ways. So the total number of cases (sample space) = ${}^{20}C_2$ = 190.

(i) There are 9 red balls out of which 2 balls can be drawn in ${}^{9}C_2$ ways. Therefore, favorable number of cases = ${}^{9}C_2$ = 36. So the required probability = $\frac{36}{190} = \frac{18}{95}$

(ii) There are 7 white balls out of which one white can be drawn in ${}^{7}C_1$ ways. One ball from the remaining 13 balls can be drawn in ${}^{13}C_1$ ways. Therefore, one white and one other colour ball can be drawn in ${}^{7}C_1 \times {}^{13}C_1$ ways. So the favourable number of cases = ${}^{7}C_1 \times {}^{13}C_1$ = 91.

So the required probability = $\frac{91}{190}$

## Practice Exercise

Q1. If the probability of A failing in an examination is $\frac{1}{5}$ and that of B failing the same examination is $\frac{3}{10}$ then the probability that either A or B fails is

(a) $\frac{1}{2}$ (b) $\frac{11}{25}$ (c) $\frac{19}{50}$ (d) None of these

Q2. A bag contains 2 red, 3 green and 2 blue balls. 2 blue balls are to be drawn randomly. What is the probability that the balls drawn the balls drawn contain no blue ball?

(a) $\frac{5}{7}$ (b) $\frac{10}{21}$ (c) $\frac{2}{7}$ (d) $\frac{11}{21}$

Q3. There are 6 positive and 8 negative numbers. Four numbers are chosen at random and multiplied. The probability that the product is a positive number is

(a) $\frac{500}{1001}$ (b) $\frac{503}{1001}$ (c) $\frac{505}{1001}$ (d) $\frac{101}{1001}$

Q4. Two dice are tossed. The probability that the total score is a prime number is

(a) $\frac{1}{6}$ (b) $\frac{5}{12}$ (c) $\frac{1}{2}$ (d) $\frac{4}{25}$

Q5. A coin is tossed 5 times. What is the probability that head appears an odd number of times?

(a) $\frac{2}{5}$ (b) $\frac{1}{5}$ (c) $\frac{1}{2}$ (d) $\frac{5}{6}$

Q6. Atal can hit a target 3 times in 6 shots, Bhola can hit the target 2 times in 6 shots and Chandra can hit the target 4 times in 4 shots. Each one of them fire one shot. If the outcomes are independent, what is the probability that atleast two of them will hit the target?

(a) $\frac{1}{2}$ (b) $\frac{2}{3}$ (c) $\frac{1}{3}$ (d) $\frac{5}{6}$

Q7. A dice is thrown 6 times. If "getting an odd number" is a "success". The probability of 5 successes is

(a) $\frac{1}{10}$ (b) $\frac{3}{32}$ (c) $\frac{5}{6}$ (d) $\frac{25}{26}$

Q8. A box contains 5 brown toys and 4 white toys. A man takes out two toys simultaneously. The probability that they are of the same colour is

(a) $\frac{1}{6}$ (b) $\frac{5}{108}$ (c) $\frac{5}{18}$ (d) $\frac{4}{9}$

Q9. A fair coin is tossed repeatedly. If head appear on the first four tosses, then the probability of appearance of tail on fifth toss is

(a) $\frac{1}{2}$ (b) $\frac{1}{7}$ (c) $\frac{3}{7}$ (d) $\frac{2}{3}$

Q10. A card is drawn at random from a well-shuffled pack of 52 cards. What is the probability of getting a jack of hearts or a jack of diamonds?

(a) $\frac{3}{26}$ (b) $\frac{2}{17}$ (c) $\frac{1}{26}$ (d) None of these

Q11. If the integers m and n are chosen at random between 1 and 200 then the probability that a number of the form $7^m + 7^n$ is divisible by 10 is

(a) $\frac{1}{5}$ (b) $\frac{1}{7}$ (c) $\frac{1}{4}$ (d) $\frac{1}{49}$

Q12. A box contains 6 white balls and 7 black balls. Two balls are drawn at random. What is the probability that both are of the same colour?

(a) $\frac{5}{13}$ (b) $\frac{6}{13}$ (c) $\frac{7}{13}$ (d) $\frac{6}{7}$

Q13. The letters B, G, I, N and R are rearranged to form the word 'BRING'. Find its probability.

(a) $\frac{1}{120}$ (b) $1/5^4$ (c) $\frac{1}{24}$ (d) $5/5 \times 4^2$

Q14. A and B play a game where each is asked to select a number from 1 to 5. If the two numbers match, both of them win a prize. The probability that they will not win a prize in a single trial is

(a) $\frac{1}{25}$ (b) $\frac{24}{25}$ (c) $\frac{2}{25}$ (d) none of these

Q15. What is the probability that a non leap year will have 53 Wednesdays?

(a) $\frac{1}{365}$ (b) $\frac{1}{53}$ (c) $\frac{1}{7}$ (d) $\frac{2}{7}$

Q16. What is the probability that a leap year will have 53 Wednesdays?

(a) $\frac{1}{365}$ (b) $\frac{1}{53}$ (c) $\frac{1}{7}$ (d) $\frac{2}{7}$

Q17. A fisherman predicts that on a rainy day, his probability of catching fishes will be only 40%. How many days in the month of April he would not be able to catch fish?

(a) 30 (b) 12 (c) 18 (d) 20

Q18. A fisherman predicts that on a rainy day, his probability of catching fishes will be only 40% and on a sunny day, his probability of catching fishes will be 80%. In the month of April, there are 20 rainy days and 10 sunny days. On how many days, would he been able to catch fish?

(a) 15 (b) 10 (c) 14 (d) 16

Q19. There was a theft in my neighborhood last night. The house owner was able to get a glimpse of the thief and recalled that the thief had curly hair. Police said that there were 10 persons in every locality with curly hair and out of them, 2 are usual suspects. If there are 8 localities in the city, how many usual suspects are there in the city?

(a) 1 (b) 80 (c) 16 (d) 64

Q20. In a random throw of a dice, what is the probability that it will show an even number?

(a) $\frac{3}{4}$ (b) $\frac{1}{2}$ (c) $\frac{1}{3}$ (d) $\frac{1}{4}$

Q21. In a random throw of two die, what is the probability that atleast one of them will show a prime number?

(a) $\frac{3}{4}$ (b) $\frac{1}{2}$ (c) $\frac{1}{3}$ (d) $\frac{1}{4}$

Q22. An airline expects that 4% of its flights will be delayed by 1 hour – 2 hour in the year 2015. Samar is supposed to take 40 flights by the same airline in a year. How many of those flights are expected to be delayed by 1 hour – 2 hours?

(a) 1 (b) 2 (c) 3 (d) 4

Q23. In a single throw of two dice, what is the probability that the sum of the numbers shown will be atleast 10?

(a) $\frac{3}{4}$ (b) $\frac{1}{6}$ (c) $\frac{1}{12}$ (d) $\frac{1}{36}$

Q24. In a single throw of three dice, what is the probability that the all of them show the same face?

(a) $\frac{3}{4}$ (b) $\frac{1}{6}$ (c) $\frac{1}{12}$ (d) $\frac{1}{36}$

Q25. There are three ways to go to Delhi from Dehradun – by car, by train and by air. Further, there are two ways to go to Shimla from Delhi – by car or by train. A family is planning to travel to Shimla from Dehradun via Delhi. What is the probability that it takes train only for the whole journey?

(a) $\frac{1}{5}$ (b) $\frac{1}{2}$ (c) $\frac{1}{6}$ (d) $\frac{1}{4}$

## Answer Grid:

| Q. No. | 1 | 2 | 3 | 4 | 5 | 6 | 7 | 8 | 9 | 10 | 11 | 12 | 13 |
|---|---|---|---|---|---|---|---|---|---|---|---|---|---|
| Answer | b | b | c | b | c | b | b | d | a | c | c | b | a |
| Q. No. | 14 | 15 | 16 | 17 | 18 | 19 | 20 | 21 | 22 | 23 | 24 | 25 | |
| Answer | b | c | d | c | d | c | b | a | b | b | d | c | |

## Solutions and Explanations:

Q1. Probability that either A or B fails = 1 – probability that both A and B pass = 1 – (4/5 × 7/10) = 22/50. Hence option (b) is the answer.

Q2. Balls can be drawn in the following ways.

1 red, 1 green or 2 red or 2 green

Required probability = $\frac{2C1 \times 3C1}{7C2} + \frac{2C2}{7C2} + \frac{3C2}{7C2} = \frac{10}{21}$

Hence option (B) is the answer.

Q3. The product of four numbers will be positive in the following ways.

1. All the four numbers are positive, then probability = $\frac{6C4}{14C4}$

2. All the four numbers are negative, then probability = $\frac{8C4}{14C4}$

3. Two numbers are negative and two numbers are positive, the probability = $\frac{6C2 \times 8C4}{14C4}$

Hence, required probability of the event = $\frac{6C4 + 8C4 + 6C2 \times 8C4}{14C4} = \frac{505}{1001}$

Hence option (C) is the answer.

Q4. Number of ways of out comes when two dices are thrown = n(s) = 36 and possible cases of event when the sum of numbers on two dice is a prime numbers are,

(1,1), (1,2), (1,4), (1,6), (2,1), (2,3), (2,5), (3,2), (3,4), (4,1), (4,3), (4,5), (5,2), (5,6), (6,1), (6,5)

So, number of events = n(A) = 15

Hence, required probability = $\frac{n(A)}{n(S)} = \frac{15}{36} = \frac{5}{12}$

Hence option (B) is the answer.

Q5. Here, $p = q = \frac{1}{2}$

Required probability = $5C1\left(\frac{1}{2}\right)^1\left(\frac{1}{2}\right)^4 + 5C5\left(\frac{1}{2}\right)^3\left(\frac{1}{2}\right)^2 + 5c5\left(\frac{1}{2}\right)^5 = \frac{1}{2}$

Hence option (C) is the answer.

Q6. Given, P(A) = $\frac{3}{6} = \frac{1}{2}$, P(B)=$\frac{2}{6} = \frac{1}{3}$ and P(C) = $\frac{4}{4} = 1$

∴ Required probability = P(A)P(B)P(C) + P(A)P()P(C) + P(A)P(B)P(C) + P(A)P(B)P(C)

$= \frac{2}{3}$

Hence option (B) is the answer.

Q7. Let A be the event of getting an odd number n(s) = 6

Favourable cases = 3 {as there are three odd numbers}

∴ Probability of getting an odd number = $\frac{3}{6} = \frac{1}{2}$

Hence, probability of not getting an odd number = $1 - \frac{1}{2} = \frac{1}{2}$

Hence, required probability of 5 successes = ${}^6C_5 \times \left(\frac{1}{2}\right)^5 \times \frac{1}{2} = \frac{3}{32}$

Hence option (B) is the answer.

Q8. Required probability = $\frac{5c_2}{9c_2} + \frac{4c_2}{9c_2} = \frac{10+6}{36} = \frac{16}{36} = \frac{4}{9}$

Hence option (D) is the answer.

Q9. Since, all events are independent. Hence required probability = $\frac{1}{2}$

Hence option (A) is the answer.

Q10. Required probability = $\frac{1}{52}+\frac{1}{52}=\frac{2}{52}$

Hence option (c) is the answer.

Q11. Required probability = ¼. Hence option (c) is the answer.

Q12. Two white balls can be selected in the following ways.

Both the balls are white or Both the balls are black

Hence, the probability = $\frac{6C2}{13C2}+\frac{7C2}{13C2}=\frac{6}{13}$

Hence option (B) is the answer.

Q13. There are total 5 distinct letters. Total number of words that can be formed using these = 5! = 120. Out of those 120 words, there will be one word 'DELHI'.

Hence favorable number of cases = 1.

Hence, probability = $\frac{1}{120}$

Hence option (A) is the answer.

Q14. Total number of ways in which both of them can select a number each = 5 × 5

Probability that they win the prize = $\frac{1\times1}{25}=\frac{1}{25}$

Probability that they do not win the a prize = $1-\frac{1}{25}=\frac{24}{25}$

Hence option (B) is the answer.

Q15. A non - leap year has 365 days = 52 weeks + 1 day extra. 52 weeks ensure that all the days from Monday to Sunday are occurring 52 times.

For 53 Sundays, this extra day should be a Wednesday.

Required probability = $\frac{\text{Number of desire doutcomes}}{\text{Total Number of possible outcomes}}=\frac{1}{7}$

Hence option (c) is the answer.

Q16. A leap year has 366 days = 52 weeks + 2 days extra. 52 weeks ensure that all the days from Monday to Sunday are occurring 52 times.

For 53 Sundays, one of these two extra days should be a Wednesday.

$$\text{Required probability} = \frac{\text{Number of desired outcomes}}{\text{Total number of possible outcomes}} = \frac{2}{7}$$

Hence option (d) is the answer.

Q17. There are 30 days in April.

Hence number of days that he would be able to catch fish in April = 40% × 30 days = 12 days

Hence number of days when he won't be able to catch fish in April = 30 days – 12 days = 18 days. Hence option (c) is the answer.

Q18. Number of rainy days that he will be able to catch fish in April = 40% × 20 days = 8 days

Number of sunny days that he will be able to catch fish in April = 80% × 10 days = 8 days

Hence total number of days = 8 days + 8 days = 16 days, Hence option (d) is the answer.

Q19. For every locality, there are 2 usual suspects and there are 8 localities.

Hence total number of usual suspects = 2 × 8 = 16

Hence option (c) is the answer.

Q20. Dice can show any number from 1 to 6. Out of these, 2, 4 and 6 are even numbers.

$$\text{Required probability} = \frac{\text{Number of desired outcomes}}{\text{Total number of possible outcomes}} = \frac{3}{6} = \frac{1}{2}$$

Q21. Dice can show any number from 1 to 6. Out of these, 2, 3 and 5 are prime numbers.

$$\text{Required probability} = \frac{\text{Number of desired outcomes}}{\text{Total number of possible outcomes}} = \frac{27}{36} = \frac{3}{4}$$

Hence option (a) is the answer.

Q22. Since 4% of the flights are expected to be delayed, hence number of flights expected to be delayed = 4% of 50 = $\frac{4}{100} \times 50 = 2$. Hence option (b) is the answer.

Q23. Sum should be atleast 10. In other words, sum should be 10, 11 or 12.

For sum of the 10 ⇒ (5,5), (6,4), (4,6) = 3 outcomes

For sum of the 11 ⇒ (6,5), (5,6) = 2 outcomes

For sum of the 12 ⇒ (6,6) = 1 outcome

Hence total number of ways a sum of atleast 10 can be made = 3 outcomes + 2 outcomes + 1 outcomes = 6 outcomes

Required probability = $\dfrac{\text{Number of desired outcomes}}{\text{Total Number of possible outcomes}} = \dfrac{6}{36} = \dfrac{1}{6}$

Hence option (b) is the answer.

Q24. Following ways, all the three dice can show the same face : - (1,1,1), (2, 2,2), (3,3,3), (4,4,4), (5,5,5) and (6,6,6) = 6 outcomes

Total number of possible outcomes = $6 \times 6 \times 6 = 216$.

Hence required probability = $\dfrac{\text{Number of desired outcomes}}{\text{Total Number of possible outcomes}} = \dfrac{6}{216} = \dfrac{1}{36}$

Hence option (d) is the answer.

Q25. Following are the total six ways to reach to Shimla from Dehradun via Delhi:

There is only one way through which we can use train for the whole journey.

Required probability = $\dfrac{\text{Number of desired outcomes}}{\text{Total Number of possible outcomes}} = \dfrac{1}{36}$

Hence option (c) is the answer.

# 16 Geometry

In this chapter, we are going to study (a) Lines and Angles, (b) Circles, (c) Quadrilaterals and (d) Triangles

## (a) Lines and Angles

## Important Definitions and Theorems:

### I. Measurement and Nomenclature

| Types of Angles | Property | Diagram |
|---|---|---|
| Acute Angle | $0° < \theta < 90°$ (∠AOB is an acute angle) | 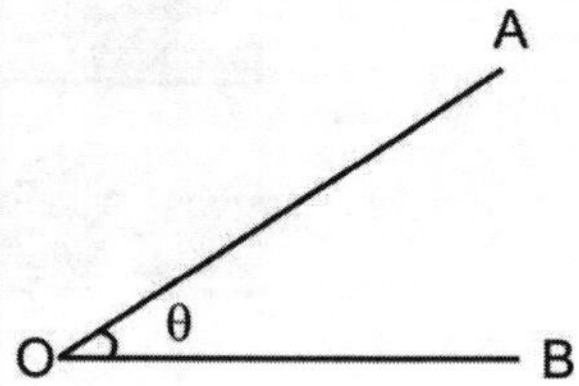  |
| Right Angle | $\theta = 90°$ | 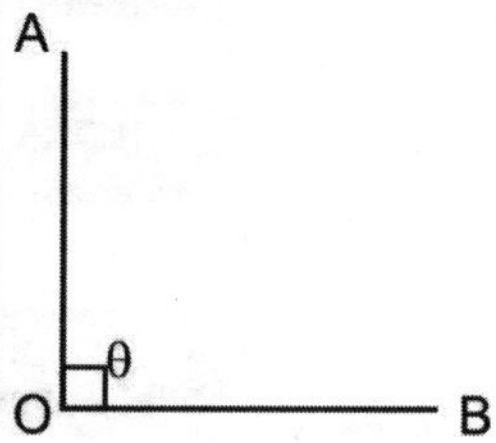  |
| Obtuse Angle | $90° < \theta < 180°$ | 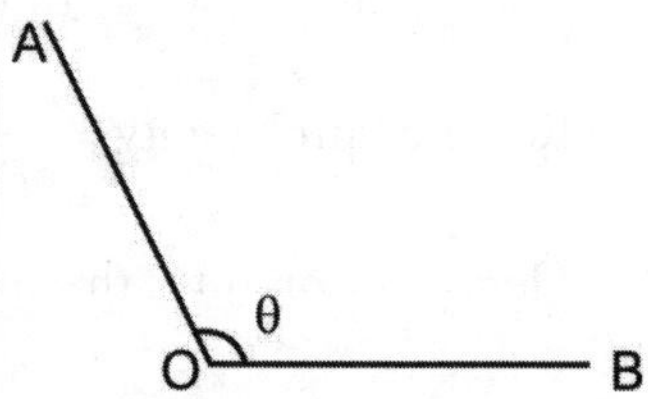  |

| | | |
|---|---|---|
| Straight Line | $\theta = 180°$ | 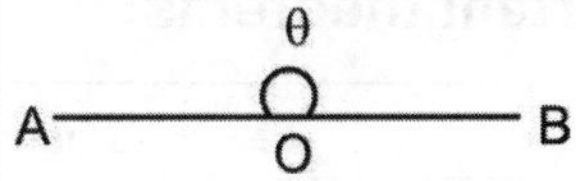 |
| Complementary Angle | $\theta_1 + \theta_2 = 90°$ | 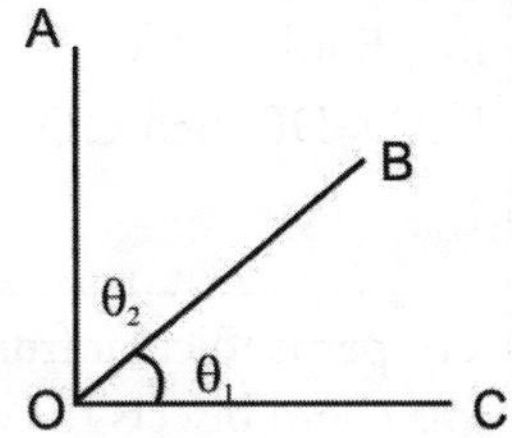 |
| Supplementary Angle | $\theta_1 + \theta_2 = 180°$ | 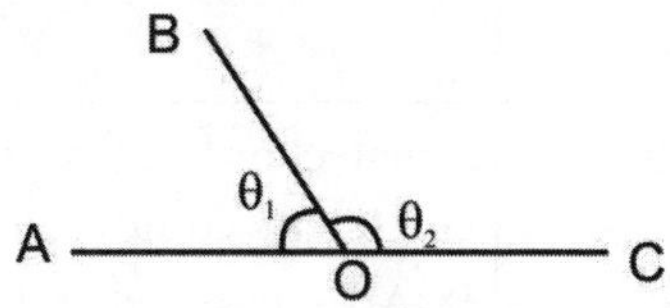 |
| Vertically opposite Angle | $\angle DOA = \angle BOC$ and $\angle DOB = \angle AOC$ | 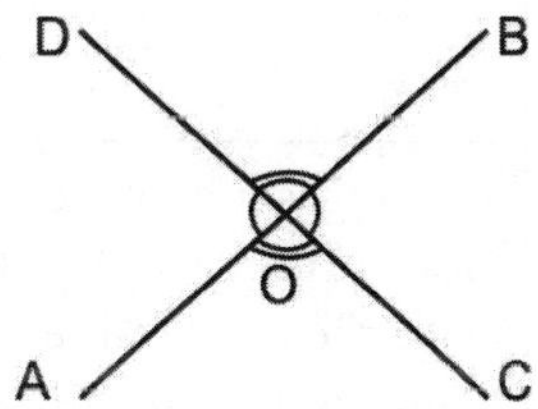 |

## (b) Circles

A circle is the path traveled by a point which moves in such a way that its distance from a fixed point remains constant. The fixed point is known as centre and the fixed distance is called the radius.

Area of circle = $\pi r^2$

Circumference of circle = $2\pi r$

Area of a sector subtending $\theta$ angle at the centre = $\pi r^2 \dfrac{\theta}{360°}$

Perimeter of a sector subtending $\theta$ angle at the centre = $2r\left(\dfrac{\pi\theta}{360}+1\right)$

## Important theorems:

| S. No. | Theorem | Diagram |
|---|---|---|
| 1. | The line joining the centre of a circle to the mid-point of a chord is perpendicular to the chord.<br>If AD=DB then OD ⊥ AB | 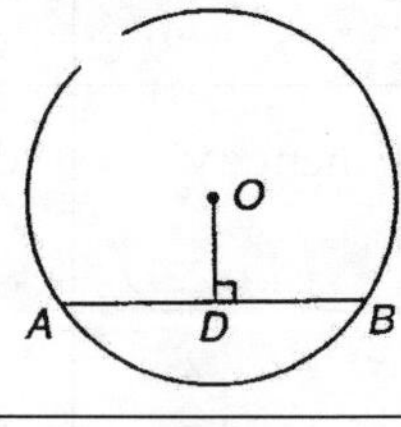 |
| 2. | The perpendicular from the centre of a circle to a chord bisects the chord i.e.,<br>if OD⊥AB, then AD = DB. | 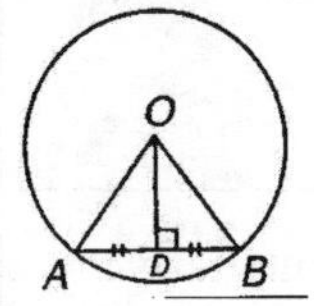 |
| 3. | Equal chords of a circle (or of congruent circles) are equidistant from the centre<br>If AB = PQ, then OD = OR | 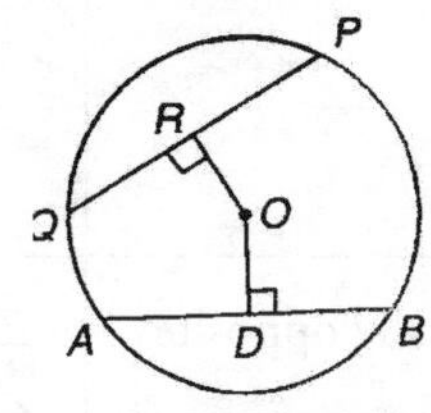 |
| 4. | The angle subtended by an arc (the degree measure of the arc) at the centre of a circle is twice the angle subtended by the arc at any point on the remaining part of the circle on the same side.<br>∠AOB = 2 ∠ACB. | 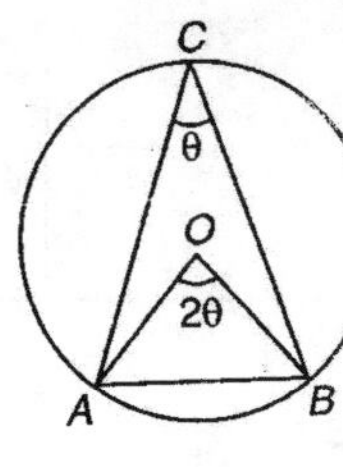 |
| 5. | Angle in a semicircle is a right angle. | 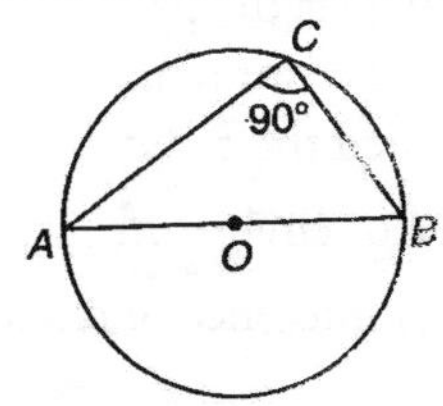 |
| 6. | Angles in the same segment of a circle are equal i.e., ∠ACB = ∠ADB | 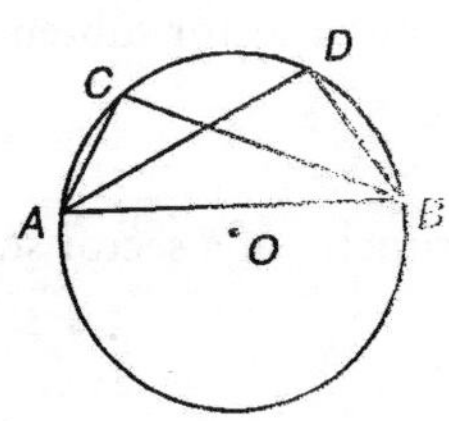 |

| | | |
|---|---|---|
| 7. | The lengths of two tangents drawn from an external point to a circle are equal i.e., AP = BP | 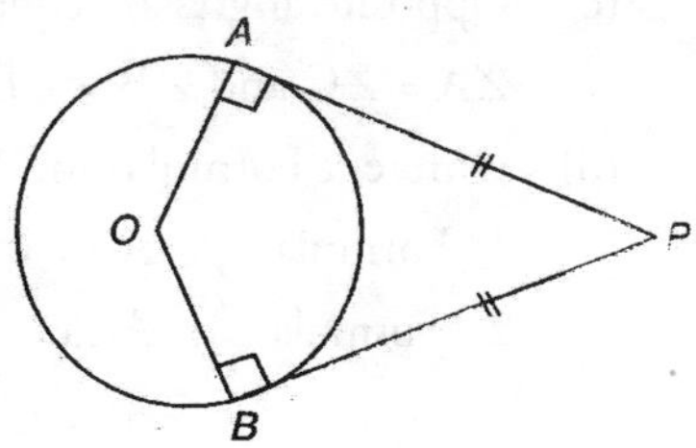 |
| 8 | Equal arcs (or chords) subtend equal angles at the centre If PQ = AB then ∠POQ = ∠AOB | 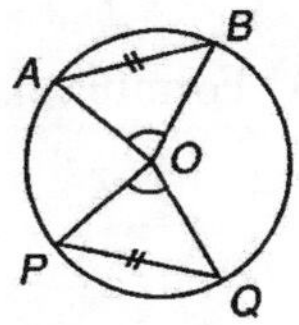 |

## (c ) Quadrilaterals

A quadrilateral is a structure bounded by four sides.

Area = $\frac{1}{2}$ × one diagonal × (sum of perpendiculars to the diagonal from opposite verticals)

$= \frac{1}{2} d\,(h_1+h_2)$

**Now we will discuss types of quadrilaterals one by one:**

1. **Parallelogram** - a quadrilateral whose opposite sides are equal and parallel.

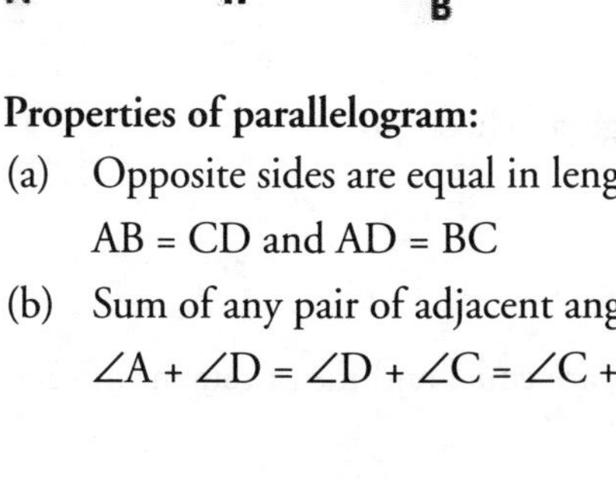


**Properties of parallelogram:**

(a) Opposite sides are equal in length and parallel.
AB = CD and AD = BC

(b) Sum of any pair of adjacent angle = 180°
∠A + ∠D = ∠D + ∠C = ∠C + ∠B = ∠B + ∠A = 180°

(c) Opposite angles are equal

$\angle A = \angle C$ and $\angle B = \angle D$.

(d) Different Formulas for Area of Parallelogram:

1st Formula : Area = Base × Height

2nd Formula : Area = (Product of adjacent sides) × (sine of the angle between them)

Area = xy sin θ, where x and y are the side lengths and θ is the angle between non parallel sides.

3rd Formula : Area $= 2\sqrt{s(s-x)(s-y)s-d)}$ where S is the semiperimeter of the triangle with sides of the parallelogram x, y and one of the diagonals d.

2. **Rectangle**

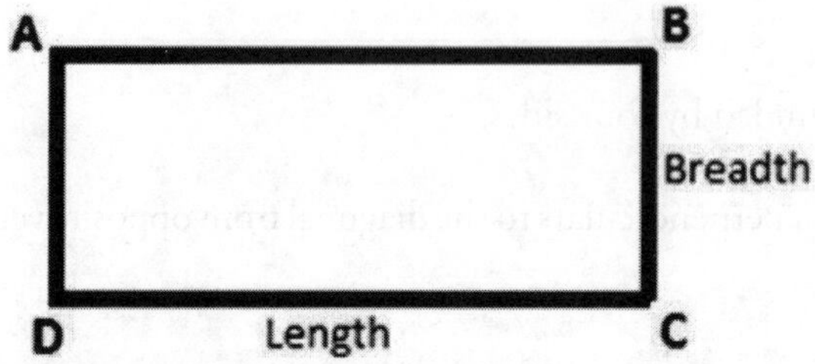


**Properties of Rectangle:**

(a) Opposite sides are equal in length and parallel to each other.

AB = CD and AD = BC

(b) Sum of any pair of adjacent angle = 180°

$\angle A + \angle D = \angle D + \angle C = \angle C + \angle B = \angle B + \angle A = 180°$

(c) All the four angles are equal.

$\angle A = \angle B = \angle C = \angle D$

Each Angle = 90 degree

(d) Area of rectangle = Length × Breadth

(e) Perimeter = 2 × (Length + Breadth)

(f) $Diagonal^2 = length^2 + breadth^2$ (Pythagoras Theorem)

$d^2 = l^2 + b^2$

$d = \sqrt{l^2 + b^2}$

3. **Square** - a quadrilateral whose all four sides are equal and measurement of each of the angles is 90°.

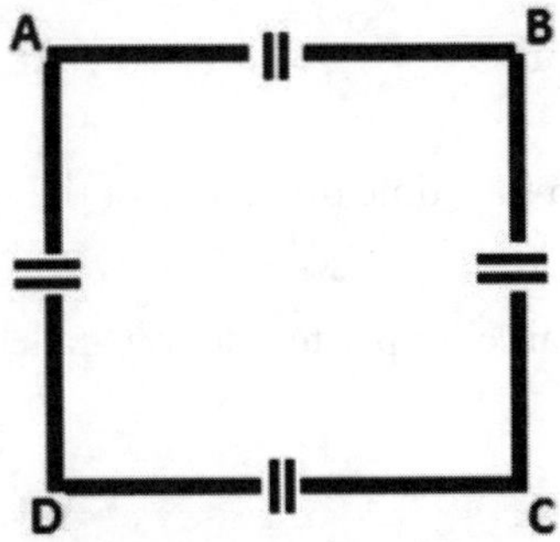


**Properties of Square:**

(a) All four sides are equal to each other.

AB = BC = CD = AD

(b) All four angles are equal to 90°

(c) Area of rectangle = (Side of length) 2 = $\frac{(\text{diagonal})^2}{2} = \frac{(\text{perimetr})^2}{16}$

(d) Perimeter = 4 × (Length of side)

(e) Diagonal = √2 × (Length of a side)

4. **Rhombus – is a quadrilateral whose all four sides are equal but none of the angles is 90°**

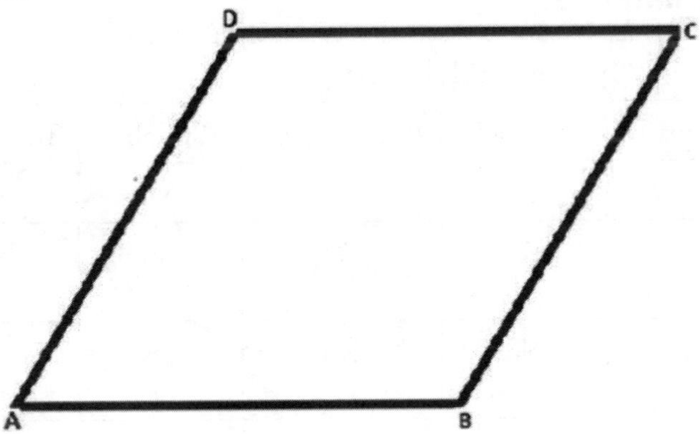


**Properties of Square:**

(a) All four sides are equal to each other.

AB = BC = CD = AD

(b) None of the angles is equal to 90°

(c) Area = $\frac{1}{2}$ × (product of the diagonals) = $\frac{1}{2} d_1 d_2$

(d) Sum of the square of the diagonals is equal to four time the square of the side i.e. $d_1^2 + d_2^2 = 4a^2$

5. **Trapezium** - is a quadrilateral in which only one pair of opposite sides is parallel.

AB is parallel to CD and h is the perpendicular distance between the parallel lines.

(a) Area = $\frac{1}{2}$ × (sum of parallel sides) × (distance between the parallel sides)

Area = $\frac{1}{2}$ (AB + CD) h

## Diagonals of the quadrilaterals:

| | Types of quadrilaterals | | | | |
|---|---|---|---|---|---|
| | Square | Rectangle | Parallelogram | Rhombus | Trapezium |
| 1. Diagonals are equal | Yes | Yes | No | No | No |
| 2. Diagonals bisects each other | Yes | Yes | Yes | Yes | No |
| 3. Diagonals bisect vertex angles | Yes | No | No | Yes | No |
| 4. Diagonals are at right angle | Yes | No | No | Yes | No |

## (d) Triangles

A triangle is a figure enclosed by three sides. In triangle ABC, AB, BC and CA sides measure c units, a units and b units respectively.

## Important Properties:

(a) Sum of all the angles of a triangle = 180°

(b) Sum of lengths of two sides > Length of third side

(c) Difference of any two sides of any triangle < Length of the third side

(d) General formula for the area of triangle

(i) Area of any triangle = $\frac{1}{2}$ × base × perpendicular to base from opposite vertex.

(ii) Area of any triangle = $\sqrt{S(S-a)(S-b)(S-c)}$, where S is the semi-perimeter of the triangle and a, b and c are sides of the triangle.

(iii) Area of any triangle = (½) × bc Sin A = (½) × ab Sin C = (½) × ac Sin B

## Note from Authors:

(a) If perimeter of different regular geometrical figures is same, then area of the structure with maximum number of sides will always be more than the area of a polygon of lesser sides.

(b) If perimeter of different types of quadrilaterals is same, then area will be maximum when all four sides are equal i.e. for square.

(c) If perimeter of different types of triangles is same, then area will be maximum when all three sides are equal i.e. for equilateral triangle.

## Worked Out examples:

Q1. Consider the figure given below:

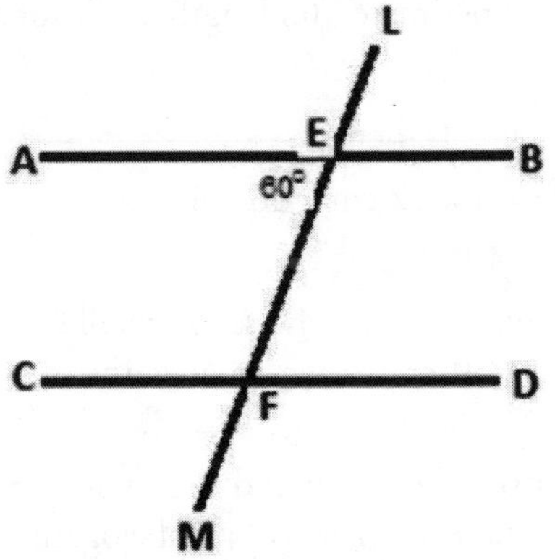

AB and CD are two parallel lines and LM is a transversal intersecting the parallel lines at points E and F. If ∠AEF = 60°, then what is the value of (a) ∠CFE, (b) ∠DFM, (c) ∠LEB

**Solution –**

(a) ∠AEF + ∠CFE = 180°. Hence ∠CFE = 180° – 60° = 120°

(b) ∠DFM = Vertically opposite ∠CFE = 120°

(c) ∠LEB = Vertically opposite ∠AEF = 60°

Q2. There are two bamboo sticks of length 10 meters and 15 meters respectively. What should be the range of length of the third bamboo stick so that a triangle can be formed using the three bamboo sticks?

**Solution** – In case of a triangle, every side should be greater than the difference of the other two sides and smaller than the sum of other two sides.

In this question, length of third bamboo stick should be greater than the difference of other two bamboo sticks and smaller than the sum of the other two bamboo sticks.

Assume length of third bamboo stick = x meter.

Then (15 – 10) meter < x meter < (15 + 10) meter ⇒ 5 meter < x meter < 25 meter.

Q3. Two sides of a parallelogram are 12 cm and 14 cm. What is its (a) perimeter, (b) area, (c) length of diagonals?

**Solution –**

(a) Perimeter = Sum of all four sides = 12 + 14 + 12 + 14 = 52 cm

(b) Area = To calculate area, we need to know the angle at which the sides are inclined at. This is not given in the question. Hence area cannot be calculated.

(c) To calculate length of diagonals, we need to know the angle at which the sides are inclined at. This is not given in the question. Hence area cannot be calculated.

Q4. Length of a side of a square shaped wooden photo frame is 12 cm. Ignoring the width of the wooden boundary, what is its (a) area, (b) perimeter, (c) length of diagonal?

**Solution –**

(a) Area of a square = $(\text{Length of Side})^2 = (12)^2 = 144$ cm

(b) Perimeter of a square = 4 × length of side = 4 × 12 cm = 48 cm

(c) Length of diagonal = length of side × $\sqrt{2} = 12\sqrt{2}$ cm

Q5. A parallelogram and a triangle have been formed between the same parallel lines and on the same base. If the area of the triangle is 30 $cm^2$, then what is the area of the parallelogram?

**Solution** – Using the following property: if a parallelogram and a triangle are drawn between the same parallel lines and on the same base, then area of parallelogram is twice the area of the triangle.

Hence area of parallelogram = 2 × (Area of Triangle) = 2 × 30 $cm^2$ = 60 $cm^2$

Q6. Area of a rhombus is 40 sq cm. If one diagonal of the rhombus is 10 cm, what is the length of the other diagonal?

**Solution** – Area of rhombus = ½ × product of diagonals = ½ × $d_1$ × $d_2$ = 40 sq cm

Or, ½ × $d_1$ × 10 cm = 40 sq cm ⇒ $d_1$ = 8 cm

Q7. Length of one diagonal of the rhombus is 10 cm. If the length of the side of the rhombus is 4 cm, what is the length of the other diagonal?

**Solution** – In the diagram given below, AC and BD are diagonals of the rhombus intersecting at N. In a rhombus, diagonals bisect each other at right angle.

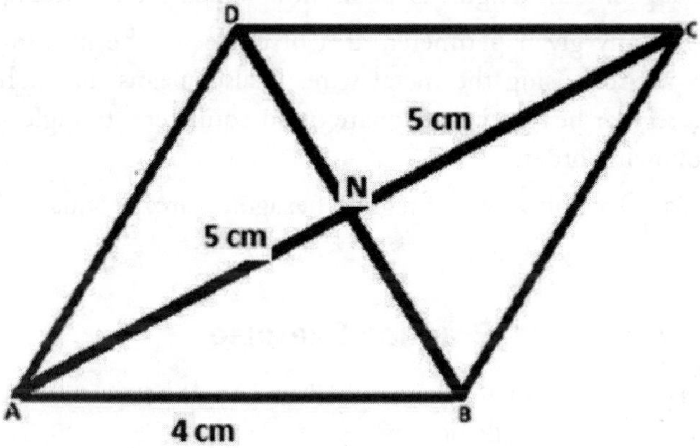


Since AC = 10 cm, AN = NC = 5 cm

V ANB is a right angle triangle and ∠ANB = 90°

Hence $AN^2 + BN^2 = AB^2$, or, $5^2 + BN^2 = 4^2$. Hence $BN^2 = 9$. So, BN = 3 cm.

Length of other diagonal = DB = DN + NB = 3 cm + 3 cm = 6 cm.

Q8. Length of a rectangle is 12 cm and its breadth is 8 cm. What is the (a) perimeter, (b) area, (c) length of diagonal of this rectangle?

**Solution** –

(a) Perimeter of rectangle = 2 × (Length + Breadth) = 2 × (12 + 8) cm = 2 × 20 cm = 40 cm

(b) Area of rectangle = Length × Breadth = 12 cm × 8 cm = 96 $cm^2$

(c) Length of diagonal = $\sqrt{Length^2 Breadth}$ = $\sqrt{12^2+8^2}$ =15 cm

Q9. Mid points of all the four sides of a square are joined by straight lines. What is the resulting figure formed by these straight lines?

**Solution** – Joining the mid points of all the four sides of square give square. Hence the resulting figure is a square.

Q10. Perimeter of a triangle is 20 cm. If all the sides of the triangle are integers, what is the maximum length of the longest side of this triangle?

**Solution** – Length of any side of the triangle will be less than the sum of other two sides.

Hence length of the longest side < ½ × Perimeter.

Or, length of the longest side < ½ × 20 cm

Or, length of the longest side < 10 cm. Since all the sides of the triangle are integers, so maximum possible length of the longest side = 9 cm.

Q11. Samar has a metal wire of length 20 cm. He wants to draw a geometrical figure so that the area of that geometrical figure is maximum. Which geometrical figure shall he draw?

**Solution** – For any given perimeter, area of circle will be maximum. Hence Samar should draw a circle using the metal wire. It also means that if he draws a regular octagon or a regular hexagon or a square or an equilateral triangle, then the area will follow the following order:

Area of Regular Octagon > area of regular hexagon > area of square > area of equilateral triangle

## Practice Exercise

Q1. Two sides of a parallelogram are 8 cm and 12 cm. Angle between non parallel sides is 30°. What is the area of this parallelogram?

(a) 24 sq cm (b) 48 sq cm

(c) 96 sq cm (d) cannot be determined

Q2. Length of side of an equilateral triangle is 10 cm. What is the height of this triangle?

(a) $5\sqrt{3}$ cm (b) $10\sqrt{3}$ cm (c) $20\sqrt{3}$ cm (d) $25\sqrt{3}$ cm

Q3. Length of the side of a rhombus is 20 cm. What is its area?

(a) 400 sq cm (b) 200 sq cm

(c) 100 sq cm (d) cannot be determined

Q4. There is a right angled triangle with perpendicular side lengths 6cm and 8cm. If a rectangle of length 6 cm has same area as that of this right angled triangle, what is the breadth of the rectangle?

(a) 4 cm (b) 2cm (c) 3 cm (d) 8 cm

Q5. Length of sides of a quadrilateral are 12 cm, 14 cm, 16 cm and 20 cm. Midpoints of all these four sides are joined to form a new quadrilateral. Name the quadrilateral formed as a result.

(a) Square (b) Rectangle
(c) Parallelogram. (d) cannot be determined

Q6. In a rectangle ABCD, mid points of sides AB, BC, CD and DA are P, Q, R and S are respectively. Quadrilateral PQRS will be a …

(a) Rectangle (b) Rhombus
(c) Parallelogram. (d) cannot be determined

Q7. In a parallelogram ABCD, non parallel sides are of length 16 cm and 8 cm. What is the area of parallelogram ABCD if angle between non parallel sides is $60^0$?

(a) $64\sqrt{3}\ m^2$ (b) $24\sqrt{3}\ m^2$ (c) $12\sqrt{3}\ m^2$ (d) $40\sqrt{3}\ m^2$

Q8. Two circles of diameters 24 cm and 16 cm touch each other internally. What is the distance between their centres?

(a) 8 cm (b) 4 cm (c) 2 cm (d) 1 cm

Q9. Area of a rhombus is 80 sq cm. If one diagonal of the rhombus is 20 cm, what is the length of the other diagonal?

(a) 8 cm (b) 4 cm (c) 2 cm (d) 1 cm

Q10. In a parallelogram ABCD, $\angle A = 60^o$. What is the value of $\angle B$?

(a) $60^o$ (b) $30^o$ (c) $120^o$ (d) None of these

Q11. A rectangular park of dimension 20 m by 12 m is to be paved with concrete path on its boundary. If width of the concrete path is 1m, what is the area of the concrete boundary?

(a) $30\ m^2$ (b) $60\ m^2$ (c) $120\ m^2$ (d) $180\ m^2$

Q12. Consider the following rectangular park ABCD of dimension 20 m by 16 m. Inside this park, a concrete pathway (in black color) of width 1 m is made. What is the area of the concrete pathway?

(a) $36\ m^2$ (b) $35\ m^2$ (c) $60\ m^2$ (d) None of these

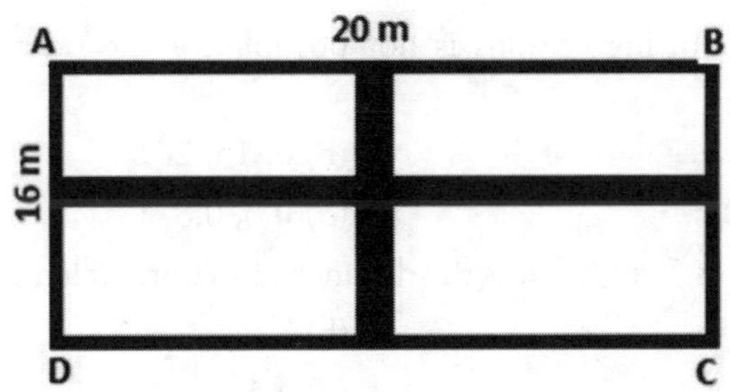


Q13. What is the ratio of the area of a rectangle and the area of parallelogram if their height is same and their base length is equal?

(a) 2:1 (b) 1:2

(c) 1:1 (d) Cannot be determined

Q14. Length of sides of a rough sheet measures 24 inches, 12 inches, 24 inches and 12 inches. Without knowing anything extra about the sheet, we can determine that the rough sheet is a -

(a) Rectangle (b) Rhombus (c ) Square (d) Parallelogram

Q15. Two circles touch externally. Sum of the areas of the two circles is $61\pi$ cm$^2$. If length of radius of one of the circles is 6 cms, what is the length of radius of the other circle?

(a) 3 (b) 4 (c) 5 (d) 6

Q16. Which of the following options is possible for the ratio of the angles of a right angled triangle?

(a) 1:2:3 (b) 3:4:5 (c) 3:5:7 (d) 1:1:3

Q17. A square shaped park ABCD is formed. In front of the park, a parking space in the shape of equilateral triangle ABE is formed. What is the measurement of the angle DEA?

(a) 15° (b) 30° (c) 45° (d) 60°

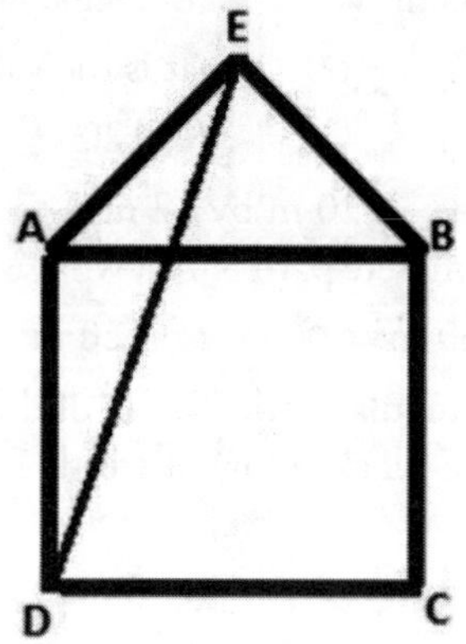


Q18. Which of the following options is not possible for the sides (all values in cm) of a triangle?

(a) 10, 15, 20 (b) 6, 15, 20

(c ) 100, 200, 80 (d) 0.6, 0.8, 1

Q19. In a circle of radius 5 cm, what is the distance of a chord of length 8 cm from the centre?

(a) 3 cm (b) 3.6 cm

(c ) 4 cm (d) 4.5 cm

Q20. Chord AC subtends equal angle at two different points of circle on the same side - B and D. It is also known that AB and CD intersect at point E. Length of chord AD = 6 cm and length of chord BC = 3 cm. If area of triangle BCE is x cm$^2$, what will be area of the triangle DAE (in cm$^2$)?

(a) 2x (b) 4x (c) x/2 (d) x/4

Q21. Two sides of a triangle are 100 units and 200 units respectively. If length of third side is N units, find the range of length of third side.

(a) $N < 300$ (b) $N \leq 300$ (c) $N > 100$ (d) $100 < N < 300$

Q22. In the figure given below, $\Delta ABC$ is a right angled triangle $BC \perp AC$. If AD = 8 cm and DC = 2cm, then what is the value of BD?

(a) 4cm (b) 4.5 cm

(c) 5cm (d) Cannot be determined

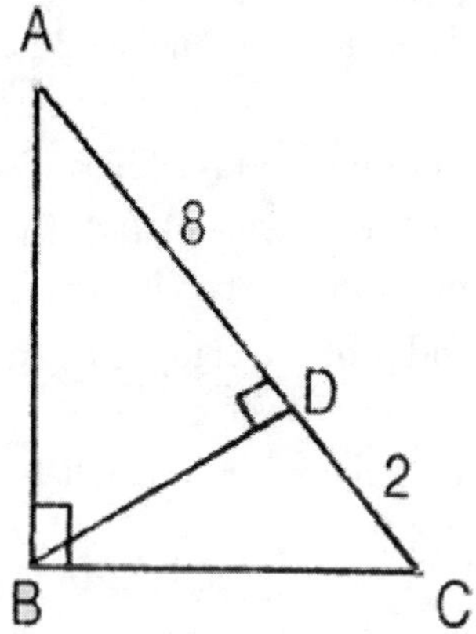


## Answer Grid:

| Q. No. | 1 | 2 | 3 | 4 | 5 | 6 | 7 | 8 | 9 | 10 | 11 |
|---|---|---|---|---|---|---|---|---|---|---|---|
| Answer | b | a | a | d | a | c | b | a | b | c | b |
| Q. No. | 12 | 13 | 14 | 15 | 16 | 17 | 18 | 19 | 20 | 21 | 22 |
| Answer | b | c | d | c | a | a | c | a | b | d | a |

## Solution and Explanations:

Q1. If lengths of non parallel sides of a parallelogram are a cm and b cm and angle between them is $\alpha$, then area of parallelogram = ab $\sin\alpha$.

Hence area of parallelogram = $8 \times 12 \times \sin 30^\circ = 96 \times ½ = 48$ sq cm. Hence option (b) is the answer

Q2. If length of side of an equilateral triangle is x cm, then its height = $\frac{\sqrt{3}}{2}a$

Hence height of the triangle = $\frac{\sqrt{3}}{2} \times 10 = 5\sqrt{3}$ cm. Hence option (a) is the answer.

Q3. To calculate the area of a rhombus, we need to have the length of diagonals. There is no way we can find the length of the diagonals with the length of side. Hence option (d) cannot be determined is the answer.

Q4. Area of triangle = ½ × base × height = ½ × 6 × 8 = 24 $cm^2$

Given that area of rectangle = Area of triangle = 24 $cm^2$ = Length × Breadth = 6 cm × Breadth

Hence breadth = 4 cm. Hence option (a) is the answer.

Q5. When mid points of a quadrilateral which has different length of all its sides are joined, the new quadrilateral formed will be a parallelogram. Hence option (c) is the answer.

Q6. When mid points of the sides of a rectangle are joined by straight lines, rhombus is formed. Hence option (b) is the answer.

Q7. Area of a parallelogram with length of non parallel sides a units and b units = ab Sin$\alpha$, where $\alpha$ is the angle between these sides.

Hence area of parallelogram = 16 × 8 × Sin 60° = 128 × $\frac{\sqrt{3}}{2}$ = $64\sqrt{3}$ $m^2$

Q8. Since they are touching internally, distance between their centres = Distance between the length of their radii = 12 cm – 8 cm = 4 cm. Hence option (b) is the answer.

Q9. Area of rhombus = ½ × product of diagonals = ½ × $d_1$ × $d_2$ = 80 sq cm

Or, ½ × $d_1$ × 20 cm = 80 sq cm Þ $d_1$ = 8 cm. Hence option (a) is the answer.

Q10. In a parallelogram, sum of adjacent angles = 180°

Or, ∠A + ∠B = 180°

Or, 60° + ∠B = 180°

Hence ∠B = 180° – 60° = 120°

Hence option (c) is the answer.

Q11. Following is the diagram:

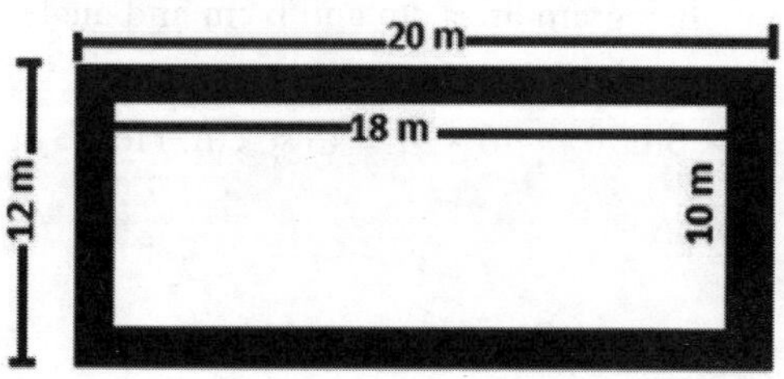

Blackened area is the concrete path.

Area of outer rectangle = 20 m × 12 m = 240 $m^2$

Width of the concrete path is 1 m.

Area of inner rectangle = 18 m × 10 m = 180 $m^2$

Hence area of concrete path = 240 $m^2$ - 180 $m^2$ = 60 $m^2$

Hence option (b) is the answer.

Q12. Area of pathway = Area of pathway along the length + area of pathway along the breadth – common area = 20 m × 1 m + 16 m × 1 m – 1 m × 1 m = 35 $m^2$

Hence option (b) is the answer.

Q13. If the height and base length are equal, then area of rectangle = Area of parallelogram = Length of base × Height. Hence option (c) is the answer.

Q14. Since all four sides are not equal, option (b) and option (c) are ruled out.

Further, none of the angles is known, so we cannot definitely conclude that it's a rectangle. We are left out with option (d) parallelogram.

Q15. Let the radii of the two circles are $r_1$ cm and $r_2$ cm.

According to the question, $\pi(r_1^2 + r_2^2) = 61\pi$

Or, $r_1^2 + r_2^2 = 61$

Or, $6^2 + r_2^2 = 61$

Hence $r_2^2 = 61 - 36 = 25$

So, $r_2 = 5$ cm. Hence option (c) is the answer.

Q16. Let us verify the options one by one:

Option (a) 1 : 2 : 3

Assume angles are x, 2x and 3x.

Or, x + 2x + 3x = 180°, or, 6x = 180°. Hence x = 30°

Hence 3x = 3 × 30° = 90°

So option (a) is possible. Since only one of the options is the answer, we are not required to check the next options.

Q17. In ΔADE, ∠DAE = 90° + 60° = 150°

Since AD = AB (sides of square) and AB = AE (sides of equilateral triangle), we can conclude that AD = AE.

In triangle ADE,

Since AD = AE, so ∠ADE = ∠DEA ——————(1)

Further∠ADE + ∠DEA + ∠DAE = 180°, or, ∠ADE + ∠AED + 150° = 180°

Or, ∠ADE + ∠DEA = 30°

Using (1), 2 × ∠DEA = 30°. So, ∠DEA = 15°

Hence option (a) is the answer.

Q18. Except option (c), all the other options satisfy "sum of two sides is greater than the length of third side length". Hence option (c) is the answer.

Q19. Following is the diagram:

Assume point O is the centre of the circle, AB is the chord of length 8 cm. Distance between the centre and chord = OC. It should be noted that whenever we talk of distance, it is always perpendicular distance.

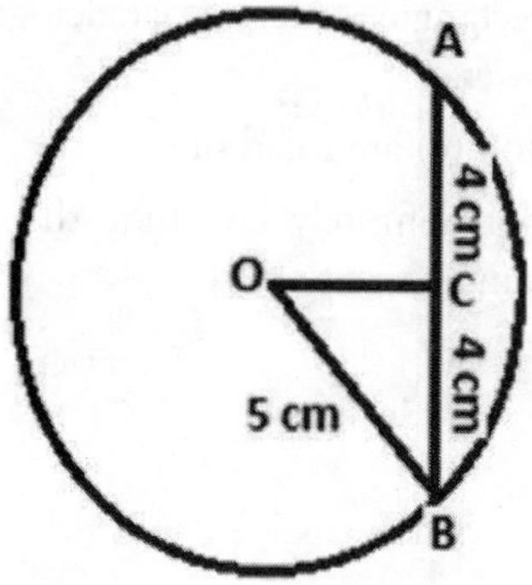


∇ OCB is a right angled triangle.

Hence $OB^2 = OC^2 + BC^2$

Or, $5^2 = OC^2 + 4^2$

Or, $OC^2 = 25$ cm – 16 cm = 9 cm

Hence OC = √9 = 3 cm. Hence option (a) is the answer.

Q20. Following figure can be drawn:

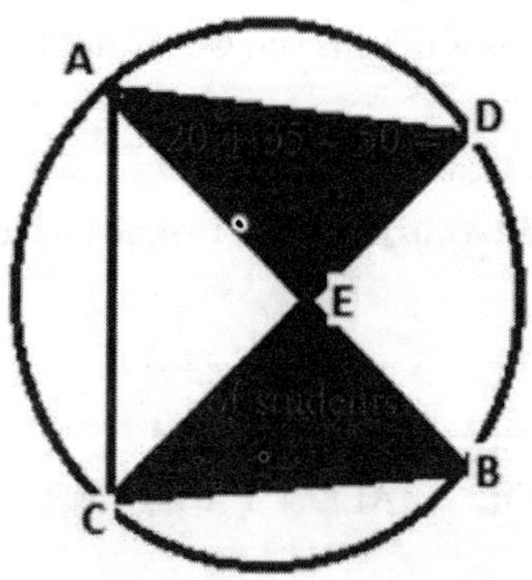

Consider ΔBCE and ΔDAE ( in black color):

∠EBC = ∠ADC (angles by the same chord AC)

∠CEB = ∠AED (vertically opposite angles)

Using AA, ΔBCE and ΔDAE are similar Δs.

We know that if two triangles are similar, then their ratio of areas = (ratio of sides)$^2$

Given that AD = 6 cm, BC = 3 cm

$$\frac{\text{Length of side ADE}}{\text{Length of side BCD}} = \frac{6}{3}\ 2:1$$

$$\text{Hence } = \frac{\text{Area of ADE}}{\text{Area of BCD}} = \frac{4}{1} = \frac{4x}{x}$$

Hence option (b) is the answer.

Q21. Third side will be greater than the difference of two sides and smaller than the sum of two sides. If length of third side = N units, then (200 – 100 ) < N < (200 + 100) ⇒ 100 < N < 300. Hence option (d) is the answer.

Q22. Using the concept of similarity, Δ ADB is similar to ΔBDC. So, $\frac{AD}{BD} = \frac{BD}{DC}$

Hence $BD^2 = AD \times DC = 8 \times 2$, or, $BD^2 = 16 \Rightarrow BD = 4$ cm

**This expression can be used as a formula too: $BD^2 = AD \times DC$**

# 17 Mensuration

In this chapter, we are going to discuss the following 3-dimensional figures:
(a) Sphere, (b) Hemisphere, (c) Cylinder, (d) Cone, (e) Cuboid and (f) Cube

## General Definitions of the terms:

(a) Volume – Volume is the holding capacity of a vessel. In other words, Volume = Quantity of water that the vessel can hold

(b) Curved Surface area – Curved surface area is the area of the curvature.

(c) Lateral Surface Area – Lateral surface area is the area of four walls of a cube or cuboid structure. For a room, Lateral Surface Area is the area of four walls.

Mathematically, Curved Surface area is same as Lateral Surface Area. Only difference between these two is – Curved Surface area is calculated for solids which are curved like cylinder or cone whereas Lateral Surface Area is calculated for solids which have flat surfaces like Cube or Cuboid.

(d) Total surface area – Total surface area = Curved Surface area / Lateral Surface Area + Area of Base + Area of top

(e) Diagonal – Diagonal is the length of the longest stick kept inside a cube or cubiod.

**Sphere**

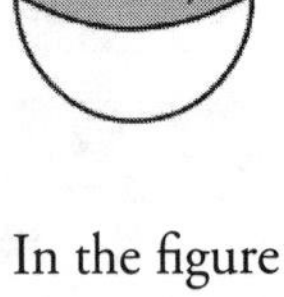


In the figure given above, r is the radius of the sphere.

(a) Volume of Sphere = $\frac{4}{3}\pi^3$

(b) Surface Area of the Sphere = $4\pi r^2$

**In case of Sphere, Surface Area or Total Surface Area of Curved Surface Area mean the same thing.**

**Hemisphere**

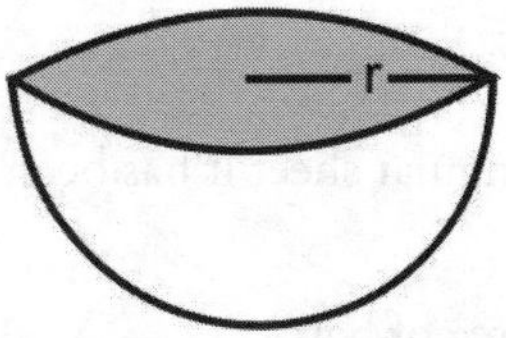


(a) Volume = $\frac{2}{3}\pi^3$

(b) Curved surface area (C.S.A.) = $2\pi r^2$

(c) Total surface area (T.S.A.) = C.S.A. + Area of top face(which is circular is shape)

T.S.A. = $2\pi^2 + \pi r^2$

T.S.A. = $3\pi^2$

## Cylinder

Cylinder is formed by rolling a rectangular sheet of paper along its length or breadth.

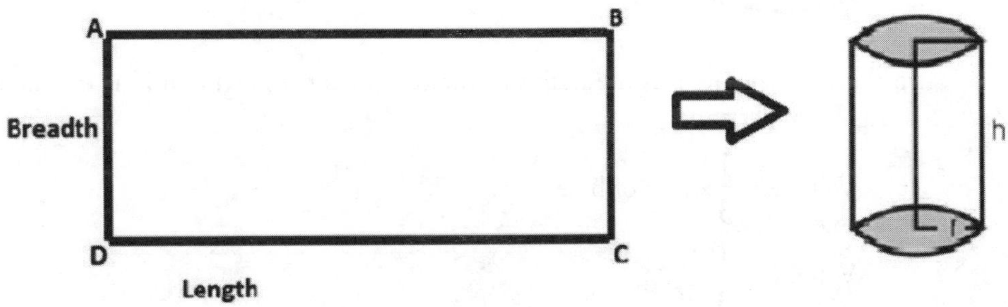


In the figure above, rectangle ABCD is rolled along its length to form a cylinder.

In the above figure r is the radius of the base and h is the height of cylinder. In this case, length of rectangular sheet = Circumference of the base of the cylinder = 2 π r and Breadth of cylindrical sheet = Height of Cylinder = h

(a) Volume = Area of base × height

Volume = $\pi r^2 h$

(b) Curved surface Area (CSA) = Perimeter of base × height

CSA = $2\pi rh$

CSA of the Cylinder is same as the area of the rectangular sheet it has been formed from.

(c) Total Surface Area (TSA) = CSA + Area of top + Area of base

TSA = $2\pi rh + \pi r^2 + \pi r^2$

TSA = $2\pi r(r + h)$

**Right Circular Cone**

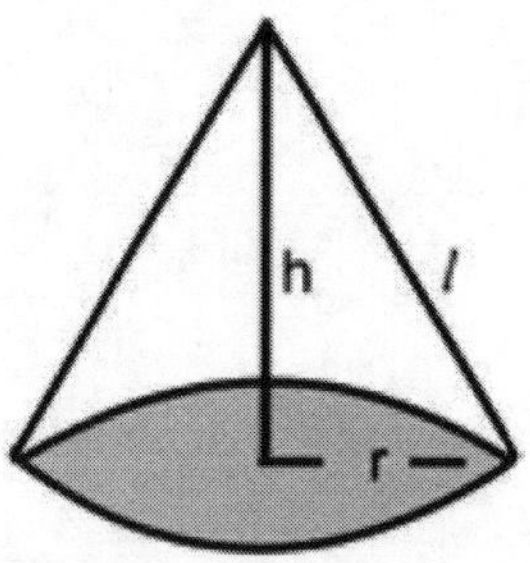


In the above figure 'r' is the radius of the base, h is the height and l is the slant height of right circular cone.

(a) Volume = $\frac{1}{3} \times$ area of base × height

Volume = $\frac{1}{3}\pi r^2 h$

It can also be seen that Volume of Cone is 1/3rd the Volume of corresponding Cylinder (with same radius and height).

(b) Slant height = $l = \sqrt{r^2 + h^2}$

(c) Curved Surface Area (CSA) = $\pi r l = \times \pi r\sqrt{r^2 + h^2}$

(d) Total Surface Area (TSA) = (CSA + Area of base) = $\pi r l + \pi r^2$

## Important Deductions

**Frustum of Cone**

A cone whose top portion is sliced off by a plane which is parallel to the base is called frustum of cone.

Formation of Frustum:

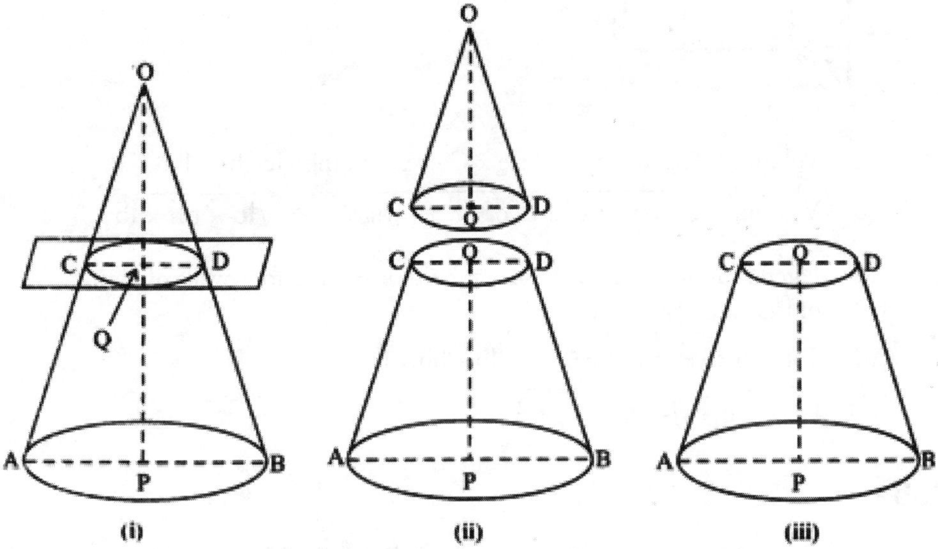


However for the sake of representing the formula, we will use another form of Frustum right now as given below:

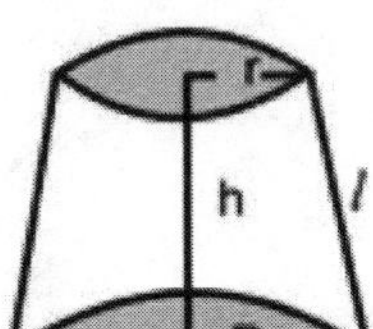


(a) Volume of Frustum = Volume of Original Cone – Volume of Cone removed

(b) Total Surface Area (TSA) = Curved Surface Area of frustum + Area of Top + Area of base

(c) Slant height ($l$) = $\sqrt{h^2 - (R-r)^2}$

## Cuboid (Rectangular Box)

A cuboid is a rectangular solid with six rectangular faces. As given in the figure below, for the sake of writing formula, assume that length breadth and height are represented by l, b and h respectively.

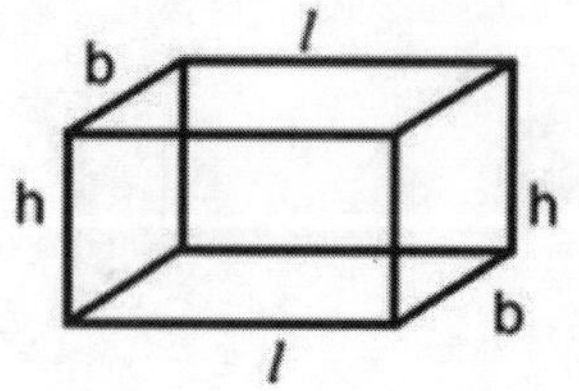


(a) Volume = Area of any surface × Corresponding Height = lbh

(b) Volume = $\sqrt{\text{Product of area of three surfaces}} = \sqrt{lb \times bh \times lh}$

(c) Lateral surface area (LSA) of a cuboid or Area of four walls of a room = Perimeter of base × height = 2 (l + b)h

(d) Total surface area (TSA) = 2 (lb + bh + lh)

(e) Diagonal = $\sqrt{l^2 + b^2 + h^2}$

## Cube

If all the three dimensions namely length, breadth and height of a cuboid are equal, then this solid is known as Cube. In the figure given below, length = breadth = height = 'a' units

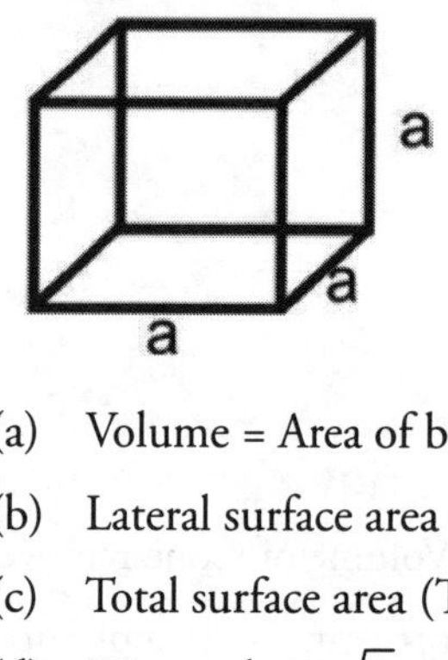


(a) Volume = Area of base × Height = $a^2 \times a = a^3$

(b) Lateral surface area (LSA) or area of 4 walls = Perimeter × height = $4a \times a = 4a^2$

(c) Total surface area (TSA) = $6a^2$

(d) Diagonal = $a\sqrt{3}$

## Worked out examples:

Q1. Radius of a sphere is 14 cm. What is the (a) volume (b) Total surface area of this sphere?

**Solution** – (a) Volume of sphere = $\frac{4}{3}\pi r^2 = \frac{4}{3} \times \frac{22}{7} \times 21^3 = 38772$ cm$^3$

(b) Total surface area of sphere = $4\pi r^2 = 4 \times \frac{22}{7} \times 21^3 = 5538$ cm$^2$

Q2. Radius of a hemi-sphere is 28 cm. What is the (a) volume (b) Total surface area, (c) curved surface area of this hemisphere?

**Solution** – (a) Volume of hemi-sphere = $\frac{2}{3}\pi r^3 = \frac{2}{3} \times \frac{22}{7}\ 28^3 = 45952$ cm$^3$

(b) Total surface area of hemisphere = $3\pi r^2 = 3 \times \frac{22}{7} \times 28^2 = 7385$ cm$^2$

(c) Curved Surface area of hemi sphere = $2\pi^2 = 2 \times \frac{22}{7} \times 28^2 = 4923$ cm$^2$

Q3. Radius of a cylinder is 10 cm and its height is 14 cm. What is the (a) Volume, (b) Curved surface area and (c) Total Surface area?

**Solution** – (a) Volume = $\pi r^2 h = \frac{22}{7} \times 10^2 \times 14 = 4396$ cm$^3$

(b) Curved surface Area (CSA) = $2\pi rh = 2 \times \frac{22}{7} \times 10 \times 14 = 879.2$ cm$^2$

(c) Total Surface Area (TSA) = $2\pi rh + \pi r^2 + \pi r^2 = 2\pi r (r + h)$

$= 2 \times (22/7) \times 10 \times (10+14) = 1507.2$ cm$^2$

Q4. Radius of a cone is 14 cm and its height is 20 cm. What is the (a) Volume, (b) Curved surface area, and (c) Total surface area of this cone?

**Solution** –

(a) Volume = $1/3\ \pi r^2 h = (1/3) \times \frac{22}{7} \times 14^2 \times 20 = 4103$ cm$^3$

(b) Curved surface Area (CSA) = $\pi rl$

We know that slant height = $l = \sqrt{r^2+h^2}$

Hence Curved surface Area (CSA) = $\pi rl = \pi r = \times \sqrt{r^2 + h^2} = \frac{22}{7}\ 14 \times \sqrt{14^2 + 20^2}$

= 1073 $cm^2$

(c) Total surface area of the cone = Curved Surface area + area of bottom surface

$= \pi rl + \pi r^2 = \frac{22}{7} \times 14 \times \sqrt{14^2 + 20^2} + \frac{22}{7} \times 14^2 = 1688\ cm^2$

Q5. Length, breadth and height of a cuboid are 10 cm, 12 cm and 15 cm respectively. What is the volume of this cuboid?

**Solution** – Volume of cuboid = Length × Breadth × Height = 10 cm × 12 cm × 15 cm = 1800 $cm^3$

Q6. Length, breadth and height of a cuboid are 12 cm, 15 cm and 20 cm respectively. What is the length of the longest pole that can be kept inside this cuboid?

**Solution** – Length of the longest pole = $\sqrt{12^2 + 15^2 + 20^2}$ cm = $\sqrt{769}$ cm = 27.73 cm

Q7. A customer, who has gone to buy a spherical ball at a sports shop, stole a white spherical solid ball from the shop. When he was about to leave the shop, he got scared that he might get caught during the search, and so he cut it into four similar pieces thinking that he would join it back using glue once he is safely out of shop. During the search, the owner of the shop claimed that it is a ball from his shop, and to prove this, he claimed that the surface area of the outer surface will be same as the surface area of the inner surfaces of all the four pieces. What is ratio of the area of the outer surface to the sum of surface area of the inner surfaces of all the four pieces?

1. 1:1 2. 1:2 3. 2:1 4. Cannot be determined

**Solution** – Let the radius of spherical ball = r, hence total surface area = $4\pi r^2$

After cutting, two surfaces of every piece will be exposed with area of each surface = ½ $\pi r^2$ Hence surface area per piece = $\pi r^2$

There are four such pieces. Hence total surface area of all four pieces = 4 $\pi r^2$

So, the ratio of the area of the outer surface to the sum of surface area of the inner surfaces of all the four pieces = 1:1

Q8. A cylinder can hold 300 litres of water. For the same radius and same height, how much water will a cone hold?

**Solution** – For the same radius and same height, volume of a cone = $\frac{1}{3}$ × (volume of cylinder) = $\frac{1}{3}$ × 300 litres = 100 litres.

Q9. A spherical metal ball of 6cm radius is melted to give rise to three small spherical metal balls. The radii of two of these balls are 3cm and 4cm. What is the radius of the third ball?

1. 4.5 cm 2.5 cm 3.6 cm 4. 7 cm

**Solution** – During the recasting process, we assume that volume remains constant unless stated otherwise.

Volume of the original ball = $\frac{4}{3}\pi r^3 = \frac{4}{3}\pi \times 216 \text{ cm}^3$ —— (i)

Let radius of the third ball = 'a' cm

So total volume of small balls = $\frac{4}{3}\pi\,[3^3 + 4^3 + a^3]$ —— (ii)

Using equation (i) and (ii):

$$\frac{4}{3}\pi \times 216 = \frac{4}{3}\pi\,[27 + 64 + a^3]$$

$a^3 = 216 - 91 = 125$. So a = 5 cm

## Practice Exercise

1. The volume of a cuboid is 1120 $cm^3$ and its height is 5 cm while the length and the breadth of the cuboid are in the ratio 8:7. The length of this cuboid exceeds the breadth by -

   (a) 2 cm (b) 4 cm (c)7 cm (d) 5 cm

2. The volume of a rectangular block of stone is 103868 $dm^2$, its dimensions are in the ratio of 3:2:1. If its entire surface is polished at 2 paise per $dm^2$, then what is the total cost?

   (a) Rs. 31.68 (b) Rs. 31 .58 (c) Rs. 63 (d) Rs. 63.36

3. A school room is to be built to accommodate 70 children, so as to allow 2.2 $m^2$ of floor and 11 $m^3$ of space for each child. If the room be 14 m long, what must be its breadth and height?

   (a) 12 and 5.5 m (b) 13 and 6 m (c) 11 and 5 m (d) 11 and 4m

4. A pool is in the shape of a frustum of a right circular cone. It is 8cm across at the top and 4 m across the bottom. It is 6 m deep. Find the area of its curved surface area.

(a) 118.4 $m^2$ (b) 162.3 $m^2$ (c) 452 $m^2$ (d) 181.6 $m^2$

5. Two cans have the same height equal to 21 cm. One can is cylindrical, the diameter of whose base is 10 cm. The other can has square base of side 10 cm. what is the difference in their capacities?

(a) 350 $cm^3$ (b) 250 cm $^3$ (c) 450 $cm^3$. (d) 300 $cm^3$

6. A Cistern of dimensions 2.4mX 2m x 1.5 m takes 2 h 30 min to get filled with water. The rate at which water flows into the cistern is

(a) 0.48000 cu m/hr (b) 800 cu m /min

(c) 800 cu m/ sec (d) None of these

7. It is required to design a circular pipe such that water flowing through it at a speed of 7m / min fills a pool of capacity 440 cu m in 10 min. The inner radius of the pipe should be

(a) 2m. (b) $\sqrt{2}$ m (c) 1/2 m. (d) $1/\sqrt{2}$ m

8. Twenty nine times the area of a square is one square meter less than six times the area of the second square and nine time the sides of it exceeds the perimeter of other square by one meter. The difference in sides of this square is

(a) 5m (b) 54/11m (c) 11m (d) 6m

9. Milk has been poured into an empty rectangular container at the rate of 8 cu ft/min for. 2.5 min. the length of the container is 3 ft and the width is one half of the length. How deep is the milk in the container?

(a) 4ft. (b) 3.86ft. (c) 3.23ft. (d) 4.44ft

10. A roller 150 cm long has diameter 70 cm. To level a playground, it takes 750 complete revolutions. The cost of leveling the playground at the rate of Rs 2 per $m^2$ is (Rs.)

(a) Rs. 5000 (b) Rs. 2950 (c) 45 (d) 4950

11. A circular swimming pool with a diameter of 28 ft has a deck of uniform width built around it. If the area of the deck is 60p sq ft, find its width.

(a) 3ft. (b) 2.8ft (c) 2ft. (d) 2.5.ft

12. An structure is in the shape of a hemisphere surmounted by a cone. If radius of base of the cone is 3 cm and its height is 4 cm, the total surface area of the structure is

(a) 33 $\pi$ $m^2$. (b) 42$\pi$ $cm^2$ (c) 66 $\pi$ $cm^2$. (d) 56 $\pi$ $cm^2$

13. The length of rectangle is increased to 3/2 times of its length and breadth is reduced to 1/3rd of its breadth. What is the change in area?

(a) 1/3 (b) 1/4 (c) 1/2 (d) no change

14. The ratio of the volume of cube to that of a sphere which can fit inside the cube is
(a) 3:4 (b) 21:11 (c) 11:22 (d) 4:3

15. Length of a rectangular chessboard is 8m more than that of its breadth. If its length is increased by 7 m and its breadth is decreased by 4m, its area remains unchanged. The length and breadth of the rectangular chessboard is
(a) 24m, 16m (b) 20m, 24m (c) 28m, 20m (d) 28m, 16m

16. A cylindrical vessel of radius 12 cm contains water up to a depth of 20 cm. A spherical ball of Iron is dropped into the flask and thus the level of water is the raised by 6.75 cm. The radius of the spherical ball is -
(a) 7.25 cm (b) 6 cm (c) 4.5 cm (d) 9 cm

17. A spherical ball of zinc, 3cm in diameter is melt and recast into three spherical balls. Radii of two balls are 1.5 cm and 2cm respectively. The diameter of the third ball is
(a) 3 cm (b) 2.66 cm (c) 2.5 cm (d) 3.5 cm

18. A rectangular farm has to be fenced on one long side, one short side and the diagonal. Given that cost of fencing is Rs 100 per m, the area of the farm is 1200 $m^2$ and the short side is 30m long. How much would the job cost?
(a) Rs. 14000 (b) Rs. 12000 (c) Rs. 7000 (d) Rs. 15000

19. A landowner increased the length and breadth of a rectangular plot of land by 10% and 20% respectively. Find the percentage change in the cost of the plot of land?
(a) 35% (b) 33% (c) 22.22% (d) none of these

20. In a swimming pond measuring 90m by 40m, 150 men take a dip. If the average displacement of water by a man is 8 cu m, what will be the rise in water level?
(a) 33.33 cm (b) 30 cm (c) 20 cm (d) 25 cm

21. A 4cm cube is cut into 1cm cubes. Find the percentage increase in surface area.
(a) 200% (b) 100% (c) 400 % (d) 300%

22. The radius of the base of a conical tent is 5m. If the tent is 12m high, then the area of a canvas required in making tent is -
(a) 300 $\pi$ $m^2$ (b) 60 $\pi$ $m^2$ (c) 90 $\pi$ $m^2$ (d) none of these

23. A wooden box of dimension 8m × 7m × 6m is to carry rectangular boxes of dimensions 8cm × 7cm × 6cm. The maximum number of boxes that can be carried in the wooden box is
(a) 9800000 (b) 1000000 (c) 7500000 (d) 1200000

24. The length of a rectangular field is double its width. Inside the field, there is a square-shaped pool 8m long. If the area of the pool is 1/8 of area of the field, what is the length of the field?
(a) 32 m (b) 16 m (c) 64 m (d) 20 m

25. Volume and height of a cone and a cylinder are same. What is the ratio of radius of cone to the radius of cylinder?

(a) 1:3 (b) 3:1 (c) 1:1 (d) 9:1

## Answer Grid:

| Q. No. | 1 | 2 | 3 | 4 | 5 | 6 | 7 | 8 | 9 | 10 | 11 | 12 | 13 |
|---|---|---|---|---|---|---|---|---|---|---|---|---|---|
| Answer | a | d | c | a | c | d | b | d | d | d | c | a | c |
| Q. No. | 14 | 15 | 16 | 17 | 18 | 19 | 20 | 21 | 22 | 23 | 24 | 25 | |
| Answer | b | c | d | c | b | d | a | d | d | b | a | b | |

## Solutions and Explanations

Q1. Let the length and breadth of a cuboid be 8x and 7x.

Volume of cuboid = L × B × H

1120 = 8x × 7x × 5

$x^2 = \frac{1120}{8\times7\times5} = 4 \quad x = 2$

Length and breadth of a cuboid are 16cm and 14cm.

Hence, length exceeds breadth by 2cm. Hence option (A) is the answer

Q2. Let dimension of a stone be 3x, 2x, x.

∴ Volume of stone = 10368

3x × 2x × x = 10368, or, = 10368

Hence = 1728. Hence x = 12

∴ Dimensions are 36 dm, 24 dm, 12 dm.

∴ Entire surface area of a stone = 2(lb + bh + hl) = 2(36×24 + 24× 12 + 12×36)

= 2(864 + 288 + 432) = 3168 $dm^2$

∴ Total cost of polishing = 3168 × 0.02 = 63.36

Hence option (D) is the answer

Q3. Let the breadth and height be b and h respectively

Then, 70 ×2.2 = 14 × b, or, b = 11m

Also, $14 \times b \times h = 70 \times 11$. Hence $h = \frac{70 \times 11}{14 \times 11} = 5m$

Hence option (C) is the answer

Q4. Curved surface area of a pool = $\pi (r + R)L$

Here, $R = \frac{8}{2} = 4m$, $r = \frac{4}{2} = 2m$

And $l = \sqrt{h^2 + (R-r)^2}$ $\quad l = \sqrt{6^2 = 2^2} = \sqrt{40}$

$\therefore$ Curved surface area = $\frac{22}{7} \times (2+4) \times \sqrt{40} = 119.26 \cong 118.4\ m^2$

Hence option (A) is the answer

Q5. Required difference = $l \times b \times h - \pi r^2 h = 10 \times 10 \times 21 - \frac{22}{7} \times (\frac{10}{2})^2 \times 21 = 2100 - 1650$

$= 450\ cm^3$

Hence option (C) is the answer

Q6. Capacity of cistern = $2.4 \times 2 \times 1.5 = 7.2$ cu m

Total time to fill the cistern $= 2\frac{1}{2}$ h

So, rate of water flow = $\frac{7.2}{2\frac{1}{2}} = 2.88$ cu m/h

Hence option (D) is the answer

Q7. A pool of 440 cu m is filled in 10 min.

$\therefore$ Flow of spirit = 44 cu m/min

$\therefore \pi r^2 h = 44 \quad \frac{22}{7} \times r^2 \times h = 44$

$r^2 = \frac{44}{22} = r = \sqrt{2}$ m

Hence option (B) is the answer

Q8. Let the sides of two squares be x m and y m.

Then, $29x^2 + 1 = 6y^2$ and $9x - 1 = 4y$

From Equations (1) and (2),

$29x^2 + 1 = 6 \times [\frac{9x-1}{4}]$, or, $29x^2 + 1 = \frac{6}{16} \times (81x^2+1-18x)$

Or, $232x^2 + 8 = 243x^2 + 3 - 54x$, or, $11x^2 - 55x + x - 5 = 0$

$(11x+1)(x-5)=0$ $\therefore$ x= 5m as $x - \neq -\frac{1}{11}$

Y = 11m $\therefore y - x = 6$ m

Hence option (D) is the answer

Q9. Let milk in the container is h feet deep.

$\therefore 3\times\frac{3}{2}\times h = 8\times 2.5$ $h = \frac{8\times 2.5\times 2}{3\times 3} = 4.44$ ft

Hence option (D) is the answer

Q10. Total area of playground = $750 \times 2\pi rh$

$= 750 \times 2 \times \frac{22}{7} \times \frac{70}{2} \times 150$

$= 2475 \times 10^4$ cm$^2$ = 2475 m$^2$

Hence option (D) is the answer

Q11. Area of swimming pool = $\pi r^2 = \pi(14)^2 = 196\pi\, ft^2$

Total area of the swimming pool and deck = $196\pi + 60\pi = 256\pi ft^2$

$= 196\pi + 60\pi = 256\pi ft^2$

So, $256\pi = \pi R^2$ R = 16 ft

Width of deck = 16 – 14 = 2 ft

Hence option (C) is the answer

Q12. Surface area of hemisphere = $2\pi r^2 = 2\pi(3)^2 = 18\pi$ cm$^2$

Now l= $\sqrt{4^2+3^2} = 5$

Surface area of cone = $\pi rl = \pi \times 3 \times 5 = 15\pi$ cm$^2$

Total surface area = $18\pi + 15\pi = 33\pi$ cm$^2$

Hence option (A) is the answer

Q13. Old length of rectangle = L — New length of rectangle = $\frac{3}{2}$ L

Old breadth of rectangle = B — New breadth of rectangle = $\frac{1}{3}$ B

Old area = L × B — New area = $\frac{3}{2}$ L × $\frac{1}{3}$ B = $\frac{1}{2}$ LB

Hence, change in area is $\frac{1}{2}$

Hence option (C) is the answer

Q14. Let the side of cube = x units

Volume of cube = $x^3$

Let the radius of sphere = r

Now, sphere can fit inside the cube, so r = $\frac{x}{2}$

$$= \frac{\text{volume of cube}}{\text{volume of sphere}} = \frac{x^3}{\frac{4}{3}\times\frac{22}{7}\times\frac{x^3}{8}} = \frac{3\times7\times8}{4\times22} = \frac{21}{11}$$

Hence option (B) is the answer

Q15. Let length and breadth of chessboard be x m and (x - 8) m

Then, x × (x – 8) = (x + 7) (x – 12)

$x^2 - 8x = x^2 - 5x - 84$

$x = \frac{84}{3} = 28\text{m, or, } x - 8 = 20\text{m}$

Hence option (C) is the answer

Q16. Volume of raised water inside the vessel = Volume of spherical ball

Or, $\pi \times (12)^2 \times 6.75 = \frac{4}{3}\pi r^3 = \pi \times 144 \times 6.75$

Solving it, we get = 729. Or, r = 9 cm

Hence option (D) is the answer

Q17. Let the diameter of third ball be 2r.

$$= \frac{4}{3}\pi \times \left(\frac{3}{2}\right)^3 = \frac{4}{3}\pi \times \left(\frac{1.5}{2}\right)^3 + \frac{4}{3}\pi \times \left(\frac{2}{2}\right)^2 + \frac{4}{3}\pi\left(\frac{2r}{2}\right)^3$$

$$= \frac{27}{8} = \frac{27}{64} + 1 + r^3 \qquad r^3 = \frac{125}{64}$$

$$r = \frac{5}{4}\text{ cm} \qquad 2r = \frac{10}{4} = 2.5\text{ cm}$$

Hence option (C) is the answer

Q18. Length of longer side = $\frac{1200}{30}$ = 40m

Length of diagonal = $\sqrt{40^2 + 30^2}$ = 50 m

Total length of fenced sides = 30 + 40 + 50 = 120 m

∴ Total cost = 100 × 120 = Rs. 12000

Hence option (B) is the answer

Q19. Using the formula for successive percentage change, percentage change in cost =

$10 + 20 + \frac{10 \times 20}{100}$ = 32%. Hence option (D) is the answer

Q20. Let water level will rise by x m.

According to the question, 90 × 40 × x = 150×8, or, x = 0.3333 m = 33.33 cm

Hence option (A) is the answer

Q21. Total number of smaller cubes = $\frac{4 \times 4 \times 4}{1 \times 1 \times 1}$ = 64

Increase in surface area = $64 \times 6 \times (1)^2 - 6 \times (4)^2$ = 288 $cm^2$

Required percentage = $\frac{288}{96} \times 100$ = 300%

Hence option (D) is the answer

Q22. Slant height l = $\sqrt{5^2 + 12^2}$ = 13 m

Surface area of tent = $\pi rl = \pi \times 5 \times 13 = 65\pi\, m^2$

Hence option (D) is the answer

Q23. Required number of boxes = $\dfrac{8\times7\times6\times100\times100\times100}{8\times7\times6}$ = 1000000

Hence option (B) is the answer

Q24. Area of the square pool = $(8)^2 = 64$

Let the width of the field be x m, then length = 2x m

Then, area of rectangular part = $x \times 2x = 2x^2$

Area of pool = of area of the field, or, $64 = \dfrac{1}{8} \times 2x^2$, or, x = 16 m

Hence length of the rectangular field = 2 × 16 = 32m

Hence option (A) is the answer.

Q25. Normally, in these situations, students go through the formula to get the answer. Though in my opinion, with a little bit of visualization, this question can be done easily without going through the actual calculation.

For the same height and same radius, Volume of cone = $\dfrac{1}{3}$ volume of cylinder.

In this question, volume of cone and volume of cylinder are equal. Since their heights are equal, radius of cone should be three times the radius of the cylinder. Hence answer = 3:1. Hence option (b) is the answer.

# 18 Set Theory

**A set is a collection of well-defined objects.**

For Example:

A = (a, b, c, d, e, f) – 1st six Letters of English Alphabet

B = (2, 4, 6, 8, 10) – 1st five even natural numbers

## Different Types of Set:

| Empty or Null Set | Singleton set | Finite set: | Infinite set: | Equal sets |
|---|---|---|---|---|
| • A set having no element is known as Empty or Null Set and it is denoted as ? or { }. | • A set having only one element is known as Singleton set. | • A set having a countable number of elements is known as Finite set. | • A set whose elements cannot be counted is known as Infinite set. | • Two sets are said to be equal sets if all the elements of set A are included in set B and all the elements of set B are included in Set A |
| • Example:- A set of irrational prime numbers. | • Example - A set of even prime number /s. | • Example - A set of odd numbers from 100 to 890. | • Example: A Set of all rational numbers between 5 and 6. | • If two sets A and B are equal then it is represented by A = B<br>• Example: A = {a, b, c} and B = {c, b, a} are equal sets. |

1. Subsets Set A is said to be the subset of another set B if all the elements of Set A are included in set B. 'Set A is subset of Set B' is shown by $A \subseteq B$. We can say now that every element of set A is a member of Set B. Example: If A = {a, b, c} and B = {a, b, c, d, e} then $A \subseteq B$, or A is a subset of B.

   **Some important results on subsets:**

   1. Every set is a subset of itself.
   2. Every set has an empty set as its subset.
   3. Total number of subsets of a set having n elements in $2^n$.

2. Universal Set: A set which contains all the sets in a given context is a Universal Set. Example: when we are using sets containing natural numbers, N is the universal set.

   If A = {a,b,c,}, B = {b,c,d}, C = {c,d}

   Then we can take U = {a,b,c,d} as universal set.

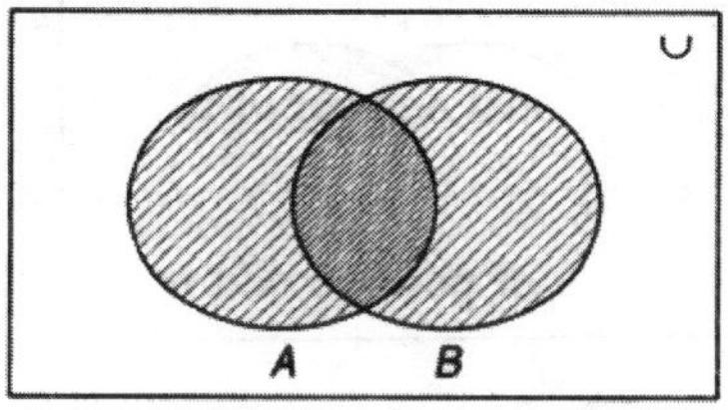


3. Power Set: The Collection of all the subsets of a set is known as the power set of that set. If A is the set, then a set containing all the subsets of A is known as the Power set of A. it is denoted by P(A).

   Let A = {1,2},, then the number of subsets of this set will be $2^2$ and the subsets are {}, {1}, {2} and {1,2} and the set containing all these four sets is known as Power set represented as P(A).

4. Venn Diagram - Swiss mathematician Euler first gave the idea of representing sets by diagram. Later on, British mathematician Venn brought this into practice. So, it is known as Euler – venn diagram or simply Venn diagram. In this way of representing sets, we use a closed curve, generally a circle, to denote sets and their operations

## Operations on Sets

1. Union of Sets - If two sets are A and B, then union of A and B is defined as the set that have all the elements which belong to either A or B or both. It is represented by $A \cup B$.

2. Intersection of sets - If two sets are A and B, then intersection of A and B is defined as the set that have all the elements which belong to both A and B.

   It is represented by $A \cap B$.

   Example: find $A \cup B$ and $A \cap B$ if A = {1, 2, 3, 4, 5} and B = {2, 4, 6}

$A \cup B = \{1, 2, 3, 4, 5, 6\}$

$A \cap B = \{2, 4\}$

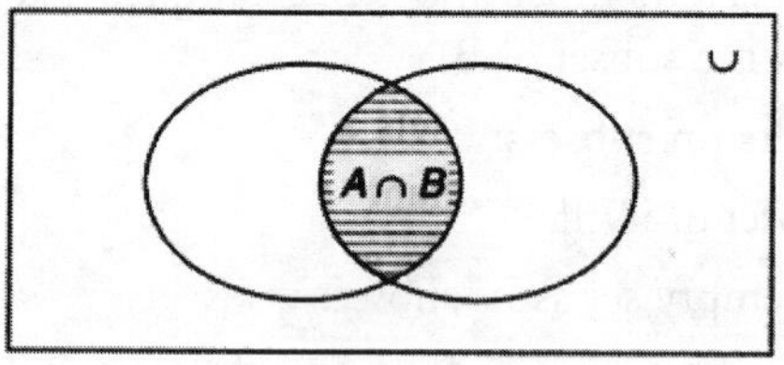


3. Disjoint Sets - Two sets are said to be disjoint if $A \cap B = 0$, that is, not a single element is common to both of these two sets.

   Example: If A = {Set of all odd numbers} and B = {Set of all even numbers} then set A and set B are disjoint sets.

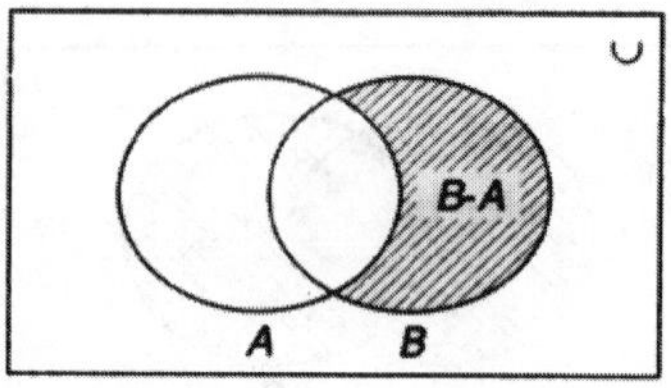


4. Difference of Sets - For two sets A and B, A – B is the set of all those elements of A that do not belong to B. similarly, B – A is the set of all those elements of B that do not belong to A.

   Example: $A = \{1,2,3,4,5,6\}$ and $B = \{2,4,8\}$,

   then $A - B = \{1,3,5,6,\}$ and $B - A = \{8\}$

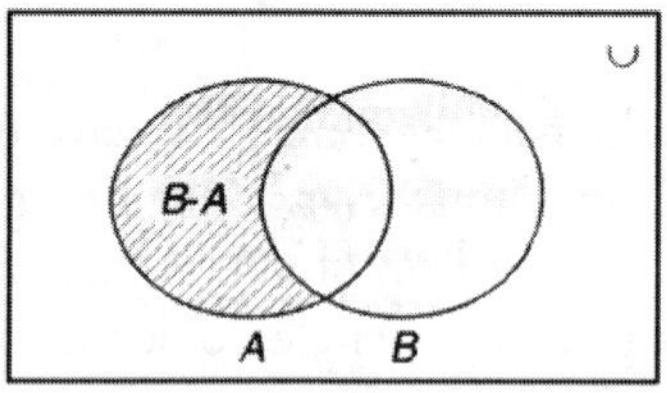


5. Complement of a set if U is the universal set and a set A is such that $A \subseteq U$ then complement of the set A is defined as U – A and represented as A' or $A^c$

   Example : U = {Set of all prime numbers} and A = {set of all even prime numbers} then U – A = {Set of all odd prime numbers}

## Algebraic Laws in set Theory

1. Commutative Laws: For any two sets A and B

   $A \cup B = B \cup A$ and $A \cap B = B \cap A$

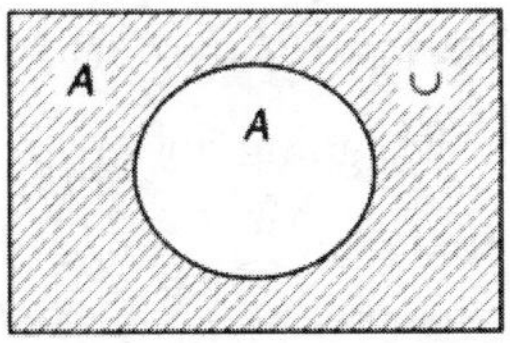


2. Associative Laws: For any three sets A, B and C,
   $(A \cup B) \cup C = A \cup (B \cup C)$ and
   $A \cap (B \cap C) = (A \cap B) \cap C$
3. Distributive laws for any three sets A, B and C
   $A \cup (B \cap C) = (A \cup B) \cap (A \cup C)$
   $A \cap (B \cup C) = (A \cap B) \cup (A \cap C)$
4. Identity laws
   $A \cup \phi = A$, where $\phi$ is the null set
   $A \cap U = A$, where U is the universal set
5. De-Morgan's law: If A and B are two sets then
   $(A \cup B)' = A' \cap B'$
   $(A \cap B)' = A' \cup B'$
6. $A \cup A = A$ and $A \cap A = A$

## Some Important Results

If A and B are any two sets, then

1. $A - B = A \cap B'$
2. $B - A = B \cap A'$
3. $(A - B) \cup B = A \cup B$
4. $(A - B) \cap B = \phi$
5. $(A - B) \cup (B - A) = (A \cup B) - (A \cap B)$

**Some important results on numbers of Elements in sets**

If A, B and C are three finite sets then

1. $n(A \cup B) = n(A) + n(B) - n(A \cap B)$
2. $n(A \cup B) = n(A) + n(B)$ if set A and set B are two disjoint sets.
3. $n(A \cup B \cup C) = n(A) + n(B) + n(C) - n(A \cap B) - n(B \cap C) - n(A \cap C) + n(A \cap B \cap C)$
4. $n(A' \cup B') = n((A \cap B)') = n(U) - n(A \cap B)$
5. $n(A' \cap B') = n((A \cup B)') = n(U) - n(A \cup B)$

## Worked Out Examples:

Q1. There are 50 students in a group going for a trip. In the morning, only tea or coffee is served. 20 drink tea but not coffee. Make a venn diagram showing this.

OR,

There are 50 students in a group going for a trip. In the morning, only tea or coffee is served, 20 drink tea only. Make a venn diagram showing this.

**Solution** –

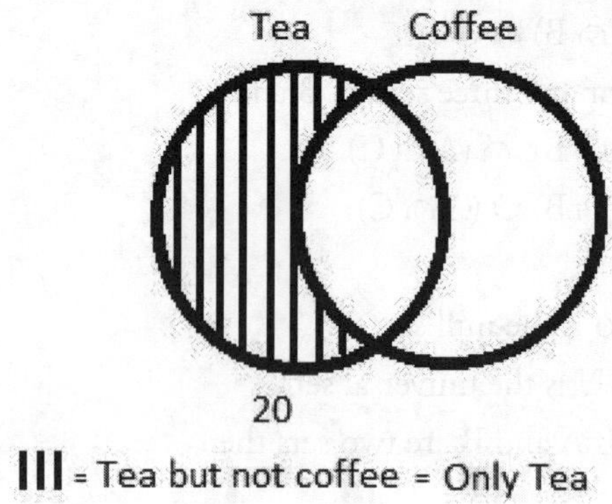


Understand that we cannot infer that remaining 30 students drink 30 coffee. In fact, we cannot infer anything about number of students drinking coffee.

Q2. In a group of 50 students drinking tea or coffee, 20 drink tea. Make a Venn diagram showing this.

**Solution** – Following Venn diagram can be drawn:

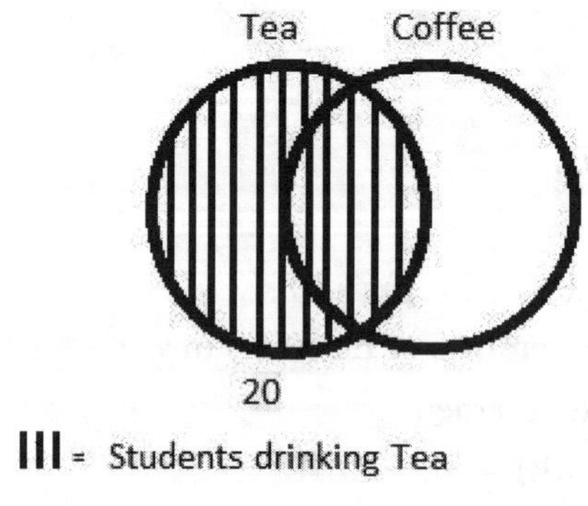


Q3. There are 50 students in a group going for a trip. In the morning, only tea or coffee is served, 20 drink tea and 30 drink coffee.

Make a venn diagram showing this.

**Solution** – Following venn diagram can be drawn:

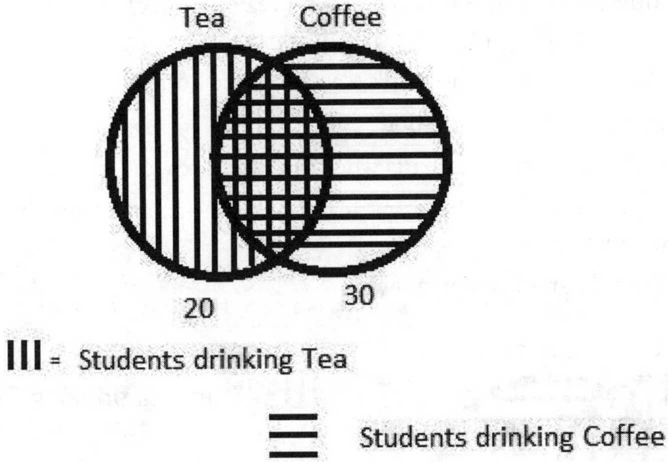


**Q4.** In the previous question, what is the number of students who drink both tea and coffee?
**Solution** – It cannot be solved because we do not know how many students drink atleast one of tea or coffee.

Q5. There are 50 students in a group going for a trip. In the morning, only tea or coffee is served, 20 drink tea and 30 drink coffee. If each one of them drink atleast one of the two, what is the number of students who drink both tea and coffee?

**Solution** – Following Venn diagram can be drawn:

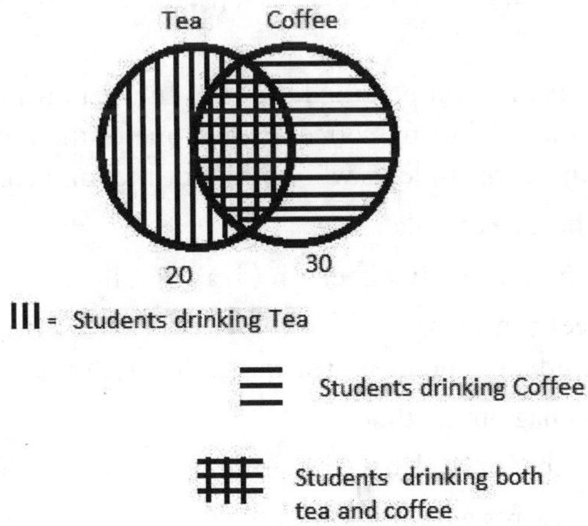

**Method 1 :** - Set Theory Formula

n (Tea ∪ Coffee) = n (Tea) + n (Coffee) – n (Tea ∩ Coffee)

Or, n (Tea ∩ Coffee) = n (Tea) + n (Coffee) – n (Tea ∪ Coffee) = 20 + 30 – 50 = 0. Hence number of students who drink tea and coffee both = 0.

**Method 2 :** - Venn Diagram method

Assume that the number of students who drink both tea and coffee = x.

Hence number of students who drink tea only = 20 – x, and number of students who drink coffee only = 30 – x.

Following Venn diagram can be drawn:

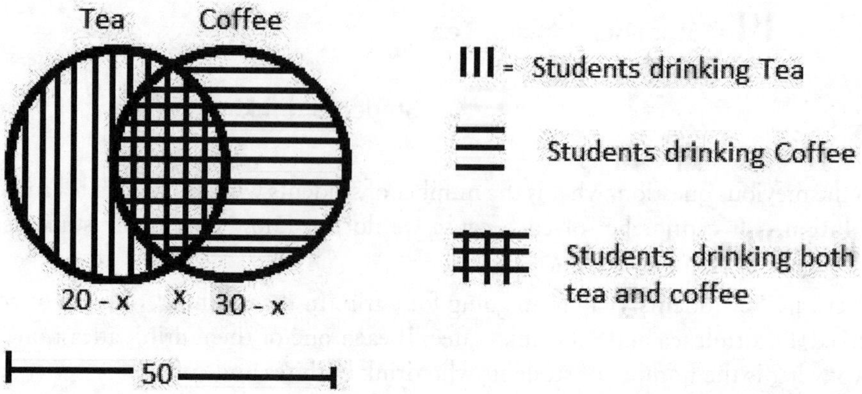


Hence 20 – x + x + 30 – x = 50, or, x = 0. Hence number of students who drink both tea and coffee = 0.

Q6. There are 50 students in a group going for a trip. In the morning, only tea or coffee is served, 20 drink tea and 35 drink coffee. If each one of them drink atleast one of the two, what is the number of students who drink both tea and coffee?

**Method 1 :** - Set Theory Formula

n (Tea ∪ Coffee) = n (Tea) + n(Coffee) – n (Tea ∩ Coffee)

Or, n (Tea ∩ Coffee) = n (Tea) + n(Coffee) – n (Tea ∪ Coffee) = 20 + 35 – 50 = 5. Hence number of students who drink tea and coffee both = 5.

**Method 2 :** - Venn Diagram method

Assume that the number of students who drink both tea and coffee = x.

Hence number of students who drink tea only = 20 – x, and number of students who drink coffee only = 30 – x.

Following Venn diagram can be drawn:

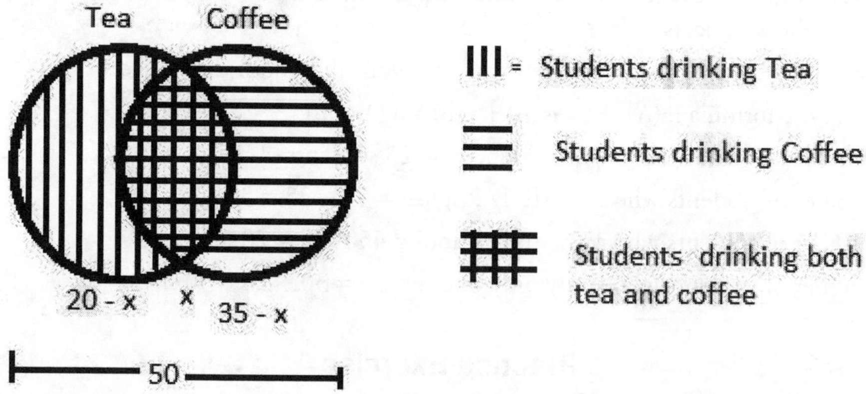


Hence 20 –x + x + 35 – x = 50, or, x = 5. Hence number of students who drink both tea and coffee = 5.

Q7. A survey on a sample of 25 new cars being sold at a local auto dealer was conducted to see which of the three popular options – air conditioning, radio and power windows – were already installed. The survey found:
15 had air conditioning, 2 had air conditioning and power windows but no radios, 12 had radio, 6 had air conditioning and radio but no power windows, 11 had power windows, 4 had radio and power windows and 3 had all three options. What is the number of cars that had none of the options?

**Solution**- From the given conditions, we have

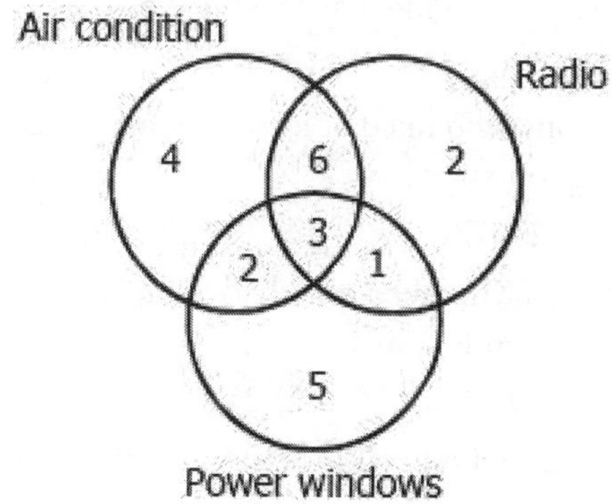


When we add all the values, we get a total of 23 cars.

So, 2 cars don't have any of Air condition, Radio, Power Windows.

Q8. In a group of 75 students where each student studies at least one of the 2 subjects, 55 study English while 45 study Hindi. Find the number of students who study exactly one of the 2 subjects.

**Solution** - Let x be the number of students who study both the subjects.

Using the formula n $(A \cup B)$ = n (A) + n(B) – n $(A \cap B)$

75 = 55 + 45-x, or, 100-x = 75. Hence x = 25 students

Number of students who only study English = 55 – 25 = 30

Number of students who only study Hindi = 45 – 25 = 20

Number of students who study only one subject = 30 + 20 = 50

## Practice Exercise

Q.1. There are two sets A and B. Set A has 21 elements, set B has 32 elements and there are 11 elements which are in both A and B. What is the total number of elements?

(a) 36 (b) 38 (c) 42 (d) 40

Q.2. In a group of 52 students, 16 students study maths but not English and 33 students study maths. Then what is the number of students who study both maths and English?

(a) 17 (b) 19 (c) 23 (d) cannot be determined

**Directions for questions 3-6 - Read the passage below and solve the questions based on it.**

Out of 10000 persons surveyed, 3700 liked movie A, 4000 liked movie B, and 5000 liked movie C. 700 persons liked movies A and B, 1200 liked movies A and C, and 1000 liked movies B and C. Each person liked at least one movie.

Q3. Find the number of persons who liked all the three movies?

(a) 100 (b) 200 (c) 300 (d) 400

Q4. Find the number of persons who liked at least two movies as a percentage of number of persons who liked exactly one movie.

(a) 31.4% (b) 29.8% (c) 20.83% (d) 33.33%

Q5. Find the number of persons who liked exactly two movies as a percentage of the number of persons who liked at least one movie.

(a) 21.5% (b) 19.16% (c) 25.5% (d) None of these

Q6. Find the number of persons who liked movie A and movie B but not movie C?

(a) 400 (b) 5500 (c) 600 (d) None of these

Q7. A survey of a hundred people was conducted to find out whether they had read the recent issues of Golmal, a monthly magazine. A summary of the information regarding the readership in 3 months is given below:

Only September: 18; September but not August: 23; September and July: 28; September: 28; July: 48; July and August: 10;

None of the three months: 24.

What is the number of surveyed people who have read exactly two consecutive issues (out of the three)?

(1) 7 (2) 9 (3) 12 (4) 14

Q8. In a group of 70 people, 37 like Inception, 52 like Dark Knight and each person likes at least one of the two movies. How many people like both Inception and Dark Knight?

(a) 19 (b) 21 (c) 17 (d) 15

**Directions for questions 9-10 – Read the passage below and solve the questions based on it.**

There are 727 students in a school. Out of them, 600 students watched The Last Samurai and 173 students watched both The Last Samurai and Life of Pi. Each student has watched at least one of the two movies.

Q9. How many students watched Life of Pi?

1. 250 2. 300 3. 280 4. 290

Q10. How many students watched Life of Pi only?

1. 300 2. 280 3. 127 4. 173

Q11. How many numbers from 1 to 100 are neither divisible by 2 nor by 5?

(a) 40 (b) 60 (c) 50 (d) None of these

**Directions for questions 12-13 – Read the passage below and solve the questions based on it:**

New Age Consultants have three consultants Gyani, Medha and Buddhi. The sum of the number of projects handled by Gyani and Buddhi individually is equal to the number of projects in which Medha is involved. All three consultants are involved together in 6 projects. Gyani works with Medha in 14 projects. Buddhi has 2 projects with Medha but without Gyani, and 3 projects with Gyani but without Medha. The total number of projects for New Age Consultants is one less than twice the number of projects in which more than one consultant is involved.

Q12. What is the number of projects in which Medha alone is involved?

(a) 0 (b) 1

(c) 2 (d) Cannot be determined

Q13. What is the number of projects in which Gyani alone is involved?

(a) 0 (b) 1

(c) 2 (d) Cannot be determined

Q14. In a party 70% of the people drank Coke, 65% drank Sprite, 27% did not drink anything, whereas 248 people drank both. What is the number of people who attended the party?

(a) 400 (b) 600 (c) 800 (d) 900

**Directions for questions 15-16 – Read the passage below and solve the questions based on it.**

In a class of 106 students, each student studies at least one of the three subjects Maths, Political science and Chemistry. 48 of them study Maths, 51 political science and 53 chemistry. 16 study Maths and political science, 17 study Maths and chemistry and 18 study Political science and chemistry.

Q15. What is the number of students who study, exactly two subjects?

(a) 31 (b) 32 (c) 33 (d) 36

Q16. What is the number of students who study more than one subject?

(a) 39 (b) 41 (c) 40 (d) 42

**Directions for question number 17-20– Read the passage below and solve these questions based on it.**

During break, 150 students go to the library which has books of only three types – books on Philosophy, Fiction books, and books on Psychology. 36 students read books on Psychology and 10 students read only Philosophy. 15 students read Fiction and Psychology, 10 students read Fiction and Philosophy, 4 students read Philosophy and Psychology but not Fiction and 11 students read Fiction and Psychology but not Philosophy. 42 students read Fiction.

Q17. How many students read atleast one of Philosophy or Fiction or Psychology?

(a) 40 (b) 73 (c) 55 (d) 60

Q18. How many students do not read any of the things?

(a) 77 (b) 73 (c) 67 (d) 63

Q19. How many students read at least books of two types?

(a) 27 (b) 30 (c)25 (d) 35

Q20. What is the number of students who read *only* one of the three types of books?

(a) 32 (b) 36 (c) 42 (d) 48

## Answer Grid:

| Q. No. | 1 | 2 | 3 | 4 | 5 | 6 | 7 | 8 | 9 | 10 |
|---|---|---|---|---|---|---|---|---|---|---|
| Answer | c | d | b | d | b | a | b | a | b | c |
| Q. No. | 11 | 12 | 13 | 14 | 15 | 16 | 17 | 18 | 19 | 20 |
| Answer | a | b | d | a | d | b | b | c | c | d |

## Solution and Explanation:

Q1. We know that n (A ∪ B) = n (A) + n (B) – n (A ∩ *B*)

n (A ∪ B) = 21 + 32 – 11 = 42. So option (c) is the answer.

Q2. 16 students study maths but not English and 33 students study maths. Following Venn diagram can be drawn:

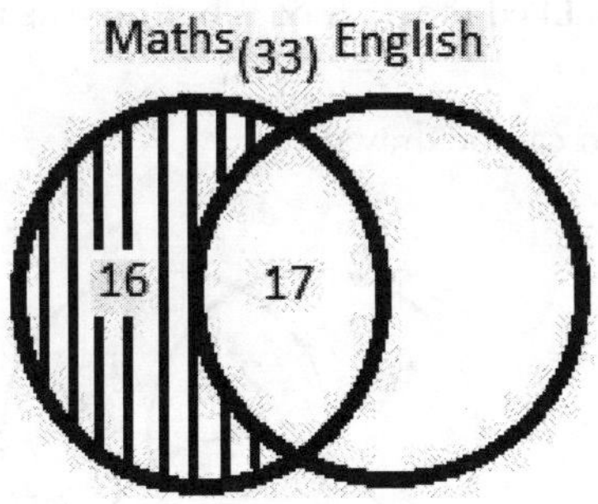


Hence there are 17 students who study both maths and English.

**Solution to Questions 3 – 6:**

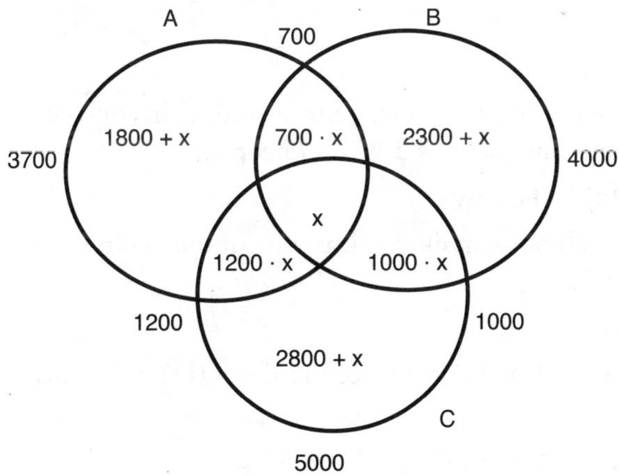


Let the number of people who liked all the three movies be x.

3700 + 2300 + x + 1000 – x + 2800 + x = 10000

x = 200. Hence option (b) is the answer.

Q4. Number of persons who liked atleast 2 movies = 500 + 800 + 1000 + 200 = 2500.

Number of persons who like exactly 1 movie = 2000 + 2500 + 3000 = 7500

Hence required percentage = $\frac{2500}{7500} \times 100 = 33.33\%$

Hence option (d) is the answer.

Q5. Number of persons who liked exactly 2 movies = 500 + 800 + 1000 = 2300

Hence required percentage = $\frac{2300}{1000} \times 100 = 23\%$

Q6. Number of persons who liked movie A & B but not the movie C = 2000 + 500 + 2500 = 5000

Q7. Following Venn diagram can be drawn:

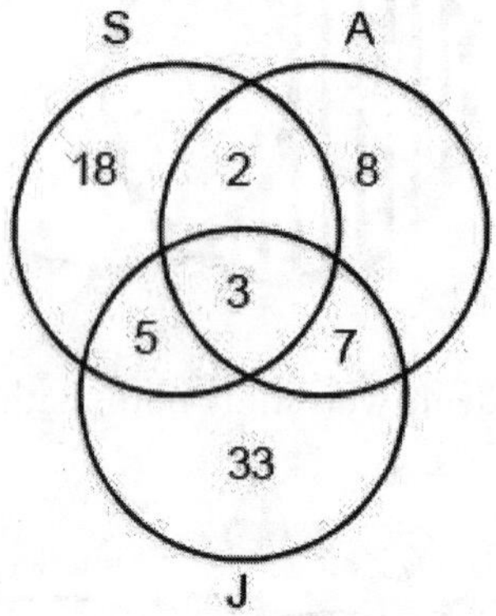


As given in the above diagram, total persons reading in consecutive months i.e. July and August and August and Sept. is 2 + 7 = 9 people.

Hence option (b) is the answer.

Q8. It is given that each of them likes at least one of the two movies. Hence n(Inception ∪ Dark Knight) = 70.

Using the formula,

n(Inception ∪ Dark Knight) = n (Inception) + n (Dark Knight) – n (Inception ∩ Dark Knight)

Or, 70 = 37 + 52 – n (Inception ∩ Dark Knight)

Hence n (Inception ∩ Dark Knight) = 89 – 70 = 19. Hence option (a) is the answer.

Q9. n (The Last Samurai ∪ Life of Pi) = n (The Last Samurai) + n (Life of Pi) – n (The Last Samurai ∩ *Physics*)

727 = 600 + n (Life of Pi) – 173

n (Life of Pi) = 300.

Hence option (b) is the answer.

Q10. Life of Pi only = 300 – 173 = 127. Hence (c) is the answer.

Q11. **Method 1:**

Total numbers = Divisible by atleast one of 2 or 5 + Divisible by neither 2 nor 5

Divisible by atleast one of 2 or 5 = $n(2 \cup 5) = n(2) + n(5) - n(2 \cap 5) = 50 + 20 - 10 = 60$

Hence neither divisible by 2 nor by 5 = Total numbers - Divisible by atleast one of 2 or 5 = 100 – 60 = 40. Hence option (a) is the answer.

**Method 2:**

Numbers which are neither divisible by 2 nor by $5 = 100\left(1 - \frac{1}{2}\right)\left(1 - \frac{1}{5}\right) = 40$. Hence option (a) is the answer.

Q12. Following Venn Diagram can be drawn:

As per the given data we get the following:

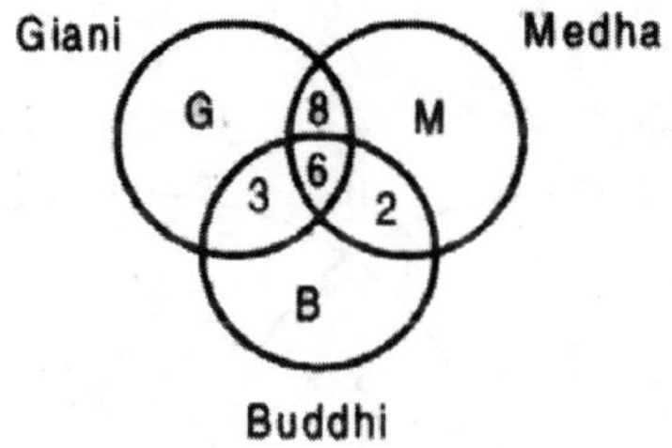


G + B = M + 16

Also, M + B + G + 19 = (2 x 19)-1 i.e. (G + B) = 18 – M Thus, M + 16 = 18 – M

Hence number of projects in which Medha alone is involved = M = 1. Hence option (b) is the answer.

Q13. Using the Venn diagram from the above question, it cannot be calculated. Hence option (d) is the answer.

Q14. **Method 1:**

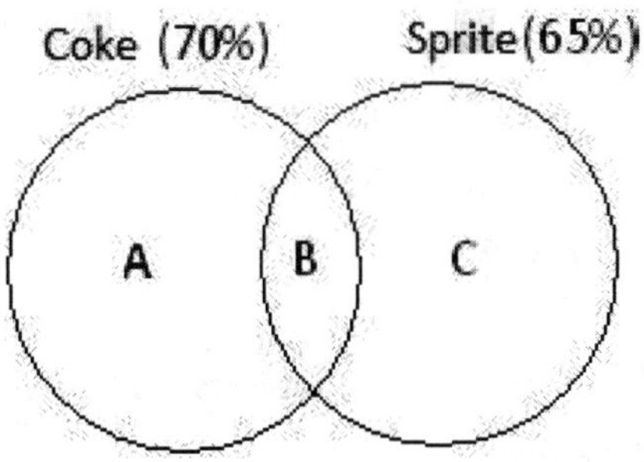


A = Only Coke, B = Both and C = Only Sprite

From the diagram A + 2B + C = 70 + 65

A + 2B + C = 135% —— (i)

It is given that A + B + C = 100 – 27 = 73% —— (ii)

Then from equation (i) and equation (ii)

B = 62% of the people and B = 248

Since 62% of the people = 248

Then 100% of the people = $\frac{248}{62} \times 100 = 400$

**Method 2:**

n (Coke ∪ Sprite) = n (Coke) + n (Sprite) – n (Coke ∩ *Sprite*)

73 = 70 + 65 – n (Coke)

n (Coke ) = 62%

62% = 248. Hence 100% = × 100 = 400.

Hence option (a) is the answer.

Q15.

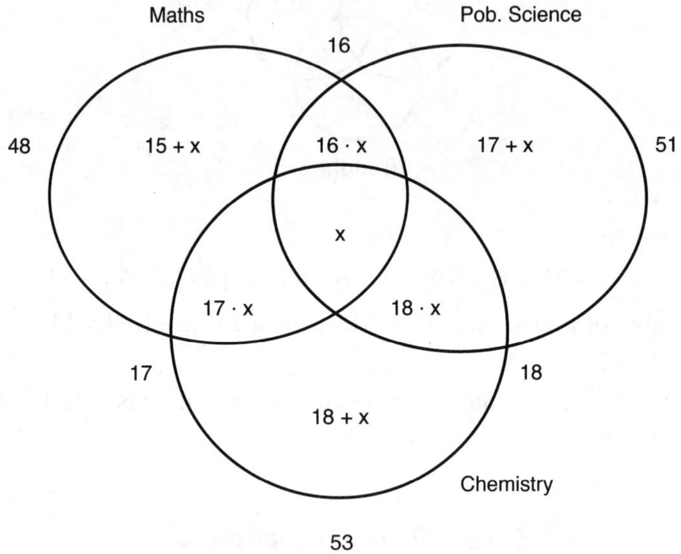


Let the no. of people who study all three be x

48 + 17 + x + 18 – x + 18 + x = 106

101 + x = 106 ⇒ x = 5.

Number of people who study exactly 2 subjects = 11 + 13 + 12 = 36.

Hence option (d) is the answer.

Q16. Number of people who study more than one subject = 36 + 5 = 41

Hence option (b) is the answer.

**Direction for the questions 17 – 20:**

Q17. Following diagram can be drawn:

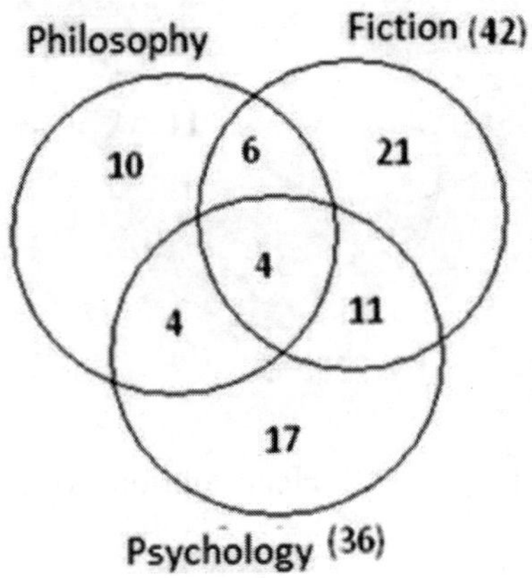


Using the diagram, $A \cup B \cup C = 10 + 6 + 21 + 4 + 4 + 11 + 17 = 73$. Hence option (b) is the answer.

Q18. Given that total number of students who go to library = 150.

So, number of students who do not read any type of book = 150 – 73 = 77

Q19. Number of students who read at least two types of books can be seen as shaded one in the diagram given below:

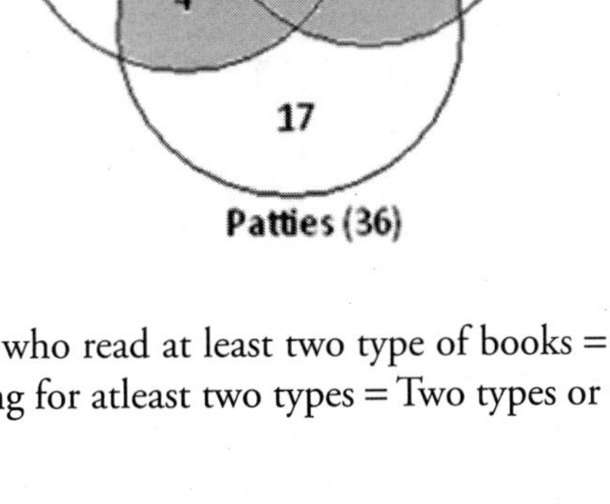


Number of students who read at least two type of books = 6 + 4 + 4 + 11 = 25 [Note that question is asking for atleast two types = Two types or three types]

Q20. Shaded area in the following venn diagram gives the required answer:

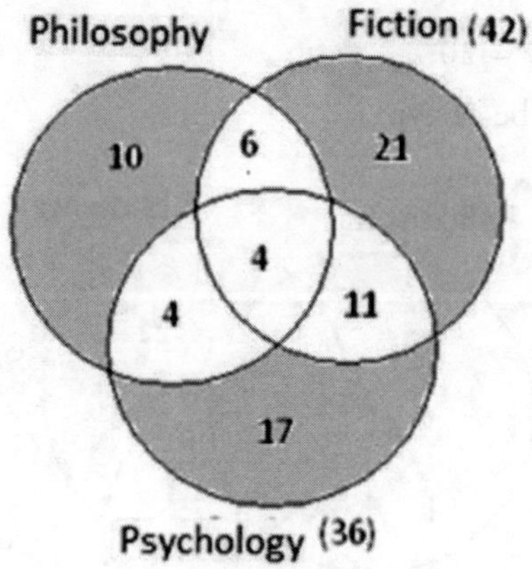


Hence answer = 10 + 21 + 17 = 48. Hence option (d) is the answer.

# 19 Previous Years Exam Paper

## Quantitative Aptitude - Year 2014

1. A bakery bakes cake with the expectation that it will earn a profit of 40% by selling each cake at marked price. But during the delivery to showroom 16% of the cakes were completely damaged and hence could not be sold. 24% of the cakes were slightly damaged and hence could be sold at 80% of the cost price. The remaining 60% of the cakes were sold at marked price. What is the percentage profit in the whole consignment?

   (1) 3.2 (2) 2.4 (3) 2.8 (4) 4.2 (5) 3.6

2. A professional institute's total expenditure on students for a particular course is partly fixed and partly varies linearly with the number of students. The average expense per student is Rs. 615 when there are 24 students and Rs. 465 when there are 40 students. What is the average expense when there are 60 students?

   (1) Rs. 370 (2) Rs. 450 (3) Rs. 350 (4) Rs. 420 (5) Rs. 390

3. The ratio of the present ages of A and B is 7 : 9. Six years ago the ratio if $\frac{1}{3}$ of A's age at that time and $\frac{1}{3}$ B's age at that time was 1 : 2. What will be the ratio of A's to B's age 6 years from now?

   (1) 4 : 5 (2) 14 : 15 (3) 6 : 7 (4) 18 : 25 (5) 22 : 25

4. A, B and C have to type 506 pages to finish an assignment. A can type a page in 12 minutes, B in 15 minutes and C in 24 minutes. If they divide the task into three parts so that all three of them spend equal amount of time in typing what is the number of pages that B should type?

   (1) 172 (2) 176 (3) 154 (4) 168 (5) 164

**Directions (Q. 5-9):** The question consists of a question and two statements I and II given below it. You have to decide whether the data provided in the statements are sufficient to answer the question. Read both the statements and choose the appropriate option.

5. **What is the base of a triangle PQR with PQ as base?**

**I. Height and base of a triangle are in the ratio of 3 : 4.**

**II. The area of the triangle is 48 cm$^2$, perimeter 36 cm and height $\frac{2}{3}$ of the perimeter.**

(1) The data in statement II alone are sufficient to answer the question, while the data in statement I alone are not sufficient to answer the question.

(2) The data either in statement I alone or in statement II alone are sufficient to answer the question.

(3) The data in statement I alone are sufficient to answer the question, while the data in statement II alone are not sufficient to answer the question.

(4) The data in both statements I and II together are necessary to answer the question

(5) The data even in both statements I and II together are not sufficient to answer the question.

6. **What is the speed of the train?**

**I. A train crosses another train coming from opposite direction at the speed of 45 kmph in 20 seconds.**

**II. The train crosses another train running in the same direction at the speed of 42 kmph in 1 minute 18 seconds.**

(1) The data either in statement I alone or in statement II alone are sufficient to answer the question.

(2) The data in statement I alone are sufficient to answer the question, while the data in statement II alone are not sufficient to answer the question.

(3) The data even in both statements I and II together are not sufficient to answer the question.

(4) The data in both statements I and II together are necessary to answer the question

(5) The data in statement II alone are sufficient to answer the question, while the data in statement I alone are not sufficient to answer the question.

7. **What is the rate of interest pcpa?**

**I. An amount invested on simple interest becomes four times in 24 years.**

**II. The difference between compound interest and simple interest for two years on an amount of Rs. 10000 at that rate is Rs. 156.25.**

(1) The data in statement II alone are sufficient to answer the question, while the data in statement I alone are not sufficient to answer the question.

(2) The data in statement I alone are sufficient to answer the question, while the data in statement II alone are not sufficient to answer the question.

(3) The data in both statements I and II together are necessary to answer the question

(4) The data even in both statements I and II together are not sufficient to answer the question.

(5) The data either in statement I alone or in statement II alone are sufficient to answer the question.

8. **What is the total strength of institute X?**

I. **Out of the total strength of Institute X, 35% are females and rest are males. The number of females in Institute X is equal to the number of males in Institute Y.**

II. **Out of the total strength of Institute Y, the no. of males is 560, which is 28% of the total strength.**

(1) The data either in statement I alone or in statement II alone are sufficient to answer the question.

(2) The data in statement II alone are sufficient to answer the question, while the data in statement I alone are not sufficient to answer the question.

(3) The data even in both statements I and II together are not sufficient to answer the question.

(4) The data in statement I alone are sufficient to answer the question, while the data in statement II alone are not sufficient to answer the question.

(5) The data in both statements I and II together are necessary to answer the question.

9. **What is the cost of fencing a rectangular plot along all four sides @ Rs. 450 per metre?**

I. **The area of the plot is 1458 $m^2$, which is 54 times the numerical value of its breadth.**

II. **The length of the plot is 200% of its breadth and the breadth is 50% of its length.**

(1) The data even in both statements I and II together are not sufficient to answer the question.

(2) The data in statement II alone are sufficient to answer the question, while the data in statement I alone are not sufficient to answer the question.

(3) The data in statement I alone are sufficient to answer the question, while the data in statement II alone are not sufficient to answer the question.

(4) The data either in statement I alone or in statement II alone are sufficient to answer the question.

(5) The data in both statements I and II together are necessary to answer the question.

**10. In the figure given below, the perimeter of the circle is 220 cm. What is the area of the shaded portion in cm²?**

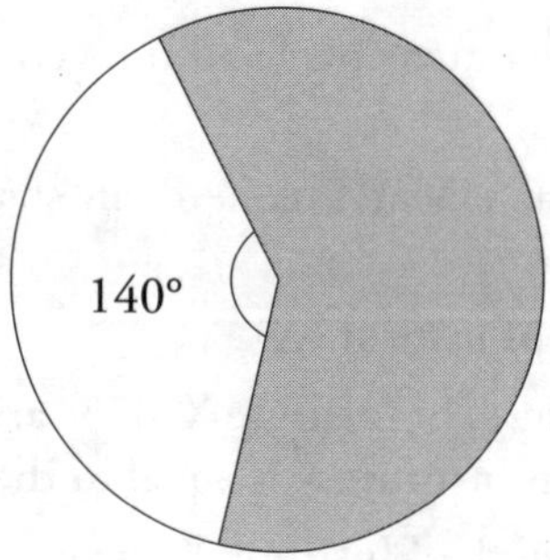


(1) $2542\frac{7}{9}$ (2) $2584\frac{1}{3}$ (3) $2447\frac{1}{9}$ (4) $2352\frac{7}{9}$ (5) $2376\frac{2}{3}$

**Directions** (Q. 11-1(5): Study the table to answer the given questions.

| City | Perecentage of people (male and female) who watch the TV Series out of the total population of the city | | | | | | | | |
|---|---|---|---|---|---|---|---|---|---|
| | Total population of the city | Big Bang Theory | | Arrow | | Breaking Bad | | Mentalist | |
| | | Male | Female | Male | Female | Male | Female | Male | Female |
| P | 40000 | 12 | 14 | 22 | 18 | 18 | 20 | 12 | 10 |
| Q | 20000 | 10 | 20 | 20 | 16 | 14 | 10 | 15 | 30 |
| R | 50000 | 18 | 12 | 10 | 22 | 16 | 12 | 16 | 22 |
| S | 30000 | 16 | 20 | 10 | 20 | 12 | 30 | 18 | 12 |
| T | 50000 | 22 | 30 | 12 | 14 | 20 | 12 | 15 | 20 |

**11. What is the difference between the total number of people living in City R, Q and T together who do not watch Arrow and the total number of people living in these three cities together who watch Arrow?**

(1) 47200 (2) 45300 (3) 47400 (4) 47600 (5) 45600

**12. What is the average number of males who watch Big Bang Theory in all the cities together?**

(1) 6320 (2) 6380 (3) 6340 (4) 6350 (5) 6360

13. The ratio of the total number of males to the total number of females in City P is 5 : 3. What percent of the female population watches Breaking Bad in City P?

(1) $55\frac{1}{3}$ (2) $55\frac{2}{3}$ (3) $58\frac{1}{3}$ (4) $53\frac{1}{3}$ (5) $53\frac{2}{3}$

14. The total population (males and females) of City R watching Mentalist is what percent more than the total population (male and female) of City T watching the same TV Series?

(1) $8\frac{3}{7}$ (2) $8\frac{5}{7}$ (3) $8\frac{4}{7}$ (4) $7\frac{3}{7}$ (5) $7\frac{4}{7}$

15. What is the ratio of the number of females who watch Breaking Bad in City Q and City S together to the number of females who watch Mentalist in the same cities together?

(1) 59 : 47 (2) 55 : 48 (3) 59 : 42 (4) 55 : 43 (5) 59 : 45

16. Raghu invested a certain sum in Scheme X for 4 years. Scheme X offers simple interest @ 12 pcpa for the first two years and compound interest (compounded annually) @ 20 pcpa for the next two years. The total interest earned by him after 4 years is Rs. 11016. What was the sum invested by Raghu in Scheme X?

(1) Rs. 17400 (2) Rs. 18400 (3) Rs. 16200 (4) Rs. 11400 (5) Rs. 9400

**Directions (Q. 17):** This question is based on the graph below:

**Number of male and female teachers in four schools**

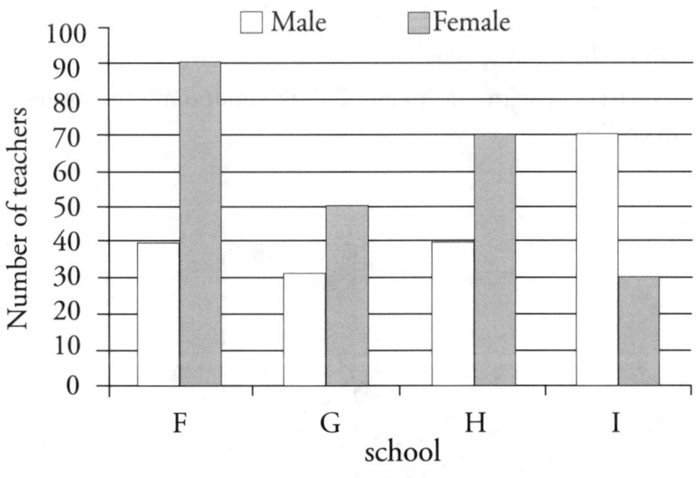


17. What is the difference between the average number of male and female teachers in the given schools?

(1) 10 (2) 20 (3) 5 (4) 25 (5) 15

**Directions (Q. 18-22):** In this question two equations numbered I & II are given. You have to solve both the equations and find out the correct option.

18. **I. $6x^2 + 41x + 63 = 0$** **II. $4y^2 + 8y + 3 = 0$**
(1) Relationship between x and y cannot be establised (2) $x \geq y$
(3) $x < y$ (4) $x > y$ (5) $x \leq y$

19. **I. $x^2 + 10x + 24 = 0$** **II. $4y^2 - 17y + 18 = 0$**
(1) $x \leq y$ (2) $x \geq y$ (3) Relationship between x and y cannot be establised
(4) $x > y$ (5) $x < y$

20. **I. $24x^2 + 38x + 15 = 0$**
**II. $12y^2 + 28y + 15 = 0$**
(1) $x \leq y$ (2) $x > y$ (3) $x \geq y$ (4) $x < y$
(5) Relationship between x and y cannot be establised

21. **I. $3x^2 - 20x - 32 = 0$**
**II. $2y^2 - 3y - 20 = 0$**
(1) $x < y$ (2) $x \leq y$ (3) $x > y$
(4) Relationship between x and y cannot be establised (5) $x \geq y$

22. **I. $x^2 - 20x + 91 = 0$**
**II. $y^2 - 32y + 247 = 0$**
(1) $x < y$ (2) Relationship between x and y cannot be establised
(3) $x \geq y$ (4) $x \leq y$ (5) $x < y$

**Directions (Q. 23):** In the figure given below:

GHI is an equilateral triangle with side 14 cm. G is the midpoint of JL. What is the area of the shaded portion (in cm(2)?

23.

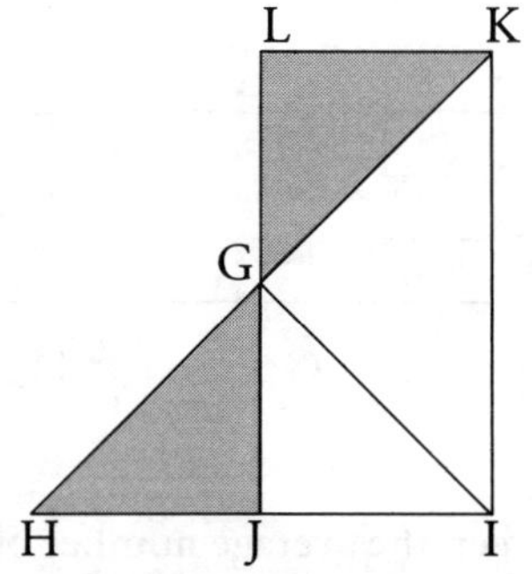


(1) $56\sqrt{3}$ (2) $70\sqrt{3}$ (3) $35\sqrt{3}$ (4) $49\sqrt{3}$ (5) $42\sqrt{3}$

**Directions (Q. 24-28):** Refer to the pie-chart and answer the given questions:

Distribution of the total number of novels (Romantic and Horror) sold by 7 stores

**Total number = 63000**

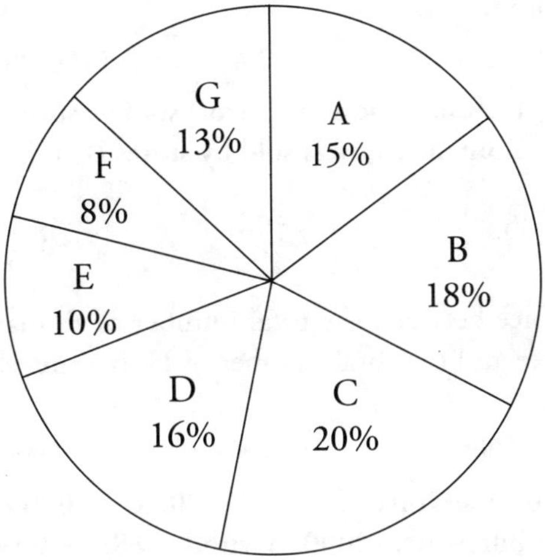


Distribution of the total number of Romantic novels sold by 7 stores

Total number = 36000

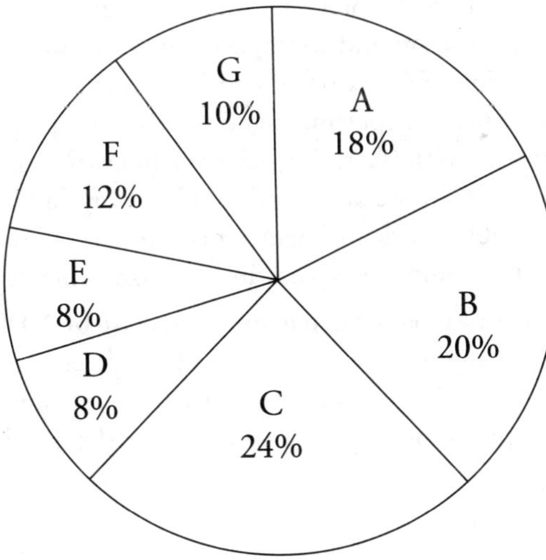


24. **What is the ratio of the number of novels (Romantic and Horror) sold by store E to the total number of Horror novels sold by stores C and F together?**

(1) 35 : 32 (2) 45 : 32 (3) 35 : 24 (4) 35 : 26 (5) 45 : 34

**25. What is the average number of Horror novels sold by stores B, C, E and F together?**

(1) 2960 (2) 3060 (3) 2680 (4) 3240 (5) 3180

**26. What is the central angle corresponding to the number of novels (Romantic and Horror) sold by store B?**

(1) 68.2° (2) 72.6° (3) 62.4° (4) 64.8° (5) 70.8°

**27. The number of novels (Romantic and Horror) sold by store F is what percent less than the total number of Romantic novels sold by stores B and G together?**

(1) $51\frac{2}{3}$ (2) $53\frac{1}{3}$ (3) $55\frac{2}{3}$ (4) $58\frac{1}{3}$ (5) $56\frac{1}{3}$

**28. What is the difference between the total number of Romantic novels sold by stores A, D and G together and the total number of Horror novels sold by the same stores together?**

(1) 2000 (2) 1600 (3) 2400 (4) 1800 (5) 2200

**29. A, B and C started a business investing Rs. 42000, Rs. 30000 and Rs. 28000 respectively. After 4 months A withdrew Rs. 12000, B withdrew Rs. 6000 and C withdrew Rs. 8000. If after 10 months a total profit of Rs. 46420 is earned, what is the share of C?**

(1) Rs. 12580 (2) Rs. 13160 (3) Rs. 13020 (4) Rs. 12540 (5) Rs. 12760

**Directions (Q. 30-34):** Study the following information to answer the questions.

In an organization there are 1700 employees. The organization has five departments - HR, Finance, Marketing, Administration and Manufacturing. Out of the total number of female employees in the organization, 34% work in HR department, 20% work in Marketing department, 18% work in Finance department and the remaining 224 female employees work in Administration department. Manufacturing department has no female employees. Out of the total number of male employees in the organization, 12% work in HR department, 35% work in Marketing department, 30% work in Finance department, 10% work in Administration department and the remaining employees work in Manufacturing department.

**30. If the male employees in Finance department increase by 10%, the male employees in Administration department increase by 20%, 23 male employees join Manufacturing department and the number of male employees in HR and Marketing department remains the same, what is the percentage increase in the number of male employees in the organization?**

(1) $7\frac{4}{9}$ (2) $7\frac{1}{9}$ (3) $7\frac{5}{9}$ (4) $7\frac{2}{9}$ (5) None of these

**31. The total number of male employees working in Marketing and Finance department together is what percent of the total number of employees (male and female) working in these two departments together? (Round off to numerical integers).**

(1) 66 (2) 63 (3) 62 (4) 60 (5) 70

**32. If 26 male employees from HR department are transferred to Administration department and 28 female employees from Administration department are transferred to HR department, what is the ratio of the number of male employees to the number of female employees in Administration department after the transfer of employees?**

(1) 23 : 49 (2) 29 : 49 (3) 25 : 49 (4) 23 : 47 (5) 25 : 47

**33. What is the average number of employees (male and female) who work in Manufacturing, Marketing and Administration departments together?**

(1) 360 (2) 392 (3) 302 (4) 368 (5) 386

**34. If equal number of female employees and male employees working in Finance department leave the job, the ratio of the number of male employees working in Finance department to the number of female employees working in the same department reduces to 40 : 19. What is the total number of employees working in Finance department who left the job?**

(1) 20 (2) 60 (3) 30 (4) 50 (5) 40

**35. A boat takes 35 minutes less to travel 28 km downstream than it takes to travel the same distance upstream. If the speed of the boat in still water is 14 kmph, what is the speed of the stream? (in kmph)**

(1) 2.5 (2) 6.5 (3) 2 (4) 9.5 (5) 10.5

**Directions (Q. 36-40):** In the following number series, only one number is wrong. Find out the wrong number.

**36. 41, 45, 61, 97, 181, 261, 405**

(1) 181 (2) 97 (3) 261 (4) 61 (5) 45

**37. 16, 30, 58, 114, 226, 496, 898**

(1) 58 (2) 226 (3) 30 (4) 114 (5) 496

**38. 15, 21.5, 46.5, 145, 585.5, 2933, 17603.5**

(1) 585.5 (2) 2933 (3) 46.5 (4) 145 (5) 21.5

**39. 5, 6, 16, 57, 246, 1245, 7506**

(1) 16 (2) 6 (3) 1245 (4) 246 (5) 57

**40. 2, 13, 46, 145, 452, 1333, 4006**

(1) 1333 (2) 452 (3) 46 (4) 145 (5) 13

41. **There are two vessels A and B. Vessel A is containing 40 litres of pure milk and vessel B is containing 22 litres of pure water. From vessel A, 8 litres of milk is taken out and poured into vessel B. Then 6 litres of mixture (milk and water) is taken out and from vessel B poured into vessel A. What is the ratio of the quantity of pure milk in vessel A to the quantity of pure water in vessel B?**

(1) 14 : 9 (2) 21 : 11 (3) 24 : 13 (4) 14 : 5 (5) 21 : 13

42. **It takes 24 seconds for a train travelling at 93 kmph to cross entirely another train half its length travelling in opposite direction at 51 kmph. It passes a bridge in 66 seconds. What is the length of the bridge? (in m)**

(1) 1065 (2) 1600 (3) 1705 (4) 1580 (5) None of these

43. **A rectangular plot, 36m long and 28m broad, has two concrete roads 5m wide running in the middle of the park, one parallel to the length and the other parallel to the breadth. What would be the total cost of gravelling the plot, excluding the area covered by the roads, @ Rs. 3.60 per sq m?**

(1) Rs. 2772.20 (2) Rs. 2466.60 (3) Rs. 2654.40 (4) Rs. 2332.60 (5) Rs. 2566.80

**Directions (Q. 44-45):** Study the following table the answer the given questions.

Number of girls studying IT and Electronics Engineering from Five colleges

| College | IT | Electronics |
|---|---|---|
| A | 240 | 315 |
| B | 350 | 285 |
| C | 260 | 225 |
| D | 325 | 255 |
| E | 275 | 220 |

44. **The total number of girls studying IT Engineering from college B, C and D together is by what percent more than the total number of girls studing Electronics Engineering from these three colleges?**

(1) $22\frac{2}{9}$ (2) $23\frac{1}{9}$ (3) $22\frac{2}{3}$ (4) $23\frac{5}{9}$ (5) $23\frac{1}{3}$

45. **What percent of the girls in college C study Electronics Engineering out of the girls studying IT and Electronics Engineering? (rounded off to the nearest integer)**

(1) 46 (2) 52 (3) 51 (4) 42 (5) 49

**Directions (Q. 46-50):** Study the following graph carefully to answer the given questions.

**Number of the flat booked in HIG, MIG and LIG categories from different cities in 2004.**

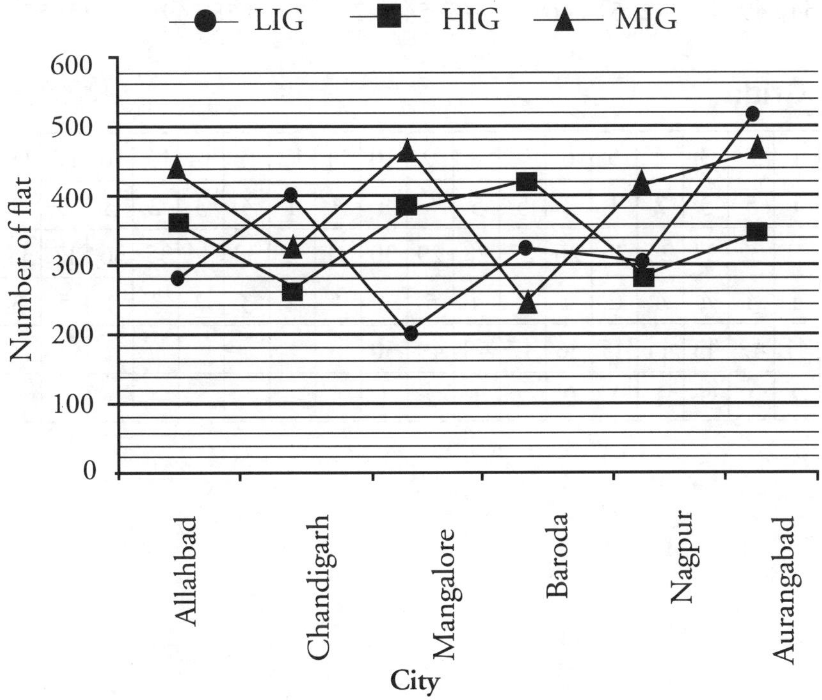


46. **If for Aurangabad the number of HIG flats booked in 2005 was more than that in 2004 by 15%, the number of MIG flats booked in 2005 was more than that in 2004 by 10% and the number of LIG flats booked in 2005 was more than that in 2004 by 20% then what was the total number of flats booked in Aurangabad in 2005?**

    (1) 1565 (2) 1521 (3) 1625 (4) 1642 (5) 1544

47. **Out of the LIG flats booked from Chandigarh, 35% were by employees of a Financial Institution and out of the remaining flats, those booked by officers from a software company and HRM department of Government of India were in the ratio of 6 : 7. What was the total no. of LIG flats booked by officers from the software company?**

    (1) 130 (2) 120 (3) 160 (4) 140 (5) 150

48. **The total number of MIG flats booked in Manglore, Baroda and Nagpur is by what percent more than the total number of LIG flats booked from these three cities together? (rounded off to the nearest integer)**

    (1) 37 (2) 35 (3) 39 (4) 32 (5) 34

49. **What is the difference between the total number of MIG flats booked in Allahabad, Mangalore, Nagpur and Aurangabad together and the total number of LIG flats booked in these four cities together?**

    (1) 420 (2) 480 (3) 460 (4) 360 (5) 260

**50. What is the ratio of the total number of flats (all three types) booked in Allahabad to that in Baroda?**

(1) 54 : 49 (2) 51 : 46 (3) 54 : 47 (4) 58 : 49 (5) 55 : 48

## Answer Grid:

| Q. No. | 1 | 2 | 3 | 4 | 5 | 6 | 7 | 8 | 9 | 10 | 11 | 12 | 13 | 14 | 15 | 16 | 17 | 18 | 19 | 20 |
|---|---|---|---|---|---|---|---|---|---|---|---|---|---|---|---|---|---|---|---|---|
| Answer | 1 | 5 | 3 | 2 | 1 | 3 | 5 | 5 | 5 | 4 | 4 | 1 | 4 | 3 | 2 | 3 | 5 | 3 | 5 | 3 |
| Q. No. | 21 | 22 | 23 | 24 | 25 | 26 | 27 | 28 | 29 | 30 | 31 | 32 | 33 | 34 | 35 | 36 | 37 | 38 | 39 | 40 |
| Answer | 4 | 4 | 4 | 4 | 2 | 4 | 2 | 4 | 5 | 3 | 1 | 2 | 3 | 2 | 3 | 1 | 5 | 5 | 4 | 2 |
| Q. No. | 41 | 42 | 43 | 44 | 45 | 46 | 47 | 48 | 49 | 50 | | | | | | | | | | |
| Answer | 2 | 1 | 5 | 1 | 1 | 2 | 2 | 1 | 2 | 1 | | | | | | | | | | |

## Quantitative Aptitude - Year 2013

**Directions (Q. 51 -55) : What will come in place of the question mark (?) in the following questions?**

**51.** **4003 × 77 – 21015 = ? × 116**

(1) 2477 (2) 2478 (3) 2467 (4) 2476 (5) None of these

**52.** **[(5√7 +√7) × (4√7 + 8√7)] – (19)2 = ?**

(1) 143 (2) 72√7 (3) 134 (4) 70√7 (5) None of these

**53.** **(4444÷ 40) + (645 ÷ 25) + (3991 ÷ 26) = ?**

(1) 280.4 (2) 290.4 (3) 295.4 (4) 285.4 (5) None of these

**54.** **200×5 + 2**

(1) 1002 (2) 33 (3) 34 (4) 28 (5) None of these

**55.** **26 + 26 ÷26**

(1) 2 (2) 305.75 (3) 26 (4) 27 (5) None of these

**Directions (Q. 56-60): What approximate value should come in place of the question mark (?) in the following questions? (Note: You are not expected to calculate the exact value.)**

**56.** **8787 ÷ 343 × Ö50=?**

(1) 250 (2) 140 (3) 180 (4) 100 (5) 280

**57.**

(1) 48 (2) 38 (3) 28 (4) 18 (5) 58

**58.** **212 + 17 - 240**

(1) -11 (2) -21 (3) 21 (4) 11 (5) 4850

**59.** **23% of 6783 + 57% of 8431 = ?**

(1) 6460 (2) 6420 (3) 6320 (4) 6630 (5) 6360

**60.** **335.01 × 244.99 ÷ 55 = ?**

(1) 1490 (2) 1550 (3) 1420 (4) 1590 (5) 1400

**Directions (Q. 61-65) : In each of these questions a number series is given. In each series only one number is wrong. Find out the wrong number.**

**61.** **5531, 5506, 5425, 5304, 5135, 4910, 4621**

(1) 5531 (2) 5425 (3) 4621 (4) 5135 (5) 5506

**62.** **6, 7, 9, 13, 26, 37, 69**

(1) 7 (2) 26 (3) 69 (4) 37 (5) 9

**63.** **1, 3, 10, 36, 152, 760, 4632**

(1) 3 (2) 36 (3) 4632 (4) 760 (5) 152

**64.** **4, 3, 9, 34, 96, 219, 435**

(1) 4 (2) 9 (3) 34 (4) 435 (5) 219

**65.** **157.5, 45, 15, 6, 3, 2, 1**

(1) 1 (2) 2 (3) 6 (4) 157.5 (5) 45

**Directions (Q. 66-70):** Study the following graph and table carefully and answer the questions given below:

**Time taken to travel (in hours) by six vehicles on two different days**

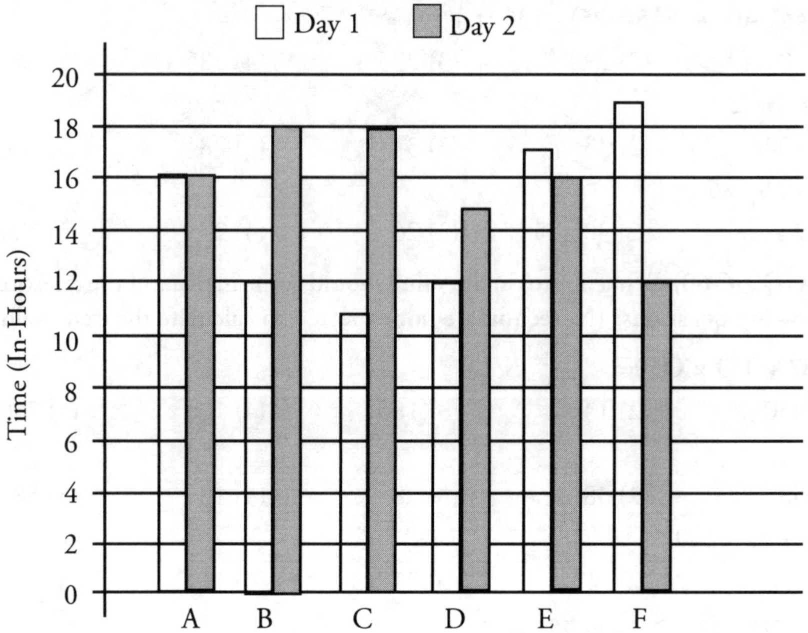


Distance covered (in kilometres) by six vehicles on each day

| Vehicle | Day 1 | Day 2 |
|---|---|---|
| A | 832 | 864 |
| B | 516 | 774 |
| C | 693 | 810 |
| D | 552 | 765 |
| E | 935 | 546 |
| F | 703 | 636 |

**66.** **Which of the following vehicles travelled at the same speed on both the days?**

(1) Vehicle A (2) Vehicle C (3) Vehicle F (4) Vehicle B (5) None of these

67. **What was the difference between the speed of Vehicle A on Day 1 and the speed of Vehicle C on the same day?**

(1) 7 km/hr (2) 12 km/hr (3) 11 km/hr (4) 8 km/hr (5) None of these

68. **What was the speed of Vehicle C on Day 2 in terms of metres per second?**

(1) 15.3 (2) 12.8 (3) 11.5 (4) 13.8 (5) None of these

69. **The distance travelled by Vehicle F on Day 2 was approximately what per cent of the distance travelled by it on Day 1?**

(1) 80 (2) 65 (3) 85 (4) 95 (5) 90

70. **What is the ratio of the speeds of Vehicle D and Vehicle E on Day 2?**

(1) 15:13 (2) 17:13 (3) 13:11 (4) 17:14 (5) None of these

71. **An article was purchased for ? 78,350. Its price was marked up by 30%. It was sold at a discount of 20% on the marked-up price. What was the profit per cent on the cost price?**

(1) 4% (2) 7% (3) 5% (4) 3% (5) 6%

72. **When X is subtracted from the numbers 9, 15 and 27, the remainders are in continued proportion. What is the value of X?**

(1) 8 (2) 6 (3) 4 (4) 5 (5) None of these

73. **What is the difference between the simple and the compound interest on Rs. 7,300 at the rate of 6 p.c.p.a. in 2 years?**

(1) Rs. 29.37 (2) Rs. 26.28 (3) Rs. 31.41 (4) Rs. 23.22 (5) Rs. 21.34

74. **The sum of three consecutive numbers is 2262. What is 41% of the highest number?**

(1) 301.51 (2) 303.14 (3) 308.73 (4) 306.35 (5) 309.55

75. **In how many different ways can the letters of the word THERAPY' be arranged so that the vowels never come together?**

(1) 720 (2) 1440 (3) 5040 (4) 3600 (5) 4800

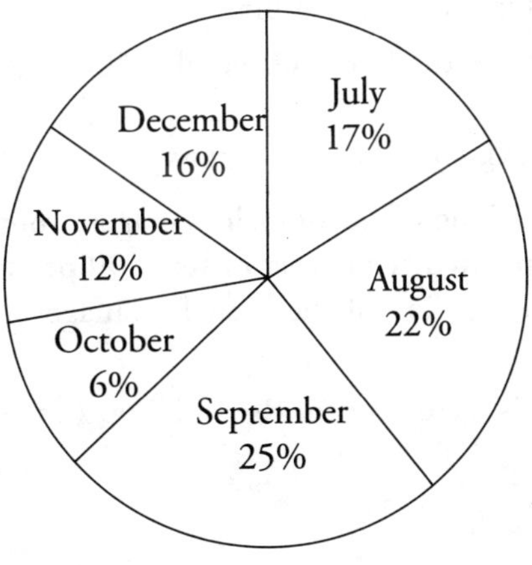

76. **What is the ratio of the number of mobile phones sold of Company B during July to those sold during December of the same company?**

(1) 119 : 145 (2) 116 : 135 (3) 119 : 135 (4) 119 : 130 (5) None of these

77. **If 35% of the mobile phones sold by Company A during November were sold at a discount, how many mobile phones of Company A during that month were sold without a discount?**

(1) 882 (2) 1635 (3) 1638 (4) 885 (5) None of these

78. **If the shopkeeper earned a profit of Rs 433 on each mobile phone sold of Company B during October, what was his total profit earned on the mobile phones of that company during the same month?**

(1) Rs. 6,49,900 (2) Rs. 6,45,900 (3) Rs. 6,49,400 (4) Rs. 6,49,500 (5) None of these

79. **The number of mobile phones sold of Company A during July is approximately what per cent of the number of mobile phones sold of Company A during December?**

(1) 110 (2) 140 (3) 150 (4) 105 (5) 130

80. **What is the total number of mobile phones sold of Company B during August and September together?**

(1) 10000 (2) 15000 (3) 10500 (4) 9500 (5) None of these

**Directions (Q. 81-85): Study the following information and answer the questions that follow:**

The premises of a bank are to be renovated. The renovation is in terms of flooring. Certain areas are to be floored either with marble or wood. All rooms/halls and pantry are rectangular. The area to be renovated comprises a hall for customer transaction measuring 23m by 29m, the branch manager's room measuring 13m by 17m, a pantry measuring 14m by 13m, a record keeping-cum-server room measuring 21 m by 13 m and locker area measuring 29m by 21 m. The total area of the bank is 2000 square metres. The cost of wooden flooring is Rs. 170 per square metre and the cost of marble flooring is Rs. 190 per square metre. The locker area, record keeping-cum-server room and pantry are to be floored with marble. The branch manager's room and the hall for customer transaction are to be floored with wood. No other area is to be renovated in terms of flooring.

81. **What is the ratio of the total cost of wooden flooring to the total cost of marble flooring?**

(1) 1879:2527 (2) 1887:2386 (3) 1887:2527 (4) 1829:2527 (5) 1887:2351

82. **If the four walls and ceiling of the branch manager's room (the height of the room is 12 metres) are to be painted at the cost of Rs. 190 per square metre, how much will be the total cost of renovation of the branch manager's room, including the cost of flooring?**

(1) Rs. 1,36,800 (2) Rs. 2,16,660 (3) Rs. 1,78,790 (4) Rs. 2,11,940 (5) None of these

**83. If the remaining area of the bank is to be carpeted at the rate of 110 per square metre, how much will be the increment in the total cost of renovation of bank premises?**

(1) Rs. 5,820 (2) Rs. 4,848 (3) Rs. 3,689 (4) Rs. 6,690 (5) None of these

**84. What is the percentage area of the bank that is not to be renovated?**

(1) 2.2% (2) 2.4% (3) 4.2% (4) 4.4% (5) None of these

**85. What is the total cost of renovation of the hall for customer transaction and the locker area?**

(1) Rs. 23,100 (2) Rs. 2,3036 (3) Rs. 2,16,920 (4) Rs. 2,42,440 (5) None of these

**86. A certain amount was to be distributed among A, B and C in the ratio 2 : 3 : 4, but was erroneously distributed in the ratio 7 : 2 : 5. As a result of this, B got 740 less. What is the amount?**

(1) Rs 210 (2) Rs 270 (3) Rs 230 (4) Rs 280 (5) None of these

**87. Muni enters a shop to buy ice-creams, cookies and pastries. She has to buy at least 9 units of each. She buys more cookies than ice-creams and more pastries than cookies. She picks up a total of 32 items. How many cookies does she buy?**

(1) Either 12 or 13 (2) Either 11 or 12

(3) Either 10 or 11 (4) Either 9 or 11 (5) Either 9 or 10

**88. The fare of a bus is Rs. X for the first five kilometres and Rs. 13 per kilometre thereafter, if a passenger pays Rs. 2402 for a journey of 187 kilometres, what is the value of X?**

(1) Rs. 29 (2) Rs. 39 (3) Rs. 36 (4) Rs. 31 (5) None of these

**89. The product of three consecutive even numbers is 4032. The product of the first and the third number is 252. What is five times the second number?**

(1) 80 (2) 100 (3) 60 (4) 70 (5) 90

**90. The sum of the ages of 4 members of a family 5 years ago was 94 years. Today, when the daughter has been married off and replaced by a daughter-in-law, the sum of their ages is 92. Assuming that there has been no other change in the family structure and all the people are alive, what is the difference between the age of the daughter and that of the daughter-in-law?**

(1) 22 years (2) 11 years (3) 25 years (4) 19 years (5) 15 years

**91. A bag contains 13 white and 7 black balls. Two balls are drawn at random. What is the probability that they are of the same colour?**

(1) 41/ 190 (2) 21/190 (3) 59/190 (4) 99/190 (5) 77/190

**92. Akash scored 73 marks in subject A. He scored 56% marks in subject B and X marks in subject C. Maximum marks in each subject were 150. The overall percentage marks**

**obtained by Akash in all the three subjects together was 54%. How many marks did he score in subject C?**

(1) 84 (2) 86 (3) 79 (4) 73 (5) None of these

93. **The area of a square is 1444 square metres. The breadth of a rectangle is 1/4 the side of the square and the length of the rectangle is thrice its breadth. What is the difference between the area of the square and the area of the rectangle?**

(1) 1152.38 sq mtr (2) 1169.33 sq mtr

(3) 1181.21 sq mtr (4) 1173.25sq mtr (5) None of these

94. **Rs 73,689 are divided between A and B in the ratio 4 : 7. What is the difference between thrice the share of A and twice the share of B?**

(1) Rs. 36,699 (2) Rs. 46,893 (3) Rs. 20,097 (4) Rs. 26,796 (5) Rs. 13,398

95. **A and B together can complete a task in 20 days. B and C together can complete the same task in 30 days. A and C together can complete the same task in 40 days. What is the ratio of the number of days taken by A when completing the same task alone to the number of days taken by C when completing the same task alone ?**

(1) 2 : 5 (2) 2 : 7 (3) 3 : 7 (4) 1 : 5 (5) 3 : 5

**Directions (Q. 96-100): Study the following information and answer the questions that follow:**

The graph given below represents the production (in tonnes) and sales (in tonnes) of company a from

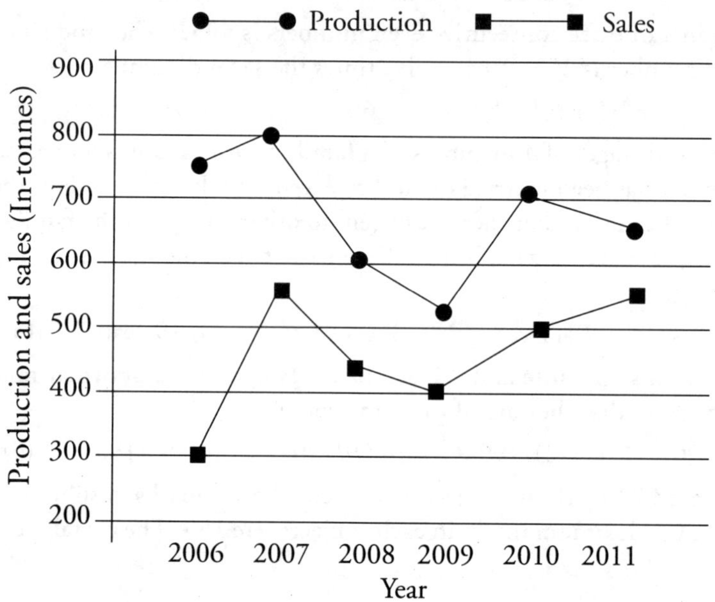

**The table given below represents the ratio of the production (in tonnes) of Company A to the production (in tonnes) of Company B, and the ratio of the sales (in tonnes) of Company A to the sales (in tonnes) of Company B.**

| Year | Production | Sales |
|---|---|---|
| 2006 | 5:4 | 2:3 |
| 2007 | 8:7 | 11:12 |
| 2008 | 3:4 | 9:14 |
| 2009 | 11:12 | 4:5 |
| 2010 | 14:13 | 10:9 |
| 2011 | 13:14 | 1:1 |

96. What is the approximate percentage increase in the production of Company A (in tonnes) from the year 2009 to the production of Company A (in tonnes) in the year 2010?

(1) 18% (2) 38% (3) 23% (4) 27% (5) 32%

97. The sales of Company A in the year 2009 was approximately what per cent of the production of Company A in the same year?

(1) 65% (2) 73% (3) 79% (4) 83% (5) 69%

98. What is the average production of Company B (in tonnes) from the year 2006 to the year 2011 ?

(1) 574 (2) 649 (3) 675 (4) 593 (5) 618

99. What is the ratio of the total production (in tonnes) of Company A to the total sales (in tonnes) of Company A?

(1) 81 : 64 (2) 64 : 55 (3) 71 : 81 (4) 71 : 55 (5) 81 : 55

100. What is the ratio of production of Company B (in tonnes) in the year 2006 to production of Company B (in tonnes) in the year 2008?

(1) 2 : 5 (2) 4 : 5 (3) 3 : 4 (4) 3 : 5 (5) 1 : 4

20

# MOCK QA Test 1

1. 12 + 22 + 32 + ... + 102 = ?

   A) 400 B) 625 C) 380 D) 625

2. 6% of 350 + (?)% of 200 = 75% of 40

   A) 5 B) 4.5 C) 5.5 D)7

3. Which number will replace (?) in the following series: 8, 10, 12, 16, (?)

   A) 15 B) 18 C) 17 D) 21

4. 5 7 11 (?) 17

   A) 13 B) 17 C) 19 D) 18

5. 11 (?) 19 23 27

   A) 14 B) 16 C) 15 D) 21

6. I. $p^2 + 7p + 10 = 0$ II. $q^2 + 11q + 30 = 0$

   A) if P is greater than q. B) if P is smaller than q.

   C) if P is equal to q. D) if P is either equal to or greater than q.

7. I. $3p^2 + 8p - 5 = 0$ II. $10q^2 + 9q + 2 = 0$

   A) if P is greater than q. B) if P is smaller than q.

   C) if P is equal to q. D) if none of the above is true.

8. Ajay can do a piece of work in 15 days and Bindu in 20 days. How much time will they take to complete the work if they work on alternate days, starting with Ajay ?

   A) 16 B) 17 C) 28 D) 30

9. A silver wire, when bent in the term of a square, encloses an area of 144 cm². How much area would the same wire include if it is bent to form a circle ?

   A) 61.7 $cm^2$ B) 25.45 $cm^2$ C) 85 $cm^2$ D) 183.43 $cm^2$

10. A bag contains 3 blue, 2 green and 1 red ball. If three balls are picked at random, what is the probability that at least one is red ?

    A) 1/4 B) 1/5 C) 1/6 D) 1/8

11. **If the digits of a two-digit number are interchanged, the number so obtained is greater than the original number by 18. If the sum of the two digits of the number is 14. What is the original number ?**

A) 68 B) 77 C) 95 D) 86

12. **If the numerator of a fraction is increased by 50% and denominator by 20%, the fraction become 9/15. What was the original fraction ?**

A) 12/25 B) 13/25 C) 3/5 D) 6/7

13. **The ratio between the present ages of a man and his wife is 4 : 3 respectively. Also, the man is 8 years older than his wife. What is the present age of the daughter who is one-eighth the present age of her mother ?**

A) 6 years B) 12 ears C) 9 years D) 3 years

14. **The number obtained by interchanging the digits of a two-digit number is less than the original number by 36. The sum of the digits of the number is 8. What is the original number ?**

A) 71 B) 62 C) 53 D) 35

15. **The Salary of an employee increase consistently by 12% per year. If his present salary is Rs. 12000 then what will his salary be after 3 years ?**

A) Rs. 15000 B) Rs. 16345 C) Rs. 16589 D) Rs. 16859

16. **In how many ways can 3 boys be chosen from 6 boys and 4 girls so as to include exactly one girl ?**

A) 252 B) 210 C) 120 D) 60

17. **A sum was lent at simple interest at a certain rate for 2 years. Had it been lent at a rate 4% higher than the previous rate, it would have fetched Rs 488 more. What was the sum ?**

A) 2700 B) 3200 C) 5400 D) 6100

18. **Two trains start at the same time from Delhi and Mumbai towards each other at the speed of 32 kmph and 48 kmph respectively. When they meet, it is found that one train has travelled 128 km more than the other one. What is the distance between Mumbai and Delhi?**

A) 600 km B) 620 km C) 640 km D) 660 km

19. **In how many different ways can the letters of the word SEQUENCE be arranged ?**

A) 64 B) 13440 C) 6720 D) 20160

20. **An amount of money is distributed among A, B and C in the ratio of 1 : 2 : 9. If C gives Rs. 400 from his share to B, the new ratio becomes 1 : 3 : 8. What is the total amount ?**

A) 4200 B) 4800 C) 5600 D) 6400

21. When a number is added to another number the total becomes 350% of the first number. What is the ratio of the first number to the second ?

A) 3 : 8 B) 4 : 9 C) 2 : 5 D) 8 : 15

22. In a five-litre mixture of milk and water the portion of water is 40%. How much milk should be added to the mixture so that the portion of water reduces to 5% ?

A) 15 litre B) 20 litre C) 35 litre D) 40 litre

23. A card is drawn from a pack of 52 cards. What is the probability of its being an ace of red suit ?

A) 1/13 B) 2/13 C) 1/26 D) 3/13

24. Ritu invested 20% more than Sonu. Sonu invested 25% less than Ajay who invested Rs. 6,000. What is the respective ratio between the amount that Rita invested and the total amount invested by all of them together ?

A) 35 : 104 B) 13 : 29 C) 101 : 36 D) 18 : 53

25. 42% of a number is 23646. What is 29% of this number?

A) 16217 B) 16327 C) 17325 D) None of these

26. The respective ratio between the speeds of a car, a train and a bus is 5 : 9 : 4. The average speed of the car, the bus and the train is 72 kmph together. What is the average speed of the car and the train together ?

A) 82 kmph B) 78 kmph

C) 84 kmph D) Cannot be determined

27. 6 women alone can complete a piece of work in 10 days, whereas 10 children alone take 15 days to complete the same piece of work. How many days will 6 women and 10 children together take to complete the piece of work?

A) 4 B) 8

C) 6 D) Cannot be determined

28. A train 300 metres long is running at a speed of 90 km/hr. How many seconds will it take to cross a 200 metre long running in the opposite direction at a speed of 60 km/hr.

A) 60 second B) 12 second C) 20 second D) None of these

29. Tina invests Rs. 48,000 to start a business. Four months later Shreya joins her by investing Rs. 62,000 and another two months later Tulika joins them both by investing Rs. 80,000. At the end of one year the business earns a profit of Rs. 20,661. What is Tulika's share in the profit ?

A) Rs. 7,668 B) Rs. 6,603 C) Rs. 7,240 D) Rs. 6,390

30. A school team has eight volleyball players. A five-member team and a captain will be selected out of these eight players. How many different selections can be made?

A) 224 B) 168 C) 88 D) 120

31. If the price of the sugar is increased by 7%, then by how much percent should a housewife reduce her consumption of sugar, to have no extra expenditure ?

A) 6.54% B) 8% C) 7% D) None of these

32. A's income is 10% more than B's and C's income is 32% more than B's. By what percent is C's income more than A's ?

A) 10% B) 15% C) 18% D) 20%

33. A person sold 3/5 of a consignment at a profit of 30% and the rest at a loss of 35%. If there was an overall profit of Rs. 615 what is the actual cost of the consignment ?

A) Rs. 1380 B) Rs. 14300 C) Rs. 15374 D) Rs. 1550

34. What will be the ratio of the simple interest to the compound interest on a certain sum of money at 28% per annum for two years ?

A) 50:51 B) 50:57 C) 21:20 D) 53:50

35. From a basket containing 5 black and 8 white balls, two draws of one ball each are made without replacement. What is the probability that one is black and the other is white?

A) 20/29 B) 8/15 C) 2/13 D) 48/85

36. 15 litres of a mixture contains 20% alcohol and the rest is water. If 3 litres of water is mixed in it find the percentage of alcohol in the new mixture ?

A) 17% B) 50/3% C) 15% D) None of these

**37-41: Study the following information carefully and answer the given questions.**

Out of 500 students, 5.4% passed in all the three papers, Physics, Chemistry and Biology. 14.4% students passed only in Physics, 21% passed only in Chemistry and 22.4% passed only in Biology. 8.6% passed only in Physics and Chemistry and 15.4% passed only in Chemistry and Biology.

37. What percentage of students failed only in Chemistry ?

A) 7.8 % B) 8.6% C) 12.8% D) 13.6 %

38. What is the difference between the number of students who passed in Biology and the number of students who passed only in Biology ?

A) 164 B) 168 C) 170 D) 172

39. The number of students who passed in Chemistry is what percentage of the number of students who passed only in Physics ?

A) 28.57% B) 122.33% C) 150% D) 350%

40. How many students are there who passed in at least two papers out of the given three ?

A) 211 B) 207 C) 203 D) 1%

41. The number of students who passed in all three papers is what percentage of the number of students who passed in at most one paper ?

A) 7.82% B) 9.34% C) 11.2% D) 13.64%

42. A train travelling at the speed of 60 kmph crosses a platform in 20 seconds. What is the length of the train ?

A) 333 m B) 300 m

C) 336 m D) Cannot be determined

43. In a college the number of students studying Arts, Commerce and Science are in the ratio of 3 : 5 : 8 respectively. If the number of students studying Arts, Commerce and Science is increased by 20%, 40% and 25 % respectively, what will be the new ratio of students in Arts, Commerce and Science respectively ?

A) 18 : 35 : 50 B) 3 : 10 : 10 C) 4 : 8 : 5 D) 32 : 35 : 25

44. In an election between two candidates, 75% of the voters cast their votes, out of which 2% of the votes were declared invalid. A candidate got 9261 votes which were 76% of the total valid votes. Find the total number of votes enrolled in that election.

A) 1000 B) 12000 C) 15800 D) 16800

45. 12 buckets of water fill a tank when the capacity of each tank is 13.5 litres. How many buckets will be needed to fill the same tank, if the capacity of each bucket is 9 litres?

A) 8 B) 15 C) 16 D) 18

**46-50:Following pie-chart shows the percentage distribution of total students who appeared in board exam from different schools. The table shows the ratio of the number of boys to that of girls and the ratio of passed to failed students.**

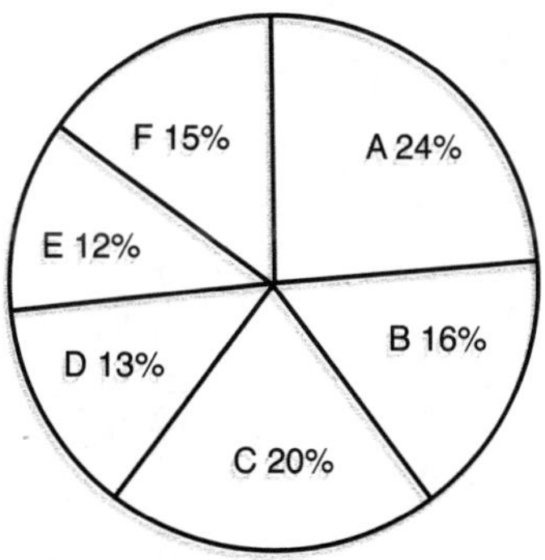

Total number of students who appeared in exam = 48000

| School | Boys : Girls | Pass : Fail |
|---|---|---|
| A | 5 : 3 | 2 : 1 |
| B | 9 : 7 | 1 : 1 |
| C | 2 : 3 | 3 : 2 |
| D | 6 : 7 | 8 : 5 |
| E | 3 : 1 | 2 : 1 |
| F | 8 : 7 | 3 : 2 |

**46. What is the total number of boys who appeared in board exam from all six schools together ?**

A) 26100 B) 26200 C) 26300 D) 26400

**47. What is the average number of students who failed from all six schools together ?**

A) 3110 B) 3120 C) 3130 D) 3140

**48. What is the total number of girls who failed from School C ?**

A) 3840 B) 1920 C) 2304 D) None of these

**49. What is the ratio of the total number of students who failed from School A to the total number of students who passed from School B ?**

A) 1 : 1 B) 1 : 2 C) 2: 3 D) 3 : 4

**50. The total number of girls appearing from School E is what percentage of the total number of students who appeared from School F ?**

A) 16% B) 18% C) 20% D) 24%

## Answer Grid:

| Q. No. | 1 | 2 | 3 | 4 | 5 | 6 | 7 | 8 | 9 | 10 | 11 | 12 | 13 | 14 | 15 | 16 | 17 | 18 | 19 | 20 |
|---|---|---|---|---|---|---|---|---|---|---|---|---|---|---|---|---|---|---|---|---|
| Answer | D | B | B | A | C | D | D | B | D | C | A | A | D | B | D | C | D | C | C | B |
| Q. No. | 21 | 22 | 23 | 24 | 25 | 26 | 27 | 28 | 29 | 30 | 31 | 32 | 33 | 34 | 35 | 36 | 37 | 38 | 39 | 40 |
| Answer | C | C | C | D | C | C | C | A | D | B | A | B | C | B | A | B | C | B | D | A |
| Q. No. | 41 | 42 | 43 | 44 | 45 | 46 | 47 | 48 | 49 | 50 | | | | | | | | | | |
| Answer | B | D | A | D | D | D | B | D | A | C | | | | | | | | | | |

## Explanations:

1. Sum of the squares of first 'n' natural number = n(n+1)(2n+1)6. Put n = 10, 10. 10x 11 x 21/6 = 55 x 7 = 385
2. Let x% of 220 = 75% of 40 – 60% of 350 = 9 or x=9x100/220 = 45/11 = 4.09
3. The series is 5, and 5 + odd prime numbers 5 + 3 = 8, 5 + 5 = 10, 5 + 7 = 12, 5 + 11 = 16, 5 + 13 = 18
4. The series is : Prime numbers starting from 3.
5. The series is : +4.
6. $p^2 + 7p + 10 = 0$

   $= p(p + 5) + 2(p + 5) = 0$

   $= p = -2, -5$

   ll. $q^2 + 11q + 30 = 0$

   $= q = -5, -6$

   $\therefore p > q$
7. $3p^2 + 8p - 5 = 0$

   $= p = -8 + \sqrt{124}/6 = -8 + 11/6 = -19/6, 1/2$

   ll. $10q^2 + 9q + 2 = 0$

   $= 5q (2q + 1) + 2 (2q + 1) = 0$

   $= (5q + 2) (2q + 1) = 0$

   $= q = -2/5, -1/2$

   None of the relations exist.
8. Work done by Ajay in one day = 1/15

   Work done by Bindu in one day = 1/20

   Total work done in 2 days = 1/15 + 1/20 = 4 + 3/60 = 7/60

   Total work done in 16 days = 7/60 x 8 = 56/60 = 14/15,

   Remaining work = 1 – 14/15 = 1/15 and this can be done by Ajay on the 17[th] day.

9. Let the side of the square be 'x' and the radium of the circle be 'r'

We have $x^2 = 144$

or $x = \sqrt{144} = 12$

We have 4x = 48 2pr

or r = 48/2p = 24/p

Area enclosed by the circle = $pr^2 = p\ (24/p)^2$ =183.43

10. Probability of having no red ball is

${}^5C_1 / {}^6C_1 = 5/6$

Probability of having at least one red ball 1 is 1 – 5/6 = 1/6

11. Let the no. be 10x + y.

No. formed by the interchange of digits = 10y + x

We have y – x = 2 .....(i)

y + x = 14 .....(ii)

Solving (i) and (ii), we get x = 6, and y = 8

∴ the no. is 68.

12. Let the fraction be x/y, We have 150x/120y = 9/15 = x/y = 12/25

13. Man = wife + 8

4x – 3x = 8

Man's age = 8 x 4 = 32 yrs

Wife's age = 8 x 3 = 24 yrs

Daughter's age = 24/8 = 3 yrs

14. Let the number be 10x + y.

∴ x + y = 8 .....(i)

10x + y – (10y + x) = 36 ∴ 9(x – y) = 3

∴ x – y = 4 .......(ii)

From equation (i) and (ii): x = 6, y = 2

∴ Number = 62

15. Salary = 12000 x 1.12 x 1.12 x 1.12 =16859

16. One girl can be chosen in ${}^4C_1$ = 4 ways and 4 boys can be chosen in ${}^6C_2$ = 30 ways

∴ Total number of ways = 4 x 30 = 120 ways.

17. Let the interest rate be 'r' and the sum

'x' Then x(r + 4) x 2/100 = X x r x 2/100 + 488

∴ 2xr + 8x – 2xr = 48800

∴ x = 40800/12 = 34000

18. The difference between the speeds of the trains to make the difference of 128 km = 48 – 32 = 16 kmph

Difference in distance = 128 km

Hence time = 128/ 16 = 8 hrs i.e. they meet after 8 hrs.

Total distance = 32 x 8 + 48 x 8 = 256 + 384 = 640 km

19. Total ways = 8!/3! = 6720

20. Let the amount received by A, B and C be x, 2x and 9x respectively.

$\therefore$ Total = 12x

x : 2x + 400 : 9x – 400 = 1 : 3 :8

ie 8x = (9x – 400) $\therefore$ x = 400

$\therefore$ Total number = 12x = 4800

21. Let the first number be 'x' and the second number be 'y'

Then, x + y = X x 350/100 = 7x/2

$\therefore$ 2x + 2y = 7x, ie 2y = 5x

$\therefore$ x/y = 2/5

22. Original mixture = 5 litre;

Milk = 3 litre; Water = 2 litre

Let x litre of milk be added so that thc

mixture becomes (x + 5) litres and the percentage of water becomes 5%

So, 2 = (x + 5) x 5/100

$\therefore$ x = 35

23. Total Number of possible selections n(s) = $^{52}C_1$

Number of ways of selection an ace of red suit, n(E) = $^{2}C_1$

$\therefore$ P(E) = $^{2}C_1$ / $^{52}C_1$ = 2/52 = 1/26

24. Ajay's investment = Rs. 6000

Sonu's Investment = 75 x 6000/100 = Rs. 4500

Ritu's Investment = 4500 x 120/100 = Rs. 5400

Therefore Required ratio = 5400 : (6000 + 4500 + 5400) = 5400 : 15900 = 18 : 53

25. Required value = (23646/42) x 29 = 16327

26. 5x + 9x + 4x = 72 x 3 = 18x = 72 x 3

$\therefore$ x = 72 x 3/18 = 12 kmph

$\therefore$ Average speed of car and train = 5x + 9x/2 = 7x = 7 x 12 = 84 kmph

27. 10W $\times$10 = 10C $\times$ 15, or, 2W = 5C

(6W + 10C) $\times$ X = 6W $\times$ 10

10W $\times$ X = 6W $\times$ 10 = X = 6 days

28. Relative speed = 90 kmph – 60 kmph = 30 km/hr

    30 x 5/18 = 25/3 m/sec

    Time taken to cover (300 + 200) m at 25/3 m/sec = (500 x 3)/25 = 60 sec

29. Ratio of the profit of Tina, Shreya and Tulika = 48000 × 12 : 62000 × 8 : 80000 × 6 = 48 × 12 : 62 × 8 : 80 × 6 = 36 : 31 : 30

    Sum of ratio = 36 + 31 + 30 = 97

    ∴ Tulika's share = Rs. (30/97 x 20661) = Rs. 6390

30. Required ways = $^8C_6 \times {}^6C_1 = 168$

31. Less % = (7/107) x 100

    700/107 = 6.54%

32. A B C

    110 100 132

    ∴ Required % = 132 – 100/110 x 100 = 22/110 x 100 = 20%

33. Let the total cost of the consignment be x.

    ∴ (3x/5 x 130/100 + 2x/5 x 65/100) – x = 615

    Or, (78x/100 + 26x/100) – x = 615, or, 104x/100 – x = 615

    ∴ 4x = 615 x 100

    ∴ x = 15375

34. Let the sum be Rs. 100.

    ∴ SI = 100 x 28 x 2/100 = 56,

    Amt at CI = 100 x 1.28 x 1.28 = 163.84

    ∴ CI = 163.84 – 100 = 63.84

    ∴ SI/CI = 56/63.84 = 5600/6384 = 50/57

35. $n(S) = {}^{13}C_2 = 78$

    $n(E) = {}^5C_1 \times {}^8C_1 = 5 \times 8 = 40$

    ∴ P(E) = 40/78 = 20/39

36. The mixture contains 3 litres of alcohol and 12 litres water. Afterwards, the mixture contains 3 litres of alcohol and 15 ltres of water.

    Percentage of alcohol = (3/18) x 100 = 50/3 %

37. k = 500 – (72 + 43 + 105 + 27 + 77 + 112) = 500 – 436 = 64

    ∴ Reqd % = 64/500 x 100 = 12.8

38. Biology = 280, Only Biology = 112,

    ∴ Difference = 280 – 112 = 168

39. Chemistry = 252
Only Physics = 72
Therefore, Reqd % = 252/72 x 100 = 350%

40. At least two = 43 + 64 + 77 + 27 = 211

41. At most one paper = 72 + 105 + 112 = 289
Therefore, Reqd % = 27/289 x 100 = 9.34

42. When a train crosses a platform the distance covered
= Length of platform and the train.
Speed = Length of (platform + train)/Time taken
Thus we have inadequate data.

43. Let the number of students in Arts, Commerce and Science be 3x, 5x and 8x respectively.
On increasing their respective numbers,
Required ratio
= 3x x 120/100 : 5x x 140/100 : 8x x 125/100
= 360 : 700 : 1000
= 18 : 35 : 50

44. Let the number of votes enrolled be x
No. of votes cast = 75% of x, valid votes = 98% of (75% of x)
75% of (98% of(75% of x)) = 9261
(75/100 x 98/100 x 75/100 x x) = 9261
x = (9262 x 100 x 100 x 100)/ 75 x 98 x 75 = 16800

45. Capacity of the tank = 12 x 13.5 = 162 litres'
Capacity of each bucket = 9 litres
No. of buckets needed = 162/9 = 18

46. Total boys = 48000 (0.24 x 5/8 + 0.16 x 9/16 + 0.2 x 2/5 + 0.13 x 6/13 + 0.12 x 3/4 + 0.15 x 8/15)
= 48000 (0.15 + 0.09 + 0.08 + 0.06 + 0.09 + 0.08) = 48000 x 0.55 = 26400

47. Total number of failed students = 18720
∴ Average = 18720/6 = 3120

48. No explanation

49. Ratio = 48000 x 0.24 x 1/3/4800 x 0.16x1/2 = 0.08/0.08 = 1/1

50. $Girls_E$ = 48000 x 0.12 x 1/4
$Total_F$ = 48000 x 0.15
= 7200
∴ Required % = 1440/7200 x 100 = 20%

# MOCK QA Test 2

1. $2 + 2^2 + 2^3 + \ldots\ldots. + 2^9 = ?$

   A) 2044 B) 1022 C) 1056 D) None of these

2. There are three persons Amit, Bimal and Chirag when the age of Amit is added to half of the age of Bimal, the result is equal to Chirag's age. One-third of the age of 'Bimal' is equal to one-fourth of the age of 'Chirag'. If one-fifth of Amit's age is added to half of Bimal's age, the result is equal to half of Chirag's age. Then what is the age of 'Bimal' ?

   A) 16 yrs B) 20 yrs C) 24 yrs D) 30 yrs

3. A train crosses a 120-metre and a 70-metre long plat form in 17 seconds and 12 seconds respectively. What is the speed of the train ?

   A) 10 m/sec B) 16 m/sec C) 20 m/sec D) 24 m/sec

4. If Andy's salary is 50% more than Ben's; then how much per cent is Ben's salary less than Andy's ?

   A) 20% B) 26% C) 32 ½ % D) 33 1/3 %

5. $25 \times 16$ is what % of 1600 ?

   A) 20% B) 25% C) 26% D) 30%

6. A shopkeeper bought an item at 10% discount on its original price. He sold it at 35% increase on the original price. What percentage profit did he get ?

   A) 25% B) 45% C) 50% D) 22 ½%

7. What number will replace the (?) in the following series:

   7, 20, 46, 98, 202, (?)

   A) 420 B) 410 C) 310 D) 320

8. A certain amount of money becomes five times at the simple interest rate of 7% per annum. At what rate per cent will it become 9 times ?

   A) 14% B) 21% C) 28% D) 17.5%

**Directions 9-13 : Following line-graph shows the ratio of import to export of two companies 'A' and 'B' during the period 1990 to 1995.**

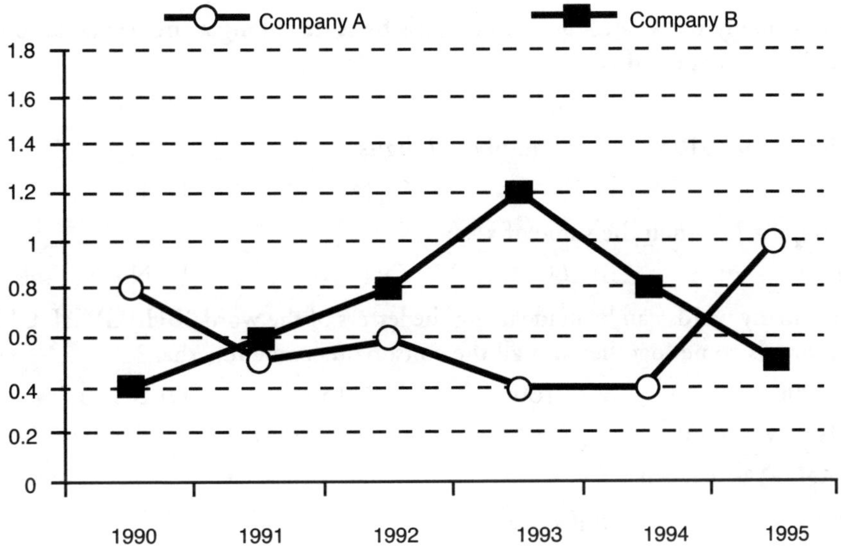


9. **If the export of Company B in year 1992 was Rs 72 lakhs then what was its import (in Rs) in the same year ?**

   A) 90 lakhs B) 57.6 lakhs C) 60 lakhs D) 56 lakhs

10. **If the import of Company B in year 1993 was Rs 72 lakhs then what was its export (in Rs) in the same year ?**

    A) 60 lakhs B) 64 lakhs C) 86.4 lakhs D) 84 lakhs

11. **In which year was the value of export of Company A less than the value of its import in that year ?**

    A) 1990 B) 1992 C) 1993 D) None of these

12. **If the import of Company A in year 1992 and the export of Company B in year 1990 was Rs 66 lakhs and Rs 166 lakhs respectively then what was the sum (in Rs) of export of A in year 1992 and import of B in year 1990 ?**

    A) 176.4 lakhs B) 178.6 lakhs C) 182 lakhs D) 184.5 lakhs

13. **If the import of Company B in year 1995 is increased by 20% and export is decreased by 20%, then what will be the new ratio of its import to export ?**

    A) 0.50 B) 0.40 C) 0.60 D) 0.75

14. **Two numbers are respectively 33% and 40% more than a third number. What percentage is the first of the second ?**

    A) 70% B) 75% C) 80% D) 90%

15. **The ratio between the sale price and cost price of an article is 7 : 5. What is ratio between the profit and the cost price of that article ?**

A) 2 : 7 B) 5 : 2 C) 7 : 2 D) None of these

16. **In how many ways can 7 boys and 7 girls be seated along a circular table so that they are alternately placed ?**

A) 7! 7! B) 14! C) 7! 6! D) 6! 6!

17. **If log 2 = 0.30103, find the number of digits in $2^{56}$**

A) 12 B) 15 C) 16 D) 17

18. **If $\log_8 x = 2/3$, then the value of x is :**

A) 3/4 B) 4/3 C) 4 D) None of these

19. **How many words can be made using the letters of the word "BHAGWADGITA" if all the vowels come together and all the consonants come together ?**

A) 2000 B) 20160 C) 20150 D) 20180

20. **I. $4x^2 - x - 5 = 0$**

**II. $6y^2 - 13y + 6 = 0$**

A) if x > y B) if x > y

C) if x D) if x = y or if there is no relation between x and y

21. **The number obtained by interchanging the digits of a two-digit number is less than the original number by 36. The sum of the digits of the number is 8. What is the original number ?**

A) 71 B) 62 C) 53 D) 35

22. **The average of 50 numbers is 38. If two numbers are 45 nad 55 the average of the remaining number is**

A) 37.5 B) 23.22 C) 11.22 D) 44.32

23. **The least number which when divided by 20, 25, 35, 40 leaves remainders 14, 19, 29, and 34 respectively is -**

A) 1200 B) 1234 C) 1394 D) None of these

24. **Six bells start ringing together and ring at intervals of 2, 4, 6, 8, 10, and 12 seconds respectively. how many times will they ring together in 30 minutes (including t = 0)?**

A) 4 B) 10 C) 15 D) 16

25. **If log a/b + log b/a = log(a + b), then**

A) a = b B) a + b =1 C) a – b =1 D) a2 – b2 = 1

26. **Neeraj is as younger to Gopal as he is older to Deepak. If the sum of the ages of Gopal and Deepak is 58 years. What is Neeraj's age ?**

A) 29 B) 30 C) 40 D) 55

27. A goods train runs at the speed of 72 kmph and crosses a 250 m long platform in 20 seconds. What is the length of the goods train ?

A) 230 m B) 240 m C) 260 m D) 270 m

28. Two pipes A and B can fill a tank in 36 and 45 minutes respectively. If both the pipes are used together, then how long will it take to fill the tank?

A) 10 min B) 20 min C) 26 min D) 34 min

29. A man rows upstream 12 km and downstream 28 km taking 5 hours each time. The velocity of the current is

A) 8/5 km/h B) 5/2 km/h C) 3 km/h D) None of these

30. A can finish the work in 24 days, B in 9 days and C in 12 days. B and C start the work but are forced to leave after 3 days. The remaining work was done by A in :

A) 5 days B) 6 days C) 10 days D) None of these

31. An accurate clock shows 7 o'clock in the morning. Through how may degrees will the hour hand rotate when the clock shows 12 o'clock in the afternoon?

A) 154° B) 150° C) 170° D) 210°

32. In what ratio must coffee at Rs. 60 per Kg be mixed with coffee at Rs. 70 per Kg so that the mixture must be worth Rs. 64.50 per Kg?

A) 1 : 2 B) 10 : 1 C) 11 : 9 D) 11 : 12

33. The ratio of the ages of a father and son is 17 : 7 respectively. 6 years ago the ratio of their ages was 3 : 1 respectively. What is the father's present age ?

A) 64 B) 51 C) 48 D) Cannot be determined

34. If $7^{(x-y)} = 343$ and $7^{(x+y)} = 16807$, what is the value of x?

A) 4 B) 3 C) 2 D) 1

35. Soumil and Yadav invest Rs. 21000 and Rs. 17500 respectively in a business. At the end of the year, they make a profit of Rs. 26400. What is the share of Soumil in the profit?

A) Rs. 14400 B) Rs. 26400 C) Rs. 12000 D) Rs. 12500

36. The product of two numbers is 120 and the sum of their squres is 289. The sum of the numbers is

A) 20 B) 23 C) 169 D) None of these

37. A certain amount of money grows to Rs. 67600 in two years and to Rs. 87880 in three years on interest compounded annually. What is the rate of interest ?

A) 15% B) 20% C) 25% D) 30%

**Direction (38-40): In the following number series only one number is wrong. Find out the wrong number.**

38. 4, 6, 18, 49, 201, 1011

A) 1011 B) 201 C) 18 D) 49

39. 8, 27, 64, 125, 218, 343

A) 27 B) 218 C) 125 D) 343

40. 48, 72, 108, 162, 243, 366

A) 72 B) 108 C) 162 D) None of these

**Direction (41-44): Following pie-charts show the distribution of the total number of students selected in an entrance exam from seven different schools in 2010 and 2011. (The total number of students selected from School S7 in 2010 and 2011 are 180 and 270 respectively.)**

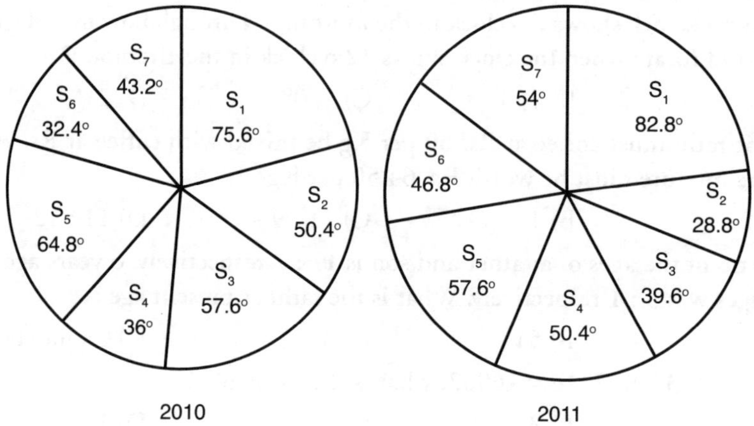


41. **The total number of students selected from all seven schools together in the year 2011 is approximately what per cent of the total number of students selected from all seven schools in 2010 ?**

A) 83.33% B) 120% C) 71.42% D) 140%

42. **What is the per cent rise in the number of students selected from School S4 from 2010 to 2011 ?**

A) 60% B) 63% C) 68% D) 72%

43. **The total number of students selected from School $S_5$ and $S_7$ together in the year 2010 is approximately what per cent of the number of students selected from School S: in the year 2011 ?**

A) 178.5% B) 247.5% C) 287.5% D) 312.5%

44. **What is the difference between the average number of students selected from school $S_1$ $S_2$ and $S_3$ in the year 2010 and the average number of students selected from schools $S_5$, $S_6$ and $S_7$ in the year 2011 ?**

A) 9 B) 12 C) 15 D) 18

45. **Ram buys 6 oranges for Rs. 5 and sells 5 oranges for Rs. 6. How much profit does he make?**

A) 20% B) 22% C) 36% D) 44%

46. **A motorist travel to a place 150 k away at an average speed of 50 km/hr and returns at 30 km/hr. His average speed for the whole journey is ?**

A) 33.5 km/hr B) 51.5 km/hr C) 81 km/hr D) 91 km/hr

47. **Dinesh, Vipul and Chandra start at the same time in the same direction to run around a circular stadium. Dinesh completes a round in 252 seconds, Vipul in 308 seconds and Chandra in 198 seconds, all starting at the same point. After what time will they again at the starting point ?**

A) 36 minutes 22 seconds B) 46 minutes 22 seconds

C) 36 minutes 12 seconds D) 46 minutes 12 seconds

48. **What is the smallest number which when diminished by 12, is divisible 8, 12, 22 and 24?**

A) 276 B) 264 C) 272 D) 268

49. **There are 6 candidates for 3 posts. In how many ways can the posts be filled?**

A) 120 B) 130 C) 100 D) 110

50. **The diagonal of a square is 8m. What is the area of the square ?**

A) 64 sq m B) 32 sq m C) 16 $\sqrt{2}$sq m D) 40 sq m

## Answer Grid:

| Q. No. | 1 | 2 | 3 | 4 | 5 | 6 | 7 | 8 | 9 | 10 | 11 | 12 | 13 | 14 | 15 | 16 | 17 | 18 | 19 | 20 |
|---|---|---|---|---|---|---|---|---|---|---|---|---|---|---|---|---|---|---|---|---|
| Answer | B | C | A | D | B | C | | A | B | A | D | A | D | C | C | C | D | C | B | D |
| Q. No. | 21 | 22 | 23 | 24 | 25 | 26 | 27 | 28 | 29 | 30 | 31 | 32 | 33 | 34 | 35 | 36 | 37 | 38 | 39 | 40 |
| Answer | B | A | C | D | B | A | D | B | A | C | B | C | B | A | A | B | D | C | B | D |
| Q. No. | 41 | 42 | 43 | 44 | 45 | 46 | 47 | 48 | 49 | 50 | | | | | | | | | | |
| Answer | B | C | B | A | D | D | D | A | A | B | | | | | | | | | | |

## Explanations:

1. This is a G.P in which a = 2, r = $2^2/2$ = 2, n = 9

   $S_n = a(r^{n-1})/(r - 1) = 2 \times (2^9 - 1)/(2 - 1) = 1022$

2. A + B/2 = C .......(i)

   B/3 = C/4 ........(ii)

   A/5 + B/2 = C/2 ........(iii)

   Solving these three equations, Amit = 20, Bimal = 24 and Chirag = 32

3. Let the length of the train be x

   ∴ 120 + x/17 = 70 + x/12

   1440 + 12x = 1190 + 17x

   ∴ x = 250/5 = 50m

   ∴ Speed = (120 + 50)/17 = 170/17 = 10 m/s

4. Required % = (150 – 100)/150 x 100 = 500/15 = 100/3 = 33 1/3%

5. (( 25 x 16 )/ 1600 ) x 100 = 25 %

6. Let the original price be 100.

   After discount it is 100 – 10 = 90

   He sells it on 35% profit of original price. So SP = 135

   ∴ % profit = 135–90/90 x 100 = 4500/90 = 50%

7. Interest rate = (9–1)/(5–1) x 7 = 8 x 7/4 = 14%

8. $I_B/E_B$ = 0.84

   ∴ $I_B$ = 0.8 x 72 = 57.6 lakh

9. $I_B/E_B$ = 1.24

   ∴ $E_B$ = 72/1.2 = 60 lakh

10. Exp < imp never occurred for company A

Only in year 1995 imp = exp

11. $I_A/E_B = 0.6$

$E_A = I_A/0.6 = 66/0.6 = 110$ lakh

$I_B/E_B = 0.4$; $I_B = 0.4 \times I_B = 0.4 \times 166 = 66.4$ lakh

12. $I_1/E_1 = 0.5 = 1/2$ .............(i)

$I_2 = I_1 + I_1 \times 20/100 = 6I_1/6,$

$E_2 = E_1 - E_1 \times 20/100 = 4E_1/5$

$\therefore$ Ratio $= I_2/E_2 = 6I_1/5 \times 5/4E_1 = 3/2\ I_1/E_1$

$= 3/2 \times 1/2 = 3/4$

$\therefore$ Ratio $= 3/4 = 0.75$

13. Let the 3rd number be 100.

So 1st number 120 and 2nd = 150

$\therefore$ % = (120/150) x 100 = 80%

14. Let CP = Rs. 5x and SP = Rs. 7x

Then. Gain = Rs. 2x

Required Ratio = 2x : 5x = 2 : 5

15. At the circular table the 7 boys can sit in (7– 1)! = 6! ways. Now there are 7 girls can sit in 7 places in 7! ways

$\therefore$ Total number of ways = 6! 7!

16. $\log (2^{56}) = 56 \log 2 = 56 \times 0.30103 = 16.85768$

Its characteristics is 16. Hence, the no. of digits is 17 (16 + 1)

17. $\log_8 x = 2/3 \Rightarrow x = 8^{2/3} = (2^3)^{2/3} = 2^2 = 4$

18. No. of words = $2! \times 4! \times 7!/3! \times 7! = 20160$

19. I. $4x^2 - x - 5$

$4x^2 + 4x - 5x - 5 = 0$

$4x(x + 1) -5 (x + 1) = 0$

$(4x - 5) (x + 1) = 0$

$x = -1, 5/4$

II. $6y^2 - 9y - 4y + 6 = 0$

$3y (2y - 3) -2 (2y - 3) = 0$

$(2y - 3)(3y - 2) = 0$

$y = 3/2, 2/3$

Hence there is no relation between x and y.

20. Let the number be $10x + y$.

$\therefore x + y = 8$ .....(i)

$10x + y - (10y + x) = 36$ $\therefore 9(x - y) = 3$

$\therefore x - y = 4$ .......(ii)

From equation (i) and (ii): $x = 6, y = 2$

$\therefore$ Number = 62

21. $((50 \times 48) - (45 + 55)) = 1900 - 100 = 1800$

$\Rightarrow$ Average = 1800/4 = 37.5

22. Here, $(20 - 24) = 6$

$(25 - 19) = 6$

$(35 - 25) = 6$

$(40 - 34) = 6$

Required no. = (L.C.M of 20, 25, 35, 40) – 6 = 1394

23. LCM of 2, 4, 6, 8, 10, 12 = 120

120 seconds = 2 minutes

Hence all the six bells will ring together in every 2 minutes

Hence, number of times they will ring together in 30 minutes =1 + (30/2) = 16

24. $\log a/b + \log b/a = \log(a + b)$

$\log(a/b \times b/a) = \log(a + b)$

$\log(1) = \log(a + b)$ Hence $(a + b) = 1$

25. $G - N = N - D$

$G + D = 2N$

$58 = 2N = N = 29$ yrs

26. Speed = $(72 \times 5/18)$ m/sec = 20 m/sec; time = 26 sec

Let the length of train be x m

Then, $(x + 250)/26 = 20 \Rightarrow x + 250 = 520 \Rightarrow x = 270$

27. Part filled by pipe A in 1 minute = 1/36

Part filled by pipe B in 1 minute = 1/45

Part filled by pipe A and pipe B in 1 minute= 1/36 + 1/45 = 1/20

i.e., both the pipe together can fill the tank in 20 minutes

28. Speed upstream = ( x – y)km/h

Speed downstream = (x + y)km/h

5( x – y) =12 and 5( x + y) = 28

On subtracting we get 10y =16, or, y = 8/5

29. (B + C)'s 1 day work = (1/9 + 1/12) = 7/36

Work done by B and C in 3 days = (7/36) x 3 = 7/12

Remaining work = (1– 7/12) = 5/ 12

Now, 1/24 work is done by A in 1 day

So, 5/12 work is done by A in (24 x 5/12) = 10 days

30. We know that Angle traced by hour hand in 12 hrs = 360°

From 7 to 12, there are 5 hours

The angle traced by the hour hand in 6 hours = 5 × 360/12 = 150°

31. Using the rule of alligation, we have

Cost of 1 kg of 1st kind coffee        Cost of 1 kg tea of 2nd kind coffee

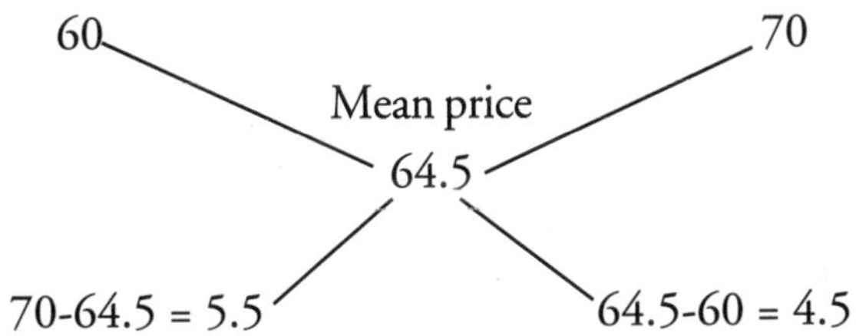


Required Ratio = 5.5 : 4.5 =11 : 9

32. Let the present ages of father and son be 17x years and 7x years respectively.

According to the question. 17x – 6/7x – 6 = 3/1

= 21x – 18 = 17x – 6

= 21x – 17x = 18 – 6

= 4x = 12

= x = 12/4 = 3

∴ Father's present age = 17 x 3 = 51 years

33. $7^{(x-y)} = 343 = 7^3$ = x – y = 3 -----------------(1)

$7^{(x+y)} = 16807 = 7^5$ = x + y = 5 -----------------(2)

(1 + 2) = 2x = 3 + 5 = 8 = x = 8/2 = 4

34. Ratio of the investment = 21000 : 17500 = 210 : 175 = 42 : 35 = 6 : 5

Share of Soumil in the profit = 26400 × (6/11) = 2400 × 6 = 14400

35. Let the numbers be x and y. Then, xy = 120 and $x^2 + y^2 = 280$

$x^2 + y^2 = x^2 + y^2 + 2xy = 289 + 240 = 529$

$x + y = \sqrt{529} = 23$

36. Difference = 87880 − 67600 = 20280 and it is the interest of one year on amount 67600.

∴ 67600 x r/100 = 20280

∴ r = 20280/676 = 30. So, rate = 30% pa

37. 4 × 1 + 2 = 4 + 2 = 6

6 × 2 + 3 = 12 + 3 = 15 = 18

15 × 3 + 4 = 45 + 4 = 49

49 × 4 + 5 = 196 + 5 = 201

201 × 5 + 6 = 1005 + 6 = 1011

38. $2^3 = 8 : 3^3 = 27$

$4^3 = 64 : 5^3 = 125$

$6^3 = 216 = 218$

$7^3 = 343$

39. 48 × 3/2 = 72; 72 × 3/2 = 108

108 × 3/2 = 162; 162 × 3/2 = 243

243 × 3/2 = 364.5 = 366

40. $Total_{2010} = 180 \times 360°/43.2° = 1500$

$Total_{2011} = 270 \times 360°/54° = 1800$

∴ Required % = 1800/1500 × 100 = 120%

41. $S_4$ = (2010) = 1500 × 36°/360° = 150

$S_4$ (2011) = 1800 × 50.4° / 360° = 252

∴ % rise = 252–150/150 × 100 = 10200/150 = 68%

42. $S_5 + S_7$ = 1500 x (64.8° + 43.2°)/360°

= 1500 × 108°/360° = 450

$S_2$ = 1800 x 28.8° / 360° = 144

∴ Required % = (450/144) × 100 = 312.5%

43. Average of $S_1$, $S_2$ and $S_3$ = (75.6 + 50.4 + 57.6)/360 x 3 x 1500 = 255

Average of $S_5$, $S_6$ and $S_7$ = (57.6 + 46.8 + 54)/360 x 3 x 1800 = 264

∴ Difference = 264 – 255 = 9

44. CP of 6 oranges = Rs. 5

∴ CP of 1 oranges = Rs. 5/6

∴ CP of 30 oranges = 5/6 x 30 = Rs. 25

Similarly SP of 30 oranges = Rs. 6/5 x 30 = Rs. 36

So he makes (36 – 25) = Rs. 11 on Rs. 25.

∴ % profit = 11/25 x 100 = 44%

45. Average speed = (2xy/x +y) = (2 x 50 x 30/50 + 30) = 37.5 km/hr

46. LCM of 251, 308, and 198 = 2772

Hence they all will be again at the starting point after 2772 seconds or 46 minutes 12 seconds

47. Required Number = (LCM of 8, 12, 22 and 24) + 12 = 264 + 12 = 276

48. $1^{st}$ post can filled in 6 ways

$2^{nd}$ post can filled in 5 ways

$3^{rd}$ post can filled in 4 ways

So, 6 x 5 x 4 = 120

49. Area = 1/2 (diagonal)$^2$ = 1/2 × 64 = 32 sq m

# MOCK QA Test 3

1. **Which number will replace the (?) mark in the following series:**
   **2, 7, 10, 22, 18, 37, 26 ?**

   A) 42 B) 52 C) 46 D) 62

2. **Which number will replace the (?) mark in the following series:**
   **5, 10, 13, 26, 29, 58, 61, ?**

   A) 128 B) 64 C) 125 D) 122

3. **Find the odd one out in the following series: 24, 36, 52, 72, 96**

   A) 72 B) 52 C) 36 D) 24

4. **Find the odd one out in the following series: 742, 743, 633, 853, 871, 990, 532**

   A) 532 B) 990 C) 633 D) 742

5. **Find the odd one out in the following series: 6, 13, 18, 25, 30, 37, 40**

   A) 40 B) 30 C) 37 D) 25

6. **A man is 24 years older than his son. In two years, his age will be twice the age of his son. What is the present age of his son?**

   A) 23 yrs B) 22 yrs C) 21 yrs D) 20 yrs

7. **The sum of ages of 5 children born at the intervals of 3 years each is 30 years. Find out the age of the youngest child?**

   A) 6 yrs B) 5 yrs C) 3 yrs D) 2 yrs

8. **The average of five numbers is 27. If one number is excluded, the average becomes 25. What is the excluded number?**

   A) 30 B) 40 C) 32.5 D) 35

9. **The average weight of 16 boys in a class is 50.25 kg and that of the remaining 8 boys is 45.15 kg. Find the average weights of all the boys in the class.**

   A) 48.55 B) 42.25 C) 50 D) 51.25

10. **In one hour, a boat goes 14 km/hr along the stream and 8 km/hr against the stream. The speed of the boat in still water (in km/hr) is:**

    A) 12 km/hr B) 11 km/hr C) 15 km/hr D) 28 km/hr

11. **A man can row at 5 kmph in still water. If the speed of current is 1 kmph and it takes him 1 hour to row to a place and come back, how far is the place?**

    A) 3.2 km B) 3 km C) 2.4 km D) 3.6 km

12. **If the first day of a year (other than leap year) was Friday, then which was the last day of that year?**

    A) Saturday B) Friday C) Tuesday D) Monday

13. **In a camp, there is a meal for 120 men or 200 children. If 150 children have taken the meal, how many men will be catered to with remaining meal?**

    A) 50 B) 40 C) 30 D) 10

14. **$109 \times 109 + 91 \times 91 = ?$**

    A) 20162 B) 18322 C) 13032 D) 18662

15. **What least number should be added to 1056, so that the sum is completely divisible by 23?**

    A) 4 B) 2 C) 3 D) 1

16. **$1398 \times 1398 = ?$**

    A) 1624404 B) 1851404 C) 1951404 D) 1954405

17. **If $a * b = 2a - 4b + 2ab$, then $2*3 + 3*2 = ?$**

    A) 2 B) 0 C) 14 D) 12

18. **In a group of ducks and cows, total number of legs are 28 more than twice the number of heads. Find the total number of cows.**

    A) 14 B) 12 C) 16 D) 8

19. **How many pieces of 75 cm length can be cut from a rod of 43.5 meters long?**

    A) 10 B) 15 C) 20 D) 58

20. **The population of town increases by 5% annually. If its population in 2011 is 138915 what it will be in 2012 ?**

    A) 150000 B) 128000 C) 140000 D) None of these

21. **If $\log_{10}2 = 0.3010$, what is the value of $\log_{10}1600$ ?**

    A) None of these B) 5.204 C) 1.204 D) 3.204

22. **A glass full of spirit contains 30% water. A part of this spirit is replaced by another containing 18% water and now the percentage of water was found to be 20%. The quantity of spirit replaced is**

    A) 1/3 B) 3/4 C) 1/2 D) 1/5

23. **There are 20 men and 35 women in an office. In how many ways can a person be selected?**

    A) 20 B) 50 C) 55 D) 150

24. **In how many ways can 9 girls be seated in a circular order?**

    A) 60 B) 120 C) 5040 D) None of these

25. **There are 20 gifts and 25 blanks in a lottery. If Behan has taken a lottery, what is the probability for him to get a gift?**

    A) 4/9 B) 3/7 C) 1/7 D) 2/9

26. **Six dice are tossed together. What is the probability of getting the same face in all the dice?**

    A) $17/6^5$ B) $1/6^5$ C) $1/6^6$ D) $7/6^4$

27. **Ayush draws a card from a pack of cards. What is the probability that the card drawn is a card of black suit?**

    A) 1/2 B) 1/4 C) 1/3 D) 1/13

28. **I. $p^2 - 12p - 28 = 0$ II. $q^2 + 12p + 36 = 0$**

    A) if p is greater than q B) if p is smaller than q

    C) if p is equal to q1111 D) if p is either equal or greater than q

**Direction (29-33): Study the following information carefully and answer the questions given below it.**

A survey is conducted on 800 people from a city. It is found that 6 1% of people surveyed speak Hindi, 54.5% people speak Bangla and 37.5% of them speak English. 16.5% people can speak only Hindi and Bangla, 14.5% people can speak only Hindi and English and 6% people can speak only Bangla and English. Answer the following questions based on this information.

29. **How many people are there who can speak only Hindi ?**

    A) 172 B) 174 C) 176 D) 178

30. **The total number of people who can speak only English is what percentage of the total number of people who can speak English?**

    A) 18% B) 24% C) 30% D) 36%

31. **Total number of people who can speak exactly two languages from the given three is what percentage of the total number of people surveyed ?**

A) 33% B) 35% C) 37% D) 39%

32. **Total number of people who can speak English and Bangla only is how many times the number of people who can speak only Bangla ?**

A) 3/2 times B) 2/3 times C) 1/4 times D) 4 times

33. **What is the difference between the total number of people who can speak exactly one language out of given three and the number of people who can speak all the three languages ?**

A) 375 B) 376 C) 377 D) 378

34. **I. $x^2 + 11x + 30 = 0$**

**II. $2y^2 + y - 1 = 0$**

A) if $x > y$ B) if $x \geq y$ C) if $x < y$ D) None of these

35. **A tank can be filled by a tap in 5 hours while it can be emptied by another tap in 10 hours. If both the taps are opened simultaneously, then after how much time will the tank get filled?**

A) 10 hrs B) 24 hrs C) 36 hrs D) 40 hrs

36. **A fodder stock lasts for 36 days for 20 cows. How long will it last for 15 cows ?**

A) 42 days B) 44 days C) 46 days D) 48 days

37. **A shopkeeper sells his goods at cost price but uses a weight of 800 gm instead of kilogram weight. What is his profit percentage?**

A) 18% B) 40% C) 25% D) 20%

38. **The simple interest occurred in 8 years on a principal of Rs. 22500 is 128 percent of the principal. What is the rate of interest per annum?**

A) 14% B) 18% C) 16% D) 20%

39. **Anuj completes 80% of a work in 20 days. Then Bimal also joins and Anuj and Bimal together finish the remaining work in 3 days. How long does it need for Bimal if he alone completes the work?**

A) 37 ½ days B) 22 days C) 31 days D) 22 days

40. **Faiz and Zoya can finish a work 30 days if they work together. They worked together for 20 days and then Zoya left. Faiz finished the remaining work in another 20 days. In how many days Faiz alone can finish the work?**

A) 60 B) 50 C) 40 D) 30

41. **In how many different ways can the letters of the word 'DIVISION' can be arranged?**

A) 6020 B) 5040 C) 6220 D) 6720

42. **Abhishek is walking at the rate of 5 km/hr and crosses a bridge in 15 minutes. What is the length of the bridge (in metres)?**

A) 1250 B) 1280 C) 1320 D) 1340

43. **A, B and C invested some money in the ratio 3 : 5 : 6 in a business. If the amount invested by B is Rs. 856560. What is the total amount invested in the business ?**

A) Rs. 2398368 B) Rs. 2423368

C) Rs. 2685420 D) None of these

44. **The surface area of the cube is 384 $m^2$. Its volume will be ?**

A) 343 $m^3$ B) 616 $m^3$

C) 512 $m^3$ D) Cannot be determined

45. **A table has two drawers. First drawer has 3 gold coins and second has 4 silver coins. Open drawer randomly and take a coin. What is the probability that it is a gold coin?**

A) 1/2 B) 3/4 C) 3/5 D) 4

**Direction (46-50): Study the graph and answer the questions that follow :**

Number of Candidates (in Thousands) Qualified in the Written Test for Admission to two Different Institutions

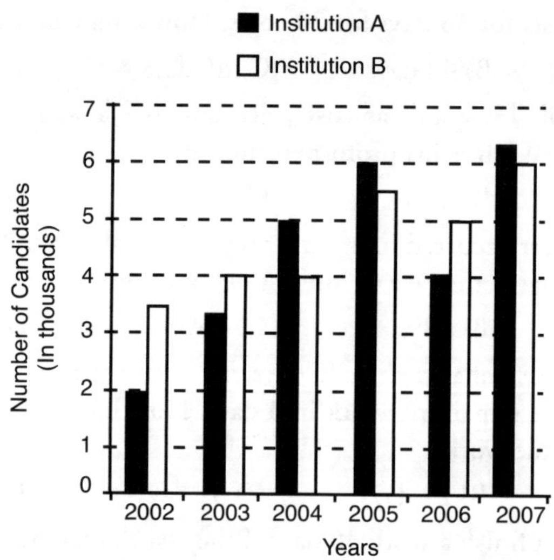


46. **What was the respective ratio between the number of candidates qualified in the written test in the year 2002 for admission in institution B and the number of candidates qualified in the written test in the year 2006 for admission to institution A?**

A) 8 : 5 B) 7 : 4 C) 7 : 8 D) 7 : 5

47. What was the approximate average number of candidates qualified in the written test for admission to institution B over all the years ?

A) 4555 B) 4200 C) 4160 D) 4667

48. In which year was the total number of candidates qualified in the written test for admission to both the institutions together the second highest ?

A) 2003 B) 2004 C) 2005 D) 2006

49. What is the difference between the total number of candidates qualified in written test in year 2006 for admission to institution A and B together and the number of candidates qualified in written test in year 2003 for admission to institution A ? In which year was the total number of candidates qualified in the written test for admission to both the institutions together the second highest ?

A) 5000 B) 3500 C) 1500 D) 5500

50. What was the total number of candidates qualified in the written test for admission to institution A over all the years together ?

A) 27000 B) 26500 C) 26000 D) 27500

## Answer Grid:

| Q. No. | 1 | 2 | 3 | 4 | 5 | 6 | 7 | 8 | 9 | 10 | 11 | 12 | 13 | 14 | 15 | 16 | 17 | 18 | 19 | 20 |
|---|---|---|---|---|---|---|---|---|---|---|---|---|---|---|---|---|---|---|---|---|
| Answer | B | D | B | D | A | B | C | D | A | B | C | B | B | A | C | D | C | A | D | D |
| Q. No. | 21 | 22 | 23 | 24 | 25 | 26 | 27 | 28 | 29 | 30 | 31 | 32 | 33 | 34 | 35 | 36 | 37 | 38 | 39 | 40 |
| Answer | D | D | C | C | A | B | A | A | C | B | C | C | B | C | A | D | C | C | A | A |
| Q. No. | 41 | 42 | 43 | 44 | 45 | 46 | 47 | 48 | 49 | 50 | | | | | | | | | | |
| Answer | D | A | A | C | A | C | D | C | D | A | | | | | | | | | | |

## Explanations:

1. There are two series here

   2, 10, 18, 26, ... (Increase by 8)

   7, 22, 37, ... (Increase by 15)

   Hence, next term is $37 + 15 = 52$

2. Numbers are alternatively multiplied by 2 and increased by 3

   $5 \times 2 = 10$

   $10 + 3 = 13$

   $13 \times 2 = 26$

   $26 + 3 = 29$

   $29 \times 2 = 58$

   $58 + 3 = 61$

   $61 \times 2 = 122$

3. All except 52 are multiples of 6

4. In all numbers except 742, the difference of third and first digit is the middle digit.

5. The difference between two successive terms from the beginning are 7, 5, 7, 5, 7, 5

   Hence, in place of 40, right number is $37 + 5 = 42$

6. Let the present age of the son = x years

   Then present age the man = (x + 24) years.

   Given that in 2 years, man's age will be twice the age of his son

   $\Rightarrow (x + 24) + 2 = 2(x + 2)$

   $\Rightarrow x = 2$

7. Let the age of the youngest child = x

   Then the ages of 5 children can be written as x, (x + 3), (x + 6), (x + 9) and (x + 12)

   $x + (x + 3) + (x + 6) + (x + 9) = 30$

$\Rightarrow 4x + 18 = 30$

$\Rightarrow 4x = 12$

$\Rightarrow x = 12/4 = 3$

8. Sum of 5 numbers = $5 \times 27$

Sum of 4 numbers after excluding one number = $4 \times 25$

Excluded number

$= 5 \times 27 - 4 \times 25$

$= 135 - 100 = 35$

9. Average weight of 16 boys = 50.25

Total weight of 16 boys = $50.25 \times 16$

Average weight of remaining 8 boys = 45.15

Total weight of remaining 8 boys = $45.15 \times 8$

Total weight of all boys in the class = $(50.25 \times 16) + (45.15 \times 8)$

Total boys = $16 + 8 = 24$

Average weight of all the boys = $(50.25 \times 16) + (45.15 \times 8)/24$

$= (50.25 \times 2) + (45.15 \times 1)/3 = (16.75 \times 2) + 15.05 = 33.5 + 15.05 = 48.55$

10. Let the speed downstream be x km/hr and the speed upstream be x km/hr, then

Speed in still water $=1/2(x + y)$ km/hr

Speed in still water = $1/2(15 + 7)$ km/ph = 11 km/hr

11. Speed in still water = 5 kmph

Speed of the current = 1 kmph

Speed downstream = $(5 + 1) = 6$ kmph

Speed upstream = $(5 - 1) = 4$ kmph

Let the requited distance be x km

Total time taken = 1 hour, so, $2x + 3x = 12$

Hence $5x = 12$, or, $x = 2.4$ km

12. Given that first day of a normal year was Friday

Odd days of the mentioned year = 1 (Since it is an ordinary year)

Hence First day of the next year = (Friday + 1 Odd day) = Saturday

Therefore, last day of the mentioned year = Friday.

13. Meal for 200 children = Meal for 120 men

Meal for 1 child = Meal for 120200 men

Meal for 150 children = Meal for $120 \times 150200$ men = Meal for 90 men

Total meal available = Meal for 120 men

Renaming meal = Meal for 120 men – Meal for 90 men = Meal for 30 men

14. $(a + b)^2 + (a - b)^2 = 2(a^2 + b^2)$

$109^2 + 91^2 = (100 + 9)^2 + (100 - 9)^2 = 2(100^2 + 9^2) = 2(10000 + 81) = 20162$

15. $1056 \div 23 = 45$ with remainder = 21

Remainder = 21. 21 + 2 = 23. Hence 2 should be added to 1056 so that the sum will be divisible by 23

16. $1398 \times 1398 = (1398)^2 = (1400 - 2)^2 = 1400^2 - (2 \times 1400 \times 2) + 2^2$

$= 1960000 - 5600 + 4$

$= 1954404$

17. $a * b = 2a - 4b + 2ab$

Hence, $2*3 = 2(2) - 4(3) + 2(2 \times 3) = 4 - 12 + 12 = 4$

$3*2 = 2(3) - 4(2) + 2(3 \times 2) = 6 - 8 + 12 = 10$

$\because 2*3 + 3*2 = 4 + 10 = 14$

18. Let the number of ducks be d

and number of cows be c

Then, total number of legs = $2d + 4c = 2(d + 2c)$

total number of heads = $c + d$

Given that total number of legs are 28 more than twice the number of heads

$\Rightarrow 2(d + 2c) = 28 + 2(c + d)$

$\Rightarrow d + 2c = 14 + c + d$

$\Rightarrow 2c = 14 + c$

$\Rightarrow c = 14$

i.e., total number of cows = 14

19. Number of pieces = 4350/75 = 870/15 = 58

20. $(138915/100) \times 105 = 145860.75$

21. $\log_{10}1600 = \log_{10}(16 \times 100)$

$= \log_{10}(16) + \log_{10}(100)$

$= \log_{10}(2^4) + \log_{10}(10^2)$

$= 4\log_{10}(2) + 2 = (4 \times 0.3010) + 2 = 1.204 + 2 = 3.204$

22. Using the rule of alligation,

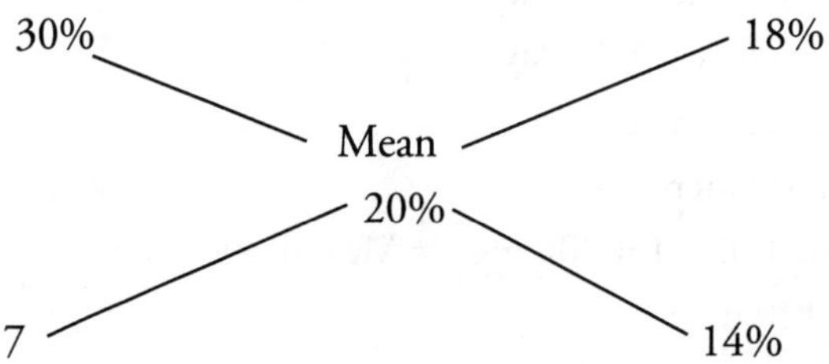


Hence ratio of 1st and 2nd quantities = 2 : 10 = 1 : 5

23. The number of ways in which a person can be selected = 20 + 35 = 55
24. Number of arrangements possible = (9–1)! = 7! = 7 x 6 x 5 x 4 x 3 x 2 x 1 = 5040
25. Total number of outcomes possible, n(S) = 20 + 25 = 45
    Total number of prizes, n(E) = 20
    P(E) = n(E)/n(S) = 20/45 = 4/9
26. P(E) = n(E)/n(S)
    $= 6/6^6 = 1/6^5$
27. Total number of cards, n(S) = 52
    Total number of black cards, n(E) = 26
    P(E) = n(E)n(S) = 2652 = 12
28. l. p2 – 12p – 28 = 0
    = p(p – 14) + 2(p – 14) = 0 = p = –2, 14
    ll. $q^2 + 12q + 36 = 0$
    = q = –6, –6
29. x + y + z + k = 800 – (132 + 116 + 48) = 504 .....(i)
    x + k = 488 – (132 + 116) = 240 .....(ii)
    y + k = 436 – (132 + 48) = 256 ......(iii)
    z + k = 300 – (116 + 48) = 136 .....(iv)
    (eqn ll + lll + IV) – eqn (l) gives
    2k = (240 + 256 + 136) – 504
    2k = 632 – 504 = 128 ∴ k = 64
    x = 240 – 64 = 176
    y = 256 – 64 = 192
    z = 136 – 64 = 72

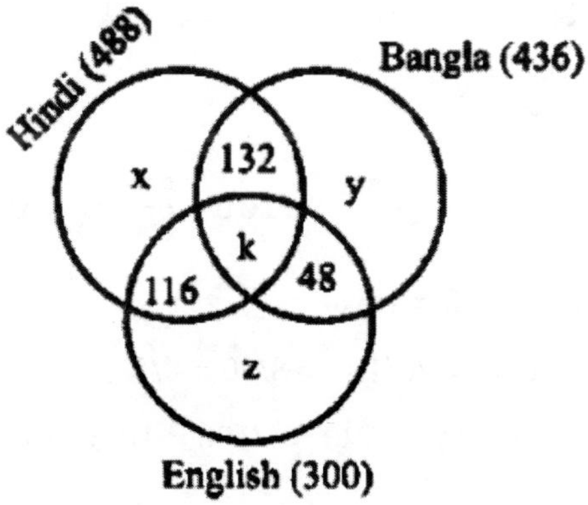

30. Required % = 72/300 x 100 = 24%

31. Exactly two languages = 132 + 116 + 48 = 296

Required % = 296/800 x 100 = 37%

32. Only Bangla and English = 48

Only Bangla = 192

∴ Required no. = 48/192 x 1/4 times

33. Only one language = 176 + 192 + 72 = 440

All three languages = 64

∴ Difference = 440 – 64 = 376

34. I. $x^2 + 6x + 5x + 30 = 0$

$x(x + 6) + 5(x + 6) = 0$

$(x + 50)\ (x + 6) = 0$

$x = -5, -6$

II. $2y^2 + 2y - y - 1 = 0$

$2y(y + 1) -1(y + 1) = 0$

$(2y -1)\ (y + 1) = 0$

$y = 1/2, -1$

$\therefore x < y$

35. Part filled by the first tap in 1 hour = 1/5

Part emptied by the second tap 1 hour = 1/10

Net part filled by both these taps in 1 hour = 1/5 - 1/10 = 1/10

i.e, the tank gets filled in 10/1 hours = 10 hours

36. $20 \times 36 = 15 \times x$, or, x = 48 days

37. If a trader professes to sell his goods at cost price, but uses false weights,

If shopkeeper sells x grams instead of 1000 grams (where x < 1000), then

Profit percentage = $\frac{1000-x}{x} \times 100$ %

So here profit percentage = $\frac{1000-800}{800} \times 100 = \frac{200}{800} \times 100 = 25\%$

38. $28800 = (22500 \times 8 \times r)/100 = 16\%$

39. Work done by A in 20 days = 80/100 = 8/10 = 4/5

Work done by A in 1 day = (4/5) / 20 = 4/100 = 1/25 --- (1)

Work done by A and B in 3 days = 20/100 = 1/5 (Because remaining 20% is done in 3 days by A and B)

Work done by A and B in 1 day = 1/15 ---(2)

Work done by B in 1 day = 1/15 – 1/25 = 2/75

⇒ B can complete the work in 75/2 days = 37 ½ days

40. Amount of work done by Faiz (F) and Zoya (Z) in 1 day = 1/30

Amount of work done by F and Z in 20 days = 20 × (1/30) = 20/30 = 2/3

Remaining work – 1 – 2/3 = 1/3

F completes 1/3 work in 20 days

Amount of work F can do in 1 day = (1/3)/20 = 1/60

⇒ F can complete the work in 60 days

41. Total number of ways = 8! / 3! = 6720

42. Speed = 5 km/hr

Time = 15 minutes = 1/4 hour

Length of the bridge = Distance Travelled by the man

= Speed × Time = 5 × 1/4 km = 5 × 1/4 × 1000 metre = 1250 metre

43. The value of 5 ratio = Rs. 856560

The value of 14 ratio = (856560/5) × 14 = Rs. 2398368

44. Surface area of cube = $6a^2 = 384 \Rightarrow a^2 = 64$

Hence a = 8 m

Volume = $a^3 = 8^3 = 512$ $m^3$

45. Probability to open one drawer = ½

Hence probability to get 1 coin of gold = (1/2 x 1 +1/2 x 0) = 1/2

46. Required ratio = 3500 : 4000 = 7 : 8

47. Average number of candidates qualified in institute B = (3.5 + 4 + 4 + 5.5 + 5 + 6)/6 thousand = 4.667 x 1000 = 4667

48. Number of candidates qualified in the year 2005 = 11.5 thousand

49. Required difference = [(4 + 5) – 3.5] thousand = 5500

50. Required number of candidates in institute A = (2 + 3.5 + 5 + 6 + 4 + 6.5) thousand = 27000

